# FASCISM

# FASCISM

## Alan Cassels
*McMaster University*

Harlan Davidson, Inc.
Arlington Heights, Illinois 60004

ISBN: 0-88295-718-X
(Formerly 0-690-00184-3)

Library of Congress Card Number: 73-13716

PRINTED IN THE UNITED STATES OF AMERICA

82  83  84  85  86MA10  9  8  7  6  5  4

For Celia and Jennifer

# PREFACE

A few years ago, I produced a book entitled *Fascist Italy* for the series "Europe since 1500." In writing it, I was aware that exigencies of space left me little or no opportunity to consider the relationship of Mussolini's movement to fascism* at large; it was a shortcoming properly observed by more than one reviewer. This present work is an attempt to remedy the deficiency by examining, not just Italian Fascism, but a cross section of modern fascisms within an international context.

Unavoidably, however, the subject matter of my earlier book and this one overlap to a slight degree. I have, therefore, used an abbreviated version of Mussolini's rise to power from *Fascist Italy* in the early part of Chapter 2 here. The further treatment of Fascist Italy's place in world fascism, as well as of the dozen or so other fascist movements, is, of course, fresh.

Since this is a general work intended for as wide an audience as possible, the editors and I resolved to do without footnotes. Instead, I have referred to a number of authorities in the text without, I hope,

---

* On the grounds that fascism is a generic noun, I have not capitalized it. I have reserved the spelling of Fascism and Fascist for those national movements which specifically employed the word in their title; for example, the Italian Fascist party, Italian Fascism, the British Union of Fascists.

vii

cluttering it unmercifully. It is an avowed purpose of this book to emphasize, in the course of a general narrative, those aspects of the topic which have occasioned the liveliest debate and to acquaint the reader with the major schools of thought. Up to a point, this is a synoptic view of a generation of scholarly research into the best-known fascist organizations, presenting both the clash of opinion and the current consensus, where it can be discerned.

But, in another respect, I have gone beyond the received wisdom. When it comes to devising a conceptual definition of fascism to serve as a frame of reference for the individual fascist movements, there is not the vestige of a consensus. There exists diagnosis enough, but the quintessence of a singular political philosophy called fascism remains elusive. In fact, the confusion grows apace as the epithet "fascist" is hurled with increasing abandon, but declining meaning, as a term of contemporary abuse. Given this imprecision, every writer who aspires to offer a general theory of fascism is virtually compelled to advance his own subjective interpretation. I have injected myself into this work in two ways—one, I think, unexceptionable, the other probably more contentious.

In the first place, I have confined my examination of fascism in action to Europe up to 1945. There can be no argument but that Europe in the period spanning the two world wars was the historical stamping ground of fascism. Indeed, it has been reasonably argued that fascism was the most distinctive feature of this European age; such is the assertion of Ernst Nolte's ambitious study, *Der Faschismus in seiner Epoche* (1963), oddly translated as *Three Faces of Fascism*. This is not to deny the presence of fascism outside Europe and after 1945. The Japanese nationalist regime of the 1930's with its racist overtones had some affinity with Nazi Germany, while Juan Perón's government in Argentina from 1946 to 1955 (which I touch on in passing) was plainly recognizable as a fascist experience. Remnants of interwar fascism survive patchily in today's Europe, and some would call the Greek colonels' regime of 1967 neofascist. Others discern fascist tendencies in both black and white Africa; still others see fascism arising out of the race problem in America. However, to take account of every conceivable and peripheral fascist movement would make a veritable encyclopedia of a book; it would also risk blurring any definition of essential fascism. Hence, my restriction to unmistakable fascisms and their principal locus.

Yet, even within the limits of a continent and a generation, the observer is still faced with a diverse array of self-styled fascist movements. Above all, he is struck by the vast difference in mood and accomplishment between German National Socialism and Italian Fascism. Some commentators have gone so far as to claim that the German and Italian forms of fascism were not parts of the same phenomenon at all. George Mosse in his *Crisis of German Ideology* (1964), for instance, argues that "the German crisis was *sui generis*" and Nazism "unique." In contrast, in this book I have expressed what I believe to be the basic ideological impulse of all fascisms, and then suggested a theoretical construct to explain Hitler-Mussolini distinctions while keeping the German and Italian brands of fascism within the same intellectual structure. This, naturally, constitutes the second major intrusion of my personal viewpoint.

One problem in specifying a generic philosophy of fascism is that the fascists themselves affected to despise systems of thought. A scientific dialectic was the forte of fascism's enemies—the nineteenth-century liberals and, even worse, the Marxian socialists. Fascists exalted action over thought, and boasted of reaching decisions intuitively. This highly charged approach stretched the definition of politics, a point observed many years ago in the title of Peter Viereck's book on Nazism, *Metapolitics* (1941). Understandably, all this "passionate thinking" (Nolte's phrase) gave rise to fanatically held convictions. In this way, the fascists were ideologues without too coherent an ideology. Broadly speaking, the fascists had a firm enough idea of where they wanted to go. Nonetheless, the fact remains that, in speaking of fascist ideology, one is often dealing with inchoate aspirations and half-formulated inferences.

With this proviso in mind, it may be asserted that all the fascist movements sprang from the same ideological source. Emerging from the breakdown of the nineteenth-century synthesis and deploring the fragmentation of modern society, they entertained one common ambition—the renewal of social cohesion (my chapter 1). But concerning the specific nature of the new unitary order, fascists were divided. Using Nazi Germany and Fascist Italy as prototypes, I have suggested that there were fundamentally two fascist visions of the ideal society (chapters 2 and 3). In Germany which, fifty years after unification, had become an industrialized and, in a material sense, modern state, the fascist revulsion against the present was almost total. The Nazis rejected the tradition of scientific rationalism which had created twentieth-century Europe. They were prepared to use modern technology, but mainly in order to achieve their premodern utopia—a *Volk* community based on peasant and small-town burgher values. In comparably backward Italy, on the other hand, Fascists rejected only certain aspects of modernity, notably the creeds of individualism and Marxist socialism. For the rest, Italian Fascism presented itself as a progressive movement which would complete the transformation of the nation into an advanced, industrialized society. Moreover, the corporative means whereby this goal was, in theory, to be achieved came directly from the mainstream of modern rationalist thought.

On the basis of this Nazi-Fascist contrast, I have then postulated a general schema: that fascism where it appeared in less advanced regions tended to look ahead to a stepped-up modernization of the community (albeit without the normal dislocations attendant on progress), while in already modernized nations fascism preferred to look back to a legendary past. I have applied this analysis to the other fascist movements which came to the fore in the 1930s and during World War II (chapters 4 and 5). In the backward Iberian peninsula and in Austria, fascism did indeed seem to follow the relatively enlightened corporative mode of Mussolini's Italy. In eastern Europe, however, circumstances peculiar to the region make this proposition only partially applicable. On the other hand, in the advanced countries of northwestern Europe, it is argued that the fascist movements showed an affinity with German Nazism in that they all harked back to a racially pure, preindustrial golden age. My conclusion is a résumé of the main factors common to all fascisms, together with some elaboration on the dichotomy between the "forward-looking" and "backward-looking" varieties.

Of late, more than one historian—Wolfgang Sauer and Henry A. Turner come to mind—has recommended that fascism be viewed, and hopefully elucidated, in terms of a response to modernization. But the author who has come closest to a systematic correlation between fascism and modernization—and whose views parallel my own up to a point—is the political scientist, A. F. K. Organski. In *The Stages of Political Development* (1965), Organski depicts Italian-style fascism as the product of tensions within a partly industrialized society, with fascism serving to protect the traditional elites from the rising forces of industrial managers and formerly subservient classes. On the other hand, national socialism, to Organski, was a function of mass democracy, enabling the government to practice intervention on a massive scale in order to preserve a balance between the masses and capital in a fully industrialized state. Nevertheless, Organski's book does not pretend to offer a comprehensive examination of fascism; there is no treatment, for example, of fascism in any advanced nation other than Germany. My differentiation of all the major European fascist movements according to economic growth is, therefore, I believe, a novel approach. I first advanced it in a paper, "Janus: The Two Faces of Fascism," delivered in 1969 at the annual meeting of the Canadian Historical Association, where I profited from discussion among the audience.

In the final analysis, though, it must be emphasized that I have not propounded my thesis of two kinds of fascism in any dogmatic fashion. Plainly, all the fascist movements contained both backward-looking and forward-looking elements. R. H. Kedward in his *Fascism in Western Europe* (1969) remarks properly on the fascists' peculiar skill in interweaving Dionysian and Apollonian strands from modern culture. My contention is merely that in modernized societies the regressive factors were inclined to overwhelm the progressive, while the reverse happened in less industrialized nations. It is, then, largely a matter of degree and emphasis. Nor have I offered my interpretation as a conclusive resolution of the riddle of fascism, although I venture to hope that future research will bear out my conjectures. In this book I have used the concept of two-faced fascism because it proved a convenient and credible framework within which to provide a narrative and historiographical survey of Europe's multifarious fascist movements. It is for the moment a working hypothesis and nothing more.

ALAN CASSELS

Dundas, Ontario, Canada
April 1973

# CONTENTS

xiii

# 1

## The Antecedents of Fascism

### The Legacy of the Nineteenth Century

In the years between the two world wars, it was customary to look back on the era before 1914 as something of a golden age in Europe. The attraction of the pre-World War I era lay in its apparent success in reconciling the contradictory goals of progress and stability. As for progress, its most obvious form was technological development, primed in the late nineteenth century by dramatic strides in steelmaking, the chemical industries, and the application of electricity. Moreover, in the half-century before 1914, the benefits of an industrial revolution began for the first time to filter down to the masses in the guise of a higher standard of living and greater leisure. The masses also made progress in political terms, as the propertied franchise in many parts of Europe gave way to virtual manhood suffrage. But this new electorate lacked enlightenment—so it was believed. Therefore state schemes of elementary education were established, and by the end of the nineteenth century, some countries could boast that their first literate generation had come of age. In international affairs, too, progress seemed discernible. Since 1815 international conflicts had been localized or contained by the Concert of Europe; possibly war itself was on the way to being exorcised.

1

The semblance of European stability before 1914 derived in large measure from the peaceful resolution of group and class conflicts which might have been expected to tear nineteenth-century Europe apart. The French and Industrial revolutions had brought to the fore a new, urban middle class which challenged the preeminence of the traditional agrarian aristocracies. Yet this clash between a "market society" and a "status society" never fully materialized. Instead, the two elites, especially in western Europe, came together to form a new ruling class —the social basis of the nineteenth-century synthesis. One factor which reconciled the old aristocracy and the *nouveaux riches* to each other was a common fear of the lower classes. However, with the advent of mass democracy and the beginnings of the welfare state, even the industrial proletariat was to some degree brought within the nineteenth-century synthesis. By the eve of World War I, the major European socialist parties had agreed, in practice if not in theory, to work for the time being within the existing parliamentary and capitalist system. The relative quiescence of class conflict reinforced belief in a natural harmony of interests, which was counted on to maintain social stability.

The combination of progress and order gave rise to a sense of the rectitude of things and of a confidence in man's ability to control both himself and nature. In intellectual terms, this trust in human reason was subsumed in the doctrines of positivism. More practically, Europe's self-confidence was expressed in the arrogant imposition of western culture on much of the rest of the world in a late nineteenth-century wave of imperialism.

This pre-1914 European order of progress, security, and certitude was shattered by the First World War—or at least so it was widely held right after the holocaust. In actual fact, the war was such a traumatic shock that it distorted perspectives and caused many of the interwar generation to depict the prewar age in sentimental, idealized, but quite inaccurate terms. For the past thirty years, scholars have been busy demolishing the roseate view of pre-1914 Europe. They have argued that World War I did not so much destroy a golden age as bring to maturity certain features of European society which were already eroding the nineteenth-century synthesis before 1914. Therefore, the roots of European civilization between the world wars can be traced back to the prewar period. So it is with fascism. For the antecedents we must look at some of the flaws and aberrations in the superficially cosy ambience of late nineteenth and early twentieth-century Europe.

It is probably best to begin with the intellectual and cultural background. The intellectual assumptions on which nineteenth-century civilization rested were essentially those of the Enlightenment of the previous century. Man was seen as a rational animal and the world as a machine which ran according to inexorable laws. These laws could be discovered by the methods of empirical science. The more man gathered data to which he applied his reason, the more he understood the nature of the universe and learned to adjust to it. Thus, progress was assured and optimism unbounded. Typically, the two most famous thinkers of the nineteenth century, Karl Marx and Charles Darwin, were proud to call themselves scientists, and they used their intelligence to conceive mechanistic systems wherein the world appeared driven by immutable principles. Significantly, too, Marxism and Darwinism both postulated a linear advance to higher and presumably happier stages of development. The nineteenth century, to be sure, was not without its intellectual doubters and pessimists—one thinks of Kierkegaard, Schopenhauer, and especially Nietzsche—but theirs were lonely voices. Not until the last decade of the century did a whole cluster of geniuses emerge who departed fundamentally from the prevailing rationalist and materialist philosophy. This is not to imply that a deliberate and concerted attack on conventional values occurred. Rather, a number of scholars working individually arrived, unexpectedly, at conclusions which collectively challenged the self-confidence of the nineteenth century.

Of this new breed of intellectuals, perhaps the most influential in the years before World War I was the French philosopher, Henri Bergson. He was critical of any theory of knowledge based on observation and reason alone. He urged a greater use of intuition which he seemed to regard as the human equivalent of animal instinct—an *élan vital*. This preference for the instinctive over the empirical was also characteristic of the German neo-idealists of the late nineteenth century. Their *Verstehen* was the counterpart of Bergson's intuition. Similarly, the versatile Italian, Benedetto Croce, found shortcomings in scientific methodology. For instance, he denied the possibility of objective history, recognizing the subjective in all historical writing in his famous dictum: "All history is contemporary history." Ultimately, the most famous of all these thinkers was, of course, Sigmund Freud. The psychoanalytical school which he inspired challenged the very basis of nineteenth-century society—its concept of man. When Freud asserted that the mainspring of human action lay not in individual will but in hidden sexual impulses, he contradicted the standard perception of man as a self-reliant, rational being. By implication, he cast doubt on both man's perfectibility through orthodox education and the inevitability of human progress. However, in his early career Freud was preoccupied with individual case studies. On the other hand, Georges Sorel, the French political economist and revolutionary writer, discerned irrationality in society at large. What moved masses of men to action, he claimed, was not objective calculation of profit and loss, or even right and wrong, but social "myths." These were beliefs or truths held by emotional conviction and not susceptible to logical explication. The German sociologist, Max Weber, too, ventured into this area with his discussion of the magic quality which enabled some men to lead others; termed *charisma* by Weber, it was another phenomenon beyond the scope of scientific rationalism.

These few examples cannot begin to do justice to a complex reorientation of European thought. But hopefully, they do illustrate that two aspects of nineteenth-century orthodoxy in particular came under fire. First, there was a reaction against positivist methodology. The nineteenth-century insistence on verifiable facts seemed needlessly restrictive, and cut off fruitful speculation and revelation by intuition. Second, and more important, there was a movement away from mechanistic philosophical constructs in which man and nature behaved predictably. Often starting from a critique of the rigid Marxian dialectic, the philosophers and social scientists of the period 1890–1914 went on to rediscover some of the mystery in life. Hence, the new curiosity about the irrational, dark side of the human psyche—"the recovery of the unconscious" to use H. S. Hughes's apt phrase. None of the intellectuals intended to promote a cult of unreason. Indeed, with the possible exception of Sorel, they positively abhorred such an idea. Nevertheless, their very choice of subject matter could not help but confer an aura of respectability on emotional thinking and instinctual habits of mind.

Much the same thing may be said of European artists at the opening of the twentieth century. Just as the intellectuals exhibited dissatisfaction with current materialist philosophy, so the artists were alienated by the environmental materialism of an industrial society. Partly, this was a reaction against the obvious ugliness of factory life and urban slums. Even more, it was a protest against the dehumanizing effect of technological change. Industrialization created in both the board room and on the assembly line "economic man": that is, a figure who responded to material stimuli but was woefully bereft of cultural appreciation.

Moreover, the creeping egalitarianism of the nineteenth century gave rise to a mass taste which many artists frankly despised. The classic statement of this cultural snobbery was to appear in Ortega y Gasset's *Revolt of the Masses*, first published in 1930. But long before World War I, many European artists were exhibiting serious alienation from contemporary society.

Some sought release from uncongenial surroundings by a return to the past; the Pre-Raphaelites set a precedent, while Wagner's operas were excursions from present reality into a romanticized past. Others tried to escape geographically; one recalls Gauguin's search in the South Pacific for a purer, less artificial world than urbanized western Europe. But the commonest expression of artistic disenchantment was a cultivation of personal sensitivity—a *culte du moi*, as one title of the day put it. Under the rubric of "the self-enchanted," G. Masur in his *Prophets of Yesterday* (1961) lists the Anglo-Irish Oscar Wilde, in France, Maurice Barrès and André Gide, and above all, the German writers, Stefan George and Hugo von Hofmannsthal. The doctrine of art for art's sake was used deliberately by all these writers to maintain a barrier between self and the everyday world. The concentration on an intensely personal vision gave rise to a great variety of fashions: for example, in writing, the stream of consciousness school; in painting, the postimpressionist flowering of synthesism, symbolism, and cubism; in music, atonal experimentation. Each new esoteric style, whatever its aesthetic merits, served to intensify the artist's divorce from his society.

There was one aspect of Europe before 1914, however, which had a strong appeal for some artists. This was the spirit of nationalism and imperialism rampant at the turn of the century. International conflict and war itself could be made to appear a high-minded adventure in contrast to the banal daily round. Thus, the Italian Futurists, led by Filippo Marinetti and Gabriele D'Annunzio, declaimed that the battlefield brought out man's finest qualities—courage, self-sacrifice, honor; their injunction to live and die nobly had a certain Nietzschean ring. French writers such as Charles Péguy, Paul Claudel, and Charles Maurras found it possible to sublimate their yearning for the heroic in love for *la patrie*—not support for the existing regime but for an abstract ideal of France. With actual war in 1914 came a sense of purpose. The English poet, Rupert Brooke, spoke for many artists of his generation when he wrote in August: "The central purpose of my life, the thing God wants of me, is to get good at beating Germans. . . .

I'm the happiest person in the world." Patriotic and warlike fervor was politically conformist; but it must be remembered that these feelings amounted to a rejection, deliberate or subconscious, of the mainstays of the nineteenth-century order—rationalism and materialism.

Besides the general run of intellectuals and artists, one other case of patent aversion to materialistic norms deserves mention. In the two decades before World War I, Europe witnessed the rapid development of the Youth Movement. Although originally a protest movement against an authoritarian elder generation, it soon became better known for a passionate attachment to nature. The most famous of the youth groups, the German *Wandervogel*, was born by no accident in the middle-class, virtually treeless Berlin suburb of Steglitz. On their country rambles and in their rural camps, the members found in communion with nature a release of pent-up emotions, often in the form of uninhibited and spontaneous sexual encounters. So the Youth Movement joined with the intellectuals and artists in deploring the stultifying atmosphere of mechanized, urban Europe, and in pioneering new ways for the fulfillment of deep-seated human emotions. Marshall McLuhan in his piquant fashion catches this spirit of disappointment and longing:

> The dwellers of the old mechanical world lived on dreams as a way of contacting a fuller world. The whole nineteenth century in a sense ended with the movies and manifested its preference for a dream world as altogether richer than real life. The workaday world was not only ugly but fragmented and specialized so that private dreaming of a better life occupied a good deal of time and energy (*War and Peace in the Global Village* [1968]).

In due course the fascist movements would promise a fantasy world to satisfy this dreaming. In place of "economic man," they would offer "heroic man." They would not usually offer concrete programs, preferring rather to project a mood which would appeal to the artistic imagination instead of the analytical mind. Fascism more than once was to be described as a "poetic" movement. Furthermore, fascism would also begin as something of a youth cult—hence the title of the Italian Fascist anthem, "Giovinezza," meaning youth—which offered to replace the worldly preoccupations of an older generation with a youthful idealism. In other words, fascism was able to flourish by exploiting those traits of anti-intellectualism and neoromanticism which began to emerge in Europe before 1914.

Yet, on the outbreak of the First World War, such notions had made little impact on the public consciousness at large. Trust in the scientific method remained strong; the pseudoscientific generalities of Social Darwinism still enjoyed wide currency; and in art and literature nineteenth-century naturalism kept its hold on popular favor. Freudians and Bergsonians, the Youth Movement, and the postimpressionists—all in 1914 were no more than minority cliques. Not until their values became general, and in the process vulgarized, would fascism's opportunity arise. For all the fascist parties aspired to be mass movements. Consequently, for further antecedents of fascism, we must turn to European society in the mass.

In the half-century before 1914, much of Europe started on the road to mass democracy. With the first halting steps toward the welfare state and extension of the suffrage, the attempt was made to integrate the masses into respectable society. Of many motives which prompted the experiment, one stood out. The increasing concentration of an urban proletariat in factory towns gave rise to a class consciousness and the possibility of revolution from below. It was largely to prevent the radicalization of the masses that the forces of law and order offered to broaden the base of nineteenth-century society and politics. Superficially though, the workers received their political rights and social benefits from the state, and it was to the nation-state, rather than to any form of social organization, that they were inclined to give their allegiance. However, so long as the nation-state system and the nineteenth-century social order were compatible, loyalty to one could be equated with loyalty to the other. Thus, popular nationalism was encouraged by the upper and upper-middle classes, and patriotism became a duty, so to speak, assumed by the masses in return for their new privileges. The state-supported elementary schools, which proliferated in the late nineteenth century, were established to educate the recently enfranchised masses, not only in the three R's but in civic responsibility too. It was but a short step from civic responsibility to national pride, which in fact became a staple diet in all public systems of elementary education. Compulsory military service, a feature of the arms race before World War I in all the major nations save Great Britain, supplied a further education in patriotism and individual subjection to the dictates of the nation state. The growth of a literate mass public sparked a journalistic revolution. Cheap, sensational newspapers came into being and, sensing their readers' inclinations, peddled a strong line of exclusive, intolerant nationalism. All of this was both a cause and effect of the general European spirit of Social Darwinism and competitiveness. By 1914 chauvinism was rife in all the principal nation-states and at all levels of society.

Although the nineteenth-century power structure might regard nationalism as a safeguard against revolution, it was a Frankenstein's monster that was conjured up. Popular nationalism was subversive of almost all nineteenth-century values, fostering intolerance, emotionalism, and violence at the expense of compromise, debate, and reason. Above all, popular nationalism must be blamed for the breakdown of that cosmopolitan and aristocratic style of diplomacy which rested on an assumed harmony of interests and the Concert of Europe. In brief, in popular nationalism lay the seeds of both world wars.

The dangers inherent in unrestrained nationalism were disclosed, even before 1914, by the increasing frequency with which the boundary with racism was crossed. This trend was especially prevalent in central and eastern Europe where national frontiers did not correspond to ethnic divisions and Pan-German contended against Pan-Slav sentiment. In this climate anti-Semitism flourished. The infamous forged plan for Jewish world domination, the *Protocols of the Elders of Zion*, began to circulate in Russia in the first decade of this century. At the same time, in Germany and Austria-Hungary, many anti-Semitic fringe groups and parties were going out of existence, but only because their anti-Semitism was now catered to by the conventional parties. Meanwhile, the Dreyfus affair in France demonstrated that western Europe was far from free of the scourge of anti-Semitism. It was a moot point whether the conventional nation-states could contain and satisfy these deep, irrational instincts. Their failure was to be fascism's opportunity. A common denominator of all the fascist movements was a strong sense of national community. Some fascists would dream of reinvigorating the traditional nation-state; others—the German Nazis providing the most egregious case—would base their whole philosophy on tribal and racial nationalism.

In the short run, however, until 1914 patriotism operated in conjunction with democracy to give the masses a stake in the nineteenth-century nation-state and to keep them for the most part reconciled to the existing order. All of which contributed to the image of a pre-World War I golden era. Yet, if revolution was not imminent in 1914, there were still definite limits to the social conciliation achieved by popular nationalism, universal manhood suffrage, and the embryonic welfare state. For one thing, the new mass democracy was not egalitarian; a vast gulf remained between haves and have-nots and between government and governed. In the words of a recent survey of these years:

> A common feature of both agrarian and industrial Europe, nevertheless, was their acceptance of the fact that society was split for its practical working into a small élite which ran things, and a large mass which was subordinate. . . .
>
> Although standards of living were rising more rapidly in the advanced countries and reducing the economic gap between élite and mass, it was still everywhere enormous. Both eastern and western Europe accepted such a gap, though some might regret it. The two parts of society lived different lives (J. M. Roberts, *Europe 1880–1945* [1967]).

Not surprisingly, proletarian discontent persisted, and it reached a crescendo in the years 1904–14. The decade was marked by violent strikes and lockouts, often involving unskilled labor. Working-class agitation seemed to take its most extreme form where representative assemblies had lost credibility as agencies of reform. In France and Italy, political scandals and constitutional crises threw the parliamentary systems into disrepute, and thereby facilitated the spread of syndicalist socialist ideas. The syndicalists took their inspiration from Sorel, who urged workers to put their faith in trade unions (in French *syndicats*) and to engage in direct economic warfare with capitalism, preferably by a general strike. Later, the fascist movements, particularly in the Latin countries, would take up this syndicalist emphasis on workers' organizations as an alternative to parliamentary democracy.

Fascism's forte lay in blending together hitherto disparate historical trends. The most fateful amalgam was, no doubt, that of nationalism and socialism, "the two great waves of the nineteenth century" in Friedrich Meinecke's phrase. Socialism here is being interpreted loosely, of course. In practice, fascism was hardly ever socialist according to accepted socialist doctrines. Nonetheless, the fascists often succeeded in preempting the orthodox socialists' appeal to the masses. Fascist propaganda always stressed that the workers belonged within the national consensus as citizens. Under fascism, worker expectations (socialism) were supposed to be fulfilled through national unity. The pre-World War I governments in their pursuit of national glory and acceptance of modest state interventionism hinted at a fusion of nationalism and generic socialism. The fascists in the interwar years would improve on these early pointers.

It has been said that basically there exist two interpretations of fascism—as a mass upheaval and as a class phenomenon. Although the fascist emphasis on national cohesion clearly indicated a desire to represent the entire community, in reality certain strata of society proved more susceptible than others to the appeal of fascism. Many commentators—Marxist and non-Marxist alike—have considered fascism to be primarily an outlet for the frustrations of the lower-middle class. For example, the sociologist Seymour Lipset in *Political Man* (1960) calls fascism an "extremism of the center." Beyond question, such groups as small shopkeepers, artisans, and independent farmers were under considerable pressure by the opening of the twentieth century from forces both above and below in the social scale. On the one hand, economic activity was coming to be dominated by large impersonal corporations—the conglomerate holding company, the department store, the scientific capitalist farm. The day of the individual entrepreneur was long past, and the small man who continued to operate on an individualistic basis found his livelihood placed in constant jeopardy by the big combines. The lower-middle class, then, was threatened with depression to the level of the proletariat. On the other hand, as the working class became organized in trade unions, it was able to improve its lot to the point where at least skilled workers were overtaking the lower-middle class from below. Moreover, the advance of the working class was accompanied by the growth of social democratic parties whose programs were aimed specifically at the eradication of class barriers. Herein lay the great alarm of members of the lower-middle class—not so much that they might become poorer than some manual workers, but that they might lose their status above the proletariat. To the lower-middle class, the fascists would appear less as national unifiers than as champions of an authoritarian and hierarchical social order which hopefully would preserve traditional class stratifications. To regard fascism as nothing but a petit bourgeois conspiracy is undoubtedly too narrow a perspective; fascism, as we shall see, drew recruits from everywhere on the social scale. Nevertheless, fascism did gain much of its popular support from the lower-middle class segment of society, the erosion of whose ego and material well-being was plainly under way by 1914. To this extent, fascism constituted a revolt of the déclassés and economic losers.

Whether one takes the mass or the class view of fascism, in reality one is discussing the collapse of liberalism. The quintessence of classical or atomic liberalism of the nineteenth century was the maximization of individual freedom consonant with good social order. This was desirable on the assumption that the educated citizen, given his freedom, would behave in a reasonable manner. However, by the end of the nineteenth century, Europe's intellectuals were beginning to undermine the notion of man as a rational creature. Mass democracy by its very nature was thoroughly inimical to liberalism; mass parties, trade union bargaining, and popular nationalism left little scope for individual scruple or initiative. And the plight of the middle class, squeezed between big business and big labor, testified to the breakdown of the liberal economic policies of laissez faire and private enterprise. Liberalism comprised a more complex set of values than can be indicated here. But, loosely interpreted, it was a creed peculiarly suited to the rising, vigorous middle class of the first part of the nineteenth century. A century later, it was outmoded, outflanked as the creed of moderate reform by social democracy. By 1914 liberalism was everywhere on the defensive, even in Great Britain, its spiritual home, despite the Liberal party's election victory in 1906. The question was what would fill the vacuum left by declining liberalism.

Perhaps the likeliest contender at the opening of the twentieth century was some form of collectivist socialism derived from Karl Marx's teachings. Marxian socialism seemed a natural step after liberalism, emerging as it did from the same historical environment of the Enlightenment and the Industrial Revolution, and sharing the nineteenth-century faith in progress to be achieved by the application of scientific principles. In due course, when and where Marxist parties grew stronger, those illiberal elements in Europe that detested Marxism as much as or more than liberalism would seek a refuge in fascism. In this sense, fascism has been adjudged the counterpoint of Marxism. "Fascism," writes Nolte, "is anti-Marxism which tries to destroy the enemy by evolving a radically opposed yet related ideology and by using almost identical and yet typically modified methods." Indeed, in a dozen and one nations, the communist scare was to be the immediate cause of the rise of fascist movements. Specifically, the fear that the Great Depression would feed the Marxist fires goes a long way toward explaining fascism's growth in the 1930s. On the other hand, as Nolte suggests, fascism was not the complete obverse of Marxism, but in some ways its kin. Fascist politics were quite as dictatorial as those of the Marxists; fascist economic theories were collectivist although, unlike Marxian blueprints, they were seldom applied in practice. In their denial of individual rights, fascism and Marxian socialism vied as the antithesis of classical liberalism. Here, in liberalism, it must be emphasized, was to be found fascism's real *bête noire*; Marxism as a "Western heresy" was only a symptom of the deeper problem of decadent liberal society. And it was the entire materialist, positivist *Weltanschauung* that the fascists were dedicated to uprooting. Although a twentieth-century cult, Fascism was conceived in the twilight of nineteenth-century liberalism and, as an ultimate rationale, held out an utterly contrary set of values.

In the same way that fascism should not be equated with simple anti-Marxism, so it cannot be dismissed as a mere extrapolation of the historic Right. Certainly, in their repulsion of liberalism, fascists found themselves voicing many of the slogans and ideas of Europe's reactionaries who regretted both the French and Industrial revolutions. Similarly, fascism and the big business conservatism which evolved in the late nineteenth century spoke the same language against Marxism. Hence, at least one writer, John Weiss, has discerned a "fascist tradition" in modern history. Yet, placing fascism within the mainstream of European conservatism threatens to obscure its populist origins. Fascism was an experiment in mass politics, and it preached its own form of collectivist democracy. The tendency was for fascist leaders to start out as socialists or social reformers. The youthful fascist movements had no intention of fighting liberalism and its socialist offshoots in order to retain or restore the privileges of the traditional aristocracies of birth and wealth. Later, wherever the conventional power structure succeeded in using and controlling local fascists—and this frequently did happen—it would be a truncated and perverted fascism that survived. If a conservative force at all, then, fascism can only be fitted into that ultramodern political category, the radical Right. Right-wing because it was antiliberal and anti-Marxian, fascism was radical in that it aimed at a total overturn of the status quo. In the last analysis, fascism must be accounted a revolutionary movement whose alliances with conservatism were tactical more than ideological and whose vision of the future was novel and drastic.

## The Great War

Fascism, as a practical political and social proposition, was spawned by World War I, the Great War as it was once known and has indeed proved in terms of its impact. The war, acting as a catalytic agent, fertilized all the antiliberal features of European civilization described above, transforming latent trends into popular cults. All wars diminish the worth of the individual, but the First World War was something new and horrendous. The problem arose from the fact that few had visualized the war of attrition which developed by the winter of 1914. Lacking the imagination to adjust to the unexpected military stalemate, most generals and politicians succumbed to the impersonal imperatives of the war. World War I appeared to evolve a dynamism of its own, sweeping away the judgment of the decision-makers as well as the lives of troops sacrificed in vain infantry attacks on the Somme and at Verdun, in the Carpathians and on the Carso. The bulk of the belligerent populations came to acquiesce in the slaughter. At the start of the war, the first casualty trains to reach the European capitals evoked shocked surprise. But as the years of war rolled by and casualty lists grew longer, public sensibilities became numbed by the repetition of horrors. Critics of the useless suffering were most often decried as cowards, pacifists, or traitors.

The conduct of the war was a convincing denial that man was master of his fate. Nor was the war reconcilable with the nineteenth-century shibboleths of man's rationality and automatic progress. Rather, Europe collectively between 1914 and 1918 seemed gripped by an unconscious Freudian death wish. One of the more depressing revelations of the war was the ease with which the governments were able to whip up emotional patriotic fervor to keep the struggle going. In the early stages, volunteers for the front were plentiful, and later on, although conscripts grumbled, they hardly ever mutinied. The steadfastness of troops and civilians alike to the bitter end in 1918 must be attributed in part to the barrage of nationalist propaganda laid down by newly established ministries of information and officially vetted newspapers. The wartime propaganda machines picked up the jingoist slogans and tricks of persuasion used by the prewar yellow press. In turn, one of the most concrete lessons that the interwar fascists learned retrospectively from the First World War concerned the techniques of manipulating entire populations by catchwords, distorted half-truths, and appeals to instinctual group loyalties.

World War I was the first total war, which meant the mobilization of all the resources of every belligerent country. This involved a drastic increase in the bureaucratization of society, exposing the average citizen to a variety of new administrative edicts. Similarly, the war emergency demanded that decisions be quickly taken and quickly executed. So the central executives of the belligerent nations were streamlined and their powers hugely extended. Two cherished liberal traditions were most directly affected by this escalation of state power. First, civil liberties—freedom of the press and speech, freedom of assembly and movement, freedom from arbitrary arrest, and so on—were seriously curtailed in the interests of national security. Second, laissez faire economics were pushed to the wall as governments, to wage total war, were forced to introduce some national planning, intervening in or controlling such vital economic activities as the import and distribution of raw materials. The best example of a rampant wartime executive occurred in beleaguered Germany where Walther Rathenau's economic planning agencies cushioned the impact of the Allied blockade for four years, and where by 1917 the duo of Field Marshal von Hindenburg and General Ludendorff exercised a virtual military dictatorship over the whole country. It was expected—indeed, it was promised—that the arbitrary regulations necessitated by war would be repealed when peace came. In truth most wartime controls were lifted after 1918, although not all (for instance, the ordinary traveler's need for a passport has continued since World War I). But what could not be easily reversed was a frame of mind—a frame of mind which took a large bureaucracy for granted, thought of individual rights in minimum terms, and expected governmental intervention in the economic process for political purposes. Generally speaking, people emerged from the war much more inclined than before to look to a central authority for guidance. In many ways fascism proposed to recapture the wartime atmosphere— the frenzied excitement, the sense of national crisis and, above all, the dependence on a supreme centralized executive backed by an extensive bureaucracy. The First World War left many minds conditioned to accept these future fascist traits as norms.

Another difficulty in trying to turn the clock back to 1914 was that Europe's prewar elite had suffered crippling blows in the war. Such was the nature of trench warfare that it took a prohibitive toll of those young officers who led the forays into no-man's-land. These lieutenants and captains, many of them the patriotic volunteers of 1914, came from the upper and upper-middle classes, and in normal times were destined twenty years later to assume the leadership posts in politics and the professions. Their decimation between 1914 and 1918 opened the door to ambitious men from other strata of society— to Benito Mussolini, son of a Romagna blacksmith, and to Adolf Hitler, son of a minor customs official in the Hapsburg Empire. Many prominent fascists hated the pre-1914 world not on ideological grounds alone, but also for the personal reason that it had refused them advancement. The war upset the conventional patterns of promotion, and the fascists intended to carry the dislocation further.

The rise of fascism was facilitated not only by the war itself but by the disappointments of its immediate aftermath. As the war had dragged on without prospect of victory, the problem of keeping up national morale at home and at the front became urgent. The solution found was for the organs of propaganda to dwell on one particular note. Increasingly, the struggle was proclaimed a moral crusade from which there could be no backsliding. The corollary was that once the forces of evil were overcome, a better morrow would be sure to dawn; and the wartime governments were lavish with promises of a rosy post-war future in order to keep the war effort rolling. The expectations were given a fillip by twin events in 1917. First, the overthrow of autocracy in Russia opened up the prospect of radical change every-where. Second, the United States entered the war for avowedly high principles—the furtherance of international law, national self-deter-mination, and democracy. For the last year of the war, the American President Wilson and the Russian Bolshevik leader Lenin appeared as rival messiahs coming from beyond Europe to announce their own brands of salvation for a ruined civilization. But even without these propagandist and revolutionary promises, the hope of a brave new world was the only possible rationalization for the carnage in the trenches—that all the sacrifice might have been in vain was too un-bearable to contemplate. By the time peace came in 1918, the con-viction was widespread, in the vanquished as well as the victorious nations, that somehow all the recent suffering would bring its just rewards.

These high hopes proved illusory for one outstanding reason. The postwar governments of Europe (and America, too) were hypnotized by the specter of Russian Bolshevism and a subversive "red tide" flow-ing westward. During 1919 the red danger was repulsed and the Soviet experiment confined within the context of Russian nationalism where its bright postwar image was dimmed by creeping totalitarianism. Mean-while, the Western powers were so afraid of encouraging radicalism at home that they shied away from any substantive reform. Moderate Wilsonian proposals—essentially the re-creation of the nineteenth-cen-tury synthesis, albeit tempered with a greater measure of social justice, and the resurrection of the old international concert in the guise of the League of Nations—received some lip service. But, in reality, they went down to defeat.

The war had, of course, utterly reshaped the European order, how-ever firmly the postwar governments were convinced that they could practice pre-1914 business as usual. But the changes wrought by the war were not immediately apparent, especially to the ordinary man in the street or returned soldier. The familiar class distinctions, or at any rate pretensions, persisted. Great disparity in wealth was still present, perhaps more noticeable than ever because of the ostentatious consumption of some war profiteers. While Europe readjusted painfully from a wartime to a peacetime economy, unemployment ran at a high level; most European governments provided a dole for the unemployed, but often grudgingly and meagerly. There were, in short, no "homes fit for heroes to live in." It was not long before disillusion and cynicism set in. If the existing power structures could not or would not fulfill the wartime promises, then extreme measures were required. Some looked to communism, others to fascism to implement the radical reorientation of society of which they had been cheated in 1919.

Quite another kind of disillusion was exhibited by those whom the war had transformed into professional warriors. Thousands of returned soldiers failed to find a niche in civilian life, either because no jobs were available or because they were no longer temperamentally suited. "What we wanted, we did not know. And what we knew, we did not want!" said a typical veteran who later joined the Nazis. Such men found the business of earning a living dull and, when left to fend for themselves, often frightening. They missed the excitement of military life with its camaraderie which had served as protection against loneliness. As soldiers in spirit, these men were intensely patriotic, which was the cause of a further grievance against the postwar world. They were fiercely critical of their own government whenever they believed that the national interest had been betrayed in the peace settlement; sometimes they resorted to violence against offending ministers. Indeed, the perpetuation of nationalist feeling after the war was one of the clearest indicators of the decay of rationalism. Since intolerant nationalism had been patently a major cause of the Great War, an abatement of unthinking patriotism might have been anticipated. Yet, on the Continent at least, nationalist prejudices survived the war unscathed. Nor was it merely "the generation of the trenches" which scorned peaceful pursuits and strove to keep alive the militant passions of war. A lot of youths just too young to have fought in the war felt chagrin at having missed the great adventure. As solace, they assumed the opinions and imitated the behavior of the disgruntled elements among the demobilized troops.

One haven for these would-be soldiers was the paramilitary formations which sprang up nearly everywhere immediately after the war. They were particularly numerous in Germany, where they went by the name of *Freikorps*, because German disarmament under the terms of the Treaty of Versailles severely curtailed regular military employment. In the long run the fascist organizations offered practically everything these misfits craved—military discipline, fellowship, and adventure for a nationalist cause. It was no coincidence that a high proportion of early members in all fascist movements were ex-soldiers and young men for whom a conventional civilian existence was tame and unsatisfying.

## The View from the Social Sciences

From the foregoing it must be clear that fascism appealed to different groups for different, even contradictory, reasons. To some extent, propaganda, at which all the fascist movements excelled, was used to disguise the inconsistencies. But there is a deeper, more subtle explanation why fascism made a success out of appearing all things to all men. The truth is that the fascist movements' attraction rested not in policies nor in precise answers to specific problems; rather, fascism won adherents because it responded to the temper of Europeans of all sorts and conditions. This is to suggest that the real antecedents of fascism lay in a deep disturbance of Europe's mass psyche. Obviously, the First World War was a traumatic shock, as the case of the maladjusted demobilized soldiery illustrates. However, most authors who have written of the causes of fascism in psychological terms consider the war as much a symptom as a cause of the general malaise. In this context both World War I and fascism become products of the stresses of the modern world.

Discussion of changing social mentalities involves generalizations of the sort that professional historians have traditionally been trained to beware of. It is hardly surprising, therefore, that the literature on this subject comes almost exclusively from the social sciences. One of the earliest and most systematic interpretations of our century's psychological distress is that propounded by the psychoanalyst Erich Fromm in his classic *Escape from Freedom* (New York, 1941). The British edition bears the perhaps more expressive title, *Fear of Freedom*. Fromm begins with the proposition that ever since the commercial and Protestant revolutions of the sixteenth century, Western man has been enjoined to be free and independent. Unfortunately, as the centuries passed, obstacles to the realization of individual freedom arose; Fromm emphasizes the moral commands of a Calvinist god and the restrictive practices of monopoly capitalism (underplaying relatively the extension of state power). At all events, the conflict between the Western aspiration to freedom and its nonfulfillment has resulted in a mass psychosis, in a subconscious dread of freedom itself. The outcome of this predicament has been the development of an "authoritarian personality." (This is a well-known sociopsychological concept and forms the leitmotif of a later collective investigation of anti-Semitism and fascism, *The Authoritarian Personality* [1950].) In Fromm's view the authoritarian personality finds release in two ways: in democratic countries mostly through "automation conformity," but elsewhere often through the mechanism of overt sadomasochism. Sadistically, the authoritarian character wishes to dominate and hurt others; masochistically, it desires to be hurt and dominated. One can readily see the relevance to fascism. The fascist submitted himself in masochistic fashion to the dictates of the movement or its personification, the leader; as a sadist he was enabled to assert himself against the rest of the population or, because fascism was imperialistic and chauvinistic, against other nationalities.

Most social scientific writers agree with Fromm regarding the mental strains of modern freedom. Thus the social psychologist, Z. Barbu, describes democracy as a "flexible society" and goes on to observe:

> But not all social groups and sub-groups belonging to our contemporary world could adjust themselves to a flexible pattern of life. Moreover, in many individuals and groups the change and fluidity of the pattern of life aroused the feeling of instability and insecurity; the desire of change has thus turned into anxiety of change, the feeling of freedom has thus become fear of responsibility (*Democracy and Dictatorship* [1956]).

Western man's insecurity is often ascribed to his feeling of rootlessness, of not knowing what to believe or where to belong. Where once the churches had provided the assurance of solid belief, the Enlightenment made a virtue out of skepticism and freethinking. Where a static agricultural society had maintained group patterns from generation to generation, the Industrial Revolution broke up old relationships and introduced social mobility. The problems of self-identification have been compounded by the crowded conditions of modern urban living. It has proved difficult to cultivate attachments amid the antlike scurry of large impersonal cities, while on the assembly line most factory workers have to recognize that they are replaceable cogs in a machine. The anxieties of a modern environment are beautifully captured in the paradoxical title of David Riesman's celebrated book, *The Lonely Crowd* (1950).

The modern individual's sense of aloneness is probably best expressed by the word *anomie* coined by the nineteenth-century sociologist, Émile Durkheim. The notion of anomie lies at the heart of Hannah Arendt's seminal work of political theory, *The Origins of Totalitarianism* (1951, 1958). Arendt postulates an ideal past situation when the state performed as aloof, olympian arbiter above the contending factions which made up society. During the nineteenth century, however, traditional group allegiances were undercut by industrialization and mass democracy. Simultaneously the old distinction between state and nation grew blurred as the state fell captive to particular interest groups, notably the bourgeoisie. These processes were hastened forward tremendously, in Arendt's opinion, by the wave of "new imperialism" at the close of the century. By the twentieth century the nation-state, as Arendt understands the term, was virtually dead, leaving a mass of "atomized" individuals cut off from past associations in a state of anomie. They supplied the human raw material for totalitarian or would-be totalitarian movements such as fascism.

Fascism, then, offered the *déracinés* or uprooted somewhere to belong and, by belonging, a sense of self-importance which they lacked in the modern urban-industrial complex. At the core of all fascist ideology was a sense of community, a spirit of brotherhood. Fascists did not relish the word party for it connoted representation of only a portion of society; they preferred all-embracing epithets such as movement or front. Similarly, they looked askance at party platforms, which implied gratification of sectional interests, insisting on the priority of united action for its own sake over political doctrine.

This is not to say, however, that the fascist movements neglected to concoct their own dogmas. On the contrary, they proved singularly adept at meeting the crisis of faith brought on by the shattering of the optimistic liberal certitudes of the nineteenth century. In this connection, J. L. Talmon, *The History of Totalitarian Democracy* (1952–60), suggests that two democratic styles emerged from the Age of Reason and the French Revolution—the liberal and the totalitarian. In the former system, democracy functions pragmatically through parliamentary debates and majorities; in the latter, democracy consists of the recognition and application of a Rousseauite general will—an absolute truth to be pursued with "messianic" fervor. It is a prerequisite of messianic politics that the general will or political creed advocated be at once simplistic and omniscient—an ideology, in fact. Fascism met the criteria of totalitarian democracy perfectly. The fascists claimed to represent a national, not a majority, will; they voiced their convictions with brutal rigidity; and their beliefs were elementary and comprehensive, the Nazi racist ideology being a classic example. Furthermore, absolute verities carry most conviction when seen to proceed from an easily recognizable but infallible source—perhaps an atavistic longing for divine revelation. This requirement the fascists met by their cult of the leader (the Nazi *Führerprinzip*), an oracular, inspirational figure.

In the interwar years there existed a disoriented popular audience aching for a secure and simple set of beliefs to which to cling. Public elementary education had alerted the masses to political and social issues, but it had lagged in developing the faculty of ratiocination to reach valid conclusions. The populace claimed the right to opinions but preferred them uncomplicated and assertive—"the comfort of opinion without the discomfort of thought," President J. F. Kennedy once expressed it. Fascism's messianic simplicities capitalized on this twentieth-century characteristic.

Theories such as those of Barbu, Arendt, and Talmon are geared, in the first instance, to explaining the twentieth-century rise of totalitarianism at large, not just its fascist variant. Indeed the social scientists must bear some of the blame for the one-time habit of regarding fascism (Nazism, in particular) and communism as two sides of the same coin—the syndrome of "red fascism" now happily discredited. In truth, social science by its very nature has been concerned not so much with precise causes of fascism as with preconditions out of which it might grow. Hence, one cannot expect—in the succeeding pages, for instance—a detailed working-out of the theme of social dislocation in the history of fascism. Yet, in the total picture, psychic alienation must remain a factor of incalculable importance.

Moreover, it is useful to have fascism placed in a broad perspective, for, if nothing else, the social scientific speculations manage to convey its scope and elasticity. They suggest that the malaise which caused fascism was spread throughout the social spectrum, although the adherents of a class definition of fascism contend that psychological strain was greatest among the lower-middle class. More important, all the sociopsychological interpretations cut across national boundaries, seconding Thomas Mann who, in 1938, called fascism "a disease of the times which is at home everywhere and from which no country is free." Regional differences and national historical vicissitudes determined which fascist movements gained power and which failed, which lapsed into genocidal racism and which did not. But incontrovertibly, fascism was an international phenomenon, and the general conditions out of which it grew were present in greater or lesser degree everywhere in Europe between the two world wars.

PEACE SETTLEMENTS
IN EUROPE 1919–1920

Territories lost by:

Germany

Bulgaria

Austria-Hungary

Russia

Plebicite areas

Demilitarized Rhineland zone of Allied occupation

# 2

# One Fascist Prototype— Mussolini's Italy

Fascism made its appearance in practically all European countries between the two world wars. But in only two nations with pretensions to major power status—Italy and Germany—did indigenous fascist movements gain power by their own efforts. (If there was a third instance, it was perhaps Vichy France between 1940 and 1942.) Prefascist conditions in Italy and Germany exhibited some broad similarities. Neither nation achieved complete unity until the Franco-Prussian War of 1870–71, and in each case belated unification seemed to leave behind a heightened concern for nationalistic self-expression. Both the new Italy and the new Germany adopted mixed monarchical constitutions, but in both countries the parliamentary branch of government functioned indifferently, giving rise to alternative authoritarian programs. And in Italy and Germany alike industrialization arrived late, for the most part after unification, and assumed monopolistic form with a close nexus between big business and government. In short, nineteenth-century classical liberalism touched Italy and Germany relatively lightly, and was therefore the more easily overcome by fascism.

22

## Problems of United Italy

A united, independent Italian state came into being in 1861, the political climax to the cultural nationalist movement known as the *risorgimento*. The fundamental problem of the new nation was forecast by one of the architects of unification, the Marquis d'Azeglio, when he remarked: "Now that we have made Italy, it is necessary to make Italians." Indeed, a gulf did exist between the unitary state and the mass of Italians; some would contend that it has not been bridged to this day. For a start, many Italians did not welcome unity at all. In the south, untouched by the *risorgimento*, unification was resented as the means whereby the alien north extended its customs and dominion over the entire Italian peninsula. On the other hand, many Italians regarded unification as a magic panacea for a host of social and economic troubles. When these did not disappear after 1861, nor after 1870 when Rome was belatedly acquired as the country's capital, disillusion with the Italian state set in. Moreover, the Catholic church, dispossessed of its temporal power by unification, placed its *non expedit* on cooperation with the secular state; for nearly half a century a large number of Italians out of religious conviction observed the ban, refusing to hold office or even to vote in the new Italy.

But most important, parliamentary institutions, which in nineteenth-century liberal politics usually provided some sort of link between populace and government, failed dismally to perform this essential function in Italy. The Italian Parliament consisted of two houses: the Senate, which was appointed and played a secondary role to the Chamber of Deputies, whose members were elected at first by a limited number of property holders. In 1882 the number of Italians eligible to vote was raised from approximately 2 to 7 percent of the population, and not until the eve of World War I was virtual manhood suffrage instituted. But it was less the restricted franchise which disenchanted Italians with their parliamentary system than the conduct of their elected representatives in Rome. In 1876 a combination of parliamentary forces on the left supplanted a coalition government of the Right. Within a few years, however, cabinet reshuffles brought elements from both right and left into the same ministry, and therafter any distinction was lost. Parliamentary allegiance was accorded personalities, not parties. Government majorities were created by parliamentary managers out of the malleable mass of representatives who occupied the center of the Chamber of Deputies. This system of *trasformismo* (transformism) depended on corruption on a grand scale; deputies were simply bought by favors—to themselves, to their families and friends, or to the districts they represented. Official chicanery reached a crescendo at election time. The electoral machinery was run by the local prefects who had been appointed by the incumbent ministry, and these officials were expected to assure that sufficient government supporters, or candidates "transformable" into supporters, were returned. Names were transcribed from gravestones to the electoral rolls, even cattle were registered, to bolster a favored candidate's total vote.

Oddly enough, in view of the lack of differences in political principles among Italian politicos, Parliament was often the scene of fiery altercations. Parliamentary decorum was notoriously fragile; personal insults and threats were frequently hurled across the floor, and so too on occasion were inkstands and rulers. The atmosphere was hardly conducive to a careful appraisal of the needs of a united Italy in the last quarter of the nineteenth century.

The one question above all others which the legislature was accused of neglecting was that of the south or *Mezzogiorno*. This region was gripped by grinding rural poverty, the topsoil of its hilly terrain eroded by centuries of overfarming. Huge estates (*latifondi*), only partially cultivated, were everywhere. The peasantry in semifeudal fashion were subservient to the titled landowners and to the southern clergy who abominated the secular authority in Rome. Indeed, the central government's writ was weak all over the south, and in parts of Sicily was null in the face of the Mafia's strength. To the urban, commercially minded northerners who wielded the most influence in Rome, the mores of the *Mezzogiorno* were backward, savage, and foreign. It was not that Parliament totally ignored the southern problem; commissions of inquiry were established, and one on agriculture in 1884 produced an admirable report full of valuable and shocking statistics. But no government plan to alleviate the plight of the south emerged. On the contrary, Rome's economic policies, particularly a pointless tariff war with France, put added burdens on southern agriculture. Sporadic peasant uprisings, a tradition of the *Mezzogiorno*, were brutally suppressed by the local authorities with the distant approbation of the central power in Rome. The populace could vote only with its feet—by emigrating in droves to the new world. Meanwhile, the south constituted a brake on Italy's economic prosperity and a latent threat to national unity.

Northern Italy, on the other hand, was undergoing an industrial revolution. Italian manufacturers, finding world markets preempted by the older industrial nations and caught in the deflation of 1873–97, appealed successfully to the national government for help. This was forthcoming in the form of protective tariffs and, even more, of official contracts; big iron and steel concerns like Ansaldo of Genoa and the Terni foundries came to rely on government orders of armaments during the international arms race before 1914. Such governmental collaboration with Italy's industrialists inevitably predisposed the state to the side of capital in the class war. The ruthless exploitation of the new proletariat in Italy's northern towns sparked numerous violent clashes between capital and labor. Invariably, in the closing decades of the nineteenth century, the central authority backed the employers, often sanctioning martial law and the suspension of civil rights. Needless to say, worker discontent was quashed superficially, but it continued to smolder beneath the surface.

Quite clearly, the parliamentary regime did not represent a broad spectrum of Italian opinion, merely the interests of a wealthy elite. Parliamentary practices reeked of corruption, and the overlapping of the political and business worlds occasioned further influence-peddling. In the eyes of many Italians, the political-business complex in Rome comprised a clique whose members were preoccupied with petty squabbles and their own self-advancement; the whole process could only be regarded with cynical detachment. It was surely no coincidence that two of the most trenchant scholarly critiques of nineteenth-century liberal parliamentarianism before 1914 came from the Italian political scientist, Gaetano Mosca, and the Italian-Swiss sociologist, Vilfredo Pareto. Both gained their firsthand impressions from the example in Rome.

In international affairs no less than domestic matters, Italy's parliamentary government failed to deliver what was expected. Unification itself had been achieved by French and Prussian arms, so that after 1870 the Italian national ego required some international triumphs on which to feed. Instead, in 1881, the territory of Tunisia, which Italians had long considered their zone of influence in North Africa, was seized by France. The most that Rome could muster by way of response was to apply to join the Austro-German alliance. This being granted, there came into being in 1882 the Triple Alliance of Germany, Austria-Hungary, and Italy. By association with Bismarckian Germany, France's archenemy and the strongest Continental power, Italy won a species of compensation for the loss of Tunisia—but at a considerable price. Now, the Triple Alliance constrained Italy to respect the susceptibilities of Austria-Hungary, which meant renouncing, temporarily at least, Italian claims to the Trentino and Trieste. These predominantly Italian-speaking regions on Italy's frontier still belonged to the Hapsburg Empire and thus constituted Italy's principal *terre irredente* (unredeemed lands). Furthermore, some upper-class Italians were prepared to defer to Berlin and Vienna not only in diplomatic but also in cultural affairs. These circles made a fashion of imitating German philosophy, music, and indeed ideas and art in general. It was a depressing foretaste of the Italian subjection to Germanic influence which was to characterize the fascist Rome-Berlin Axis half a century later. Of course, to many Italians the Hapsburg Empire continued to be the traditional enemy that it had been during the struggle for unification, and the Triple Alliance represented a betrayal of Italy's true, irredentist goals. In many quarters the foreign policy of the liberal regime was castigated as misguided and ignominious.

All the shortcomings of Italian parliamentary government seemed to conspire together in the final decade of the nineteenth century to produce a major constitutional crisis. In 1889 a parliamentary committee indicated that for some time certain Italian banks had been issuing currency beyond the legal limit to cover their own speculations. However, for three years Parliament kept the report from public gaze, and not until the yellow press got hold of it did a full-scale scandal break, implicating financiers, deputies, even ministers, and bringing the law courts into action. While the entire political system was under indictment at these revelations, working-class outbursts among both the Sicilian peasantry and northern proletariat became chronic. The then transformist premier, Francesco Crispi, himself a Sicilian by birth and an erstwhile member of the Left, nevertheless refused to admit any validity to lower-class grievances. But despite the use of the state's coercive power and the outlawry of the recently founded Italian Socialist party, the unrest persisted. At this point in the mid-1890s, Crispi resolved to distract attention from the domestic turmoil by launching an adventure abroad. This was the conquest of Ethiopia, which Italians had eyed as potential booty since first establishing a colony on the shores of the Red Sea in 1882. But the Ethiopian campaign was poorly conceived and supplied by Rome, and badly directed in the field. The result was the Battle of Adowa (1896), in which the Ethiopian army routed the invading Italians, who lost 6,000 men. As humiliating as Adowa itself was the Italian parliamentary state's failure, mainly for economic reasons, to remount the invasion of Ethiopia. It would be forty years before Mussolini tried to avenge Adowa.

It was only natural that the sorry combination of bank scandals, ongoing civil disorder, and foreign disaster should give rise to a movement to scrap the liberal political system which was held responsible. Its rallying cry was the slogan of the conservative politician, Sidney Sonnino: "Back to the constitution." By this was meant a return to the monarchical prerogative as defined in the original Italian constitution, and an end to the drift of parliamentary sovereignty. A ministry responsible to the crown and untrammeled by Parliament would be relieved of the sordid business of constructing a transformist majority and free to deal summarily with strikers and rioters. And presumably an incorrupt and strong regime at home would be a strong one abroad.

An attempt to put this program into practice was begun in 1898, largely in response to further street demonstrations in Milan. A right-wing ministry headed by General Luigi Pelloux proposed certain "exceptional laws" which curtailed the constitutional liberties of free speech and assembly, as well as drastically reduced the government's accountability to Parliament and the judiciary on a permanent basis. (By contrast, Crispi had gone outside the law only in spasmodic, ad hoc manner.) With royal support and by the usual method of buying votes, Pelloux was able to win a majority for his scheme in the Chamber of Deputies. But the opposition quickly banded together in a spirit of unity rare in Italian politics and began to talk in unfamiliar parliamentary language of the sanctity of law and the rights of the legislature. The opposition filibustered; then, in imitation of the ancient Roman plebs's gesture of protest—withdrawal to the neighboring Aventine Hills —the opposition deputies en masse walked out of the chamber. This was the government's opportunity, for the exceptional laws could be approved by the rump assembly. Of course, this would have been tantamount to a coup d'état, and civil war might well have ensued. Faced with this possibility, the Right lost its courage. Pelloux, who was no Napoleonic figure, quietly resigned in 1900, and a more moderate and transformist ministry was created.

The constitutional crisis of 1898–1900 was the harbinger of Fascism in Italy. The Right's alternative to parliamentary government—a strong executive above vice and the law, able to suppress unrest at home and assert Italy's interests abroad—was the future Fascist program in outline. The authoritarian elements in Italian society, thwarted in 1900, would be among Mussolini's firmest supporters in the aftermath of World War I.

In the short run, however, the parliamentary regime appeared to have gained from the crisis. A good deal of public support had rallied to it under attack, and there was a general belief that the liberals had been frightened into correcting the regime's worst abuses. It was almost like a bright new beginning for united Italy. One who seemed conscious of a fresh opportunity was Giovanni Giolitti, who held sway over a succession of ministries between 1901 and 1914. Giolitti was responsible for a positive effort to remove the impression that Parliament spoke only for narrow interest groups. In most labor disputes the government, instead of lending military and police support to the employers, now adopted a hands-off policy. As a result, for a few years Giolitti even received some socialist backing. But the most daring stratagem to reconcile the Italian masses to the political system was the extension of the suffrage in 1912 to all adult males over thirty. In addition to these progressive measures, Italy in the first decade of the twentieth century enjoyed an increased rate of economic growth with a consequent improvement in working-class living standards, which owed something to Giolitti's economic policies.

Modern scholarship has tended to applaud Giolitti's accomplishments, suggesting that he might well have saved Italian liberalism but for the unforeseeable catastrophe of the First World War. On the other hand, there remains some substance to the charge of an older school that Giolitti's reforms counted for little beside his methods of maintaining power. For Giolitti was an old-fashioned parliamentary manager who governed by conventional and corrupt means; the word *Giolittismo* was used to imply a refinement of *trasformismo*. It was suggested that the suffrage law of 1912 was deliberately calculated to enfranchise the southern peasantry whose votes were most easily controlled by the Giolittian machine. This suspicion seemed to be borne out in the 1913 elections when Giolitti, to compensate for loss of support on the left, entered into a working alliance with conservative Catholics whose influence was greatest in the *Mezzogiorno*. It was the premier's satisfaction with the unreconstructed state of the south, together with his debasement of parliamentary life, which lay behind the famous judgment of Gaetano Salvemini, the historian and contemporary critic of Giolittian rule, who described Giolitti himself as "*il ministro della mala vita*" (the minister of the underworld). Harsh though Salvemini's verdict may be, it nonetheless conveys the sense of bitter disillusion which arose at the dissipation of the high expectations of 1900. Insofar as Giolitti failed to overcome the Italians' basic cynicism toward liberal politics, he prepared the way, however unwittingly, for Fascism.

Moreover, another precursor of Fascism flourished in the Giolittian era. Italian nationalism and imperialism had not been dampened by Adowa; rather, the reverse occurred. The environment for sustained patriotic sentiment was, to a great extent, created by avant-garde artists whose elevation of feeling over reason was encapsulated in Marinetti's Futurist Manifesto of 1909: "We sing the love of danger. Courage, rashness, and rebellion are the elements of our poetry. Hitherto, literature has exalted thoughtful immobility, whereas we are for aggressive movement, febrile insomnia, mortal leaps, and blows with the fist. . . . There is no beauty now save in struggle, no masterpiece can be anything but aggressive, and hence we glorify war, militarism, and patriotism." However, the most articulate nationalist spokesman at this time was Enrico Corradini, whose journal *Il Regno* drew an explicit contrast between the spirituality and nobility of war and the arid materialism of the bourgeois regime in Rome. In 1910 Corradini came together with other nationalists such as Luigi Federzoni, later Mussolini's minister of colonies, and an artistic coterie headed by D'Annunzio to found the *Associazione nazionalista italiana* (Nationalist party). The organization's immediate purpose was to agitate for the seizure of Libya in North Africa, which was still part of the Turkish Empire. Giolitti, who was convinced that Libya was due Italy by "historical fatality," succumbed in 1911 to the demand for war, although he lived to regret the step. Libya was, in fact, won and a fairly punitive peace settlement forced on Turkey. But the nationalists were far from satisfied, and decried first the decision to make peace and then the treaty itself. Giolitti thus failed to appease the nationalists who scarcely paused in their corrosive denunciations of Italy's liberal system.

The parliamentary regime's inability to cope with nationalist feeling was further exposed by World War I. At the outbreak of war, Italy was still a member of the Triple Alliance. Yet, since the turn of the century, Italy had been drifting steadily away from her nominal allies, Austria-Hungary and Germany. The rising Italian nationalist movement had reawakened the demand for Austrian-held Trieste and the Trentino; and with the mounting Anglo-German rivalry, Italy found herself a partner in a potentially anti-British bloc, which she dared not countenance out of fear of British naval strength in the Mediterranean.

It was, then, no surprise when Italy proclaimed neutrality in August 1914. But, at once, a clamor for intervention began, trading on an undercurrent of feeling that it was somehow undignified for a major power, as Italy claimed to be, to stay out of such a titanic contest. Most of the specific arguments advanced were in favor of intervention on the side of the Triple Entente and against Italy's late allies; the nationalists thought the moment propitious to capture *Italia irredenta*, while the more democratic interventionists wanted to join in a crusade against Teutonic authoritarianism. As a result of diplomatic maneuvers in the spring of 1915, Austria-Hungary offered, in return for Italy's continued neutrality, a general undertaking to satisfy Italian irredentist claims at the end of the war. On the other hand, Britain and France held out as reward for intervention a blanket promise of the Trentino and Trieste, plus more territory on the eastern shore of the Adriatic and in Africa. Accordingly, by the Treaty of London of April 26, Italy undertook to join the Entente powers at war. To describe this action, the Italian premier, Antonio Salandra, coined the unfortunate phrase "*sacro egoismo*," thus implying that Italy's allegiance could be, indeed had been, bought by the higher bidder. This was exactly the sort of tainted image that had bedeviled liberal Italy for forty years.

Furthermore, the decision for intervention was taken in barely constitutional fashion. Parliament was called into session to approve the Treaty of London, but was never informed of the actual terms. The Chamber of Deputies possessed a clear neutralist majority, many members taking their cue from Giolitti who, although now out of office, remained Italy's dominant parliamentary figure. However, faced with pressure from the crown and also from street mobs inflamed by such demagogues as D'Annunzio and Mussolini, this neutralist majority evaporated within a few days, and the legislature compliantly and overwhelmingly voted for intervention. Thus, in effect, Italy's most crucial decision since unification was made outside Parliament.

The war was unpopular with many Italians. The Vatican condemned it, and so did most socialists. The bulk of the populace found little to cheer about as the Italian army became locked, for over two years, in a cruel struggle of attrition on the Austrian Alpine frontier. Then, in October 1917 the Austrians and Germans broke through at Caporetto, and in three weeks advanced one hundred miles in the direction of Venice. There were military reasons for Caporetto, although the disaster also seemed to signify a complete collapse of Italian national morale. But whatever the cause, scapegoats had to be found in the persons of liberal politicians and military advisors. After Caporetto a wave of pop-ular patriotism, generated by the Austrian presence on Italian soil, swept the country and contributed to some Italian victories in the closing months of the war; but the government in Rome was given little credit for these. Some Italians damned the parliamentary regime for allowing the nation to be dragged into war, others for its misman-agement of the war effort. Overall, the liberal system emerged from the war even more embattled than before.

## Mussolini's Socialist Youth

World War I was a fateful turning point not only for Italian liberal-ism but also for Mussolini, its destined executioner. Mussolini was born in 1883 in the village of Predappio in the Romagna, a region known throughout history for its rebellious spirit. Mussolini's father, an anticlerical, radical blacksmith, christened his son Benito after the Mexican revolutionary Juarez, and Amilcare Andrea after the Italian socialists Cipriani and Costa. He had much more influence over the young Mussolini than did his pious schoolteacher mother. Benito's mother managed to secure his entrance to various clerical academies, but he chiefly distinguished himself by his use of violence against teachers and fellow pupils. He always became incensed at the privileges accorded wealthier children; this resentment of Italy's plutocracy would stay with him all his life.

Despite his scholastic difficulties, Mussolini in 1902 gained an ele-mentary school teacher's certificate. But, within a few months, he fled to Switzerland, possibly to escape compulsory military service. There he was arrested for vagrancy. Ultimately, destitute, he approached some Italian socialists in a Lausanne café, who befriended him and set him to his lifelong vocation of political agitation. He became involved in the fight for the rights of Italian immigrant laborers in Switzerland; he was tutored in socialism by the Russian exile, Angelica Balabanov; and he may have attended a few lectures by Pareto at the University of Lausanne. In due course, Mussolini returned to Italy, completed his army service, and briefly taught school. Then in 1908 he was appointed editor of an Italian socialist paper in the Austrian city of Trent. In less than a year he was expelled by the authorities, not for his irredentism, as he was later to claim, but for his anticlericalism; he had written and published a serialized story entitled "Claudia Particella or The Cardinal's Mistress." However, his brush with the Austrians brought him some notoriety and helped to win for him the secretaryship of the Socialist federation in his native province of Forlì. This post gave him the opportunity to found and edit a local socialist paper, *La Lotte di Classe* (*The Class Struggle*), in which he polished his use of invective and displayed an extreme political dogmatism. These attributes were to bring him into national prominence within two years.

The *Partito socialista italiana* (PSI), in common with most European socialist parties before 1914, was split between the reformists and the revolutionaries. The former, who were willing to work pro tem within a bourgeois parliamentary system in return for immediate working-class gains, were excoriated as traitors by the latter, who clung to the letter of Marxism and urged uncompromising class war. In the Italian context, the reformists tended to prevail in the early years of the twentieth century, and the PSI often supported Giolitti. But Giolitti's embrace of imperialism in the Libyan War of 1911–12 cut the ground from beneath the feet of the reformists. Imperialism was anathema to almost all socialists, and the revolutionaries seized on the issue in a bid to gain control of the PSI at its biennial congress held in 1912 at Reggio Emilia. The hatchet man they chose to lead the attack on the reformist leadership was Mussolini, whose credentials for the job were ideal. He had consistently advocated the achievement of socialism by revolutionary violence, although his stand arose less from an attachment to Marxian principles than from his personal hatred of Italy's middle classes. He was renowned as an anti-imperialist, having just spent several months in prison for sabotaging a section of railroad track in order to impede the transport of troops and supplies for the Libyan War. And, not least, he had shown in his journalism a ruthless intolerance of all who disagreed with him. The revolutionaries' confidence was not misplaced. Mussolini's histrionic performance at Reggio Emilia played a substantial part in the expulsion of four prominent reformists from the party and the capture of the party executive by the revolutionary socialists. Mussolini's reward was the editorship of *Avanti* (*Forward*), the Italian Socialist party's national daily paper published in Milan.

On more than one occasion Mussolini admitted his true métier to be that of a journalist—albeit of the persuasive and not the reportorial kind. For two years Mussolini was a successful editor of *Avanti*, more than tripling its circulation. His editorials mirrored the current mood of Italian Socialism—fiery and revolutionary. *Avanti* was instrumental in stirring up a wave of labor unrest in the summer of 1914, the high point of which was the famous "Red Week" in June at Ancona. These disturbances were credited with fortifying the Italian government's resolution for neutrality at the outbreak of World War I. The PSI opposed intervention in what it considered a capitalist war, and Mussolini apostrophized in *Avanti*: "It is in the name of the International and of Socialism that we invite you, proletarians of Italy, to uphold your unshakable opposition to war." But, within a few weeks, Mussolini reversed himself totally. On October 18 in an editorial entitled "From Absolute to Active and Working Neutrality," he championed the Entente cause and queried whether socialists could afford to hold aloof from the war. He was at once relieved of his editorship of *Avanti*. A month later he produced the first issue of a new paper, *Popolo d'Italia* (*People of Italy*), in which he termed neutrality cowardice and demanded "with my full voice, with no attempt at simulation, with a firm faith, a fearful and fascinating word: *war!*" For this offense he was shortly afterward expelled from the Italian Socialist party.

Although Mussolini has often been condemned as opportunistic, his conversion to intervention was probably sincere. It is true that his *Popolo d'Italia* was established with funds from the Italian nationalist Right and French socialists, but there is no evidence that Mussolini received, or was promised, money before his volte-face. In any case, throughout his whole life he was impervious to wealth and material comfort, living in a positively abstemious fashion. He was, on the other hand, hungry for power. But his espousal of intervention wrecked a promising career which, in time, would surely have taken him close to the top of the PSI; his prospects after expulsion by the party were uncertain to say the least. Mussolini's conversion, then, is hardly explicable in terms of personal ambition.

The fact of the matter is that Mussolini did not regard his actions in the fall of 1914 as a betrayal of socialism at all. He merely changed his brand of socialism. Now, he adopted the tenet of the syndicalists, who had long since been expelled from the PSI, that World War I could be transformed into a "revolutionary war." That is, by participating in the war effort, the Italian masses would be brought for the first time within the national community. Indeed, they would be in a position to take over the state, or as Mussolini was to express it near the end of World War I: "We, the survivors, we who have returned, demand the right of governing Italy." Thus, nationalism would cease to be the exclusive preserve of the Right; Mussolini's new-found integral nationalism, embracing all strata of society and requiring the whole being of every citizen, was intended to be a radical force. He was still, as the title of Renzo De Felice's biography of these years has it, *Mussolini: Il revoluzionario* (1965).

In the meantime, Mussolini joined with more conventional nationalists to push Italy into war. Having succeeded in May 1915, he was soon after inducted into the army where, as in his term of military service in 1904, he seemed to lose his restlessness and find security in the discipline of military life. As a soldier, he performed competently and was promoted to the rank of corporal. He was badly wounded when a shell exploded inside a howitzer during firing practice. Invalided out of the army, he returned to the editor's desk at *Popolo d'Italia* in time to engage in the post-Caporetto burst of patriotism. Mussolini's recommendations for dealing with the war crisis included the imprisonment of pacifists, censorship of the socialist press, and the replacement of parliamentary government with some form of dictatorship. Yet, at the end of the war, Mussolini was far from being a leader of Italian nationalism; he was only one of innumerable professional patriots, and one with a short record at that. With the coming of peace, the flow of funds for the *Popolo d'Italia* from domestic and foreign sources began to dry up. In truth, Mussolini was only saved from likely political oblivion by the fact that Italy's liberal regime creaked to a virtual standstill in the aftermath of World War I.


## Postwar Chaos

The root of the difficulty with the parliamentary regime was that transformism became outmoded and no substitute could be found. The drastic increase in the number of voters by the suffrage law of 1912, however much it served Giolitti's immediate southern electoral strategy, in the long run was bound to make control of elections vastly more difficult. Then, in 1919, in a frank reformist effort to rid Italian politics of some of its corruption, another electoral law initiated a system of broad proportional representation and multimember constituencies. Henceforth, neither the incumbent government nor any other interest group could guarantee the election of more than one or two candidates in large multimember districts. Manhood suffrage and proportional representation spelled the end of traditional parliamentary management and opened the door to mass parties.

Indeed, the elections of 1919 saw the Italian Socialist party win 156 seats out of 508 in the Chamber of Deputies, while a brand-new Catholic party, the *Popolari* or Popular party, gained 100 seats. In effect the survival of Italy's liberal political system depended on these two parties with grass-roots following. Together, the Socialists and *Popolari* could have formed a solid coalition government. However, the possibility of cooperation was never really canvassed. To Catholics, the PSI smacked of atheistic Marxism, while in Socialist eyes, the *Popolari* represented a backward peasantry and their conservative landlords. Each party caricatured the other—and thus had an excuse to refuse collaboration.

Even so, the parliamentary situation might have been saved if either the Socialists or *Popolari* alone had been prepared to form the nucleus of a coalition ministry. But both parties shied away from office, and for roughly the same reason in each case. The Socialists were even more divided than before 1914. Not only was the rift between reformists and revolutionaries still extant, but the Russian Bolshevik Revolution introduced further dissension over how far the PSI should follow Bolshevik policies and how far it should submit to directives from Moscow. (Ultimately, in 1921 those who advocated compliance with Lenin's stringent terms for admission to the Third Socialist International or Comintern broke away and formed the *Partito communista italiana* [PCI].) Given this factionalism, it was almost impossible for the Socialists to enunciate a consistent and definite program which they might implement in office. Moreover, as the PSI remained formally Marxian and revolutionary (although rejecting Moscow's orders), the party theoretically was committed to the overthrow of the bourgeois parliamentary system itself. The *Popolari*, for their part, were also split and found it extremely difficult to construct a policy platform congenial to all shades of Catholic opinion. At one extreme, the higher clergy, particularly those close to the Vatican, were outright reactionaries; at the other, many priests, such as the Popular party's secretary, Don Luigi Sturzo, who had worked among Italy's poor, voiced radical and even socialist opinions. But the chief obstacle to the *Popolari* taking office was simply papal disapproval. In view of the papacy's erstwhile ban on all Catholic participation in Italian public affairs, its tolerance of a Catholic political party was a significant concession—motivated largely by alarm at the spread of socialism. But whether the papacy would retreat so far as to countenance a Catholic role in an Italian secular government was, in 1919, very dubious. No explicit pronouncement on the subject was made, but it was general knowledge among the *Popolari* that the Vatican's attitude was negative.

With the refusal of both Socialists and *Popolari* to assume the burden

of office to which their electoral successes entitled them, Italian politicians fell back on the method of government which they knew best
—transformism, but now executed in quite inimical circumstances. All
five ministries between the end of the First World War and the
Fascist entry into office in 1922 were palpably unstable, even when
headed by such notables as the economist and reformer, Francesco
Nitti, or the seventy-eight-year-old Giolitti, who had one last term as
premier. Not surprisingly, there was a distinct lack of official vigor,
verging at times on a complete abdication of authority. The inefficacy
of these last pre-Fascist ministries can be usefully subsumed under two
headings—socioeconomic policy and diplomacy.

Italy's economy emerged from World War I in a sorry plight. The
war had been financed out of revenues only to a small extent and,
by 1920, the public debt had increased sevenfold. Even after the war,
expenditures continued to run far ahead of receipts, at times by a ratio
of three to one. Italy's export trade had been severely dislocated, while
the costs of her essential imports, such as British coal, soared. In some
three years the cost of living rose by over 50 percent. Wages rose too,
but not all occupations benefited, nor did the millions who lived by
casual work. With two and a half million demobilized soldiers thrown
on to the labor market, unemployment was rife; by the end of 1921,
the official figure reached half a million, although almost certainly this
was a considerable underestimation. Against this mass penury was set
the conspicuous consumption of some war profiteers, poisoning the
social atmosphere. The liberal governments drifted through the crisis
and provided little leadership. Legislation to compel the rich to assume
a fair share of the country's economic burden was proposed, but out
of deference to powerful vested interests, only minor changes were
effected in Italy's regressive tax structure. On the other hand, Rome
hesitated to remove traditional but expensive bread subsidies for the
poor lest such an action produce revolution. Here, indeed, was the
rub, for all the ingredients of a revolutionary situation seemed to be
present.

The trouble began in the countryside where peasants, often ex-
soldiers wearing their war medals, occupied the uncultivated fringes
of the latifondi. But a more sensational attack on property rights took
place in the towns. During the first half of 1920, strikers began increasingly to respond to lockouts by camping in their factories. At the end
of August, workers at the huge Alfa Romeo plant in Milan reacted in
this way to unusually provocative action by management, and the tactic

spread like wildfire. Within a few weeks strikers had seized 280 factories in Milan and some 200 more in Turin. Yet, these sit-in strikes seldom lasted more than a few weeks. And as the winter of 1920–21 saw a gradual upturn in the Italian economy, working-class unrest began to subside. But the passing challenge in both town and country to the sanctity of private property appeared to lend credence to the great bourgeois fear of the time—a bolshevik conspiracy. In the case of Italy this was, for all practical purposes, a fictitious threat. There was no organization or plan behind the rural squatters or the sit-in strikers. Italian Socialists were too divided among themselves to formulate a coherent revolutionary program, and no direction was forthcoming from Moscow because Lenin considered the Italian proletariat immature. Furthermore, the revolutionary temper of the rank and file of Italian Socialists was suspect, as indicated by their lukewarm response to the several attempts between 1919 and 1922 to launch a general strike. Nevertheless, these factors were overlooked at the time, and Italy's propertied classes remained a prey to the antibolshevik panic.

Their alarm was fed by the inactivity of the central power. Although the government did intervene to play an arbitral role in some sit-in strikes, official policy was to keep out of the battle between capital and labor. This was the precept laid down by Giolitti before 1914, when it seemed an enlightened and prudent policy. After the war, however, the government's hands-off attitude was roundly condemned as an invitation to revolution and chaos. The industrialists and landowners were not content with verbal criticism, but proceeded to take the law into their own hands through the use of paramilitary groups, notably the Fascist Black Shirts, as a private police force. Thus, the liberal regime's inertia led straight to anarchy and civil war.

Italy's postwar ministries were also held to be remiss in foreign affairs. At the close of World War I, Italy was, in a sense, the most victorious nation of all, for her hereditary enemy, Austria-Hungary, had ceased to exist. To Italian nationalists, the demise of the Hapsburg Empire opened up the long-term prospect of Italian penetration into the Danube Valley as well as immediate territorial gains. At the Paris Peace Conference, where Italy occupied a privileged position as one of the Council of Four, she was granted the entire Trentino up to the strategic Brenner Pass, a settlement which consigned over 200,000 Germans in the Alto Adige to Italian rule. Moreover, the British, French, and Americans suggested an Italo-Yugoslav border which not only placed half a million Slavs within Italy's frontiers but also satisfied

Italian strategic requirements. These were rewards far in excess of the terms of the Treaty of London of 1915. In return, Italy was asked to forego her claims under the Treaty of London to Dalmatia across the Adriatic and to accept token satisfaction in the colonial field. On balance, the bargain was an advantageous one for Italy, whose overburdened treasury was scarcely in a position to sustain a military occupation of Dalmatia and the administrative costs of new colonies or mandates. The government in Rome was inclined to accept the Allied proposals. But the Italian nationalists reacted promptly and furiously against any compromise; liberal ministers were denounced as "*rinunciatari*" (renouncers), and Italy's victory declared "mutilated."

In the eye of this hyperpatriotic storm lay the question of Fiume, an Italian urban outpost on the eastern Adriatic shore amid a sea of Slavs in the new state of Yugoslavia. The Treaty of London, not anticipating the disintegration of the Hapsburg Empire, had made no provision for the city. At the Paris Peace Conference, President Wilson was adamant that Fiume should not be Italian on grounds of national self-determination. In response to nationalist pressure at home, the Italian delegation led by Premier Orlando and Foreign Minister Sonnino ostentatiously walked out of the Council of Four and refused to return for a fortnight. Yet, when the peace conference broke up in the summer of 1919, the Fiume dispute was still unresolved; the Italian government did not dare concede the city to Yugoslavia, and the Allies would not yield it to Italy.

Fiume thereupon enjoyed a semiautonomous status until September when the long-time Italian Nationalist leader, D'Annunzio, led a private army of a thousand legionnaires into the city. There, he proclaimed a regency "in the name of the Italian people." Yugoslavia took no action out of fear of Italy's military strength; the authorities in Rome felt powerless to move against D'Annunzio in the face of the acclaim with which Italians greeted the coup. In fact, the Nitti and Giolitti ministries in succession tried to curry favor with Italian nationalists by covertly supplying D'Annunzio in Fiume. Not until the D'Annunzio regency began to collapse of its own accord, helped along by the prevalence of cholera and influenza in Fiume, did Rome take stern action. In December 1920 the Italian government, having just concluded a frontier agreement with Yugoslavia which provided for an independent Fiume, dispatched a naval squadron which drove the legionnaires out of the city. But D'Annunzio's escapade had spotlighted the futility of the liberal regime's foreign policy. Unable to satisfy

Italian jingoism by imitating D'Annunzio, it was also clearly incapable of curbing nationalist excesses.

The prevalence of irrationally held opinions was a common feature of the post-World War I era. Italians gave a powerful illustration by their credulous twin beliefs—in an imminent Bolshevik coup and in the "mutilated victory." These were, in fact, perfect examples of Sorelian "myths." It was a special fascist talent to sense and exploit popular myths and moods. Beyond doubt, the key factors in Mussolini's accession to the Italian premiership in 1922 were the middle-class fear of revolution and the nationalist grievance.

In addition, another less precise kind of discontent should be mentioned. In terms of modernization, Italy had passed the "take-off" point. But, compared to Europe's advanced nations, Italy had traveled only part way along the road; she was really still in the transitional stage between an agrarian and an industrial society. In the first two decades of the twentieth century, Italian business groups and economists pressed for an acceleration and fulfillment of modernization; Nitti was a prominent spokesman for this cult of "productivism." Yet, increasingly, many of these progressives felt frustrated by the complacency and stagnation of Italian officialdom. They demanded efficiency and drive from the central government. Instead, they perceived an anachronistic political system, and endured ministries which preached traditional laissez faire and failed utterly in the *Mezzogiorno* where the chief obstacle to Italy's full entry into the twentieth century lay. Moreover, liberal Italy's lack of assertiveness in international affairs could be ascribed to a failure to modernize and become a truly major power. In contrast, Fascism appeared a young, vigorous movement, untrammeled by obsolete customs. Admittedly, the Fascists had no very clear program of modernization. But they managed to project a modernist image with such slogans as "*largo alle competenze*" (make way for the competent) and rhetoric about "*combattenti e produttori*" (fighters and producers). And at the height of the sit-in strikes, Mussolini argued that the criterion of judgment between capital and labor should be economic performance: "I only ask that there should be a clear conscience and technical capacity, and that production be increased. If this is guaranteed by the trade unions, instead of by the employers, I have no hesitation in saying that the former have the right to take the latter's place."

Europe's first fascist movement was inaugurated on May 23, 1919, when Mussolini, in a building off the Piazza San Sepolcro in Milan, addressed his new creation styled a *fascio di combattimento* (battle group). The word *fascio* was commonly used in Italy by social and political action groups; the Sicilian peasant rebels in 1894 had formed themselves into *fasci*, and so had the interventionists of 1914–15. Mussolini himself in December 1914 had established a *fascio d'azione rivoluzionario*, while the artistic exponents of nationalist violence, who were among the first to rally to Mussolini in 1919, had been banded together in *fasci politici futuristi*. *Fascio* derived from the Latin *fasces*, denoting the bundle of rods with protruding ax head carried by the magistrates of ancient Rome. The original *fasces* symbolized justice, but the binding together of the separate rods could also imply unity. It was this latter connotation which was appropriate to a movement whose principal object was to reintegrate a society rent by the class war and political factionalism.

The first meeting of the Milan *fascio di combattimento* attracted about a hundred people. Much in evidence were *arditi*, Italian shock troops renowned for their bravery, brutality, and patriotic zeal. A few weeks earlier, they had joined with Mussolini's followers to break up a meeting of Socialist *rinunciatari*; now they served as stewards at this first Fascist assembly. Shortly, Mussolini would adopt the *arditi* black shirt as the uniform of his own shock troops, the *squadristi*. The prominence of the *arditi* at the birth of Italian Fascism guaranteed that the movement would be ruthless and violent. Mussolini harangued the first Fascist audience on the two uppermost problems of Italian life—international affairs and the state of the working class. On the former subject he was predictably chauvinistic; Dalmatia, including Fiume, and colonies were demanded as of right. More interesting were Mussolini's pronouncements on the social question. These were unequivocally radical —antimonarchist, anticlerical, and anticapitalist. He was sarcastically critical of the PSI for being "obviously reactionary, completely conservative," and he advanced his own brand of "economic democracy." This hinted at worker control of industry: "We want the workers to become accustomed to managerial responsibilities." Political representation should be, not by geography, but by "occupational outlook"; Mussolini conceded that "such a program implies a return to the guilds (*corporazioni*)." Thus, from the start, Italian Fascism looked back to syndicalist socialism and forward to the corporative state.

At first, the Fascist line seemed a continuation of Mussolini's wartime endeavor to combine nationalism with drastic socioeconomic change. Quickly, however, Fascism became associated with Italy's men of property. Mussolini's alliance with the nationalist Right provided the initial link; the hall in which the inaugural Fascist meeting was held belonged to a "Club for Commerce and Industry," and was often leased to patriotic groups. The young Fascist movement was unable to resist the lure of conservative money for uniforms, transport, arms, and for the continued publication of *Popolo d'Italia*. The first donors were the *latifondisti*, who were not unduly disturbed by Mussolini's proposals for worker participation in factory management. But, in the face of mounting labor unrest, the industrialists, too, decided on stern measures and, in 1919, a General Confederation of Industry (*Confindustria*) was founded expressly to combat revolutionary agitation. As part of this campaign against the Left, funds from big business as well as the Po Valley landowners began to flow into the Fascist treasury. Initially, these subventions were to pay for the services of the Fascist squads in driving squatters off estates and strikers out of factories. But the *squadristi* went much further. They made a regular weekend sport of raiding trade union buildings, chambers of labor, headquarters of agrarian cooperative, and socialist press offices; the *Avanti* offices in Milan were wrecked several times. Individuals were beaten with *bastone* and *manganello*, clubs favored by the Fascists, and forcibly fed castor oil to purge them of their wrong opinions. Apart from some "white" or Catholic trade unions, the institutions and persons attacked were designated "red."

All this effectively destroyed Fascism's radical image, somewhat to the displeasure of Mussolini, who still aspired to be the Lenin of Italy. However, he was powerless to stop Fascism's drift rightward. In August 1921 he negotiated a pact with the PSI for the renunciation of violence; it would not be the last time that Mussolini would try to retrace his steps back to his leftist youth. But he was immediately opposed by many of his lieutenants, Fascist bosses in various regions of Italy who liked to call themselves *ras* after Ethiopian tribal chiefs. Such men as Dino Grandi in Bologna, Roberto Farinacci in Cremona, and Italo Balbo in Ferrara acted quite independently of Mussolini in Milan; they made their own financial arrangements with the local plutocracy and ran *squadristi* raids as they saw fit. At this stage Fascism was far from a monolithic, hierarchical phenomenon, and it certainly could not be equated with Mussolinianism. Faced with opposition from the *ras* —especially Balbo and Grandi—to his pact with the Socialists, Mussolini offered his resignation. But Mussolini's charisma was too valuable to lose, and he was prevailed upon to remain as Duce, the title of leader he had always craved both as Socialist and Fascist. On the other hand, on the substantive issue Mussolini capitulated. Although the arrangement with the Socialists to abjure violence was never formally repudiated, the *ras* were assured that they need not abide by it. It would be wrong, however, to assume that the revolt of the *ras* had sprung from their antisocialist principles; their main concern had been that Mussolini might stop their sport of knocking heads. Grandi and his fellows were just as much antiestablishment figures as Mussolini himself; their irreverence for constituted authority and convention was expressed pithily in their slogan, "*Me ne frego*" ("I don't give a damn"). Nonetheless, to maintain momentum, Fascism needed backing from the rich and for the time being had to dance to the paymasters' tune.

Mussolini himself seemed to bow to this necessity in November 1921 at a Fascist congress in Rome which saw the establishment of a formal party, the *Partito nazionale fascista* (PNF). Taking the opportunity to redefine policy, the Duce disclosed that Fascists were now "decidedly antisocialist" and "economic liberals." As for the masses: "We do indeed wish to serve them, to educate them, but we also intend to flog them when they make mistakes." The *squadristi* hardly required this encouragement. Italy was plunged into a veritable civil war between Fascist Black Shirts and Socialist Red Shirts. Undoubtedly, there were provocations on both sides, but there can be no question but that the major aggression came from the Black Shirts. Growing bolder each month, the *squadristi* took to expelling elected Socialist town councils and mayors and imposing a Fascist military occupation for several days; Ferrara, Ravenna, and Ancona were all "captured." Italy's new Slavic and German territorities received special attention because there the Black Shirts could beat up Socialists and non-Italians at the same time; in 1922 the regional administration of the entire Alto Adige was usurped by the Fascists. Military operations of this scope succeeded for the simple reason that they were almost always executed with the connivance of the police, and sometimes that of the military as well. Here was proof for many Italians that the Fascists, not the government in Rome, represented authority and a safeguard against revolution.

Meanwhile, Fascism was moving to take over the Italian nationalist cause. Of course, there already existed a thriving Nationalist party, and by his descent on Fiume, D'Annunzio had staked a clear claim to speak for Italian nationalism. D'Annunzio was a romantic figure, a poet of violence, and a renowned amorist; during World War I he had made daring flights to drop leaflets over unredeemed Italy, and he wore a black patch over one eye due to a wound sustained in these exploits.

He seemed on the surface a much more inspirational figurehead for the nationalists than Mussolini, an uncouth upstart with a humdrum war record. Moreover, while the Fiume regency was at its height, D'Annunzio hinted he might be willing to lead the Nationalist Blue Shirts in a coup against Italy's parliamentary regime. Yet, within a year of leaving Fiume, D'Annunzio fell into eclipse.

In the main, this was because D'Annunzio found domestic politics a pettifogging business. While in Fiume, he neglected to build up a power base in Italy, and he refused to be bought by the anti-Bolsheviks. Consequently, he was outmaneuvered by Mussolini. Mussolini plainly perceived D'Annunzio as a potential rival *duce*, and his attitude was always reserved. During the Fiume occupation, he had extolled D'Annunzio in *Popolo d'Italia* as "the Intrepid One," visited Fiume briefly, and solicited funds for the regency (although a good part of the money collected went into Fascist coffers). But when the enterprise collapsed, Mussolini showed scant regret—"We must be thankful that the tragedy has not turned into a catastrophe," he editorialized—and he proceeded to turn the situation to his advantage. He took over many of the trappings of D'Annunzio's regency—the leader's tirade from the balcony above the piazza, the flags and insignia, the ritual and incomprehensible war cries—all of which made it easier to enroll the Fiume legionnaires in the Fascist *squadre*. When D'Annunzio tried to take up the project of a joint attack on the liberal government in Rome, Mussolini turned him down flat.

What confirmed Mussolini's victory over D'Annunzio was the national elections of May 1921. In 1919 Mussolini, the only Fascist candidate, had polled under 5,000 votes out of 270,000 in Milan. But he had made light of the setback: "I prefer 5,000 rebels to 5 million votes," he quipped. He proved right. Two years later, Fascism was important enough to warrant an electoral pact. The premier, Giolitti, resolved to transform the Fascists as he had transformed the reformist Socialists before 1914, and he included Fascists in the government list of candidates. As a result, while the main parties continued to be the PSI and the *Popolari* with 147 and 106 seats, respectively, Mussolini and 34 other Fascists were also returned to Parliament. Giolitti's expectations were not fulfilled, however. Their electoral success did not deflect the Fascists from pursuing violence in the country at large, nor did they support Giolitti's coalition in Parliament. The Fascist deputies joined with the Nationalists on the extreme right of the Chamber of Deputies, a working alliance that was to culminate in the absorption of the

Nationalists into the PNF in February 1923. Mussolini's liaison with the parliamentary Nationalists, in effect, gave him dominance within the Italian nationalist camp. D'Annunzio retired to private life. In the summer of 1922, as Fascism's final push for power began, D'Annunzio was incapacitated as the result of a fall from his balcony; contemporary rumor had it that he was pushed—either by an irate husband or by the *squadristi*.

By 1922, having cornered the markets in antibolshevism and nationalism, Fascism was accepted by practically the whole Italian power structure. The pattern was set at the very top of the social hierarchy. The Italian court possessed a number of Fascist sympathizers, led by the queen mother, Margherita, who had been active on the side of the Right in the crisis of 1898–1900. Another was the king's cousin, the Duke d'Aosta, who dreamed that Fascism might engineer a palace revolution to put him on the throne. King Victor Emmanuel III, anticipating the same contingency, accommodated the Fascists to avert it. Across the Tiber, the Vatican was no less complaisant; its press organ, the *Osservatore Romano*, regularly condemned Socialist violence but was usually silent on Fascist atrocities. Moreover, Pope Pius XI had been, before his elevation in February 1922, Archbishop of Milan, in which capacity he had been known to tolerate Fascist banners in the Duomo. Mussolini played skillfully on these sympathies, curbing as best he could his more irreligious followers and dissociating himself from former allies among the anticlerical and republican freemasons. Finally, in September 1922, Mussolini announced his belated conversion to monarchism.

It was not that Fascism went unrecognized as something alien to many traditional Italian values. Rather, it was accepted as a disagreeable necessity in a critical situation, which could be—and probably would be—discarded in due course. An analogous rationalization was that Fascism, given responsibility and even office, would automatically grow more respectable and less violent. Such arguments were advanced from every quarter: by senior civil servants sublimely confident of their ability to control Mussolini if he became premier; by liberal newspapers like Milan's famous *Corriere della Sera*, which had backed the parliamentary regime in 1898–1900; by intellectuals ranging from the antidemocratic Mosca to the liberal bellwether, Croce.

In addition to possessing powerful allies, Fascism claimed to be a mass movement. At the end of 1921, the Fascist party calculated its membership at 320,000 enrolled in 2,300 local *fasci*. Undoubtedly, the

PNF succeeded in engaging the interest of large pockets of Italians previously cut off from or disenchanted by the liberal state. But the Fascist following remained distinctly less than that of either the Socialist or Popular party. Nonetheless, Fascist propaganda kept up the pretense of an irresistible force from below pushing the Fascists into power, even while they relied overwhelmingly on the traditional power structure. A perfect illustration of this technique was the "March on Rome" which supplied the final impetus for Fascism's entry into office.

On August 1 in desperation the Socialists called a general strike. The workers' response was so disappointing that it was called off after twenty-four hours; it was aptly termed "the Caporetto of Italian Socialism." But the episode was a godsend to the Fascists, for it revivified the middle classes' terror of bolshevism. On August 3 the *squadristi* responded by invading the city hall of Milan and expelling the Socialist administration. Milan was Italy's richest city, the home of both Italian Socialism and Fascism, and the real capital of Italy. Obviously, it was only a matter of time before an attack on the legal capital, Rome. On October 3 the *Popolo d'Italia* published a series of military regulations for the *squadre*, creating a regular Fascist milita. On the 24th the Duce addressed a monster rally in Naples and indicated that his private army was about to march: "Either they will give us the government or we shall seize it by descending on Rome: it is now a matter of days, perhaps hours."

The March on Rome was entrusted to a quadrumvirate which reflected the disparate social strands which had come together to form Fascism—Emilio de Bono, a nationalist general still on the active list; Cesare de Vecchi, a conservative Piedmontese landowner; Michele Bianchi, a syndicalist socialist; Balbo, the adventurer and *ras* of Ferrara. Operating from headquarters in Perugia, the quadrumvirs were to coordinate the advance of three Fascist columns on Rome, after the Black Shirts in the towns had captured or immobilized nerve centers such as police stations, post offices, radio stations. Mobilization of the Fascist units was set for October 27, with the start of the march itself to take place the next day. Although this plan was, in fact, set in motion, its completion was never required, for the liberal regime in Rome surrendered too swiftly.

Although the quadrumvirate's strategy was kept a secret, rumors of a Fascist coup were rife in Rome toward the end of October. The first instinct of the liberal politicians was to ward off the threat by bringing the PNF into the government itself. Giolitti, despite his unfortunate

Mussolini with members of the quadrumvirate in charge of the March on
Rome. Note the mixture of black-shirt uniform and civilian dress;
rambunctious Italian Fascism in 1922 was also trying to present a
respeetable image.

experience in trying to transform Fascism in the 1921 elections, was
eager to make the attempt. So, too, was Salandra who, as a member
of the Right in 1898 and an associate of the Nationalists, felt specially
qualified to negotiate with the Fascists. The current premier, Luigi
Facta, a lawyer by profession and head of a stopgap ministry, fell in

with the trend and offered Mussolini a place in his cabinet. However, all these overtures were aimed at bringing Fascism into a coalition as a junior partner. Actually, Mussolini seemed tempted by these offers, but Bianchi warned him that the Fascist hierarchs disapproved. After all, the March on Rome was planned not merely to bring Fascism into office, but to ensure that it entered office at the top level.

So October 27 arrived without any compromise. News of the Fascist mobilization brought King Victor Emmanuel back to Rome, where he was presented with the Facta ministry's offer of resignation. In the first instance, the king revived their flagging will to resist by agreeing to put Rome under martial law. But then, the following morning, the king refused to sign the promised proclamation; the announcements of martial law which had been posted on the walls of the capital overnight had to be hastily removed. Clearly, the persuasive powers of the pro-Fascists at court had been applied to the king, and very likely Facta's lack of resolution had something to do with the royal *volte-face*. News was reaching Rome of police and military fraternization with the marching Fascists, whose numbers hearsay put at 100,000. In reality, they numbered less than 20,000 and were under Mussolini's instructions not to fight in the event of resistance by army units. Furthermore, the commandant of the Rome garrison was sure his men would obey the king's commands if not those of the politicians. In other words, by ruling out martial law, the authorities threw away a positive advantage and left the liberal regime defenseless.

On October 29 the logic of the situation prevailed. On the advice of the leading politicians, the king, using De Vecchi as an intermediary, invited Mussolini to form his own ministry. No one in Rome seemed mortified, for Fascism was scarcely anathema to any of the participants. Since October 26, the Duce had been waiting and negotiating in Milan, which was understandable inasmuch as Milan was the home of Fascism; it was also, as his critics observed, close to the Swiss frontier in case things went wrong. At all events, Mussolini displayed extreme caution when the royal invitation to form a government reached him by telephone. Not until he received it in writing would he leave for Rome. On receipt of the appropriate telegram, he traveled overnight by wagon-lit and arrived in Rome wearing a bowler hat with his black shirt. His first ministry was drawn up and accepted by the king while the Fascist columns were still more than twenty miles from the capital. These were transported on October 31 by special train to Rome, and there they paraded in rather bedraggled condition—they had been drenched for several days by the autumn rains—before the king and the Duce. In this fashion the March on Rome provided an epilogue to Mussolini's actual accession to office.

## Mussolini: From Premier to Dictator

In spite of the background of violence, it could be maintained that Fascism had come into office by due legal process. Moreover, Mussolini at first was plainly anxious to portray his regime as constitutional and moderate. He himself submitted meekly to lessons in deportment and protocol at the hands of Italy's aristocratic career diplomats, for Mussolini had become, pro tem, foreign minister. On ceremonial occasions he took to wearing conventional statesman's attire—frock coat, striped trousers, spats, and top hat—although he always looked profoundly uncomfortable. And twice a week he reported regularly to King Victor Emmanuel as constitutional usage demanded of the premier.

In addition to the premiership and the Ministry of Foreign Affairs, Mussolini also took over the key portfolio of the Ministry of the Interior. Of the fourteen members of his first cabinet, only three besides Mussolini were actually Fascists. Other posts went to Nationalists, right-wing Liberals, and *Popolari*. It seemed a veritable transformist cabinet. On presenting his ministry to Parliament, Mussolini asked for extraordinary powers in the budgetary and taxation fields for a period of one year. It was not an unprecedented request, and it was granted by an overwhelming majority. Apart from a veiled Cromwellian hint by the Duce that he had the means to dispense with Parliament if it proved too obstreperous, parliamentary sovereignty seemed reasonably secure.

It was not clear what use the government would make of its special powers. Mussolini spoke literally when he said on the eve of the March on Rome: "Our program is simple—we want to rule Italy." And on his first appearance before the Chamber of Deputies, as premier, he boasted that Fascism had no set policy, only "will, firm and decisive." The hint of a conventional approach appeared in the appointment of Alberto De' Stefani, an economic liberal of the old school, as finance minister. His aim was to balance the budget, which he accomplished by cutting government expenditure. The civil service was streamlined and severely reduced; in fact, an entire ministry, the Ministry of Labor and Welfare, was abolished. These changes were acceptable to conservative businessmen, for their burden fell mostly on the working class and weakened the position of labor within the public administration. But De' Stefani's orthodox economic policy made little appeal to those progressives who believed Fascism to be an agent of modernization. Their spokesman within the PNF at this time was Massimo Rocca, who persuaded Mussolini to accept the institution of *gruppi di competenza*. These were supposed to bring together politicians, bureaucrats and, above all, representatives of the managerial and technological elites. However, Rocca became embroiled in a quarrel with Farinacci, the *ras* of Cremona, as a result of which he was dismissed from the party in May 1924. His *gruppi di competenza* were supplanted by analogous *consigli tecnici*, which quickly proved to be much more subservient cadres. The Rocca case was a microcosm of the difficulties faced by Mussolini during his first two years in office. He could not begin to pursue a coherent policy until the problem of the distribution of power within the Fascist party was settled. In turn, this resolution depended on the relationship between Fascism and those elements in Italian life which had helped Mussolini into office in October 1922.

Mussolini's deference to constitutional forms and prescriptive rights aroused the ire of the *ras*. By and large, they were activists, not politicians, and saw little merit in Mussolini's compromise with the *ancien régime*. To them, Fascism was a revolutionary movement destined to sweep away vested interests and traditional authority. In short, they eagerly awaited the "second wave" of the Fascist revolution. Mussolini was well aware of their impatience and tried to bring them under his control. In December 1922 the creation of the Grand Council of Fascism strengthened the Duce's hand somewhat. The Grand Council was elected by the party congress and was therefore responsive to political considerations. Almost its first action was to decree the incorporation of all paramilitary units into a *Milizia voluntaria per la sicurezza nazionale* (Volunteer Militia for National Security). The MVSN was a state organization, publicly financed, although every militiaman took his oath to Mussolini as head of the government. By appearing to abolish the *squadre*, the measure formed part of the campaign to allay suspicions about Fascism's violent nature; but it also served to deprive the independent *ras* of their private armies. Yet they were far from vanquished. Still wielding great power in their respective bailiwicks and often indulging in unauthorized acts of violence, they continued to exert considerable pressure on the Duce to establish an exclusively Fascist regime.

Mussolini was not impervious to this agitation, but he preferred to continue to operate gradually within the limits of constitutional law. He therefore addressed himself to the position of the PNF in Parliament. The 35 seats won in the 1921 elections were increased by 10 on amalgamation with the Nationalists, but this still constituted a miniscule power base in a Chamber of Deputies of 535 members. Admittedly, Mussolini's government had won its initial vote of confidence by a margin of 306 to 116. But then, Italian parliamentary majorities were notoriously apt to vanish almost overnight, a point underlined in the spring of 1923 when a rift opened between Mussolini and the *Popolari*, many of whom were distressed by continued Fascist brutality in the countryside. The upshot was that Mussolini dismissed the Popular ministers from his cabinet. The Popular party's reaction was muted. It announced that, while it could no longer support Mussolini's ministry, it would not join the opposition. Nevertheless, some repair of Fascism's parliamentary strength was in order.

New elections were held in April 1924. Mussolini followed the standard practice of submitting a government-approved list of candidates drawn from diverse political groupings; in this case Fascists and non-Fascists were included. He also used the standard methods of electoral manipulation; in places, the ballot was anything but secret and the opposition severely hindered in presenting its case. In brief, the Duce gave the local Fascist bosses free rein. Italian elections in the past had often been marked by violence. The elections of 1924, however, saw intimidation systematized and used on a hitherto undreamed-of scale. Under the circumstances, the result was a foregone conclusion: the government list of candidates won 403 seats and 65 percent of the vote, giving Mussolini a commanding parliamentary majority. But just as significant—and ominous for the future of the Fascist regime—was the fact that 2.5 million Italians defied official pressure and voted against Mussolini's government.

Yet, in the short run, Mussolini's strategy of working, nominally at least, within the framework of the Italian constitution appeared to have paid another rich dividend. Ironically, in this moment of triumph, the aftermath of the election propelled Mussolini into a blatantly illegal course of the sort that he had so far skillfully avoided. Protests naturally were voiced about Fascist violence in the elections. One of the most articulate critics was a Socialist deputy, Giacomo Matteotti. His remarks in the new Chamber of Deputies sparked fisticuffs and incensed Mussolini into threatening physical violence: "That man should not be permitted to walk around," the Duce is reported to have remarked to

Cesare Rossi, his press secretary, who occupied an office in Mussolini's own Ministry of the Interior. Matteotti confided to his friends that he feared for his life. On June 10, as Matteotti stepped out of his house, he was attacked by five men who hustled him into a waiting car. Witnesses provided the number of the car, which was found a few days later with a bloodstained interior. Further police investigation revealed the kidnappers to be five ex-*arditi* led by one Amerigo Dumini. Dumini was an assistant to Rossi, and indeed the whole Dumini gang had operated from the Ministry of the Interior as a strong-arm squad with the express purpose of terrorizing the opponents of Fascism into silence during the election campaign. Appropriately, they were known in Fascist circles as the "Cheka" after the Soviet political police. Although Matteotti's body with its knife wounds was not found until August 16—in a shallow grave north of Rome—long before then all Italy assumed he had been murdered. The blame was placed not only on Dumini and his associates but on Mussolini himself.

In all probability the Duce did not specifically order the assassination. Nonetheless, Mussolini was in the habit of instructing his henchmen "to make life difficult" for the more outspoken foes of Fascism, and he had singled out Matteotti as a particular enemy. Mussolini's moral guilt was beyond question. It remains, however, an interesting speculation whether Matteotti's murder was a fortuitous or a deliberate exaggeration of the Duce's orders. In the wake of his electoral success, Mussolini apparently was once more dreaming of an overture to the Left. As in 1921 when Mussolini had sought to heal his breach with the PSI, the Fascist zealots, who hated any sort of compromise, could be expected to object strenuously. These intransigents may well have calculated that the Fascist murder of a well-known Socialist was an excellent means of short-circuiting Mussolini's proposed rapprochement. Whatever the truth, the Duce was certainly taken aback by the storm aroused by Matteotti's killing.

Matteotti was not the first to die at Fascist hands, although in 1924 he was the most prominent. But equally important was the timing of the crime; coming twenty months after the March on Rome, it made a mockery of all the earlier reassurances that Fascism would grow tamer with time and the responsibilities of office. The revived suspicion of Fascism was manifest in Parliament. On June 13 the Socialists, the *Popolari*, and some Liberals—all led by a Liberal deputy, Giovanni Amendola, who had once been beaten by the "Cheka"—walked out in an Aventine secession. It was a conscious imitation of the tactic which had defeated the Right in the crisis of 1898–1900. What the Aventines of 1924 lacked, however, was a leader of greater national stature than Amendola to blend the diverse opposition factions into a united anti-Fascist front. In view of King Victor Emmanuel's crucial part in making Mussolini premier, many looked to the crown for guidance. But having made his choice in 1922, the king decided for safety's sake to stick with it. And both Giolitti and Salandra advised him to bide his time. In general, the parliamentary mandarins avoided taking a positive stand; Orlando, Giolitti, and Salandra slowly and gently dissociated themselves from Mussolini's regime, but none joined the Aventines. Another hypothetical rallying-point against Fascism was the Vatican. But, in September, Pope Pius emphatically warned the Popular party against participating in an anti-Fascist front if it meant collaboration with the atheistic Socialists. The Aventine secession, then, remained no more than a gesture. Like its counterpart a quarter of a century before, it relied on moral suasion to bring down the regime. It also, in effect, dared the government to proceed to a coup d'état—if the government had the nerve for it.

In 1900 the Right had proved too fainthearted to seize such an opportunity. For six months after Matteotti's murder, Mussolini, distraught at evidence of popular discontent, displayed the same timidity. As a journalist, he was distressed when the middle-of-the-road newspapers printed hostile editorials. Crowds gathered outside the Palazzo Venezia, which Mussolini had made the seat of his administration, shouting: "Give us back Matteotti's body!" The timeservers of the Fascist regime stayed away, awaiting developments, and occasional visitors found the Duce alone, unshaven, and red-eyed. Lack of resolution was a Mussolinian trait; one recalls his vacillation at the time of the March on Rome. It was not that Mussolini was a physical coward—he had demonstrated his courage in the First World War, and would again later when assassination attempts were made on his life—but in moments of crisis, he lacked mental fortitude. His colleagues perceived this behind his bluster; one of his erstwhile socialist acquaintances summed him up as "a rabbit, a phenomenal rabbit; he roars."

During the latter half of 1924, then, the Fascist regime was incapacitated by paralysis at the center. Mussolini's chief preoccupation was to absolve himself of blame for the Matteotti crime. He resigned as minister of the interior, and forced Rossi to resign his press post. He then went on to dismiss Aldo Finzi, the Fascist undersecretary of the Ministry of the Interior, and also General De Bono, the director of public security. This blatant attempt to exonerate himself by providing scapegoats misfired, however, for both Rossi and Finzi circulated memoranda implicating the Duce in the activities of the "Cheka." Mussolini became lavish with conciliatory promises about the "normalization" of Italian political life. In the nadir of his depression in November, he made it clear that, if requested by the king to resign, he would do so.

As both the Aventine opposition and Mussolini declined to take forcible action against each other, a deadlock ensued that was broken only by the intervention of the Fascist hierarchs. To the zealots in the PNF, the Matteotti affair was welcome because it drove a wedge between Mussolini and many moderates who had supported Fascism in 1922. And the Aventine secession presented a golden opportunity to establish genuine Fascist control over Italy—to embark on the long-awaited "second wave," in fact. Apart from instituting press censorship, Mussolini made no gestures to propitiate the Fascist extremists. On the contrary, in order to mollify liberal sentiment, he set curbs on the MVSN, which was expected to be the spearhead of further Fascist revolution. This militia, into which the *squadristi* had been merged in 1923, was now obliged to swear its oath of allegiance to the king instead of to Mussolini. Moreover, in December 1924, Balbo, the darling of the activists, was forced out of his post as commander in chief of the MVSN. The reaction within the Fascist party took the form of the "revolt of the consuls"—the *ras* now dignified by the title of Fascist consuls. On December 31 the Fascist bosses of Tuscany staged a gigantic rally in Florence, at which a motion was carried expressing loyalty to the Duce "conditional on the decisive action of the government which must be demonstrated, if necessary, by dictatorial action." On the same day, a deputation of thirty consuls visited Mussolini in Rome on the pretext of conveying new year's greetings. In reality, they came to expostulate at his continued deference to liberal scruples, and they made it quite plain that if Mussolini was not prepared to impose Fascism on the country by force, he might be deposed in favor of a more energetic *duce*. It has been suggested that Mussolini was a party to the consuls' agitation in order to pave the way for strong action which he had already decided on. But this is doubtful. More likely, capitulation to the consuls seemed the line of least resistance, and he took it.

On January 3, 1925, Mussolini addressed the rump Chamber of Deputies. For the first time, he accepted the onus for Matteotti's death: "I declare before all Italy that I assume full responsibility for what has happened." He did not hide the fact that this disregard of moderate opinion presaged a dictatorship: "Italy wants peace and quiet, and calm in which to work. This we shall give her, by love if possible, by force if necessary." Within forty-eight hours, Mussolini promised, the situation would be clarified. Indeed, the militia was mobilized at once and began its hunt for anti-Fascists. A few days later, the cabinet was purged of its remaining non-Fascist members. Nothing was done to oppose these moves. Over the past years, there had been too much compromise by non-Fascists and too much hesitation by anti-Fascists to mount resistance now. When, in 1926, the Aventine secessionists finally tried to return to Parliament, they were turned away by armed Black Shirts who informed them they had forfeited their seats. This, too, was accepted without demur. During 1925–26, four assassination attempts were made on Mussolini's life, but none sprang from a deep-rooted opposition movement. In fact, one was probably a charade staged by the government to justify extension of the dictatorship.

It took the better part of two years to build the foundations of the Fascist dictatorship. In this period, Parliament was reduced to a decorative body. Ministerial accountability to Parliament was specifically repealed, and rule by executive decree became the norm. The decision-making process was effectively transferred to the Grand Council of Fascism, although not until 1928 was this body given constitutional status. Anti-Fascist parties were proscribed and, in reality, all parties save the PNF ceased to exist. Local elections were stopped; the prefect and a new official named the *podestà*, both appointed in Rome, took over from elected mayors and councils. Independent trade unions, socialist and Catholic, were outlawed. Perhaps most important, however, was suppression of the free press. Independent newspapers, rather than a malleable Parliament, had always been the true forum of Italian public opinion. Now, not only was censorship imposed, but Fascist stooges were put in charge of such famous liberal dailies as Milan's *Corriere della Sera* and Turin's *La Stampa*. To enforce the regulations of the dictatorship, a secret police force was created, which went by the initials OVRA. It was never exactly clear what these letters stood for; the likeliest guesses were *Opera vigilanza repressione antifascismo* and *Opera volontaria per la repressione antifascista*. In any case, it was a body designed to combat antifascism. Behind the OVRA stood a new Special Tribunal for the Defense of the State, composed not of jurists but of militia officers and similar political appointees, who dispensed justice arbitrarily and sometimes secretly. By the end of 1926, which

The Duce became the personification of
Italian Fascism; therefore he was always
presented in an heroic light. Here he is (left)
as an athlete, and (above) as a productivist
laborer.

LEFT: P. & A. PHOTOS
ABOVE: WIDE WORLD PHOTOS

Mussolini termed his "Napoleonic year," the machinery had been set
up to stamp the *stile fascista* on every facet of Italian life.

All of this, on the surface, constituted a supreme triumph for the
Fascist consuls. Yet, paradoxically, the construction of a dictatorship
undercut their influence, for, by embracing their extremist policies,
Mussolini removed any grounds for challenge. Henceforth, there would
be no radical and moderate versions of Fascism; Fascism was now
synonymous with Mussolinianism. Mussolini's reconciliation with his
lieutenants was sealed in March 1925 with the appointment of Farinacci
as party secretary. Farinacci, always an uncompromising Fascist, had
been a leader of the "revolt of the consuls." But he was also a firm
believer in a disciplined and rigidly structured party under a dominant

leader. During the single year in which he held the party secretaryship, Farinacci succeeded in imposing this pattern on the PNF and, in doing so, broke the power of his former confederates, the independent *ras*. Correspondingly, Mussolini's position at the apex of the Fascist hierarchy was stabilized, which was illustrated by the degree to which the Fascist Grand Council now fell under his control. The Duce was accorded the right to choose the members of the Grand Council; he served as its permanent president; and he alone determined what matters it should deal with.

Mussolini's supremacy was further enhanced by the campaign to instill Fascism into the entire Italian population. To accomplish this, the Duce was portrayed as the embodiment of Fascist virtues with the considerable Fascist propaganda apparatus devoted to projecting the image of a selfless, resolute statesman. Mussolini was photographed absorbed in paper work at his desk in his cavernous office in the Palazzo Venezia, although his enthusiasm for the administrative routine of government was never sustained for long. To epitomize his virility, he was often pictured as a sportsman: riding horses over jumps that appeared higher than they were because the camera was placed at ground level, driving fast cars and airplanes, or playing with a lion cub that someone gave him as a present. Presumably to emphasize his manliness still more, no secret was made of his sexual prowess and innumerable mistresses. In actual fact, Mussolini was far from physically strong; he suffered perennially from a gastric ulcer, which necessitated an operation during the Napoleonic year and compelled him to adhere to a strict diet. But such human frailties had to be concealed from the public, for the Duce had to appear superhuman. Above all, he had to seem omniscient, giving rise to the ludicrous slogan which was plastered all over Italy: "Mussolini is always right." Through this cult of the Duce, the fortunes of Fascism and Mussolini became inextricably linked. So long as Mussolini continued as the cynosure of Fascism, it would be virtually impossible to topple him without bringing down Fascism itself.

The Duce's ascendancy over his fellow Fascists meant that the Fascist revolution would be carried forward, not by those who had consistently preached a radical approach, but by Mussolini, who had only accepted the need for a "second wave" opportunistically on January 3, 1925. Not only was Mussolini's commitment to a drastic restructuring of Italy in doubt, but the obstacles inherent in the situation were formidable. To the ingrained traditionalism of Italian society at large could be added the vested interests of those powerful groups which were already allied with Fascism and which expected to go on using the movement for their own ends. It is hardly surprising that, in reality, *fascistizzazione* was practiced sometimes in half-hearted fashion and with haphazard success.

## From Corporativism to Militarism

Fascist insistence on the priority of action over doctrine, especially during the years of struggle for power, militated against the formulation of a systematic theory for the reordering of Italy. Indeed, not until after the consolidation of the Fascist dictatorship in 1925–26 did corporative ideology emerge in the forefront of the Fascist program. Its enunciation then was bound to appear a belated effort to give a patina of doctrinal respectability to an otherwise unprincipled movement. Hence, commentators have traditionally dismissed Fascist corporativism as of little consequence. Yet corporativism, as recent studies by Michael Ledeen, Roland Sarti, and Edward Tannenbaum have indicated, was the projection of some of the basic, albeit vague, aspirations which lay at the heart of Italian Fascism. Ideally, the corporative state was to be the means of satisfying the radicals' demand for the end of class distinctions and exclusive privileges as well as the progressives' dream of modernizing the entire Italian economy.

Corporative ideas in the twentieth century come from two sources. The Roman Catholic church has always regarded mankind as a corporate body—that is to say, as an organic whole in which every being has an ordained and necessary role to play. And this sense of communal interdependence acquired fresh urgency with the growth of industrial societies. The corporative concept could be used to recall the rich and successful to their obligations to less fortunate brethren in a ruthless competitive world. Such was the laudable purpose behind the classic modern restatements of Christian corporativism—the papal encyclicals *Rerum Novarum* in 1891 and *Quadragesimo Anno* in 1931. Also and, to some, more important, corporativism was useful to counter the spread of godless socialism. Against the socialist glorification of the class war was set the vision of Christian corporative unity. Yet, although they might exploit these religious sentiments, few Fascists arrived at corporativism by the Christian route. As the case of Mussolini himself illustrated, Fascist corporativism derived in the main from syndicalist socialism. As their name implied, the syndicalists emphasized the role of the trade unions. It was a cardinal tenet of Georges Sorel, the philosopher of syndicalism, that representation and authority in the modern state should correspond to economic function. Mussolini liked to claim Sorel as one of his mentors, although he did not really move close to the syndicalists until his famous conversion to intervention in October 1914 when he appropriated their program of a "revolutionary war." Mussolini also borrowed from the syndicalist aspect of the Italian Nationalist movement, which manifested itself in the theoretical corporations established under D'Annunzio's Fiume regency. In imitation, Mussolini, well before the March on Rome, had created half a dozen embryonic Fascist corporations as rivals to the socialist and Catholic trade unions.

The immediate function of each of these corporations was to provide a medium of interchange between capital and labor. Within the corporations, spokesmen for rival groups and classes would be brought face to face more directly than in traditional parliamentary institutions. It was also intended that the corporations would offer a more permanent and friendlier forum for negotiation than that in which trade union bargaining usually occurred. All parties would have every opportunity to perceive the common good, and harmony would ensue more or less spontaneously.

Needless to say, both sides in the class war were reluctant to give up their independence; the *Confindustria*, in particular, objected to meeting with workers' representatives on a regular basis. Consequently, the first Fascist corporations were composed of disparate "syndical confederations" for employers and employees, which met together only occasionally. The real foundation of Mussolini's corporative system was laid in 1925 by the Vidoni Pact, named after the Palazzo Vidoni where it was signed. By the terms of the pact, the *Confindustria* and the Confederation of Fascist Syndicates recognized each other as sole legitimate bargaining agents for capital and labor respectively. As the Fascist trade unions were opposed to strikes and militant working-class action, the employers' dislike of joining with proletarians in corporations declined. In 1926 Alfredo Rocco, a distinguished jurist who had been made minister of justice during the Matteotti affair, introduced legislation consummating the Vidoni Pact. The Rocco law officially outlawed strikes and designated seven areas of national economic activity —industry, agriculture, banking, commerce, internal transport, the merchant marine, and intellectual life. In the first six occupations separate confederations of employers and workers were created; among the intellectuals the distinction was difficult to make, so one genuine corporation was born there and then. Nonetheless, the intention to proceed to mixed corporations for every activity was clearly expressed. A Ministry of Corporations was established, with Mussolini as its first minister. In 1929 he handed over the position to Giuseppe Bottai, a former Futurist who had aspirations to be Fascism's leading theoretician. Both Rocco and Bottai were vocal in arguing that a corporative system would facilitate the rise of a new, imaginative managerial elite.

Fascism's promise of far-reaching social and economic change was reinforced by Mussolini's resolve to give his regime a formal doctrine. The task of composition was entrusted to a variety of writers, although principally to Giovanni Gentile, a philosopher and one-time colleague of Croce. Gentile was a much more open supporter of Fascism than Croce; he had, in fact, been Mussolini's first minister of education from 1922 to 1925. However, the Duce, who fancied himself an intellectual and a political theorist, constantly amended the work of Gentile and others, and the completed essay on Fascism in volume XIV of the *Enciclopedia italiana* (1932) appeared over Mussolini's signature. A short while later, extracts from this article were brought out in an authorized English translation under the title "The Political and Social Doctrine of Fascism." Although these articles did not spell out the details of corporativism, they emphasized its central role in Fascism: "Now, is it not a singular thing that even on that first day in the Piazza San Sepolcro the word 'corporation' arose, which later in the course of the Revolution came to express one of the creations of social legislation at the very foundation of the regime?"

The enunciation of Fascist theory coincided with the onset of the Great Depression, so that these two developments together spurred the construction of corporative institutions. In 1934 mixed corporations of employers and employees, covering the whole range of Italian economic activity, at last came into existence. There were twenty-two of them, created by subdividing the original seven specified in the Rocco Law. These corporations, in addition to meeting individually to discuss their respective vocational problems, occasionally congregated together in a National Council of Corporations where matters of general economic concern were discussed. Then in 1938 the capstone was set on the corporate edifice. The regionally based Chamber of Deputies was abolished, to be replaced the following year by the Chamber of Fasces and Corporations. Some members of this new body were elected directly by the corporations, while others were appointed by the government or the Fascist Grand Council. But all were supposed to stand for some corporative interest, so that the Chamber of Fasces could claim to be Italy's long-awaited occupational Parliament.

On paper, corporativism was a sound sociopolitical philosophy with a respectable ancestry. It seemed a credible, even intelligent, answer to the problem of the fragmentation of modern society and a step along the road to what Gentile liked to call the "ethical state." Moreover, the novel corporative institutions contributed to the image of Italian Fascism as a movement unhampered by tradition and acting imaginatively to renovate a decrepit Italy. This impression was successfully conveyed abroad where Mussolini won popular renown for making the trains run on time. Many "pragmatic liberals" in Europe and America came to advocate corporative remedies for their own sluggish communities, even at the loss of some individual liberty.

Unfortunately, however, Fascist Italy's corporative state in practice was far from what it purported to be in principle. The corporative agencies had very little independent power. Government officials sat in the corporations quite properly as guardians of consumer interests and the commonweal at large, but their role was disproportionately great. They conveyed to their corporative colleagues key economic decisions taken elsewhere, and the corporations were expected to place a rubber stamp of approval on policies set in the cabinet or the Fascist Grand Council. Nor were the corporations any more satisfactory in bridging the gulf between capital and labor. While the corporations contained traditional and independent spokesmen of the propertied classes, the workers were not genuinely represented at all. Most of the original trade union leaders, socialist and Catholic, were anti-Fascist; after 1925, if not in prison or exile, they were forced to retire from public affairs. The Fascist syndical labor representatives were no more than party hacks who submitted readily to the industrialists and landowners who backed Mussolini's regime. The result was that capital was kept on a light leash whereas labor's freedom was heavily curbed. The corporative state in this way supplied the cloak for ruthless worker exploitation.

All this, of course, was an utter betrayal of the hopes of the radical wing of the PNF. The revolutionary syndicalists were forced to take a back seat—a situation epitomized in the decline of Edmondo Rossoni, the architect of the first Fascist trade unions and secretary of the Confederation of Fascist Syndicates. In 1928 Mussolini, in response to

*Confindustria* pressure, dissolved the national organization of the Fascist labor syndicates, thus eliminating the power base of Rossoni and the left-wing syndicalists. Ironically, Mussolini in due course was to undergo the same disillusionment. After his overthrow in 1943, he tried belatedly to recapture his former radicalism and found cause to lament: "The greatest tragedy of my life came when I no longer had the strength to repel the embrace of the false corporativists who were in reality acting as agents of capitalism. They wished to embrace the corporative system only in order to destroy it."

But if ineffectual in its avowed purposes, the corporative system provided a vast arsenal of bureaucratic jobs for the party faithful. Moreover, many of these officeholders, in collusion with a sizable segment of the business community, discovered in the corporative state opportunities for peculation of massive proportions. The most celebrated parasites were the so-called "Petacci clan." Clara Petacci was the young wife of an air force officer who, in 1936, became Mussolini's last mistress. Apparently, Mussolini found her schoolgirl prettiness and gaiety a relief from the grim public events of the closing years of his life, for she was rewarded with much more respect than the Duce usually accorded his amorous conquests, including her own apartment in the Palazzo Venezia. La Petacci's privileged position was seized upon by a horde of her relatives and acquaintances who acquired corporative and other official posts, and caused a national scandal by their shady business dealings. Plainly, in one respect, Fascism had not changed the nature of Italian government at all: the machinery of the Fascist corporative state, like that of the pre-1922 liberal regime, was oiled by bribes, the sale of favors, and corruption in general.

At least, the lip service paid to corporativism indicated that the Fascist regime would have no qualms about intervening in Italy's economic processes. In 1925 Mussolini replaced the laissez faire economist De' Stefani as finance minister with Giuseppe Volpi. Volpi, a spokesman for business and commerce, molded state action for the benefit of these interests. Higher tariffs, lower corporate taxes, and government contracts provided a further likeness to liberal Italy, wherein the links between government and capital had been notoriously close. The trend to government patronage of selected businesses was quickened by the Great Depression of the early 1930s, the most notable innovation being the *Istituto per la ricostruzione industriale* (Agency for Industrial Reconstruction), a state-financed rescue operation for shaky concerns. For the most part, it was the big companies that received IRI help, while small businesses were allowed to go to the wall. The result was a significant increase in monopolies and trusts.

Fascist economic policy was constantly bedeviled by Mussolini's obsession with prestige. Thus in 1926 Mussolini insisted that for reasons of national pride the international value of the lira should be kept up. Its stabilization by the end of 1927 at an artificially high rate created boundless difficulties for Italian exporters as well as serious deflation at home. Similarly, land reclamation was at the mercy of the Duce's showmanship. The Pontine Marshes, close to Rome and within the range of foreign visitors, were the subject of a model project. But elsewhere, money and good intentions were dissipated by dishonest contractors. And the *Mezzogiorno*, where land reclamation was crucial, remained sunk in poverty. Mussolini liked to envisage his economic plans as military campaigns. There was the "battle for births," although Italy was grossly overpopulated in relation to her economic resources and her main emigration outlet to the New World had just been closed. There was also a "battle for grain," whereby increased domestic production enabled grain imports to be cut by 75 percent in the decade following 1925. On the other hand, this was accomplished at the cost of reducing Italy's total agricultural output because so much land suitable for fruit and grazing was foolishly planted with wheat. Both these "battles" were launched in support of a militaristic foreign policy. Mussolini openly admitted that the goal of his demographic campaign was more cannon fodder, while the concentration on grain stemmed from the desire for autarchy, or self-sufficiency, in case of war.

Mussolini's economic policies were of such dubious inspiration that a consistent pattern of growth could hardly be expected. Indeed, between 1925 and 1938, owing to a combination of Fascist ineptitude and the Great Depression, Italy's national income rose a mere 15 percent; on a per capita basis the increase was only 10 percent. In the two years before Italy's entry into the Second World War, the national income rose faster, but this was brought about by the artificial stimulus of war preparations. Overall, the annual growth rate was far too small to support the budget deficits and the substantial increase in the public debt during the 1930s. The cost of the failure of Mussolini's economic policies bore heavily on the lower classes. Early on, labor was left vulnerable by the Fascist reversal of gains made in the pre-Fascist era— gains such as the eight-hour factory day and checks on eviction and rack-renting in the countryside. The Fascist Charter of Labor in 1927

and the Charter of *Mezzadria* (rural share tenancy) in 1933 only codi-
fied how far labor had been set back since 1922. Unemployment was
always high with exact figures hard to come by; in the midst of the
Great Depression in 1932, a reasonable estimate was two million. In
1927 the government decreed across-the-board wage reductions, which
were only partially restored when prices rose steeply in the late 1930s.
In fact, the index of real wages fell by some 11 percent between 1925
and 1938. The consumption of basic foodstuffs by the workers dropped,
bringing on an inevitable decline in the standard of public health. By
comparison, the Italian business community was only mildly incon-
venienced by the folly of Fascist economics. For instance, with the
Ethiopian crisis of 1935–36, Mussolini determined to put the country
on a war footing, necessitating economic controls which dismayed some
freewheeling businessmen. In particular, there was grumbling at the
imposition of strict state supervision over banking. Yet, in any objective
reckoning, Italian moneyed interests were consistently and enormously
favored under Fascism.

The fact that industrialists and *latifondisti* retained their influence
and even extended their privileges was a symptom of a larger truth;
namely, that the traditional Italian power structure succeeded in
keeping its identity and bargained with Fascism on equal terms. In
consequence, Fascist experimentation was persistently hampered by
long-established Italian forces and institutions. Above all, neither the
monarchy nor the church ever really came under Fascist control.

Mussolini had made his conversion to monarchism in 1922 for political reasons and, although King Victor Emmanuel had backed the
Duce staunchly in the Matteotti crisis, tension always existed between
the Fascist regime and the monarchy. After the establishment of the
Fascist dictatorship, Mussolini set about undermining the royal prerogative. Legislation in 1928 transferred from the king to the Fascist Grand
Council the power to nominate a premier. Even more startling, the
Grand Council was granted cognizance of all constitutional questions, including the succession to the throne. What Mussolini openly
aspired to was a dyarchy—equal status for the Fascist Duce and the
Italian king. This ambition, and indeed its achievement, was illustrated after Fascist Italy's conquest of Ethiopia when a new title, "marshal of the empire," was created; the honor was conferred on both
Mussolini and Victor Emmanuel.

While preserving correct formal relations, a thinly disguised rivalry
developed. Mussolini made no secret of his chagrin when he was forced

to give precedence to the king on ceremonial occasions. On the other hand, he loved to pose alongside Victor Emmanuel because, although only five feet six inches in height himself, he seemed to tower over the diminutive monarch. The king, for his part, was not averse to cultivating his own constituency in society. Italian aristocrats, who tended to look down their noses at the Fascists, continued to give their prime allegiance to the monarchy. This was true of many civil servants, especially in the prestigious foreign ministry. It was even more true of the armed forces, for the king remained the legal commander in chief until 1940 when Mussolini usurped the post on Italy's entry into World War II. The navy, especially, was always more royal than Fascist. Apparently, even many in the MVSN, the militia which had grown out of the Fascist Black Shirts, felt obligated to the king as the real head of state. During the 1920s and 1930s, with the royal prerogative being continually eroded by a triumphant Fascism, it was difficult to estimate what influence the king still wielded. Not until 1943 when, as we shall see, Victor Emmanuel was a major instrument in Mussolini's downfall, did it become clear how decisively the Fascists had failed to make the Italian royal house their creature.

The Catholic church, more emphatically and openly than the monarchy, was able to stand aside from the Fascist revolution, and continued to play an independent role in Italian life. Such was the price that Mussolini was constrained to pay for one of the undeniable triumphs of his regime—the final reconciliation between the papacy and the secular Italian state. By 1922, while the church-state relationship was still nominally one of mutual hostility, a convenient modus vivendi had evolved in practice. The state had long since ceased to obstruct the appointment of bishops, nor did the courts enforce the legal restrictions on landholding by the church. Church wealth was increasing, and clerical influence showed no signs of dwindling across the broad spectrum of Italian society. Catholics participated in secular public affairs, as the existence of "white" trade unions and the Popular party attested. The liberal oligarchy and the Vatican drew together in a common fear of revolutionary socialism, and, during Orlando's premiership in 1919, the first official feelers for a church-state rapprochement were put forth. At most, then, Fascism speeded up what had already been started.

Nevertheless, the Fascist regime was peculiarly well-suited to realize the incipient conciliation. For Fascism appealed to the instincts of those higher clergy, the future Clerico-Fascists, who formed part of the Italian plutocracy. They naturally admired Fascist antibolshevism, and they also sympathized with Fascist imperialism which, it was hoped, would provide opportunities to spread Christianity in the colonial world. Clerico-Fascist influence was plainly discernible in the Vatican's covert support of Fascism at the time of the March on Rome and the Matteotti crisis. It was still more evident in Pope Pius XI's supreme gestures of good will toward Mussolini's regime in 1925–26—his acquiescence in the Fascist dissolution of Catholic trade unions and cooperatives and in the demise of the Popular party. Mussolini, as part of his campaign to woo the Italian establishment, had begun to propitiate the Vatican with words as early as May 1920. Once in power, action followed: among other measures the crucifix and catechism were restored in elementary schools, Milan's Catholic university was officially recognized, and state allowances for priests were raised. In 1925 Mussolini made a token personal gesture by going through a religious wedding ceremony with Rachele Guido, the plain and unobtrusive country woman who had been his common-law wife since 1910.

The feasibility of a church-state treaty was accepted from the moment Mussolini took office. In January 1923 the Duce and Cardinal Gasparri, the papal secretary of state, held a secret meeting. But not until the Fascist dictatorship was consolidated in 1926 did formal negotiations open. They lasted three years and were closely supervised by Mussolini. The result was the Lateran Accords of February 11, 1929, which comprised three agreements. A convention dealt with a financial settlement for the church. A treaty guaranteed the sovereign independence of Vatican City, and in return the Vatican accorded de jure recognition to the Italian state. Included in the treaty was a reconfirmation of the clause in the Italian constitution that recognized Catholicism as "the sole religion of the state." But the most important and extensive document was the concordat, which spelled out the church's new status in detail and repealed most of the anticlerical legislation of the liberal era. The Vatican obtained great freedom in episcopal appointments, as well as substantive jurisdiction over marriages and wills. Ecclesiastical corporations gained tax relief, and religious orders recovered legal entity. In education, church schools were put on the same footing as state institutions, and compulsory religious instruction was extended to all secondary schools. R. A. Webster in *The Cross and the Fasces* (1960) has gone so far as to term Italy after the Lateran Accords "a confessional state." On the other side of the ledger, the church lost spiritually through its close association with a movement whose worship of force was so blatantly alien to Christian teaching and whose leaders were always anticlerical at heart. The compromise with Italian Fascism naturally inhibited the church. At worst, it seems to have stood in the way of the Vatican taking a firmer stance than it did against the greater evil of the Nazi variety of fascism. At the very least, it impaired the papacy's ability to be heard when it did preach against the unchristian aspects of fascism.

In the short run, however, the Lateran Accords gave the church security, enabling it to express itself unreservedly. On occasion, the papacy used this freedom to challenge Fascism—greatly to Mussolini's pained surprise. Predictably enough, trouble arose over youth education. The concordat of 1929 specifically recognized the right of the lay organization, Catholic Action, to operate in this sphere. But two years later, Mussolini deemed Catholic Action too politically oriented and a rival to Fascist youth groups, so he unleashed a furious propaganda attack and decreed the dissolution of Catholic Action's youth corps. The pope responded bitterly in an encyclical, *Non abbiamo bisogno*. Whereupon the Clerico-Fascists intervened to fabricate a compromise in September 1931 by which Catholic Action forswore political activity but remained operational. Indeed, although forced to act inconspicuously, Catholic Action—and similar lay Catholic groups in the universities—were able to provide for the political education of a whole generation of Christian Democratic politicians who took office in Italy after World War II. From 1931 to 1938, relations between the Duce and the Vatican were more or less undisturbed. But when Mussolini fell under the sway of Hitler to the extent of introducing racist laws into Italy, Pope Pius XI was explicit in his denunciation. His successor in 1939, Pius XII, was closer to the Clerico-Fascists and somewhat muted the criticism; notwithstanding, the Vatican's continued opposition to racism was well-known.

The relative independence of both monarchy and church indicated the limits of *fascistizzazione*. Many important subgroups in Italian society were neutralized, but without being either annihilated or absorbed into the PNF. In the south the Mafia put on black shirts, became quiescent while preserving their organizational framework intact, and in so doing outlived the Fascist regime. This was the pattern adopted by a myriad Italian institutions under Fascism, which called into question Mussolini's claim to be a totalitarian ruler. Mussolini can be credited with popularizing the term "totalitarian," and it was certainly his avowed intention to build a totalitarian state. The famous Mussolini-Gentile article on Fascism in the *Enciclopedia italiana* reads:

For the Fascist the State is all-embracing; outside it no human or spiritual values exist, much less have worth. In this sense Fascism is totalitarian, and the Fascist State—a synthesis and a unity of all values —interprets, develops, and gives power to the whole life of the people.

The same essay goes on to offer one very pertinent criterion of totalitarianism: "Neither individuals nor groups (political parties, cultural associations, economic unions, social classes) exist outside the State." But in fact, particular interest groups, classes, and institutions did maintain their identity in Fascist Italy. Consequently, the scholarly consensus on Mussolinian totalitarianism is that expressed in Alberto Aquarone's authoritative work, *L'organizzazione dello Stato totalitario* (1965): "The Fascist state proclaimed itself constantly and with great vocal exuberance a totalitarian state; but it remained until the end a dynastic and Catholic state, and therefore not totalitarian in the Fascist sense."

Mussolini's pragmatic compromise with traditional Italy was welcome to most Italians (if not all Fascists), for it provided national harmony in place of the civil strife of the pre-1922 era. The Lateran Accords were especially popular. Ivone Kirkpatrick, the British diplomat who served in the Rome embassy in the early 1930s, rightly calls these Mussolini's "halcyon years." Opposition within Italy to the Fascist regime, never great, became negligible. This was, in part, due to the fact that many articulate, potential anti-Fascist leaders had either been driven into exile or else taken refuge abroad of their own accord. These *fuorusciti* or outsiders—the word was used derisively by the Duce, proudly by the expatriates themselves—included a galaxy of illustrious Italian names: the ex-premier, Nitti; the former foreign minister, Count Sforza; the Aventine leader, Amendola; the first party secretary of the *Popolari*, Don Sturzo; almost the entire roster of past and future socialist leadership; the historian, Salvemini; Enrico Fermi, the physicist; Arturo Toscanini, who had run for Parliament as a Fascist candidate in 1919 but rebelled in no uncertain fashion when expected to play "Giovinezza" at his concerts. The *fuorusciti*, through their writings, may have marginally damaged Fascist Italy's reputation abroad, but they had no capacity to disturb the stability of Mussolini's regime at home.

Anti-Fascist activity in Italy was confined largely to individual gestures. In 1931 the writer Lauro de Bosis showered Rome with anti-Fascist leaflets from the air and immediately disappeared—probably because his plane crashed. Truth to tell, one critical domestic voice was heard constantly throughout the Fascist era. It belonged to Croce who, after the Matteotti affair, sponsored an intellectuals' anti-Fascist manifesto, and then went on to subject the regime to increasingly scathing comment as time passed. Mussolini tolerated this one dissenter either because he considered Croce too important to silence or else because he calculated him too ineffectual to be dangerous. Moreover, Croce's freedom of speech served as a rejoinder to foreign critics of Fascist censorship. At any rate, Croce was left an intellectual crying in the wilderness, for out of 1,200 university teachers required to take a loyalty oath in 1931, only 11 refused, and they were quickly forced into retirement and silence.

Behind the conformity of Fascist Italy in the 1930s stood the apparatus of the police state and the threat of brutality. Yet, in gaining power, Mussolini had shown that, while certainly not averse to violence, he also appreciated that the apprehension of force was sometimes more effective than its indiscriminate use. In Fascist Italy police terror always hung like a menacing shadow over the heads of potential rebels, but its actual implementation fell far short of that in Nazi Germany or Soviet Russia. The Special Tribunal for the Defense of the State, in its first five years of operation, dispensed only nine death sentences. In the same period, however, the tribunal sentenced almost 2,000 to prison terms, and it was calculated that even more were imprisoned without trial. Although not commensurate with Nazi concentration camps or Stalinist labor camps, prison conditions for Fascist Italy's political prisoners were wretched, particularly on the penal islands off the Italian coast. An unknown number died in these jails. The most famous prisoner, the Communist theoretician Antonio Gramsci, was released in 1937 mortally ill and died three days later. A Fascist penalty specifically tailored for independent-minded intellectuals was confino— banishment to a remote district where a man could live a normal life, albeit under the surveillance of the local police. The vast disparity between one region of Italy and another made this a more severe imposition than it might seem at first. The psychological frustration of an enforced sojourn in a primitive, disease-ridden southern village has been hauntingly captured in the famous memoir Christ Stopped at Eboli (1947) by Carlo Levi, an anti-Fascist artist from Turin sentenced to confino in 1935.

To complement the authoritarian methods of the police state, Italy was also blanketed by a profusion of official propaganda. It might almost be said that Mussolini spent the 1920s coming to terms with the

Italian establishment, while in the 1930s he devoted himself to winning over the Italian masses. This propagandist task was congenial to the Duce. On becoming premier, he had handed over the editorship of *Popolo d'Italia* to his brother Arnoldo. But when the latter died in 1931, he gladly resumed direction of the paper. However, exposure by newspaper was limited in Italy where much of the population was still functionally illiterate. Mussolini reached his largest audience through handbills and posters; the walls of Italy became the bearers of countless Fascist slogans. On both radio and film, something of Mussolini's magnetic oratory came across; state money was poured into the development of Italian radio and cinema solely, one suspects, in order to broaden the channels of propaganda. To bring all the mass media within his purview, Mussolini invented the Ministry of Popular Culture—a euphemism for ministry of propaganda.

Like every dictator who imagines his regime to be permanent, Mussolini took great heed of the rising generation. Needless to say, school curricula were laid down by the state and teachers carefully watched by local officials. However, the real Fascist indoctrination was given in the party's youth cadres: the *Balilla* for boys of eight to fourteen years of age; the *Avanguardisti* for fourteen- to eighteen-year-olds; and the *Giovani Fascisti* for those between eighteen and twenty-one. After 1928 admission to the PNF itself was denied to all but graduates of these youth organizations, and without party membership many a career was blighted. By the party's own estimate in 1939, enrollment in Fascist youth groups was the highest in the north—in some places as high as 60 percent of those eligible. But the figures fell off in the south where work in the fields left little time for school, let alone youth clubs. At this point it was decided to make membership obligatory. The Second World War, however, intervened to abort this experiment in the forced *fascistizzazione* of an entire generation.

Outwardly, the Fascist propaganda barrage achieved its purpose; by the mid-1930s, the Italian masses seemed to have accepted Fascism completely. There was no working-class subversion to speak of, although the Communists managed precariously to maintain a network of cells. Maybe the best depiction of the popular mind in Fascist Italy is to be found in works of fiction. An example is provided by Ignazio Silone's classic *Bread and Wine* (1937). The hero of this novel is a *fuoruscito* who returns to Italy in 1935, the year of Mussolini's attack on Ethiopia. The plot turns on his despair at failing to rouse either urban workers or peasants to indignation against Fascist rule. Silone

*Fascism, in would-be totalitarian fashion, sought to control the youth of Italy. Here, the Balilla are being taught to fight and die for their cause.*

was a member of the Communist underground until he took refuge in Switzerland in 1930. But he kept up his contacts with individual anti-Fascists in Italy, and he knew whereof he wrote. Alberto Moravia, on the other hand, stayed in Italy throughout the Fascist era. Afterward, he published *The Conformist* (1952), a psychological novel about a university graduate who seeks a career in Mussolini's Italy. He can do so only by submitting to PNF dictates, whereby he also assuages an inbuilt compulsion to conform. As a result, he finds himself involved in a Fascist plot to kill his former professor, now a *fuoruscito* in France—an episode modeled on the real murder of the Rosselli brothers in Normandy in 1937.

Yet, from another perspective, the outward calm and uniformity of Fascist Italy was dangerously deceptive. The general run of Italians did not habitually exhibit their ingrained cynicism toward the central authority in Rome. Through the ages, they had learned to adapt to political change with the minimum of fuss. There is an Italian word, *garbo*, untranslatable really but signifying recognition of the inevitable and adjustment to it with tact and discretion. Luigi Barzini in his national character sketch *The Italians* (1964) places it in a political context: "It is, for instance, the careful circumspection with which one slowly changes political allegiance when things are on the verge of becoming dangerous." Such a custom confounds the historian's effort to gauge the commitment of the Italian masses to Fascism. Did spasmodic outbursts of popular enthusiasm mask a traditional weary resignation? One suspects that all along there was restrained expectation that Mussolini's regime of gestures would substantially change the way of life of the ordinary Italian—and that the popular practice of *garbo* deluded Mussolini into believing that he had bridged the familiar Italian gap between people and state. The true situation was perhaps epitomized in an anecdote dating from the Fascist era. A high Fascist official visited a factory and asked the manager: "What are these workers' politics?" "One third Communist, one third Socialist, and the rest belong to small parties," was the reply. "What!" cried the livid party official. "Is none of them Fascist?" The manager hastened to reassure him: "All of them, Your Excellency, all of them."

Insofar as so many Italians seemed to harbor lingering mental reservations about Fascism, this constitutes a further specific in which Mussolini's regime fell short of genuine totalitarianism. For the very essence of a totalitarian system is that it commands the whole citizen, soul as well as body, his spiritual as well as outward conformity. Of course, the illusion of Fascist Italian totalitarianism would not be broken until it was put to the test, which came with Italy's entry into the Second World War. Then the performance of Italian troops between 1940 and 1943 revealed beyond question that they did not consider Mussolini's Fascism a cause worth dying for—a truth underscored by Italian heroism in the resistance to the Nazi occupation of 1943–45. Significantly, too, at the close of World War II, there seemed little reason for an Italian version of the denazification proceedings in Germany. The one postwar Italian ministry to apply a mild dose of *defascistizzazione* found that it helped to bring down the government.

Mussolini's failure both to liquidate the traditional Italian power structure and to integrate the masses fully into the Fascist state amounted to the demise of the Fascist revolution. The "second wave"

begun in the Matteotti crisis was never completed. Although compromise and half measures might be conducive to perpetuating Mussolini's hold on office, they did not sit well with the more ardent spirits
in the PNF. One disillusioned group was comprised of those idealists
who believed it Fascism's mission to rescue Italy from stagnation.
Especially disturbing was the corporative state's degeneration into a
complex of corrupt business-government relationships and its consequent inability to effect any significant change in Italy's modes of
production. The sense of frustration on this score deepened as the
effects of the Great Depression were felt throughout the 1930s.

In addition, not a few Italian intellectuals regarded corporativism
as the ideological essence of Fascism which would enable the movement to become ecumenical. This was the rationale of *universalfascismo*, advocated by Bottai, minister of corporations, and by writers
such as Asvero Gravelli and Camillo Pellizzi. Mussolini himself more
than once in the 1930s openly proclaimed that Fascism was exportable.
The nearest that *universalfascismo* came to realization was in December 1934 when, on the initiative of interested Italian intellectuals, a
Fascist International met in Montreux, Switzerland. Fascists from thirteen countries attended, and at the end of the gathering, a communiqué
announced their united attachment to "a revolution inspired by a true
mysticism and an elevated ideal founded on corporativism." However,
in private discussions the Italian delegates were horrified to discover
that many non-Italian fascists were largely indifferent to corporative
socioeconomic theory; on the contrary, their ideology was racist and
their preoccupation the Jewish question. The chief spokesman for this
view came from the Rumanian Iron Guard. The German Nazis were
conspicuous by their absence from the Montreux congress; but plainly,
Nazi racism was already threatening to dominate world fascism, at least
ideologically. The split into two camps at Montreux, for all practical
purposes, wrecked the Fascist International. Certainly, the prospect of
universalizing fascism through corporative doctrine died in December
1934.

The nonfulfillment of corporative dreams both within Italy and on
the world stage prompted something of a movement away from Mussolini's regime by Italy's youthful intellectuals—which, of course, made
it still easier for the hangers-on and sinecurists to take over Italian
Fascism. But this elitist aversion was purely passive and academic. Much
more immediately critical to Mussolini was the discontent of party
activists—those whose brutality had helped Fascism into power and

who waited in vain for a violent onslaught on the Italian establishment to follow. By the mid-thirties, Mussolini deemed it necessary to give his military desperadoes an outlet for their brutal energies. He chose an overseas location.

During the first Fascist decade, there had been frequent signs of Mussolini's restless ambition in foreign affairs. In 1923 he had tried to seize the Greek island of Corfu only to be thwarted by the threat of the British fleet. But, within a few months, he managed to browbeat Yugoslavia into ceding Fiume to Italy. Then, after overcoming the Matteotti crisis at home, he turned his attention to Albania which, by 1927, had become a pliant Italian satellite. It was to be expected that, sooner or later, the Duce would move on to East Africa seeking revenge for the Italian defeat at Adowa at the hands of the Ethiopians. The timing of his decision to embark on the conquest of Ethiopia, though, was questionable. In 1932 Mussolini assumed once more the post of foreign minister and, over the next two years, made it perfectly plain to his officials that he was not to be deflected from an early attack. Thereby, Mussolini chose to commit his country's strength to East Africa at the very moment that Nazi Germany began to pose a real danger to Austrian independence and, by extension, to Italy's possession of the Alto Adige with its quarter of a million Germans. It cannot be said that the Duce was unaware of the German problem. Within weeks of Hitler's accession to the German chancellorship in January 1933, Mussolini had proposed a four-power pact of Britain, France, Italy, and Germany, partly to appease Hitler but partly to contain him. Although the four-power pact was emasculated by France and her allies, the overture was testimony to Mussolini's prescience of the Nazi menace. Furthermore, in July 1934 the Austrian Nazis attempted a *Putsch* whose ultimate purpose was Anschluss (the union of Austria and Germany), and they appealed to Berlin for aid. On this occasion it was Mussolini, more than anyone else, who deterred Hitler by threatening to send Italian troops across the Brenner and to invoke the Concert of Europe against Germany. Nonetheless, the writing was on the wall; everyone knew that Anschluss might become a live issue again at a moment's notice.

At this critical juncture, then, Mussolini planned to subjugate Italy's interests in the north to the luxury of a colonial adventure. Obviously, he was gambling on a swift Ethiopian coup after which the watch on the Brenner could be resumed before the Anschluss question flared up again. But the motive which induced the Duce to gamble in the first place, the latest scholarship agrees, must be sought in domestic Italian circumstances. In sum, glory and conquest in East Africa were to compensate the PNF radicals for their arrested revolution at home and the Italian people generally for the miseries of the Great Depression. Mussolini's prescription was anything but novel; in seeking a distraction in Ethiopia from Italy's internal problems, he was following the disastrous precedent set by Crispi in 1896.

National self-assertion had been a cardinal feature of Italian Fascism from the start. When neither social revolution nor genuine corporative reform materialized at home, nationalism and empire were left as Fascism's only raison d'être. This became apparent as Fascist propaganda increasingly conceived Italian life in terms of struggle. Partly, the struggle was against the environment, to which the celebrated economic "battles" bore witness. But mainly, it was struggle against external enemies because, in Mussolini's words, "nothing has ever been won in history without bloodshed." Hence, discipline and service were called for, and the Fascist credo was reduced to the injunction: "Believe! Obey! Fight!" The supreme Fascist virtues were Spartan. In the national recreational organization created by the Fascists, the *Dopolavoro*, the stress was all on masculinity and physical prowess. Even the Fascist hierarchs were required to perform elementary gymnastics in public, although, as they were mostly middle-aged, the result was usually low comedy rather than high example. Mussolini, for his part, went back after 1925 to wearing uniforms as much as possible. By always standing ramrod straight, tilting back his head, and thrusting out his lower lip and jaw, he tried to cut a figure of belligerent strength. Cultural and intellectual pursuits were tolerated in Fascist Italy only insofar as they enhanced martial values. This was the purpose of the Fascist Institute of Culture and the School of Fascist Mysticism. Not surprisingly, the so-called *stile fascista* in art and thought never amounted to anything; the regime's objectives remained overwhelmingly material. Mussolini, who was bored by museums, complained that tourists were impressed by Italy's art treasures instead of the modern war machine that Fascism was supposedly building. In short, the Fascist state was a bleak one. It demanded sacrifice and duty, and held out the distant hope of national conquest and honor as a reward. Its unity was more that of an army than a civil community.

The emphasis on militarism at home for the sake of expansion overseas bred something of a new ideology for Fascist Italy—the inspiration of what Mussolini termed a "Third Rome." Certainly, Mussolini with growing frequency harked back to the glories of the ancient Roman

Empire and, to a lesser extent, to the heyday of Rome as the capital of a united Christendom, although it may be doubted whether the "idea of Rome" was ever more than a façade for conventional Italian nationalism. In any event, by the middle of the 1930s, the Roman ideology was pushing corporative ideas into the background, thereby postponing indefinitely the social changes which corporativism might have effected. Yet, ironically, the realization of a new Roman empire hinged on the modernization and thoroughgoing transformation of Italy which Fascism had spurned. In his pursuit of imperial expansion, Mussolini felt compelled to assert that somehow Fascism had transmogrified Italy into an efficient industrial and military power. Hence, his boasts about an army of "eight million bayonets" and an air force able "to blot out the sun." Hence, too, his claim that his autarchic economic policies after 1935 guaranteed that Italy would be virtually self-sufficient in wartime. It was all fiction, of course. After a decade and a half of

*Further lionization of Mussolini in propaganda: a picture postcard shows Mussolini as helmsman of the ship of state.*

COURTESY OF F. W. PARRY

Fascism, Italy remained what she had always been in international affairs—a major power by courtesy title only.

## International Realities

This unpleasant truth began to dawn between 1935 and 1938, as the Ethiopian adventure set in motion an unexpected train of events. In the first place, to conquer Ethiopia, Fascist Italy required the approval, explicit or tacit, of the principal colonial powers in East Africa—Britain and France. Both of these states were alarmed by Germany's military revival under Hitler and, in broad terms, they were inclined to humor Italy outside Europe if Mussolini would promise to adhere to an anti-German front in Europe. In essence, this bargain was struck—first through a visit to Rome of the French premier, Pierre Laval, in January 1935, and then in April at Stresa where Britain, France, and Italy met to consider Nazi Germany's recent announcement of massive, open rearmament. The Stresa declaration pledged the three powers to uphold the international status quo "in Europe"—but not, by inference, in Africa. These schemes, however, took no account of public sentiment in favor of collective security through the League of Nations, to which Ethiopia appealed when Italian troop movements on her border became blatantly aggressive. In Britain, where a general election was imminent, the government was particularly sensitive. So, on September 11, 1935, Sir Samuel Hoare, the British foreign secretary, treated the annual meeting of the League of Nations Assembly to a ringing panegyric on the merits of collective security. Rather to his surprise, his listeners took his words as an endorsement of League action against Fascist Italy in the Ethiopian question. Thus encouraged, the League in October branded Italy an aggressor and voted economic sanctions against the offender. The British and French governments, scarcely daring to protest, were swept along. Mussolini, who had always despised the League of Nations as a hotbed of pacifism, was furious.

Yet League sanctions were irresolutely applied, due in the main to British and French reluctance to make them work. Furthermore, London and Paris never envisaged progressing from economic to military sanctions. The Anglo-French official position came clearly to light in December 1935 after the British election was over. Hoare visited Laval in Paris, and together they concocted a scheme to offer Mussolini approximately two-thirds of Ethiopia if he would call off the invasion.

Mysteriously, this Hoare-Laval plan was leaked to the press, and the resultant popular indignation forced the British cabinet to disavow Hoare's work. Whether the Duce would have accepted the Hoare-Laval plan must be doubted; his need for a military diversion and victory to placate his activist Fascists was too great. However, the Hoare-Laval plan, by revealing Anglo-French duplicity vis-à-vis the League, scuttled any possibility of firm collective action against Italy. Ethiopia's fate was now sealed. The Italian campaign in East Africa had been making little headway, provoking rumbles of discontent in Rome. But early in 1936, Italian forces under Marshal Badoglio began to advance swiftly. Aerial gas attacks on Ethiopian villages shocked liberal consciences everywhere, but proved effective. On May 5 the Ethiopian capital was taken and, a few days later, Mussolini proclaimed the Italian Empire of Ethiopia from the balcony of the Palazzo Venezia. In July the League of Nations lifted its by-now farcical sanctions.

On the surface, the Ethiopian campaign was a tremendous success for the Fascist regime. It had received the blessing of the Vatican and the enthusiastic support of the Italian populace. The British and French governments, obviously against their better judgment, had been forced to pay lip service to collective security, and the tension generated between Fascist Italy and the Anglo-French side would take some overcoming. But, in reality, League of Nations sanctions had proved only a mild inconvenience to Italy's Ethiopian expedition. And with the whole question now settled in Mussolini's favor, there was no objective reason why, in due course, Fascist Italy should not return to the policy of cooperation with London and Paris to ward off the danger from Nazi Germany.

Any prospect for a return to the Stresa Front, however, was thwarted by the outbreak of the Spanish Civil War in July 1936. Mussolini had long postulated an unavoidable rivalry between the two "Latin sisters," Italy and France, and, since the 1920s, it had been his ambition to replace French influence in the western Mediterranean— including Spain—with that of Fascist Italy. Civil war in Spain seemed to provide an opportunity. Italian troops and military supplies began to pour into Spain in support of the Nationalist revolt led by General Francisco Franco against the radical coalition government which the Spanish parliamentary regime had thrown up in Madrid. Because Nazi Germany as well as Fascist Italy intervened on Franco's behalf, it appeared that in Spain a titanic struggle was joined between international fascism on the one hand and the forces of the Left and democracy on the other. This opinion, it will be shown later, was a travesty of what the Spanish Civil War was about. The important thing here is that Mussolini was one of those swept away by this ideological interpretation. It appealed to his melodramatic and simplistic mind which was prone to see matters in stark black-and-white terms. Although Britain and France ostentatiously refrained from intervening against Franco and his fascist allies, the Duce persuaded himself that these countries, merely because they were parliamentary democracies, were his sworn foes. His animus was fed by the conviction that the vacillation of the British and French in both the Ethiopian and Spanish questions proved that they were effete and fated to yield their world position to the virile fascist states. The breach with England was the more serious. It was largely the cordial relationship between Mussolini and the British Conservatives which had kept Italy loyal to her partners from the First World War. Italy, as Mussolini was about to discover, was not strong enough to go it alone in world affairs. Without the Anglo-Italian entente, Fascist Italy, always a discontented element in international politics, might easily drift into the orbit of those powers (Germany was the chief) dedicated to undoing the peace settlement of 1919.

In June 1936 Count Galeazzo Ciano, son of one of the first Fascists and husband of Mussolini's favorite daughter, Edda, was made Italian foreign minister. It was a sign that a distinctively Fascist foreign policy was in the offing. In short order, Nazi Germany gave diplomatic recognition to Fascist Italy's Ethiopian empire; together, Berlin and Rome recognized Franco's regime as the legitimate Spanish government; a secret Italo-German protocol was signed pledging vague cooperation in a variety of questions around the globe; and Ciano visited Germany where he had a cordial exchange with Hitler. Then, on November 1, Mussolini made his first public reference to a "Rome-Berlin line [which] is not a diaphragm but an axis, around which can revolve all those European states with a will to collaboration and peace." The Rome-Berlin Axis was an Italian invention born of Mussolini's new-found belief that the fascist states must stand together against decadent western liberalism and menacing eastern bolshevism. It conveniently ignored the ideological divisions within the fascist world which had appeared at the Montreux meeting of the Fascist International in 1934, as well as the fact that Germany and Italy harbored incompatible diplomatic goals in Austria and the Balkans. But for the time being, the superficial ideological affinity between the two self-styled fascist states was a sufficient bond. In November 1937 ideology was again operative as Fascist Italy joined the Anti-Comintern Pact which had been concluded a year earlier by Germany and Japan.

There was another dimension to the budding Italo-German rapprochement. While Mussolini, out of a mixture of umbrage at Britain and France and ideological principle, deliberately opted for the Rome-Berlin Axis, he was also being forced into it willy-nilly. On the occasion of Fascist Italy's adherence to the Anti-Comintern Pact, the Nazi diplomat Joachim von Ribbentrop visited Rome and took the opportunity to bring up the question of an Austro-German Anschluss. To his delighted surprise, Mussolini, instead of bursting into his customary tirade against an Anschluss, now intimated that it was of no great interest to him at all. The heart of the matter was that Ethiopia and Spain had grossly overtaxed Fascist Italy's military resources. For instance, by mid-1937, 50,000 of Italy's armed forces were on Spanish soil, and over the course of the entire civil war Franco received Italian military supplies worth approximately twenty million dollars. Even if Mussolini had a mind to repeat his anti-Anschluss stratagem of July 1934—Italian mobilization on the Brenner to scare Hitler off—he no longer had the means to mount a credible deterrent. In March 1938, when Hitler finally moved on Austria, he sent Mussolini a message apprising him of the impending Anschluss. The logic of Italy's military weakness, coupled with the spell of a common fascist ideology, carried the day. "The Duce accepted the whole thing in a very friendly manner," Hitler was informed. "He sends you his regards." Responded the Führer: "Please tell Mussolini that I shall never forget him for this."

The Anschluss of March 13, 1938, marked the beginning of the end of the Fascist regime in Italy. With German troops on the Brenner Pass, the shadow of predatory Pan-Germanism fell over the Italian peninsula. Not only was the Italian hold on the Germanic Alto Adige threatened but also Italy's very integrity. Fascist Italy, in brief, was ready to become a satellite of Nazi Germany. Nonetheless, Mussolini kept up his propaganda—perhaps with a hint more desperation than before the Anschluss—that Fascist Italy constituted a strong, independent power of major proportions. Moreover, he continued to convince many at home and abroad; his major accomplishments were always in the realm of salesmanship. Unfortunately, the chief victim of this masquerade was the Duce himself. It was the supreme irony and triumph of this "artist in propaganda" that he should end by deluding himself.

Mussolini's obstinate clinging to a false image of Fascist Italy's strength was a fatal error. His ambitious and feckless foreign and colonial policy between 1934 and 1938 had brought on the disaster of Anschluss. To persist on this expansionist course, as Mussolini did, was the height of folly. For having rejected experimentation and reform at home in favor of conquest abroad, Italian Fascism and its Duce, in a manner of speaking, asked to be judged by their record in the international arena. When the Second World War exposed to the full the diplomatic pretentiousness of Fascist Italy, the downfall of Mussolini and his regime followed almost as a matter of course.

# 3

# Another Fascist Prototype— Nazi Germany

The rise of fascism was strikingly similar in both Italy and Germany. Two general reasons for this may be suggested. First, in the immediate prefascist years, certain objective circumstances were present in each country—nationalist discontent, economic dislocation, intensification of the class war—all of which rocked an existing liberal regime. In these like situations, Mussolini and Hitler made strong appeals to roughly the same societal groups in Italy and Germany. Second, Hitler achieved office just over ten years after Mussolini became Italian premier. In the intervening decade, the German Nazi leader closely studied the manner in which the Duce had come to power and deliberately set out to imitate it. The resemblance between events in Italy 1919–25 and Germany 1930–34, therefore, is hardly surprising.

Yet, despite the coincidence of their paths to power, Italian Fascism and German Nazism were markedly different in temperament and in their vision of the future, reflecting the national environments of the two movements. This divergence was always present, although it did not come into clear view until after 1934, the year of the consolidation of the Nazi dictatorship. Then, in thought and deed, Nazism proved unmistakably to be of a different order of fascism from that observed in Italy. In the following section of this book, while dealing with the parallel progress of the Mussolinian and Hitlerian movements, we are concerned in the last resort with the ideological distinction between them.

## The Second German Empire

It goes without saying that both the Mussolinian and Hitlerian varieties of fascism had their roots in certain national traditions in Italy and Germany. In the latter case, however, a more extreme argument has sometimes been advanced, namely, that Nazism was nothing more than a natural culmination of German history. On occasions, this school of thought has tried to trace German national traits all the way back to the Teutons described by the writers of classical Rome; hence the view has been called the "Tacitus syndrome." More reasonably, attention has also been focused on the mode of Germany's unification, particularly on the part played by German liberals. It was the failure of the liberals to bring about unification in the *annus mirabilis* of 1848 that opened the door to the *Realpolitik* of Otto von Bismarck, who achieved the task by defiance of Prussian constitutional law and through use of the Prussian military machine in three wars in six years. Between 1866 and 1870, Prussian liberals, enraptured by Bismarck's nationalist successes, retroactively endorsed his authoritarian and bellicose policies. In doing so, they announced that liberal principles were subordinate to *raison d'état*. The example set by Prussia's liberals carried over into the new united Germany. After 1871, the German National Liberal party seemed to set more store by national consensus than individual liberties and minority rights, assenting to repressive laws against Catholics and socialists who were suspected of owing allegiance to international—that is, non-German—causes. Moreover, the business section of the Liberal party departed so far from laissez faire as to sanction imperialism and protective tariffs in return for government contracts, especially for armaments. At the crux of the problem of German liberalism was the speed of industrialization in the German Empire. At the time of unification, well over half of the German labor force was engaged in agricultural pursuits; by 1914, the figure was about 30 percent, while among European nations Germany was second only to

Great Britain in coal production and first in the production of steel, pig iron, and new chemical synthetics. This phenomenal growth occupied a mere two generations—too short a time for the building of a solid middle class which provided the social basis for liberalism in western Europe.

The obverse of the endemic weakness of German liberalism was the autocratic nature of the Second German Empire—a "pseudo-constitutional absolutism" as the contemporary historian Theodor Mommsen called it. Although the new Germany was given parliamentary institutions and the Reichstag or lower house was elected by universal manhood suffrage, this was largely a façade. The Reichstag's power to deny the government funds was not constitutionally established, while ministerial responsibility was specifically avoided; ministers were legally responsible only to the chancellor, the chancellor only to the emperor. The result was that political and administrative power became centered in one of two persons—either the emperor himself or the chancellor backed by the emperor. So from 1871 to 1890, Bismarck, with the unswerving support of William I up to 1888, dominated German life. From 1890 to 1918, William II, who would tolerate no rivals and surrounded himself with courtierlike politicians, tried to fill Bismarck's shoes, although he critically lacked the Iron Chancellor's application and judgment.

Because of William II's spasmodic attention to official business and the dearth of German statesmen of stature, something of a power vacuum developed at the core of German government. It tended to be filled by special interest groups—above all, by the military. Thus, army officers were able to determine policy far beyond the limits of normal military planning. The most notorious instance was that of the evolution between 1892 and 1906 of the Schlieffen Plan which, by committing Germany to make war on France by an invasion of Belgium, put German diplomacy in a straitjacket in the international crisis of 1914. The military's political weight was a reflection of their standing in German society at large. As the main instrument of German unification, the army was assured of a high reputation in the new empire. In fact, the army officer corps was almost an aristocracy unto itself. Officership in the army reserve was a goal of middle-class social climbers, for it gave entrée to high society. But it was also the means by which the German bourgeoisie became imbued with militarist values. The status of an army officer is nicely portrayed in Carl Zuckmayer's famous comedy, *The Captain of Köpenick* (1931), based on an actual incident in 1906. A drifter and petty criminal, having purchased and donned the secondhand uniform of an officer in the prestigious Imperial Guard, is enabled to commandeer a squad of soldiers as they march along a Berlin street and use them to occupy temporarily the town hall of Köpenick, a small town nearby. Such is the respect engendered by a military uniform that no one sees fit to challenge the bogus officer in his escapade.

Between 1871 and 1914, the Second German Empire was undeniably the most powerful state on the European continent. Plain for all to see was German military prowess, demonstrated in the wars of unification, which was supplemented by the spectacular growth of Germany's industrial might. Not surprisingly, united Germany exuded self-confidence and a somewhat blind faith in material strength. Furthermore, Germans demonstrated not merely the consciousness of power but also the will to use it. The belated but swift acquisition of power seemed to produce a sort of national intoxication, most apparent in the neurotic swaggering of Emperor William II. And it found even more concrete expression in Germany's prewar adoption of *Weltpolitik* (world policy), whereby this quintessential European state, despite preoccupation with potential enemies on both western and eastern borders, nevertheless set out to found an overseas empire, built a navy to service this empire, and demanded a voice in international questions all over the globe. Critics called this restless ambition German arrogance—a charge which was to be a staple of anti-German war propaganda. However, during the last decade a new school of German historians has refurbished this time-honored image of Wilhelmine Germany. Their most outstanding spokesman, Fritz Fischer, contends that a spirit of *Weltpolitik* pervaded all strata of German society and that German bellicosity was a major cause of World War I.

The salient features of pre-1914 Germany, then, were political authoritarianism, a taste for militarist values, and a belligerent and expansionist foreign policy. All of which can be said to have prepared the German people for the nationalist dictatorship created by Hitler after 1933. Undoubtedly, the Nazi regime capitalized on the traditions of imperial Germany. On the other hand, it was also very much more than the Prussian parade-ground mentality reincarnated. It is significant that most recent investigations of the roots of Nazism have gone behind the material surface of nineteenth-century Germany in order to concentrate on certain deep-seated cultural patterns. Specifically, Nazism has been interpreted as the fruit of a century or more of *völkisch* culture.

The German word *Volk* has no true counterpart in the English language; "people" and "folk" are far too vague to convey the elaborate connotations. G. L. Mosse, whose *Crisis of German Ideology* emphasizes the *völkisch* content of both German thought and Nazism, writes:

> "Volk" signified the union of a group of people with a transcendental "essence." This "essence" might be called "nature" or "cosmos" or "mythos," but in each instance it was fused to man's innermost nature, and represented the source of his creativity, his depth of feeling, his individuality, and his unity with other members of the Volk.
>
> The essential element here is the linking of the human soul with its natural surroundings, with the "essence" of nature. The really important truths are to be found beneath the surface of appearances. An example —and one that is ultimately crucial in the development of Volkish thought—will serve to illustrate what is meant by this linking. According to many Volkish theorists, the nature of the soul of a Volk is determined by the native landscape. Thus the Jews, being a desert people, are viewed as shallow, arid, "dry" people, devoid of profundity and totally lacking in creativity. Because of the barrenness of the desert landscape, the Jews are a spiritually barren people. They thus contrast markedly with the Germans, who, living in the dark, mist-shrouded forests are deep, mysterious, profound. Because they are so constantly shrouded in darkness, they strive toward the sun, and are truly *Lichtmenschen*.

The ties among the *Volk* were felt rather than rationally apprehended. Appropriately, *völkisch* thought gained impetus from the German romantic movement of the early nineteenth century; its early spokesmen were such literary giants as Johann Fichte and Johann von Herder. Another romantic, Father Jahn, was the inspiration behind the *Burschenschaften* (university student associations or fraternities) which, from the start, adopted *völkisch* and exclusive attitudes. Indeed, the German educational systems were perhaps the main channel by which *völkisch* traditions were handed down from generation to generation. The mystical element of *völkisch* thought seemed to appeal to the idealist strain in German philosophy and learning generally. Toward the end of the nineteenth century, an important segment of German youth, in revulsion against the growing materialism of everyday life, turned naturally to *völkisch* ideas. They regarded the countryside and the peasantry as the repositories of the "true soul" of Germany; their concern was to recapture the spiritual essence of the German people.

To some extent, *völkisch* culture flourished in nineteenth-century Germany because it served to fill the gap left by the failure of the Germans to find fulfillment in political terms. Before 1871, it plainly served as a surrogate for long-deferred unification. And what Bismarck achieved in 1871, it must be remembered, was no more than a *kleindeutsch* (small German) solution to the national problem; a united state was made but at the cost of leaving some nine million Germans in the Hapsburg Empire outside the German Empire's frontiers. *Völkisch* theorists satisfied the need to assert the unity of all Teutonic people, regardless of artificial and temporary divisions. Here was the seed of Pan-Germanism. A Pan-German Association was, in fact, founded in 1890, and proved to be a powerful lobby in the years before the First World War. For political reasons the association did not campaign openly for the German acquisition of Hapsburg territory, but its aim of a Greater Germany with a *völkisch* identity implied as much. It was a dream to be realized by Hitler in 1938.

In its emphasis on the uniqueness of different peoples, *völkisch* ideology was virtually synonymous with racism. Although racial theories were enormously popular in nineteenth-century Germany, the most systematic thinkers in this field were not German. The Comte de Gobineau was French, and Houston Stewart Chamberlain was born an Englishman although, in due course, he became a naturalized German. Practically all *völkisch* and racist writers extolled the inherent superiority of the Aryans. The word *Aryan* properly referred to a group of Indo-European languages, but was appropriated to denote roughly the Nordic or Anglo-Saxon branches of mankind or, even more narrowly, the Germans alone. The counterpart was the Jew, destined by nature to be inferior physically and culturally, and, according to some extreme racists, the deadly enemy of the Aryan.

During the nineteenth century, many European Jews profited from the spirit of egalitarianism engendered by the French Revolution, gaining emancipation and almost full citizens' rights before the law. Furthermore, the secularization of European society continually eroded the religious barrier between Jewry and the rest of the community, and Jews increasingly assimilated with their neighbors. German Jewry shared in these broad developments, with Jews accepted in most walks of German life. Emperor William II, for example, was on friendly terms with several wealthy Jewish businessmen. On the other hand, the very emergence of Jews from their traditional ghettos made them more noticeable than ever before and increased the awareness of the population at large of Jewry's distinctive presence. At the same time, the popular transference of Darwinian theories from animal species to social groups and races—Social Darwinism was especially widespread in Germany—heightened race consciousness further. In consequence, a great deal of latent anti-Semitism existed in pre-1914 Germany, although there were those who tried to make explicit and give form to the anti-Semitic undercurrent. The writers Paul de Lagarde and Julius Langbehn became obsessed with the suspected Jewish danger, and Adolf Stoecker, the imperial court chaplain, made a career out of anti-Semitic rancor. In the last quarter of the nineteenth century, several specific anti-Semitic movements and associations, albeit all of them short-lived, made their appearance in Germany.

However, the importance of anti-Semitism before World War I lies less in its degree or its visibility than in its radically new quality. Traditional European anti-Semitism condemned the Jew for religious reasons; in contrast, modern anti-Semitism has been based on racial grounds. Above all, German *völkisch* cultists excoriated Jews as "a pestilence and a cholera" which threatened to pollute the race. To accomplish this corruption, Jewish males were supposed to lust perpetually after Aryan women. A logical recommendation to be drawn from this view was the destruction of German Jewry in order to preserve the purity of the German race—a proposal made by some fanatics before 1914 and ultimately implemented by the Nazis. Racist anti-Semitism also hinted at the later totalitarians' "objective crime." The Jew was to be persecuted neither for his actions nor his beliefs (the rationale of old-fashioned Christian anti-Semitism), but simply for what he was.

## Hitler's Youth: The Artist *Manqué*

Before 1914, the Teutonic propensity for race-thinking and anti-Semitism was much more blatantly displayed in the German-speaking areas of the Hapsburg Empire than in the Second German Empire itself. Significantly, it was in prewar Austria-Hungary that Adolf Hitler underwent his youthful, formative experiences. Hitler was born in 1889 at Braunau am Inn, a small Austrian town near the German border. Although his family was long established in Upper Austria, there was mystery in Hitler's ancestry: his paternal grandfather was illegitimate and until middle age used his mother's name of Schicklgruber. This grandfather's paternity remains uncertain. Probably Hitler's great-grand-father was Johann Hiedler (Hitler) who ultimately married Maria Schicklgruber—or he may have been an unknown Jew. The latter supposition, made by some of Hitler's enemies, lacks concrete evidence, but one can legitimately speculate as to how the accusation might have affected the anti-Semitic Hitler. His father, Alois Hitler, was born a peasant, but advanced steadily through a modest civil service career in the customs and revenue division to the social position of a typical petit bourgeois. However, his family life was less ordered than his professional career. He was married three times, the last time to a second cousin; for this union special ecclesiastical dispensation had to be obtained. Adolf Hitler was the first child of this marriage to survive infancy.

The young Hitler quarreled often with his father, not surprising since Alois Hitler was over fifty when Adolf was born, and the generational gap was huge. According to the son's later complaints, Alois showed no sympathy for his aspirations to become either a painter or an architect. But since the father died before his son reached fourteen, their disputes more likely concerned poor school results. Adolf Hitler remained in school until 1905 but left without gaining a graduation diploma. After two years of idle living with his mother in Linz, passing his time in sketching, he moved, in 1907, to Vienna. Twice he applied to enter the Academy of Fine Arts but was turned down ("test drawing unsatisfactory" ran the verdict), and the School of Architecture would not consider him without a school-leaving certificate. However, he stayed on in Vienna. When his mother died, he inherited her few savings and acquired an orphan's pension. He eked out a living by casual labor (shoveling snow, carrying luggage, and so on), by painting stereotyped postcard views of Vienna which he hawked in taverns and fairs, and by drawing advertising posters for small tradesmen. For some of his years in Vienna, he lived in a mens' hostel where, in Hitler's own words, "only tramps, drunkards and such spent any time." He soon broke away from his sole close acquaintance, a school friend from Linz who had come to Vienna with musical ambitions; later he entered into partnership with another vagabond, but the association broke up when Hitler prosecuted his colleague for cheating him out of the proceeds of his pictures. By 1910 Hitler had become a lone drifter.

Thereafter, the youthful Hitler led such a solitary existence that our knowledge of his Viennese days is fragmentary. A recently discovered but unpublished memoir by the Irish wife of Hitler's stepbrother asserts that he spent the winter of 1912–13 with them in Liverpool, paying one visit to London where he was fascinated by the machinery of Tower Bridge. The tale is just credible, for firm evidence of his activity in these months is lacking, and although Hitler himself never mentioned his trip to England, he had good reason not to—he was on the run from the Austrian military authorities. Like the young Mussolini, Hitler objected to performing compulsory military service for a state of which he disapproved. Not long after his return to Vienna in 1913, he left for Munich, again probably to evade the military draft. Early the following year, he was deported to Austria-Hungary, but at Salzburg was rejected for military service on medical grounds.

Despite the imprecisions and lacunae in Hitler's life story between 1910 and 1914, we nonetheless know enough to form a general impression of his developing character. Hitler could not admit that, while he might have an artist's inclinations and temperament, he did not have the talent to match. Fits of uncontrollable enthusiasm, in which he would indulge in romantic daydreams about his future triumphs, were followed by periods of utter depression and total inactivity. In brief, he was quite incapable of sustained application. Most important, though, he relieved his frustration by blaming his failures, not on his own shortcomings, but on society. Vienna, with its art galleries and concert halls representative of the glittering world of culture which he craved to enter, both fascinated and repelled him. Vienna also was a microcosm of the polyglot Hapsburg Empire. To some, this variety was an attraction; to others, like Hitler, Vienna's cosmopolitanism indicated only that aliens were corrupting and supplanting the worthy Germanic Volk.

Because of the lack of a common national identity in Austria-Hungary, allegiance was often accorded ethnic groups and dissatisfaction was expressed in racial terms. Thus the Germans, despite their predominance in the western half of the Hapsburg Empire, voiced their grievances through völkisch movements. One such was the German Workers' party founded in 1904 in northern Bohemia. It sprang out of resentment at the use of cheap Czech labor which eroded the status and security of German railwaymen, miners, metal and textile workers. Although the party remained local, it is of interest because its members were the first to call themselves National Socialists and because their hatred of the Czechs was absorbed by Hitler to resurface in Nazi diplomacy in the 1930s. More influential within the Hapsburg Empire was Georg von Schönerer's Pan-German movement which, in the guise of the Nationalist party, succeeded in 1901 in electing twenty-one deputies to the Austrian Parliament. Schönerer's politics were vehemently anti-Slav and, in the short run, he proposed the subjugation of all national minorities in the empire to a German *völkisch* regime. But in the long term, he anticipated with pleasure the demise of Austria-Hungary, which was to pave the way for a gigantic new empire of *Mitteleuropa* composed of all Germanic peoples. Schönerer was also, perhaps needless to add, an extreme anti-Semite. Hitler admired Schönerer immensely, although with an important reservation. The Austrian Pan-German movement was mostly upper and upper-middle class, and evidenced an aloof, paternalistic attitude to the masses. Hitler despised the masses, especially the proletariat of the industrial towns. Working-class solidarity had no appeal for him, and his drifter's course proclaimed his refusal to be regarded as a worker. Nevertheless, Hitler perceived early that the masses could be manipulated, and indeed had to be manipulated to provide the basis for a successful political movement in the modern world. This was the lesson he learned from the real hero of his Viennese days, Mayor Karl Lueger.

Lueger, the most prominent figure of the new Christian Social party, served as mayor of Vienna from 1897 until his death in 1910. He was a flamboyant, charismatic leader, but his policies as much as his personality accounted for his electoral victories. He cultivated and won a mass following with a program of "municipal socialism," legalizing trade unions and providing workers' accident and sickness insurance out of public funds. As for the clash of national minorities in his capital city, Lueger met the problem by diverting hatred toward the one group everybody despised—the Jews. This proved to be a convenient tactic because it was widely believed that Jewish finance—especially the *Kreditanstalt*, the Viennese branch of the Rothschild financial domain —was underwriting the burgeoning Austrian industrial revolution. Since one of the first effects of this industrialization was to put small traders and entrepreneurs out of business, this independent artisan class—a source of solid Lueger support—laid all its woes at the door of the Jews. At the same time, this lower-middle class felt threatened by the advance of the workers, often led by Jewish Social Democratic leaders. Quite likely, Lueger used anti-Semitism opportunistically. He himself was certainly not a racial anti-Semite; "I decide who is a Jew," he once remarked. But whatever his motives, a large part of his legacy to Vienna was an inflamed spirit of anti-Semitism.

It was in Lueger's Vienna that Hitler cultivated his anti-Semitism—

a sweeping hatred of the Jews that was to blame them for every modern calamity. Hitler has described his Viennese conversion to anti-Semitism in his autobiography, *Mein Kampf* (*My Struggle*):

> Once, as I was strolling through the Inner City, I suddenly encountered an apparition in a black caftan and black hair locks. Is this a Jew? was my first thought. For, to be sure, they had not looked like that in Linz. I observed the man furtively and cautiously, but the longer I stared at this foreign face, scrutinizing feature for feature, the more my first question assumed a new form: Is this a German? As always in such cases, I now began to try to relieve my doubts by books. For a few hellers I bought the first anti-Semitic pamphlets of my life.

Then, after detailing some particulars of Viennese anti-Semitism, especially fantasies about Jewish sexual designs on the Aryan race, Hitler concluded: "All this had but one good side: . . . my love for my people inevitably grew. For who, in view of the diabolical craftiness of these seducers, could damn the luckless victims?"

Hitler was in no way a political activist during his stay in Vienna, but in externalizing his discontent, he gave it a political form. The Hapsburg Empire, the symbol of Hitler's personal disappointments, became the object of his bitter hatred. Above all, the empire's ethnic mélange aroused his scorn, and the Jew was singled out for vituperation as the personification of Austro-Hungarian cosmopolitanism. To escape these horrors, Hitler adopted Germanic tribal nationalism. His loathing of the Hapsburg Empire and his response to its nationality problem informed the rest of his career. In a way, Nazism was the transference of Hitler's reactions to Vienna on to the German scene at large. Not a few German historians—Gerhard Ritter being perhaps the most distinguished—have seized on these Austrian roots of Nazism in order to absolve traditional Prussian conservatism from the charge of having spawned Nazism.

It was the First World War that supplied Hitler's bridge from Austria to Germany. On the outbreak, he expressed his contempt for the Hapsburgs by volunteering for service in the German army; he spent the next four years with a Bavarian regiment. For the first time in his life, he felt a sense of spiritual security and belonging with his fellows under fire. The war he later described as "the greatest of all experiences. For, that individual interest—the interest of one's own ego—could be subordinated to the common interest—that the great, heroic struggle of our people demonstrated in overwhelming fashion." His new-found purpose in life enabled him to fulfill his job conscientiously in a way he had found impossible in civilian life. He was a messenger, constantly in and out of the trenches and in frequent danger. As early as December 1914, he won the Iron Cross, Second Class, and in 1918 he was awarded the Iron Cross, First Class—an uncommonly distinguished decoration to be conferred on a corporal, which was the highest rank Hitler reached. In view of his enthusiasm for the war and the dearth of officer material during the late stages of the conflict, one may wonder why Hitler was never commissioned. Apparently, he never tried to become an officer, being loath to relinquish the bonhomie of the orderlies' mess where he was popular enough even though regarded by some as a "peculiar fellow." Hitler thus insulated himself in army life, and the armistice of 1918 found him, wounded for the second time in the war, in a military hospital where he had been taken after being temporarily blinded following a British gas attack.

The armistice, embodying the German surrender, came as a shock to Hitler. Like the rest of the German population, he had believed the wartime propaganda that victory was inevitable and imminent, a claim which seemed justified by events until almost the end of the war. In March 1918 the German triumph on the eastern front was sealed by the punitive peace of Brest-Litovsk with Bolshevik Russia. As late as July, the German armies were advancing on the western front. And when the fighting ceased on November 11, German forces still occupied substantial tracts of France and Belgium and, save for a small area in Alsace, had nowhere been pushed back across the German border. The fact that imperial Germany had simply run out of supplies of men and matériel was announced at the last minute, in October 1918, and was imperfectly comprehended by many Germans. With dramatic suddenness, Hitler, among others, was forced to contemplate a swift return to a civilian existence. The prospect of resuming his prewar vagrancy appalled Hitler and, by his own account, it was at the close of the First World War that he resolved to enter politics. His old nemesis, the Hapsburg Empire, was in the process of disintegrating into its component national parts—a rump Austrian state, a truncated Hungary, and various "successor states." Now, Hitler's attention was fixed on Germany. Although the unitary German state survived the war intact, the country was in social and political ferment. The revolutionary turmoil provided an opportunity for an obscure newcomer to politics to make his way. It also threatened the subversion of traditional German values. In fact, Hitler conceived his call to politics as a mission to save the historic Volk in their hour of need.

## Weimar

German popular unrest was generated by wartime sufferings which, in the closing days of the war, proved to have been in vain. Trouble occurred first in the port of Kiel, where the ratings of the German high seas fleet got wind of a rumor that they were to sail against the British in a final, suicidal gesture. They mutinied and joined with local troops and workers to form a workers and soldiers council, akin to a bolshevik soviet, which seized the municipal government of Kiel. During the first week of November 1918, similar workers and soldiers councils sprang up and seized power in various German cities. Their prime demand was for the ending of the war, although patently this was seen as a prelude to some sort of revolution. Such was the turbulent, grass-roots background to the death of the Second German Empire.

Yet, an air of contrivance hung over the November revolution. On November 9 Emperor William II was prevailed upon to abdicate, while the chancellorship passed into the hands of Friedrich Ebert, leader of the Social Democrats. On the same day, another prominent Socialist, Philipp Scheidemann, on his own initiative proclaimed a republic, and the new Social Democratic cabinet accepted the republic as a *fait accompli*. So, on the surface, did the rest of Germany. The republic came into being within a matter of hours, more or less without bloodshed, and on the basis of a limited amount of popular agitation. In other words, the entrenched imperial establishment failed to mount any opposition. It was not only the kaiser who abdicated but the entire conservative power structure. Having led Germany into war and to defeat, the Wilhelmine generals and statesmen deemed it politic to fade discreetly from the public scene for a while. Their concern was as much for international as for domestic opinion.

During its final year and a half, World War I had taken on a distinctly ideological complexion, which on the Allied side was reflected in the entry of the United States. America joined the fray not as an Allied but as an "associated" state, thereby signifying that her war aim was not—like that of Great Britain, France, and Italy—territorial aggrandizement, but the triumph of those political principles which were to be enunciated most famously in President Wilson's Fourteen Points. When the German high command in October 1918 saw fit to sue for an armistice, they first approached the American president, who was adjudged to be the least vengeful of the leaders of the anti-German coalition. In coming to terms with the Allies through Woodrow Wilson, the German authorities had to take into account the ideological purposes for which the United States claimed to be fighting. Wilson, openly dedicated to the destruction of German militarism and imperialism, and determined to establish democracy in Germany, announced that he would treat only with "the veritable representatives of the German people." The institution of a republic on November 9 was intended to be a guarantee of a new democratic Germany. By allowing the republic to come into existence, German conservatives hoped to appease Wilson and to win a lenient peace settlement. Thus, an important motive behind German republican democracy was transitory and artificial, which called into question the viability of the new political experiment from the start.

The German republic was burdened with the stigma of defeat; not only was it born amid the confusion attendant on Germany's surrender, but it came to be blamed for the defeat itself. Many Germans remained incredulous about the military collapse since the presence of German troops on French and Belgian soil when the armistice was signed implied that the German army had not been defeated. Instead, so the argument ran, it was betrayed by the civilians at home. The revolutionary upheaval in the days leading up to November 11 was used by the German military and its admirers to foster the totally fallacious but enormously influential *Dolchstoss* or stab-in-the-back legend. In this conspiratorial perspective, special opprobrium was visited on the left-wing Jewish intelligentsia. Much of the Social Democratic leadership in November 1918 was indeed Jewish, and this fact played its part in the application of the epithet "November criminals" to Germany's republicans.

Furthermore, the calculation that a republican government could cajole the Allies into a lenient peace settlement was not borne out—at least not to Germany's satisfaction. In the first place, the treaty was not negotiated but drawn up by consultation solely among the victors, and only then presented to the German delegation at the Paris Peace Conference. Written German comments were invited, but for the most part were peremptorily brushed aside. Germany, in her disarmed state, was to be constrained to accept a *Diktat*. Under these circumstances, any treaty, whatever its terms, was likely to provoke a storm of controversy. But in addition, the substance of this treaty provided grounds for further German indignation. Germany lost 14 percent of her prewar area containing 10 percent of her population, the major beneficiary being the new state of Poland. The most deeply resented territorial provision was that affording Poland access to the sea by means of a corridor averaging some thirty miles wide which cut off East Prussia from the rest of Germany. Largely to satisfy the French demand for security, inroads were made into German national sovereignty. The left bank of the Rhine, although remaining German, was to be permanently demilitarized, while bridgeheads across the Rhine were to be occupied by Allied troops for fifteen years. Germany was disarmed totally in the air, forbidden submarines and warships over 10,000 tons, and her land forces restricted in numbers and weapons to what was necessary to maintain internal order—particularly against a bolshevik coup which was the great fear of the day. Supervision of the disarmament clauses was entrusted to an Allied military control commission stationed on German soil. But the issue that, in the long run, would cause the most controversy and anguish was reparations. The relevant section of the treaty was introduced by Article 231 which, although its framers did not intend it, appeared to lay the entire blame for the outbreak of World War I on German shoulders, thus supplying a justification for the collection of heavy war damages. The peace treaty itself laid down the principle of reparations, but did not stipulate how much the Germans should pay; the exact tabulation was left to the Allied Reparations Commission. However, the Allies indicated that the cost of their own pensions would be included in the sum demanded. Understandably, the Germans anticipated the worst.

The first reaction of the German republican government was to reject the peace terms offered, and some consideration was even given to an overture to Bolshevik Russia for a common front against the western Allies. But in her weakened postwar condition, there was no real alternative open to Germany and, after several weeks of agonizing, Berlin accepted the *Diktat*. The Allies, with a sense of the melodramatic, set the signing ceremony for June 28, 1919, the fifth anniversary of the assassination of the Austrian archduke, the event which had precipitated the First World War. For the location, the Allies insisted on the famous Hall of Mirrors at Versailles where the German Empire had been proclaimed in 1871—a gesture which affronted German pride. Beyond question, the Germans were unduly sensitive to slights and totally insensitive to other nations' feelings, while their criticism of the Treaty of Versailles was often exaggerated and self-pitying. On the other hand, it was exceedingly impolitic of the Allies, committed as they were to the furtherance of German democracy, to inflict diplomatic humiliation on the republic at its very inception. For German revulsion against the peace settlement was swiftly extended to the regime which acquiesced in its imposition. The passions aroused were illustrated by two political assassinations—of Matthias Erzberger in 1921 and Walther Rathenau in 1922. Erzberger had been leader of the German armistice delegation in November 1918 and the first finance minister of the German republic; Rathenau was the spectacularly successful organizer of Germany's economic war effort. Both men advocated fulfillment of the Versailles Treaty, and for this they were murdered by nationalist fanatics.

Arranging a peace settlement was the first order of business for the postwar German regime. In fact, not until after the signing of the Treaty of Versailles did Germany formally acquire a republican constitution: on July 31, 1919, a national constituent assembly, meeting at Weimar, agreed on a constitution. The assembly had chosen to meet at Weimar in order to escape the tumultuous atmosphere of Berlin, but Weimar was also a suitably symbolic birthplace for the new democratic Germany. Weimar, the home of Goethe and Schiller, was regarded as the capital of German culture and the liberal antithesis of the Prussianized military empire which had gone down to defeat in 1918. The Weimar constitution thus aimed to break drastically with the recent autocratic past.

For the first time, all German citizens obtained a legal guarantee of basic civil liberties—equality before the law, freedom of speech, freedom of religion, and so on. Direct popular sovereignty won a measure of approval in the provision that by petition of 10 percent of the electorate any public issue could be submitted to a national referendum. But the main thrust of the Weimar constitution was to transform Germany into a parliamentary state, with the Reichstag the crux of the republican system. The new constitution extended the Reichstag suffrage to all Germans male and female over twenty, introduced proportional representation for the Reichstag parties and, most important, specifically enunciated the dependence of "the chancellor and all other ministers on the confidence of the Reichstag for the exercise of their offices." A president, elected every seven years by universal suffrage, replaced the emperor, although oddly the German state was still called the Reich (after 1918 in the sense of nation rather than empire). The president could dissolve the Reichstag and call for elections, but he was expected to do so only at the behest of the chancellor. On the other hand, Article 48 of the Weimar statute read: "Should public order and safety be seriously disturbed or threatened, the President may take the necessary measures to restore public order and safety; in case of need he may use armed force, . . . and he may, for the time being, declare the fundamental rights of the citizen wholly or partly in abeyance." In short, the president could rule by decree in an emergency. In 1919 few stopped to consider the potential of this "suicide clause" of Weimar democracy.

Until 1918 Germany was the most glaring exception to the nineteenth-century pattern that saw the industrialization of a society followed by the dominance of middle-class liberal values. The November revolution and the Weimar constitution were intended to bring Germany ideologically into line with the western industrialized nations. That Weimar was an experiment in liberalism was somewhat obscured by the visibility of the German Socialists who were not only the republic's instigators but, over the years, were to prove its only consistent defenders. However, the German Socialist party (SPD), although theoretically pledged to Marxian revolutionary ideas, had always in practice pursued a very moderate course. Before the war, the SPD had concentrated on building its strength in the Reichstag and, in August 1914, the parliamentary party had advertised its attachment to the Wilhelmine state by voting unanimously for war credits. The German Socialists under Weimar continued in this cautious vein. Broadly speaking, they were satisfied with the institutional and liberal reforms of 1918–19, and mounted no serious campaign to effect commensurate social and economic changes. As a middle-of-the-road regime, Weimar found itself in much the same position as liberal Italy between 1918 and 1922. In both cases the center turned out to be too narrow a base on which to rest. Constant attacks were made from right and left. After the credibility of the liberal system was sufficiently eroded by criticism from both flanks, a fascist movement of neither the traditional Right nor the orthodox Left was able to move into the vacuum.

The first attempt to subvert the German republic was made by the Left, which looked forward to a repetition of what had happened in 1917 in Russia where a limited revolution was swiftly followed by a more radical one. A loose coalition of German Bolsheviks and Independent Socialists (that is, socialists who had not backed the war effort) was formed and took its name from Spartacus, the leader of a Roman slave revolt in 73 B.C. This Spartacist union, recognizing that the Majority Socialists who controlled the government were not about to embark on the radicalization of German society, took to the streets of Berlin in the new year 1919. Gustav Noske, a leading SPD member of the provisional government, was charged with the job of pacification.

Forced to call in the military, Noske turned not to regular troops but to the *Freikorps*. These were private armies usually commanded by junior officers of the Imperial German army and composed of soldiers hastily demobilized in accordance with the disarmament terms of the armistice. The *Freikorps* were superpatriotic and violently antibolshevik, and for the latter characteristic they were tolerated by both the Allies and the German government. Their employment against the Spartacists was analogous to the Italian power structure's use of Mussolini's *squadristi* against the Italian Left. In a week of fighting, the *Freikorps* smashed the Spartacist uprising with great ferocity. The rebel leaders were summarily executed, and their bodies thrown into the rivers and canals around Berlin.

After the debacle, many Spartacists joined the newly founded German Communist party (KPD). Indeed, this party grew prodigiously in the early Weimar years and, by 1923, was able to poll three and a half million votes. Yet the KPD was inhibited somewhat from plotting Weimar's overthrow by its dependence on Moscow through membership in the Comintern. For, about mid-1920, a diplomatic rapprochement began to develop between the two outcasts of Europe—defeated Russia and defeated Germany—ideological differences notwithstanding. It was not that the Soviets renounced all hope of a German proletarian uprising, but rather that they temporarily set aside the prospect. On occasions, notably in 1923, the KPD stepped up its preparations for revolution, but it is probably safe to say that the main danger to Weimar came, not from the leftists, but from rightist groups which enjoyed the advantage of a secure position in German society.

In March 1920 the German government, under pressure from the Allies to fulfill its disarmament obligations, moved to dismantle the *Freikorps*. This was the signal for a determined attack on the Weimar structure which the *Freikorps* condemned as pacifist and socialist. Two *Freikorps* brigades, just back from the Baltic provinces, seized Berlin and announced the formation of a new government headed by a Dr. Wolfgang Kapp, a right-wing politician from East Prussia. The Weimar government called on the regular army to suppress this Kapp *Putsch*. However, the army flatly refused, and General Hans von Seeckt, the *Reichswehr* commander, explained: "Troops do not fire on troops. . . . When *Reichswehr* fires on *Reichswehr*, then all comradeship within the officer corps has vanished." Within a few days the immediate crisis passed. The trade unions called a general strike in Berlin, and the Kapp regime, unable to operate the capital's services, collapsed. But, of course, the most significant facet of the Kapp *Putsch* was the role played by the military. The German army's independence of civilian control had been established before the Kapp *Putsch*, and even antedated Weimar. What was clearly disclosed for the first time in 1920 was the partial manner in which this independence was to be deployed. The *Reichswehr* could be depended on to deal with a bolshevik uprising; indeed, in the wake of the Kapp *Putsch*, the army was very active against unruly left-wing elements in the Rhineland. But plainly, the *Reichswehr* could not be counted on to protect Weimar against a rightist *Putsch*, especially if it included a military component. Moreover, as the army officer corps had historically embodied German conservatism, it could be assumed that many Germans shared the *Reichswehr's* offhand attitude to the Weimar Republic.

The basic difficulty was that the Weimar regime, having renounced a radical reorganization of German society, had to fall back on the imperial bureaucracy to run the state. Not surprisingly, a civil service trained in Wilhelmine Germany carried over its conservative values into the postwar era. The police and judiciary, in particular, flaunted their sympathies by a notorious laxity toward right-wing agitators, which contrasted with the brutal severity accorded bolsheviks and leftist demonstrators. Schoolteachers were fond of reminding their pupils of the glories of the Bismarckian era—usually to the detriment of Weimar's reputation. Another conservative group which found little to praise in the Weimar experiment was the business community. Yet, ironically, German corporations enjoyed as many advantages under Weimar as before the war. Indeed, so eager were the early Weimar governments not to offend big business that they allowed the national economy to drift into the crisis of 1923.

Heavy government borrowing and deficit spending during the war began the process of destroying the German mark. Then, the loss of industrial areas in the peace settlement coupled with the revolutionary turmoil of 1919 undermined Germany's productive capacity. Immediately, a trade deficit opened up. Serious inflation ensued and, by 1920, the mark was worth approximately one tenth of its value in 1914. Finance minister Erzberger tried to tackle the problem by an overhaul of the system of direct taxation, which substantially increased the tax burden on the wealthy. But Erzberger's measures, sensible though they were, availed little as reparations loomed increasingly large as the major inflationary factor. In 1921 the Allied Reparations Commission presented Germany with a bill for war damages totaling 132 billion gold marks—approximately 33 billion United States dollars—to be paid over an indeterminate number of years. The Germans at first refused to accept any such obligation, but were forced to acquiesce when Allied troops occupied several towns in the industrial valley of the Ruhr in the Rhineland. Germany's asserted incapacity to pay won from the Allies a moratorium during 1922 on the collection of reparations in specie. Nonetheless, the continued reparations drain on German coal and timber, together with the prospect of the resumption of currency payments, caused the mark to go on falling. In the twelve months following July 1921, its exchange rate against the United States dollar rose from 75 to an unimaginable 500. What Germany desperately needed was strict governmental control of the economy. Unfortunately, this was never seriously considered. Even the SPD was divided on the merits of national economic planning. And while ministries procrastinated in the face of the objections of German businessmen, many of the latter were profiting from and even encouraging the inflationary spiral.

A climax was reached in 1923 because, on January 9, the Reparations Commission declared Germany to be in "wilful default" of her reparations payments in kind. Under the Treaty of Versailles, such a verdict entitled the Allies to take "measures as the respective Governments may determine to be necessary in the circumstances," and the French pounced on the opportunity to occupy the entire Ruhr valley. The Germans, who considered this a French device to continue World War I on German soil, responded with passive resistance in the Ruhr. Without the cooperation of local officials and labor, France was effectively prevented from wresting substantial reparations from Germany in the form of Ruhr coal. But also, without the Ruhr, the German economy was crippled. Inflation now grew completely out of hand, as the Reichsbank authorized the printing of more and more paper money. The exchange rate of the mark to the American dollar ran into trillions. Currency distortion was just as grotesque at home. To carry the money for her daily shopping, the German housewife needed a valise or even a wheelbarrow, and it was cheaper to burn paper money in the fireplace than to use it to buy a pittance of coal or wood.

German passive resistance in the Ruhr continued until September 1923, when Gustav Stresemann became chancellor. To restore a measure of international harmony, Stresemann called off passive resistance and held out the hope of at least partial fulfillment of the Versailles treaty. To solve the fantastic inflation problem, he introduced a new official currency whose basic unit, the *Rentenmark*, was backed by a mortgage on agricultural property and industrial resources. It was a dramatic although realistic step. However, by redeeming old marks at their current, virtually nonexistent value, the currency reform confirmed the annihilation of the savings of the middle class. The well-to-do, whose investments were in real property which did not depreciate, were only marginally affected, but the small, thrifty saver who had put his nest egg into a savings account or an annuity lost everything. For such people, the great inflation killed whatever credibility the Weimar regime had possessed. It has been truly said: "The crisis of 1923 shattered traditional German society; it constituted the real German revolution, dividing old from new in a far more profound fashion than had the brief and largely superficial political revolution of 1918" (H. S. Hughes, *Contemporary Europe* [1966]).


## Nazism in Bavaria

Automatically, the difficulties of 1923 stimulated activity at the extremes of the political spectrum. In Saxony and Thuringia leftist coalition governments, which included KPD representatives, sprang up. The authorities in Berlin, alert to Communist intrigues, dispatched state commissioners to apply martial law to the affected areas. More prophetic of future developments, however, was the emergence of a Bavarian right-wing plot. It was not so much that the Bavarian Right was a more immediate threat than Saxon and Thuringian Communists, but that the Munich *Putsch* was usurped by Adolf Hitler who, in 1923, was making his first bid for national prominence.

The Weimar constitution deliberately curbed much of the local autonomy which had obtained in the Bismarckian empire; nevertheless, regional differences and politics remained strong in republican Germany. And in its early days, Hitler's Nazi movement was an unmistakable product of the peculiar circumstances of Bavaria. In the aftermath of World War I, Munich was one of the centers of revolution. Indeed, an independent Bavarian republic was proclaimed under the leadership of the Independent Socialist Kurt Eisner. In February 1919 Eisner was shot by a counterrevolutionary—a portent of things to come. Despite this murder and the suppression of the Spartacists elsewhere in Germany, revolutionary agitation persisted in Munich, and at one stage a Soviet republic was announced. Yet, intrinsically, Bavaria was anything but a radical province. Cosmopolitan Munich's relation to the rest of Bavaria was very like that of Hitler's prewar Vienna to Austria. The attitudes of the rural areas tended to prevail over those of the metropolis. As in Austria, the villages and small towns of Bavaria were overwhelmingly Catholic and *völkisch;* social patterns were relatively static and hierarchical, with the father's authority within the family unchallenged. The detestation of this *bürgerlich* (small-town, middle-class) Bavaria for the political experimentation in Munich is hard to exaggerate; it can perhaps be best appreciated in fictional form for it provides a graphic backdrop in Richard Hughes's fine novel, *The Fox in the Attic* (1961). The intensity of political feeling was revealed by the vicious backlash which set in against the Bavarian Left in May 1919. In a veritable white terror organized by the regular army and *Freikorps* units, hundreds were killed. Not content, the Bavarian Right threatened further violence, and ultimately, as the result of pressure from the local *Reichswehr* commander, Gustav von Kahr became premier of Bavaria in March 1920. Kahr's extreme right-wing ministry went out of its way to embarrass and thwart the Weimar regime. Thus, after the failure of the Kapp *Putsch,* Kahr's Bavaria became a sanctuary for the *Freikorps* and other anti-Weimar groups. It was in the service of Bavarian reaction and under the protection of conservative Bavarian officials that Hitler began his political career.

After his demobilization in Munich, Hitler flirted with the ascendant Left. But he never compromised himself in the eyes of the army whose political department hired him in mid-1919 as an "instruction officer"; his task was to indoctrinate troops against left-wing opinions and the Treaty of Versailles. In this capacity, he was ordered to investigate a group the army thought might be useful in spreading patriotic propaganda—the German Workers' party. This small faction was mainly the creation of Anton Drexler, a Munich locksmith, whose ambition was to form a German nationalist party that had a genuine appeal for the workers. At the first meeting he attended, Hitler distinguished himself by an impassioned speech against a proposal for Bavarian union with Austria. As a result, he was invited to join the party's executive, which he did, becoming the seventh member of the committee. It was an ideal situation for Hitler. In a larger, better-known party, he would have begun as a nonentity. In the tiny, obscure German Workers' party, he was able to dominate from the start.

All Hitler's pent-up energies were released in building up the German Workers' party. He immediately showed a flair for publicity and was soon put in charge of the party's propaganda. In public speaking he was gauche at first, but he improved quickly in the harsh school of Munich beer halls and street corners. Having learned to sense and adjust to the mood of an audience within a few minutes, he seldom indulged in rational discourse; his forte was the declaratory sentence and his appeal an emotive one. In less than a year, he was addressing audiences numbered in the thousands. As his reputation grew, he was patronized by some of Bavaria's plutocracy—such as Putzi Hanfstaengl, scion of an art publishing family, and Frau Bechstein, wife of the head of the piano manufacturing company—who advanced money to the party. Of even greater consequence, however, were the contacts Hitler maintained with the military. For instance, the army was the chief source of funds which, in 1920, enabled the party to buy a racist weekly, *Völkischer Beobachter* (*People's Observer*), which henceforth became Hitler's mouthpiece. Hitler's principal intermediary with the military was Major Ernst Röhm, an extremely political-minded soldier closely associated with the *Freikorps*. Röhm assiduously sent along ex-servicemen to join the German Workers' party. In due course, such recruits were formed into a "gymnastic and sports division" called the *Sturm Abteilung* (Storm Section) or SA. The SA, later to adopt a notorious brown shirt uniform, became the counterpart of Mussolini's black shirt *squadristi*. Used first to cope with hecklers at Hitler's meetings, the SA grew into a paramilitary force charged with intimidating leftists and all Hitler's other enemies.

A great many of the future Nazi elite who joined Hitler in the immediate postwar years came with recent military experience: Rudolf Hess and Max Amman had even served in the same regiment as Hitler; Hermann Göring had been the last commander of Baron von Richthofen's celebrated squadron of fliers. This militarization of the German Workers' party was symptomatic of a broader transformation. For Hitler went far beyond the proletarian movement originally envisaged by Drexler, bringing in what Daniel Lerner has called the "marginal man"—that is, he who "deviates from a substantial number and variety of predominant attributes in his society." All sorts and conditions of the disaffected came together in Hitler's "armed Bohemia." These changes did not please Drexler and his colleagues and, in the summer of 1921, they forced a showdown with Hitler. But they were at a distinct disadvantage because whatever success and influence the party enjoyed was due almost entirely to Hitler's efforts. The upshot was that Hitler's opponents were expelled from the party's executive, while he was made president with dictatorial powers. Thenceforth, the party was Hitler's creature. There would be challenges in the future, and others that Hitler imagined, but his control was never to be seriously shaken.

Hitler was always more of a *Führer* (leader) than was Mussolini a *duce*. Until 1925 at least, the Italian Fascist party had a will of its own; moreover, in 1943, as we shall see, it was the Grand Council of Fascism which triggered the actual downfall of Mussolini. Hitler, on the contrary, commanded the Nazi party's loyalty to the end. It follows that a biography of Hitler tells much more about Nazism than the life story of Mussolini can reveal about Italian Fascism. Fittingly, Alan Bullock in his classic biography, *Hitler: A Study in Tyranny* (1952, 1962), sums up the Führer's quintessential role in Nazism:

> . . . the evidence seems to me to leave no doubt that no other man played a role in the Nazi revolution or in the history of the Third Reich remotely comparable with that of Adolf Hitler.
>
> The conception of the Nazi Party, the propaganda with which it must appeal to the German people, and the tactics by which it would come to power—these were unquestionably Hitler's.

Hitler's egotistical determination to brook no rivals made cooperation with other *völkisch* movements, which were legion in postwar Germany, extremely difficult. In fact, it was Drexler's attempt to merge his party with analogous groups that precipitated his clash with Hitler. The latter's objective was to bring all radical nationalist groups under his own sway. In this, he was markedly successful. Due largely to Hitler's intrigues, Otto Dickel's party based in Augsburg collapsed in 1922, and his followers were absorbed into Hitler's movement. Also in 1922, the Weimar authorities dissolved a racist organization, the *Deutschvölkischer Schutz-und Trutzbund* (German Peoples' Defense and Offense League), an offshoot of the prewar Pan-German Association and influential throughout Germany. Its members were advised to join Hitler, who thus acquired the services of such future luminaries as the Jew-baiter, Julius Streicher, and the warped musician, Reinhard Heydrich. Hitler did maintain amicable relations with empathetic groups beyond Germany's frontiers. The most important of these were the descendants of the Bohemian National Socialist party founded in prewar Austria-Hungary. With the dissolution of the Hapsburg Empire, the movement split into two main sections—one operating in the original locale (now the Czech Sudetenland), the other in Vienna under the leadership of Walther Riehl.

It was in imitation of Riehl's group that, in 1920, the German Workers' party added to its name the phrase National Socialist, thus becoming the *Nationalsozialistische Deutsche Arbeiterpartei* (NSDAP) or Nazi party. Simultaneously, Hitler's movement began to emphasize the *Hakenkreuz* (hooked cross) or swastika as its emblem. Originally and variously, the swastika had represented an oriental sun device, a fertility symbol, and a simple good luck charm. It adorned the Benedictine monastery near Linz where Hitler had briefly attended school and presumably had first set eyes on the hooked cross. But also, since before the First World War, *völkisch* factions in both Germany and Austria had been using it as a mark of their Aryan purity and anti-Semitism. After the war, the practice spread; the racist Thule Society (another group destined to be swallowed up by Hitler's Nazis) helped to popularize the swastika, Drexler's followers sported it, and many *Freikorps* painted it on their helmets to flaunt their anti-Semitism. In adopting the swastika, Hitler also deliberately seized on the design by which it would become world famous—the black *Hakenkreuz* in a circle of white upon a blood-red field. Hitler thereby recalled the red, black, and white of the Bismarckian Reich, and symbolically rejected the Weimar Republic's red, black, and gold flag, which was indeed spurned by many patriotic Germans. In addition, the striking red background of the Nazi ensign was reminiscent of the red flag of socialism—which was Hitler's way of conveying that his movement was to be based on the masses.

At the same time that Hitler's party garnered a title and insignia, it was also formulating a program. In February 1920, the Twenty-Five Points, a document drawn up under Hitler's supervision, was adopted. This program resembled the first eclectic manifestoes of the Italian Fascist party. On the one hand, it appealed to the traditional Right by its nationalism—the Treaty of Versailles was execrated—and by its authoritarian call for "the creation of a strong central state power." On the other hand, left-wing sentiments abounded in such propositions as "abolition of incomes unearned by work," "ruthless confiscation of all war profits," "nationalization of all trusts," "sharing-out of profits from wholesale trade," and the like. By way of social and economic reform, the Twenty-Five Points advocated the formation of *Stände*, roughly translatable as chambers of professions or estates (the equivalent of the corporations which figured in the Italian Fascist program). A state based on *Stände* had long been touted by *völkisch* theorists as a "third way" between capitalism and socialism. The cement which held together the program's disparate elements was its *völkisch* spirit. Thus, citizenship in the Leviathan state was to depend on race: "None but members of the nation may be citizens of the state. None but those of German blood . . . may be members of the nation."

Of course, the significance of the Twenty-Five Points depended entirely on how far Hitler was prepared to abide by them. And in due course, Hitler would see fit to jettison many of the specifics of the original Nazi program. Nonetheless, in their racism, the Twenty-Five Points accurately reflected what was to remain the fixed point of the Führer's creed until the end. Hitler's anti-Semitism, nurtured in prewar Vienna, reached maturity in the early 1920s through his acquaintance with such pamphleteers of race hatred as Dietrich Eckart, a Munich journalist whose life was twisted by drink and drugs, and Alfred Rosenberg, a former architect from the German community in the Baltic town of Reval, whose pretentious writings were later collected under the title *Myth of the Twentieth Century* (1930). Anti-Semitism now colored Hitler's attitude on every issue. Capitalism, for example, he divided into two categories. First, there was "interest capital," a blight attacked particularly by Gottfried Feder, leader of the left-wing Nazis in the early days. But Hitler applied the concept almost exclusively to Jewish finance, which he proceeded to castigate as parasitic and exploitative. In contrast, he regarded Aryan capitalism as healthy and productive—a nice distinction which paved the way for his later cooperation with German big business. When Hitler turned to fulminate against the socialists, the Jew figured as the instigator of bolshevism. Had not many of the Spartacist leaders as well as Eisner and his Munich colleagues in 1919 been Jewish? In Hitler's vision, Jewish capitalism and Jewish socialism were linked together in a gigantic conspiracy against the German people. As he wrote in 1924 in his autobiography:

> And so the Jew today is the great agitator for the complete destruction of Germany. Wherever in the world we read of attacks against Germany, Jews are their fabricators, just as in peacetime and during the War the press of the Jewish stock exchange and the Marxists systematically stirred up hatred of Germany until state after state abandoned neutrality and, renouncing the true interests of the peoples, entered the service of the World War coalition.
>
> The Jewish train of thought in all this is clear. The Bolshevization of Germany—that is, the extermination of the national *völkisch* German intelligentsia to make possible the sweating of the German working class under the yoke of Jewish world finance—is conceived only as a prelim-

inary to the further extension of this Jewish tendency of World conquest.

Both in his capacity as captain of industry and Marxist agitator in the class war, the Jew was the agent of a detestable modernity. Consequently, the longing to return to a simple, *völkisch* past centered on the expulsion (*Entfernung*) of the Jews.

The Führer's fixation on the Jewish question has naturally engaged the interest of psychoanalysts. Most concentrate on Hitler's dislike of his father, who allegedly ridiculed his son's artistic pretenses, and deduce that Hitler suffered from a massive Oedipal complex. It has been observed that he seldom referred to Germany as the Fatherland, nearly always as the Motherland. The psychologist Erik Erikson has contended that, as a leader, Hitler shied away from a father image, preferring to pose as "the glorified older brother, who replaces the father . . . a gang leader who keeps the boys together by demanding their admiration, by creating terror, and by shrewdly involving them in crimes from which there is no way back." The tragedy was that Hitler transferred hatred of his real father to the Jewish race at large. One explanation is that, in Hitler's mind, his father was interchangeable with the family physician, a Jewish Dr. Block, who tended Frau Hitler in her last painful battle with cancer; both father and doctor thus had stood in the way of Hitler's possession of his mother. Alternately, it is possible that Hitler associated the archetypal Jew with his father because the Jew appeared as the father figure of Judao-Christian Europe. In either case, anti-Semitism was a species of parricide.

An Oedipal complex has been considered to lie behind Hitler's sexual peculiarities. Precisely what these were is still a topic of avid conjecture. Hanfstängl was probably wrong to assert he was impotent, and Werner Maser, the most reliable authority on Hitler's personal habits, estimates his sex life to have been rather conventional. But it is not hard to believe that so unusual a character had some odd cravings—arising perhaps out of an observable preoccupation with the elimination of bodily wastes. If so, his petit bourgeois soul, or superego, was no doubt inwardly ashamed, although his sense of guilt was projected onto the convenient hate object, the father figure Jew. The Führer repeatedly accused the Jews of incest, prostitution, blood pollution, and every kind of sexual abnormality. In reality, he may have been accusing himself.

It has often been suggested that Hitler is to be understood in terms of retarded mental growth or protracted infantilism. His alleged sexual inadequacy bespoke an arrested development. His fear and detestation of Jewry, unreasoning and destructive, was like a grotesque childish tantrum. Similarly, his refusal to tolerate any contradiction and his passionate self-righteousness smacked of infantilism. Having once arrived at his racist conclusions, Hitler clung to them as sublime and absolute truths: "The racial question gives the key not only to world history but to all human culture," he wrote with glib confidence. He was, in Hajo Holborn's phrase, "a doctrinaire of the first order." Hitler's convictions were rooted in a romantic, adolescent belief that he was an agent of destiny, which had chosen him to salvage German *Volkstum* (nationhood). "I go the way that Providence dictates with the assurance of a sleepwalker," he remarked once in a flash of self-revelation. Sure in his own mind of his ultimate triumph because he rode an irresistible tide of history, he dedicated himself utterly to his mission. His youthful artistic ambition became sublimated in politics. In lieu of a full and normal sex life, he found a substitute in public affairs. Once launched on a political career, Hitler more than ever avoided normal human entanglements lest they interfere with his historical purpose. Unlike the frankly sensual and easily distracted Mussolini, the Führer was a political fanatic twenty-four hours a day.

Not·unnaturally, Hitler in 1923, the year of the Ruhr occupation and the great German inflation, believed that the appointed moment to act had arrived. Signs of anti-Weimar activity all around him in Bavaria reached a crescendo after the lifting of passive resistance in the Ruhr, which the German nationalists considered a shameful capitulation. The Bavarian government itself, in defiance of the federal power in Berlin, appointed Kahr as state commissioner, a position of virtual dictator. More important, the local *Reichswehr* units under General Otto von Lossow backed the Bavarian government. Outwardly, it seemed that Bavaria was on the verge of seceding from the Weimar Republic. However, most of the Bavarian Right—including Hitler— thought less of separatism than of a march on Berlin, and Kahr, Lossow, and their fellow conspirators hesitated to act until they were sure of the cooperation of antirepublican elements outside Bavaria. The delay while negotiations were conducted irritated Hitler, and he resolved to give the national revolution a push forward.

On the evening of November 8, 1923, Kahr addressed an overflow crowd in one of Munich's better-known beer cellars, the *Bürgerbräu*. The audience half expected Kahr to issue the long-awaited call to arms. However, soon after the meeting began, Hitler, accompanied by a number of SA, burst in and fired a pistol at the ceiling. Announcing the start of a revolution, he forced Kahr and Lossow at gunpoint to endorse his venture. But the *Putsch* lacked organization; within a couple of hours, Kahr and Lossow managed to escape from the beer hall, whereupon they promptly disavowed Hitler. Nevertheless, the SA and other sympathetic paramilitary formations were now mobilized and had already occupied some key positions in the city, including the military's headquarters. Many university students and junior *Reichswehr* officers were known to be enthusiastic for Hitler, and the Nazis had the backing of the wartime military hero, General Erich Ludendorff. Therefore, to rally latent support, it was decided that Hitler and Ludendorff should lead a march through Munich on the morning of November 9. At eleven o'clock, a column of over two thousand set out from the *Bürgerbräukeller*. The army kept in the background, but in the Odeonsplatz the procession was faced by a cordon of Bavarian police. A shot rang out, then a fusillade. Sixteen marchers and three policemen were killed. Among the seriously wounded was Göring, who was shot in the leg. Hitler was dragged to the ground in the melee and suffered a dislocated shoulder, but he was able to reach the rear of the column and escape by car. Ludendorff, unscathed and unperturbed, walked up to and through the police line.

Two hours later, Röhm surrendered army headquarters and the *Putsch* was over. The Nazi leadership scattered. Some fled abroad; Göring, for instance, found Fascist Italy a comfortable refuge in which to recuperate. Hitler hid in the Hanfstängl house outside Munich but, on November 11, the police arrested him there. In February 1924 those who had been apprehended were brought to trial for high treason. The German judiciary's customary tenderness to nationalist agitators prevailed: Ludendorff was acquitted outright; others were sentenced to terms of "honorable detention." Hitler, who refused to be cross-examined by a Jewish lawyer and was allowed to regale the court with political harangues, received five years. But by the end of 1924, he was released on parole. In any event, the year Hitler spent in Landsberg prison constituted little hardship. He was permitted a constant stream of visitors and was accorded much better than the usual prison fare; he emerged from Landsberg probably healthier than when he went in.

Jail afforded Hitler the leisure to reflect on his political career to date, and apparently he reached some momentous conclusions in comparing his own failure in 1923 with Mussolini's successful March on Rome a year earlier. He perceived that Mussolini, despite the aura of violence surrounding his rise, in the final analysis had obtained power constitutionally; the Duce had accepted his mandate in 1922 at the hands of the Italian king and with the blessing of Italy's traditional elite. In his beer hall *Putsch* Hitler had employed force alone. He resolved henceforth to make his way within the framework of the law until, like Mussolini, he gained a strong enough constitutional position to dispense with legal proprieties. A further consideration which exercised Hitler's mind in Landsberg was that of Nazism's allies. F. L. Carsten has remarked that it is wrong to describe the events of November 8–9, 1923, as the Hitler *Putsch*. What Hitler had attempted was to set in motion a national revolution which would be carried to fruition by a coalition of nationalist forces. In the beer hall *Putsch* the Nazis had been joined by other Bavarian *völkisch* groups, but Hitler had counted chiefly on the *Reichswehr* and, in this, had been disappointed. True, the army had not fired on the Nazis in Munich, but the high command, particularly General von Seeckt, had made no secret of its opposition to Hitler's escapade. Yet, if Hitler was to imitate Mussolini and win office legally, he needed the help of Germany's respectable conservatives, for whom the professional army officers frequently seemed to speak. At his trial, therefore, he went out of his way to praise the army, rejoicing that it was the police and not the *Reichswehr* that had shot at him. On the other hand, Hitler was acutely conscious that the army and the conservatives had let him down in 1923. His youthful distrust of establishment forces was now accentuated and would persist, whatever tactical alliances he might later make. Above all, Hitler's skepticism of the aristocratic officer corps was to run like a thread through Nazi history after 1923.

Hitler spent much of his time in prison composing the first volume of *Mein Kampf*, a long rambling statement of his political views interspersed with bits of autobiography. It expressed pretty much what he had been peddling in public for several years. Race was the dominant motif; bigoted anti-Semitism was allied to a crude biological Social Darwinism. In a world doomed to eternal struggle among the races, fate decreed victory to the strongest. Force was always justified, there being no room for humanitarian scruples. The relevance of these sentiments to international politics was spelled out clearly in a second volume of *Mein Kampf* written in 1926. Wilhelmine diplomacy was roundly blamed for diverting German energies outside Europe. For the future, Germany's first task was to bring all Teutonic peoples within the Reich. In practice, this amounted to absorption of all of Austria and large parts of Czechoslovakia and Poland. But Hitler's dreams of glory did not stop at the notion of a Germanic *Mitteleuropa*. A growing Germany would require *Lebensraum* (living space), and the dynamics of

Nazi Social Darwinism indicated that it should be found in the east. There, racially inferior Slavs (Hitler liked to call them not *Slawen* but *Sklaven*, meaning slaves) were deemed suitable for colonization. Moreover, expansion to the east would undoubtedly end in an attack on Hitler's favorite enemy—"Jewish bolshevism" or the U.S.S.R. *Mein Kampf* can be regarded as an extremely frank disclosure of Hitler's ulterior ambitions. Nevertheless, one must remember that such romantic maunderings were commonplace in every Bavarian coffeehouse, while all German nationalists were agreed after 1919 that priority should be given to revising Germany's frontiers in central and eastern Europe. *Mein Kampf* sold respectably—several thousand copies annually at first—and reflected the mood not only of one man but of a sizable segment of the German population.

On emerging from prison, Hitler faced two tasks—to rescue the foundering NSDAP and to reestablish his personal control of the party. Hitler gave priority to the latter. During his term in prison, he had obstinately refused to allow his lieutenants to take firm action to hold the party together lest an alternative *Führer* should emerge. Soon after his release from Landsberg, he quarreled with Ludendorff and Röhm, both of whom left the Nazi party. However, the real threat to Hitler's authority came from the north German wing which, during Hitler's inactivity, really kept the Nazi movement alive. The guiding spirits of north German Nazism were the Strasser brothers, Gregor and Otto Gregor was the more prominent; as a Reichstag deputy he was a figure of some influence and independence of mind. A Bavarian by origin, he had become a Nazi in 1920 but, since moving north, his allegiance to Hitler diminished markedly. It was almost inevitable that sooner or later Hitler would confront the presumptuous Strassers.

It was not solely a question of personalities. The Strasser brothers took the socialist content of the Nazi program seriously; they advocated the nationalization of heavy industry and large estates ("state feudalism") and the substitution of a chamber of corporations for the Reichstag. Significantly, the Hitler-Strasser dispute came to center on the agitation for the expropriation of the property of Germany's former royalty—which the Strassers endorsed, but Hitler did not. The Strassers' extremist views were embarrassing to Hitler now that he was committed to working within the existing constitutional system. Furthermore, in January 1925, Hitler won permission from the Bavarian authorities to resume his political career only by promising to curb his radical north German colleagues and by parading his own anti-Marxism.

The tension between Hitler and the Strassers mounted until February 1926 when Hitler called a meeting of the Nazi leadership in Bamberg in south Germany, making it difficult for the north German leaders to attend. Of these, only Gregor Strasser was present, accompanied by his private secretary, a young Rhinelander from the fringes of the literary and film world called Joseph Goebbels. Goebbels did not speak at the Bamberg meeting, leaving Strasser isolated, and the assemblage overwhelmingly backed Hitler's cautious approach to social and economic change. In May Hitler consolidated his victory when a further meeting explicitly recognized the Munich Nazis and their leader, namely Hitler, as supreme over the entire German NSDAP. Just as important, about the same time Goebbels fell completely under Hitler's spell. In his diary, where once Goebbels had railed at the Munich "swine," he now rhapsodized over Hitler: "He is a genius, the automatically creative instrument of a divine fate. I stand before him deeply shaken. Thus he is: like a child, dear, good, merciful; like a cat, cunning, clever, agile; like a lion, roaring, great, and gigantic." In November 1926 Hitler rewarded Goebbels with the post of district party leader (*Gauleiter*) for greater Berlin. To some extent, Goebbels even took the place of the Strassers as spokesman of the Nazi Left, although he always advanced his views cautiously. And partly due to his activity, the NSDAP in the later 1920s continued to grow less Bavarian and more north German in its orientation. Yet, fundamentally, Goebbels was never anything other than Hitler's man, now strategically placed to keep in check any potential northern rivals to the Führer. The affair of the Strasser brothers comprised the last serious challenge to Hitler's authority within the Nazi movement; henceforth, Nazism was notable for its unmitigated *Führerprinzip*.

The job of rebuilding the NSDAP after the beer hall fiasco suffered, of necessity, from the intraparty squabbling. Nor for that matter was Hitler in a position to offer much leadership to the party whose absolute obedience he required. The Nazi party and its paper, *Völkischer Beobachter*, had been proscribed in 1924. Although this ban was rescinded the following year, a new prohibition was soon placed on public speaking by Hitler himself. For a party whose appeal rested so much on its leader's oratory, this was a serious handicap. Because of this restriction, Hitler often left Munich to reside at "Haus Wachenfeld," a rented villa on the Obersalzberg above Berchtesgaden in the Bavarian Alps. (In 1929 he would buy the house and, later still, rebuild it and rename it the "Berghof.") On money derived mostly from his writings, Hitler established at Berchtesgaden a household run by his widowed half-sister, Frau Raubal. For several years Hitler experienced for the only time in his adult life something like a conventional domestic existence. Yet even now his aberrant personality came to the fore. He conceived a romantic passion for his housekeeper's good-looking, brunette daughter, Geli Raubal, and very likely made her his mistress. However, it was rumored that Geli was upset by Hitler's sadomasochistic habits with a whip and by his intense jealousy at her constant flirtations. In 1931 she committed suicide. Sudden death was the fate of virtually every woman who was intimate with the Führer.

Between 1925 and 1928 Hitler's political career marked time. He faded from the world headlines; for example, in the years 1926 and 1928 he rated only one mention in the London *Times* and none at all in the *New York Times*. With the Führer's relative eclipse, the growth of the NSDAP was automatically stunted. In round numbers Nazi party membership actually climbed after 1925, but much of the increase was due to the continual absorption of other, minor *völkisch* groups. Little headway was made outside those sections of the populace already sympathetic to Nazism.

Herein lay the clue to Nazi fortunes. In 1923 the economic crisis seemed to have undercut the Weimar regime and disposed many moderate Germans to consider extreme solutions. After 1923, in contrast, Weimar began to provide economic stability, even prosperity, and the attraction of radical movements such as Nazism subsided proportionately. Germany's economic recovery was made possible by an interim solution to the reparations imbroglio. The Ruhr occupation had not brought France the coal and reparations expected, while in thwarting France by passive resistance, the Germans had destroyed their currency. The way out of this stalemate was found through American mediation. The Dawes Plan—Colonel Dawes was a U.S. financier—supplied a compromise which went into effect on September 1, 1924. Germany won evacuation of the Ruhr and the concession that annual reparations payments be geared to a capacity to pay; annuities were to vary according to a statistical index of German economic health. France, in return, was given pledges of German payment; certain state revenues, mostly from railroads, were allocated for reparations payments and were to be paid directly to an Allied agent general in Berlin. But what made the Dawes Plan viable was not written down; it was the tacit understanding that German prosperity and capacity to pay reparations would be secured by the injection of American capital. So, in the next five years, German states, municipalities, and the private sector of the economy borrowed approximately seven billion dollars abroad, mostly in short-term loans from the United States. The result was a boom that saw German industrial production surpass its prewar level and outstrip Great Britain's postwar recovery, the unemployment rate drop to around 3 percent of the labor force, and real wages rise by 10 percent in four years.

In addition, the Dawes Plan marked the beginning of a Franco-German rapprochement whose most glittering achievement was the series of agreements negotiated at Locarno in October 1925. At the core of the Locarno Pacts was a multilateral guarantee of the Franco-German and Belgian-German frontiers established in 1919. Unlike the Versailles *Diktat*, Locarno was accepted voluntarily by the German government; indeed, the initial overture had been made by Stresemann. Despite the ominous silence about Germany's sensitive eastern borders, Locarno appeared the genuine end of World War I. Within the next few years, Germany was admitted to the League of Nations, and the Allied Military Control Commission was withdrawn from German soil, as were Allied troops from the Rhineland. The Locarno years of international good will and economic prosperity were the "golden twenties." The Weimar Republic basked in the sunshine, as the forces of disaffection, including the Nazis, were forced to bide their time.

Yet, notwithstanding the euphoria of Weimar Germany between 1925 and 1929, the innate problems of the republic were not really laid to rest. Those groups which had reluctantly tolerated the November revolution of 1918 were still unreconciled to the democratic regime. Both the military and big business continued to carp even while enjoying preferential treatment. The army officer corps operated as freely as ever of civilian control, most notoriously in the area of Russo-German relations where arrangements were reached with the Red Army for secret military training. However, the toasts drunk in German army messes regularly recalled the good old days under the kaiser. On the economic front, the crisis of 1923 had forced many weaker concerns to sell out to the corporate giants, thus exaggerating the already monopolistic nature of German business. Weimar governments regarded this tendency with complacency and, not unlike ministries in pre-Fascist Italy, were often accused of favoritism toward the *Bonzen* or big business lobbyists. Nevertheless, the board rooms of *I. G. Farbenindustrie* and the *Vereinigte Stahlwerke* rang with denunciations of Weimar as a dangerous socialist experiment.

More unexpected was the failure of the German cultural and intellectual communities to rally to Weimar. In imperial Germany the artist and man of letters had been held in low esteem. In contrast, the liberating atmosphere of Weimar was expected to offer a congenial home for artistic experimentation and the intellectuals' rational discourse. To use Peter Gay's metaphor, the outsider became an insider. Unfortunately, many of these natural friends of Weimar were alienated by the republic's compromises with the old order and by the power brokerage of the parliamentary system. Some, such as the cartoonist George Grosz or the playwright Bertolt Brecht, expressed their disgust in bitter satire. But most of the liberal intelligentsia simply turned away from politics with weary cynicism. They became *Vernunftrepublikaner* (republicans of the mind), tolerant of the regime but not emotionally engaged; they were not surprised, nor even unduly alarmed, when Weimar showed signs of collapsing. The great historian, Meinecke, was perhaps the archetypal *Vernunftrepublikaner*, while Mann's classic novel, *The Magic Mountain*, first published in 1924, can be interpreted as an allegory of failed political commitment. Then again, German culture, because of its *völkisch* traditions, possessed an unusually high proportion of outright antirationalists of the sort condemned in Julien Benda's contemporary tract, *The Betrayal of the Intellectuals*. To these minds, Weimar and its liberal values were completely alien. Their influence was considerable, as evidenced by the popularity of the antihumanistic prognostications of Oswald Spengler, whose *Decline of the West* quickly went through several printings after its first appearance in 1918. Another critic of western liberalism was Moeller van den Bruck whose chief work bore the prophetic title, *The Third Reich* (1923). A microcosm of the Weimar intellectual scene could be found in the German universities. Recent investigation has disclosed, on the one hand, a faculty formally aloof from politics while, on the other, an academic atmosphere shot through with *völkisch* and anti-Weimar assumptions.

The frailty of Weimar, even amid Locarno prosperity, was further exposed by the practice of entrusting the government of the republic to conservative, basically antirepublican figures. Confidence in the SPD, the founder and real mainstay of Weimar, had been eroded by the crisis of 1923, and thereafter the Socialist party lost its position as dominant member of coalition governments. In fact, no Socialist served as a minister between 1923 and 1928. Although Hermann Mueller, a Socialist, was chancellor between 1928 and 1930, the SPD remained on the defensive. By the end of the decade, the faction around which ministries were most likely to be built was the Center party, the moderate conservative, Catholic party. Similarly, the single most powerful politician to emerge in the twenties belonged to the moderate Right. Stresemann, who was foreign minister in every German government from 1923 until his death in October 1929, came from a conservative business background in Berlin and, as a staunch monarchist, had at first deplored the revolution of November 1918.

But by far the most incongruous Weimar officeholder was Field Marshal Paul von Hindenburg who, in 1925, was elected president of the republic by the direct vote of the German people. It would be hard to imagine anyone less symbolic of the spirit of Weimar than this wooden, autocratic professional soldier from Prussia, whose appearance and every mannerism recalled his past. In 1914 he had been the pride of the imperial army for his victories on the eastern front and three years later, with Ludendorff, he had presided over Germany's wartime military dictatorship. This is not to suggest that Hindenburg did not try to fulfill the Weimar presidential oath honestly; moreover, the presence of such a respected traditional figure as head of state added some luster to the Weimar regime. But when all is said, Hindenburg's election must be seen first and foremost as a candid vote of no confidence in Weimar—in A. J. Nicholls's words, "an attempt by the German people to flee from the responsibilities of parliamentary government back to the comforting safety of prewar authority" (*Weimar and the Rise of Hitler* [1968]).

Hitler's aspiration was to usurp the place of Hindenburg as Germany's hero. It was, however, a delicate task to use the German conservatives' distrust of Weimar to undermine the republic, while at the same time plotting to replace the establishment itself. Hitler was enabled to perform this legerdemain because the opportunity arose to exploit the same two propaganda themes which had carried Mussolini to power—nationalist dissatisfaction and fear of bolshevism.


### The Great Depression

In 1929 a committee of international financial experts concocted a fresh scheme for German reparations payments to supersede the interim Dawes Plan. The new Young Plan removed some of the liens placed on Germany's economy in 1924, but called for annuities to be paid until 1988 for an irreducible sum total of 8 billion dollars. The Young Plan was intended to be a definitive settlement and, as such, it served as a reminder of the Versailles *Diktat*, especially the war guilt clause on which reparations depended. German memories of national humiliation were deliberately stirred by a virulent campaign against the Young Plan directed and financed by Alfred Hugenberg, press mogul and leader of the German Nationalist Peoples party (DNVP). Other right-wing nationalist groups besides the DNVP—including the Nazis—were welded into an alliance to fight all reparations payments, Stresemann as the architect of "fulfillment," and Weimar itself. The nationalists' agitation successfully promoted a petition to submit the Young Plan to a popular referendum, as provided in the Weimar constitution. In the event, Hugenberg's coalition failed to kill the Young Plan either by referendum (under 6 million contrary votes were cast when 21 million were required) or in the Reichstag where ratification was achieved in March 1930. However, there were important side results. The vendetta against Stresemann probably hastened his death, which occurred in October 1929. On the other hand, the chief beneficiary of the entire affair was Hitler. He received funds from Hugenberg and, more significant, massive publicity in Hugenberg's newspapers and magazines. Moreover, association with the DNVP brought the Nazis some priceless respectability. In sum, the campaign against the Young Plan began the elevation of the NSDAP into a truly national party and Hitler into the principal spokesman for Germany's nationalist grievances.

The Young Plan was predicated on continued German prosperity. But even while the plan was being negotiated, the post-Locarno boom began to fade—providing useful ammunition for the nationalist opponents of any reparations settlement. By the summer of 1929, industrial production and stock market prices were on the decline and unemployment stood at 6 percent. What at first seemed a mild recession turned into a major disaster after the Wall Street crash in October 1929. As American investors sought desperately to realize their assets, short-term loans to Germany were speedily recalled. The result was catastrophic, with Germany the European storm center of the Great Depression. The German gross national product plummeted by 40 percent between 1929 and 1932, and prices and wages dropped in lesser but significant proportions. In 1923 the rate of inflation had been the index of German misery; in the Great Depression unemployment was the key statistic. In September 1929 over one and a quarter million were listed as unemployed; two years later, the number had more than tripled; and by early 1932 the nadir was reached at over six millions. These figures, it must be remembered, reflected only those officially registered as unemployed. There was a vast amount of "unseen unemployment," made up of those who for one reason or another did not apply for state relief or who managed to find casual, part-time work. Trade union officials in 1932 estimated that two-fifths of their membership had no job at all and another one-fifth were merely partially employed.

The conventional economic wisdom of the day held that governments faced with a depression should cut expenditures and concentrate on balancing the national budget. Such was the instinctive reaction in official Berlin. When in March 1930 the state insurance system reached the edge of insolvency, pressure built up to cut benefits. It was over this issue that the SPD resigned from the government, and a new coalition ministry was formed under the chancellorship of Heinrich Brüning, leader of the Center party. But henceforth, no Weimar government could count on a stable majority in the Reichstag, which in the midst of the Great Depression seemed a sufficiently grave hazard to warrant use of the presidential emergency powers under Article 48 of the constitution. On Brüning's advice, President Hindenburg first invoked Article 48 to implement the budget in July 1930, and then a series of financial measures—to increase taxes and cut prices and wages —was promulgated. Between 1930 and 1932, Germany was ruled almost entirely by edict. In other words, for some time before Hitler gained office, the Weimar parliamentary apparatus had ceased to function, and the German people were thus conditioned for the greater authoritarianism to come.

In the meantime, Brüning's severe deflationary policies had little success in checking the depression; on the contrary, they doubtless aggravated it by contracting trade at a time when some artificial stimulus was needed. Brüning was unkindly dubbed the "hunger chancellor." As in 1923, the government's apparent insensitivity to mass misery caused antirepublican revulsion and a rise in extremism. Given the conservative temper of Germany, it is not surprising that more attention was paid to the danger from the left than from the right. In the elections of September 1930, the KPD increased its standing in the Reichstag from 54 to 77 seats, sowing consternation among the propertied classes. Only a few months earlier, Hitler had refurbished his anti-Bolshevik credentials by challenging the radical Otto Strasser's endorsement of a general strike in Saxony. The upshot had been Strasser's departure from the NSDAP and the foundation of his own Black Front organization. The episode redounded to the Nazis' credit among Germany's rich and powerful who, in their alarm, turned to the professional anti-Marxist Hitler, just as their counterparts in Italy had turned to Mussolini a decade earlier.

One sign of the times was an increased tolerance of SA terrorist activities against alleged Communists. In 1930 Röhm returned from Latin America to rejoin the Nazi party and impose some much-needed discipline on the unruly Brown Shirts. Goebbels took several verses of a young Nazi idealist killed by the Communists (actually he was murdered in a quarrel over a prostitute), and transformed them into an immensely popular SA anthem, the "Horst Wessel Lied." From the ranks of the unemployed flocked new recruits, for the party supplied, in addition to a sense of direction and purpose, clothing in the form of a uniform and a few pfennigs and a bowl of soup daily. By 1932 the SA numbered close to 400,000. For three years before Hitler won office, the SA rampaged through the streets, provoking clashes with left-wing forces and storming and looting the offices of socialist and communist organizations. Thus was created an atmosphere of civil war and a popular siege mentality. This, indeed, was Hitler's conscious purpose—not to seize power on the barricades, but to create an aura of confusing violence conducive to the acceptance of the Führer as the simple solution of all Germany's ills.

A wide variety of influential groups and figures succumbed to Hitler's nationalist and antibolshevik blandishments, thereby smoothing his path to the chancellorship. One Nazi link with the German establishment was provided by the largely upper-class Nationalist party which maintained, albeit uneasily at times, the loose alliance with Hitler forged during the campaign against the Young Plan. In 1931, after Brüning had failed to gain international approval for an Austro-German customs union, the DNVP and the Nazis moved closer together in the "Harzburg Front," a coalition for right-wing nationalist political agitation. Also highly nationalistic were the Junkers, the Prussian landowning caste, although it was more their obsession with the Marxist danger which drew many of them to Hitler. Concentrated in East Prussia and cut off from the rest of Germany by the Polish Corridor, the Junkers saw themselves in the front line against the enemy described by Hitler as Jewish bolshevism. When Brüning, by way of economy measures, proposed to redistribute some bankrupt East Prussian estates and to curtail *Osthilfe* (help for the East)—lavish governmental subsidies payed out to favored East Prussian landowners—the standard Junker reaction was to denounce these moves as "agrarian bolshevism." Such an attitude assumes added significance when it is realized that President Hindenburg, having been awarded an estate at Neudeck for his wartime services, was now a Junker, and that his son Oskar was implicated in the Junkers' misappropriation of *Osthilfe* funds. Hitler's readiness to ignore the *Osthilfe* scandal did much to commend him to the Junkers.

The Führer's aristocratic following was not confined to Prussia, however. Franz von Papen, whose political ambitions were to loom large in Hitler's rise, came from an old Catholic family in Westphalia; he was typical of those scions of German nobility who believed Hitler could be used. Papen's Christian scruples offered no bar to his collusion with Nazism and, in the summer of 1933, he would negotiate a concordat between the Vatican and Hitler. Here was an indicator that for many German Catholics, indeed for the German Catholic church itself, Hitler was a tolerable ally in the fight against the modern antichrist, bolshevism. The German Protestant churches were less inclined, by historical conditioning, to take a political stand. But many a fiery Lutheran pastor in northern Germany used his own initiative and his pulpit to extol the spirit of national dedication to be found in the Nazi movement.

Among all the disparate elements in the German power structure accused of helping Hitler into office, two stand out: the industrialists and the army, respectively, have been the subject of a vast literature. The role of the industrialists has occasioned a major controversy because it goes to the heart of Marxist historical argument. According to this dialectic, every fascist regime is a manifestation of the last and decadent stage of capitalism—in the official Soviet phraseology "an open terrorist dictatorship of the most reactionary elements of monopoly capital." In the German context, Hitler was the tool of capitalists driven to desperate straits by the Great Depression; on their behalf, he was to quell the workers' uprising and find new economic opportunities outside overcompetitive Germany by means of an expansionist foreign policy. For an unabashed presentation of this view, one cannot better Bertolt Brecht's *The Resistible Rise of Arturo Ui* (1941). In this vastly entertaining play, the Hitler figure is a Chicago gangster who begins his career in the protection racket run by crooked businessmen known as the Vegetable Trust.

Certainly, the structure of German business was more monopolistic than almost anywhere else in the industrialized world, and the German capitalist elite, being relatively few in numbers, was in a position to speak with one voice and act as a compact lobby. However, it is on precisely this score that the Marxist analysis is weakest. For while it can be proved that individual businessmen contributed to the Nazi party—among the plutocrats to imitate Hugenberg were Fritz Thyssen, Emil Kirdorf, and Hjalmar Schacht—it does not follow that German big business as a collective unit was so eager to subsidize Hitler. On the contrary, the business community at large evinced a marked reserve, at least until January 27, 1932, when Hitler addressed the Industry Club of Düsseldorf. On this occasion, the Führer made by all accounts one of the most persuasive speeches of his career: for two and a half hours, he played unerringly on the patriotic and antibolshevik instincts of his audience of coal and steel barons; at the end he had convinced them of his respect for private property, and they stood and cheered him. Afterward, the main body of German businessmen became vocal supporters of Nazism; particularly enthusiastic were the heavy industrialists who stood to gain most from Hitler's proposed rearmament program. Business contributions to the NSDAP increased, too, although they were never lavish enough to satisfy all the party's needs. Goebbels in his diary and other Nazis at their postwar trial in Nuremberg have testified that financial difficulties haunted the Nazi party up to the very moment it took office. On January 4, 1933, only weeks before he became chancellor, Hitler at an important meeting in the Cologne house of the banker, Kurt von Schröder, was still soliciting funds.

The truth of the matter is contained in an excellent summary article by H. A. Turner, "Big Business and the Rise of Hitler," in the *American Historical Review* (1969). Turner demonstrates quite conclusively that the German financiers and industrialists throughout 1932 gave money to many parties besides the NSDAP. They were, in reality, trying to hedge their bets against any and all political contingencies. Backing Hitler was insurance lest the businessmens' preferred parties, the DNVP or the German Peoples party, should prove incapable of protecting propertied interests. Rather than deliberately plotting to bring Hitler to power, as the Marxists suggest, Germany's capitalists jumped on the Nazi bandwagon belatedly and desperately in 1932 simply because, for the first time, Hitler appeared a credible contender for office. And most assuredly, Hitler the revolutionary did not regard himself as beholden to German big business.

Indeed, if Hitler felt any obligation at all, it was probably not to the industrialists but to the army. The officer corps, not content with its status of an *imperium in imperio,* was tempted by the parliamentary paralysis in Berlin to intrigue at first hand in party politics. G. A. Craig writes in his *Politics of the Prussian Army* (1955): "Indeed there is no period in German history in which representatives of the army intervened more frequently and more directly in the internal politics of the country." Several political generals—men such as Kurt von Schleicher, Wilhelm Groener, and Werner von Blomberg—gained the ear of their former commander in chief, Hindenburg, and the president grew accustomed to consulting these self-styled spokesmen of the *Reichswehr* in matters of cabinet-making and breaking. Thus, the army was strategically placed either to hasten or to block Hitler's drive to constitutional power.

Although the officer class never ceased to despise Hitler as an upstart Bohemian corporal, they shared with the Nazis the common goal of remilitarizing the German nation. Cooperation to this end was nothing new; during the 1920s, there had been a considerable movement of personnel back and forth between the SA and the "Black *Reichswehr*" (troops illegally mustered beyond the 100,000-man limit imposed by the Versailles treaty). The question of armaments became an exceedingly live issue after 1930, culminating in the meeting of a general disarmament conference in February 1932. But the hope that France would countenance some equalization of arms between Germany and the Allies of World War I proved vain and, before the year was out, the German delegation withdrew temporarily from the conference. Disillusioned with international cooperation as a means of reaching arms parity, the *Reichswehr* turned back to the policy it had been pursuing surreptitiously for years—unilateral German rearmament. Hitler's patriotic and militarized mass movement seemed too useful a partner to ignore. Of course, in defense of the army, it can be argued that its oldfashioned Prussian military ideal was very different from the nation in arms which Hitler had in mind, and also that those politically-minded generals who most forcefully advocated collusion with Nazism did not truly represent the bulk of the army officer corps. Nevertheless, in January 1933, with Hindenburg poised to offer Hitler the chancellorship, it was the small coterie of politico-military intriguers who were invited to endorse or disapprove of the contemplated step. Their approbation committed their fellow officers and reassured Hindenburg at the moment when a negative reply might have crippled Nazism's political prospects, perhaps fatally.

All that has been said so far in explanation of the Nazis' meteoric advance recalls the circumstances of Mussolini's rise—a backdrop of violence, the appeal of nationalist and antibolshevik propaganda, the sympathy of traditional power brokers. There was, however, one weapon which Hitler possessed in much greater abundance than Mussolini, namely, mass support. Italian Fascism's claim to a popular following always had a hollow ring; so many Italians seemed to accept fascism fatalistically rather than enthusiastically. That the PNF at the time of the March on Rome held a mere 35 seats out of over 500 in the Chamber of Deputies cannot be ascribed entirely to a distaste for parliamentary tactics; and it must be remembered that Mussolini's election victory in April 1924 was obtained with the help of intimidation at the polls and a national—not an exclusively Fascist—list of candidates. In contrast, the Nazi party singly made spectacular gains after 1929; the Reichstag elections of 1930 saw its standing increase from 12 to 107 seats. During the year before Hitler gained office, the NSDAP regularly polled one-third of the votes in local and national elections. In February 1932 the state of Brunswick, where the Nazis' electoral successes had gained them a foothold in the government, conferred German citizenship on Hitler, thus allowing him to challenge Hindenburg who, in April, ran for reelection as president. In fact, he forced the war hero into a runoff; in this second election the Führer captured 13.5 million or 36.8 percent of the total vote. A few months later, in July, the Nazi vote hit a peak in the Reichstag elections—37.4 percent of the poll and 230 seats out of 608.

At this juncture, the Nazi and Communist vote, taken together, indicated that almost 60 percent of the German electorate were voting for parties openly dedicated to the overthrow of parliamentary democracy. Hitler, especially, seemed the people's choice. The Nazi vote in July 1932 constituted the highest share of the national poll achieved by a single party in the history of Weimar. If Hitler did not secure an absolute popular mandate, his electoral position was phenomenally strong in the context of Weimar politics. Understandably, one of the key debates among historians of Nazism concerns the source of Hitler's electoral support.

It is significant that Nazism made no inroads into the traditional left-wing vote. National electoral support of the SPD did decline but was offset by the rise in the KPD vote. Rather, the statistics reveal clearly that the Nazis gained nearly all their new votes from the conservative parties and the Nationalists. This suggests a desertion of traditional parties by white-collar workers trying to keep up appearances on a proletarian salary, by retailers squeezed by department and chain stores, by yeoman farmers plunging ever deeper into debt. These were the small men of property, and only by broadening the definition of capitalism to include the bourgeoisie or its German variant, the *Mittelstand*, does the Marxian view of Nazism as a class conspiracy make much sense. Even so, the *Mittelstand* was not synonymous with German capitalism, and it saw in Hitler a bulwark not only against presumptuous labor but also against overbearing monopolies. In Lipset's view: "The ideal type of Nazi voter was an economically independent Protestant of the middle class who lived either in the country or a small town, and had previously voted for a party of the center or a regional party that had campaigned against both big industry and trade unions" ("Faschismus," *Kölner Zeitschrift für Soziologie und Sozialpsychologie* [1957]).

Another school of thought, however, finds such a class interpretation of Nazism's growing popularity too narrow. For example, K. O'Lessker, "Who Voted for Hitler?" *American Journal of Sociology* (1968), argues convincingly that the social discontent which produced votes for the NSDAP was not restricted by vocation or social status. This view is reflective of the fact that Nazism was to a great degree a youth movement, with the bulk of its active support located in the eighteen to thirty-five age group. This was the generation, or as Peter Loewenberg prefers to call them, "youth cohort," disoriented in childhood by the First World War, who had come of age. The strong Hitler served as a surrogate for familial paternal authority already undermined by absence during war and impotence in the face of economic upheaval. Now, beginning in 1928–29, those who left school and university found jobs particularly hard to come by and, out of frustration, voted for the NSDAP in huge numbers. Such was the scope of the Great Depression that the unemployed young, voting for the first or second time, came from all ranks of society.

The scholarly controversy over the nature of Nazism's mass support is perhaps most instructive because it illustrates perfectly the two-faced character of Hitler's appeal. He won backing with equal skill from the young and the socially maladjusted, and from the middle class and those with a position in society to protect. To the former, Hitler appeared dynamic and his *völkisch* fantasies were an exciting romance. To the latter, he was a guarantor of historic, including *völkisch*, values. His attraction, as another social scientist has pointed out, was an uncanny blend of adventure and stability, of the "charismatic" and the "bureaucratic."

Election statistics, revealing though they are, cannot reflect the full measure of Nazism's public support. Obviously, they do not take account of those who, out of habit, continued to vote for the traditional parties, but nevertheless considered Hitler tolerable or even indispensable. Nazism responded to a mood in the country at large, a sense of frustration endemic in all strata of the German community at the complexities of modern life epitomized in the Great Depression. The predicament seemed to demand a return to the eternal verities albeit by drastic and vigorous means. The image that the Nazis projected was one of vigor and action above all else. Despite the drain on financial resources and human energy, the NSDAP contested every election with the utmost fervor, held endless noisy parades and rallies, and relentlessly bombarded the eye and ear with propaganda slogans. In short, the Nazis took great pains to remain in the forefront of public consciousness. The cumulative impression was of a movement with the energy and strength of will to do something about social, economic, and international problems—a general message much more compelling than the specifics of any program Hitler put forward. In this way Nazism became a more visible and credible alternative to tired conservatism and Weimar liberalism than even the election results suggest.

The acquisition of a mass following in one form or another was vital to Hitler's strategy of achieving office within the framework of the Weimar constitution; but the path of legality was long and tortuous, trying the patience of the more activist Nazis who would have preferred a seizure of power through the SA. A popular book in Germany at this time was Curzio Malaparte's *Coup d'État: The Technique of Revolution* (1931), and there was a widespread conviction that Hitler would not be able to forswear a *Putsch*. The SPD, for this reason, kept its own paramilitary force, the *Reichsbanner*, in readiness to repulse a full-scale SA onslaught on Weimar which never came and, in doing so, badly underestimated the chance of the Nazis' lawful accession to office. For a different reason, the Communists also ignored Nazism's popular backing and constitutional strength. Both the Kremlin and the KPD were blinded by the Marxian dogma which held that Nazism was a product of monopoly capitalism. Should Hitler come to power, it would simply confirm that capitalism was on its last legs and that therefore a revolution was imminent which would sweep away Nazism and all capitalism's works. The real Communist enemy, then, was not the

Nazis, who could only hasten an inevitable historical process, but the Social Democrats, who might abort a proletarian uprising as they had done in 1918–19. In the Marxist dialectic, Social Democrats were dubbed "social fascists," a greater threat to the true revolutionary than the real fascists. It was hardly surprising that left-wing opposition to Hitler proved stunningly ineffective. The SPD miscalculated the di-

*Democracy in Germany was undermined by economic troubles.*
*The Great Depression created millions of German unemployed in the*
*1930s; the Nazis went out of their way to show their concern with*
*typical propagandistic flair, providing mobile soup kitchens and even*
*a band to entertain the poor.*

UNITED PRESS INTERNATIONAL PHOTO

rection from which the Nazi danger was coming, while the KPD rationalized away the danger itself; and the mutual antipathy between the two leftist parties rendered a united anti-Nazi front impossible. Here was yet another set of circumstances which eased Hitler's advance.

The Nazi drive to constitutional power did not really gather momentum until May 1932 when the Brüning government fell. Ironically, one immediate cause was a controversial decree, instigated by Brüning, banning the SA. The aristocratic Franz von Papen and the military politician, General von Schleicher, seized the moment to convince Hindenburg of Brüning's unpopularity; jointly they planned a government of the far Right and anticipated Nazi backing. So Papen's "cabinet of the barons" came into being. It immediately showed its colors by repealing the ban on the SA and by arbitrarily suppressing the state government of Prussia headed by the Socialist Otto Braun. Braun's cabinet, based on an alliance of the SPD and Center, was recognized as a bulwark of German democracy; it had proved its mettle by leading the campaign to clear the streets of Nazi brown-shirted thugs. The SPD considered responding to Papen by calling out the *Reichsbanner* or the trade unions, but in the end decided against the use of force. By default, the usurpation of Braun's lawfully elected government under Article 48 was accepted. It was a shattering blow both to German Socialism and to Weimar parliamentary democracy; Hitler was delighted.

As a result of the elections of July 1932, the NSDAP emerged as the largest party in the Reichstag, and Papen and Schleicher moved to consummate their alliance with Hitler. But the latter, playing the same game that Mussolini had played precisely ten years earlier, heatedly refused to join any ministry as a junior partner. In an interview with Hindenburg on August 13, Hitler demanded carte blanche to form his own government, to which Hindenburg replied coldly that he regarded the Nazis as undisciplined and irresponsible, and that in a crisis he preferred a government less responsive to the mob. Moreover, this rebuke was conveyed to the world in the official communiqué of the meeting. In face of this setback, many Nazis recommended entering office under the tutelage of Papen and Schleicher. But the magnetism of the Führer was enough to keep the party in line, and his resolution to come to power only on his own terms was upheld.

Without the Nazis, Papen had no hope of a majority in the Reichstag. He could only govern by presidential decree, and in the process he made himself even more unpopular than Brüning. In desperation, he called another Reichstag election in November. On this occasion, for the first time since 1930, the NSDAP lost votes, two million of them. The likeliest explanation is that, after three years of constant electioneering and agitation, the Nazi rank and file, like the party treasury, were near exhaustion. In addition, a drop in the unemployment figures in the autumn of 1932 may have lessened the sense of desperation which drove so many to Hitler, although the other extremist party, the KPD, gained votes. Nonetheless, after the November elections, the NSDAP with 196 seats out of 594 remained the largest party in the Reichstag, and its support was still essential for any cabinet that aspired to rule by parliamentary majority. Papen, heartened by the electoral results, was confident the Nazis could now be persuaded to accept a secondary role in his ministry. But Papen's colleagues were less optimistic and, prompted by the Machiavellian Schleicher, forced his resignation. On December 2 Schleicher himself became chancellor, gambling that he could win Nazi backing where Papen had failed.

For several months Schleicher had been assiduously courting the Nazis through Gregor Strasser, the darling of the anticapitalist wing of the NSDAP. Although earlier in 1932 Schleicher had assisted in the creation of Papen's ministry of aristocrats, he presented himself to Strasser as a radical, talking of cooperation with the trade unions, East Prussian land reform, and price controls on meat and coal. Strasser swallowed the bait and urged Hitler to accept Schleicher's offer of a junior cabinet post. Hitler refused, and for a moment the possibility loomed that Strasser might lead a revolt against the Führer and bring a substantial bloc of Nazis over to Schleicher. This would have suited Schleicher almost as much as an alliance with Hitler himself. But Strasser had no taste for confrontation: in 1930 when his brother Otto had been drummed out of the NSDAP, he had submitted meekly. On December 8, 1932, Gregor Strasser capitulated again; he wrote a letter of resignation from the party and left with his family for a holiday in Italy. The Nazi party, albeit shaken, survived intact. Just as important, Schleicher was left high and dry.

Schleicher resumed his overtures to the Socialists, but time was running out for him. Papen had not forgiven Schleicher's intrigue which had forced him out of the chancellorship, and he was ready to pay back the general in kind. On January 4, 1933, big business interests, alarmed at Schleicher's socialist tendencies, arranged a meeting between Hitler and Papen; there began several weeks of hard bargaining which soon embraced Hugenberg's Nationalists. To impress the conservatives, Hitler and Goebbels threw all the resources of the NSDAP into the state elections in Lippe; there, on January 15, the Nazis secured almost 40 percent of the poll. It was a brilliant propaganda coup which served to disguise the recent decline in the Nazi vote elsewhere. Papen and Hugenberg were compelled to recognize that, if they wanted to get rid of Schleicher and of dependence on presidential rule under Article 48, the bases of their own support were far too narrow for a popular government. Hitler alone, as Lippe had shown, could deliver votes in sufficient quantity. By the last week of January, they agreed to serve under Hitler as chancellor. Reluctantly, President Hindenburg set aside his earlier reservations about the Nazis and allowed himself to be persuaded by Papen and Hugenberg that Hitler was indispensable. Hindenburg was glad enough of the chance to bring down Schleicher whose intrigues, particularly against Papen, had disgusted him. But he wanted assurance that Schleicher would not, or could not, raise the army against a Hitler government. Suddenly, the key figure became General von Blomberg. When he gave his promise to take the Ministry of Defense under Hitler, Hindenburg felt confident of the *Reichswehr*. On January 30, 1933, President Hindenburg appointed Hitler Reich chancellor with authority to choose his own ministry.

Hitler's strategy was vindicated. His maintenance of a delicate balance between strident propaganda and violence in the streets on the one hand and, on the other, astute handling of the factions within the legal constitution betokened a rare grasp of modern political methods. The word *Fingerspitzgefühl*, or fingertip-feeling, was often and with justice used to explain Hitler's skill. Yet, in the last analysis, the Nazi triumph arose out of a combination of extraneous circumstances which played into Hitler's hands—the breakdown of the Weimar parliamentary system in the Great Depression, the failure of the German Left to oppose Nazism effectively, and, above all, the willingness of Germany's conservatives to enter into partnership with Hitler.

## Totalitarianism in the Third Reich

Hitler was in no hurry to discard the techniques which had brought him the chancellorship. In particular, his alliance with respectable conservatives and his adherence to constitutional forms served to disguise Nazism's revolutionary essence. It is a cardinal tenet of K. D. Bracher's numerous writings that the revolution that Hitler set in motion in 1933 was made palatable by appearing at once "national" and "legal." The first Hitler cabinet was "national" in the sense that it contained only three Nazis out of eleven members. Hitler was, of course, chancellor; an ex-civil servant, Wilhelm Frick, was appointed minister of the interior, although in this capacity he had no control over the police in individual states; Göring became minister without portfolio, and was also made Prussian minister of the interior which gave him command of two-thirds of the security forces in the Reich. There seemed to be plenty of countervailing forces to undue Nazi influence: Papen as vice-chancellor and also state commissioner for Prussia (in the latter office he was expected to curb Göring); Hugenberg in charge of the three chief economic ministries; Blomberg at the Ministry of Defense; and an aristocratic career diplomat, Baron von Neurath, at the foreign ministry. But on the first issue which faced the new government, the Nazis prevailed. While most of the cabinet believed that the current Reichstag could be made to yield a ministerial majority, Hitler held out successfully for yet another election. Hugenberg, especially, had some inkling of what the Nazis might do in an election with the power of the state at their disposal; his fears were quickly justified.

The central figure in this last election held under Weimar rules was Göring. During February 1933, he purged hundreds of non-Nazis from Prussia's civil service. He ordered the police not to obstruct the Nazi SA or the Nationalists' paramilitary force, the *Stahlhelm*, "as these organizations contain the most important constructive national elements." His crowning measure was the creation of an auxiliary police force of 50,000, made up of 40,000 Nazi storm troopers and 10,000 from the *Stahlhelm*. Thus, the machinery for the intimidation of Hitler's enemies, and indeed of the general public, was already established in most of Germany when the Reichstag went up in flames in the evening of February 27. The arsonist, who was apprehended on the spot, was a demented former Dutch communist. Göring seized his cue to declare the Reichstag fire a Communist plot, although he had no evidence of this. Nor had the Communists any evidence later when they succeeded in persuading many that the Nazis themselves had set the fire. (Göring would later claim credit, but his boasting can hardly be taken on trust.) Although most likely a case of simple arson, the Reichstag fire was used the next day as the pretext to obtain President Hindenburg's signature on a decree "for protection of nation and state" which suspended all civil liberties. Simultaneously, Nazi storm troopers and the "auxiliary police" unleashed a reign of terror. Known and suspected opponents of Nazism were rounded up in the thousands, beaten and incarcerated, and many killed outright. Reichstag deputies were not immune. The left-wing press was forcibly silenced. In an atmosphere of tension and violence, Germans went to the polls on March 5.

In spite of the ominous presence of storm troopers at the polling stations and a sudden flow of business money to the NSDAP, the Nazis secured less than 44 percent of the vote in an unusually high turnout (88.8 percent of those eligible voted). The DNVP won 8 percent, giving the Nazi-Nationalist bloc a slim majority in the Reichstag. Under the decree of February 28, however, Hitler was enabled to secure his position by declaring excluded all KPD elected representatives and a score of SPD deputies as well.

The Left en masse was absent from a ceremony inaugurating the new Reichstag session which Goebbels staged in the Garrison Church at Potsdam on March 21. The symbolic antithesis of Weimar, Potsdam was the home of the Hohenzollern monarchy. Indeed, the crown prince was in the audience on March 21, and during the ceremony wreaths were laid on the royal tombs. The setting was calculated to recall Prussia's military and imperial past, which was personified in Hindenburg in his field marshal's dress uniform. But the president had to share the spotlight with the new chancellor who, for this occasion, wore a frock coat and carried a top hat. They both made speeches, Hitler at greater length, at the end of which Hitler shook Hindenburg's hand fervently. Afterward, the chancellor and the field marshal stood side by side for two hours on the reviewing stand as units of the *Reichswehr*, police, and sundry paramilitary forces marched by. It was all a blatant attempt to cast Hitler as heir to the German nationalist tradition and to suggest a thread of historical continuity beween the Nazi Third Reich and both the Germanic Holy Roman Empire and Bismarck's imperial creation.

Two days later the Reichstag assembled in Berlin's Kroll Opera House. The atmosphere was still highly charged, and Hitler capitalized on it by formally presenting a "Law for Relieving the Distress of People and Reich," otherwise known as the Enabling Act. Its purport was to give the government, initially for four years, legislative authority to do what Hitler had been doing by presidential decree since the Reichstag fire. Such a law to act "apart from procedures provided for in the Reich constitution" amounted to a change in the constitution itself and thus required a two-thirds majority in the Reichstag. Even with

the forced exclusion of some one hundred left-wing deputies, passage
of the bill was not assured. However, the Catholic Center party, with
seventy-three seats, decided hesitatingly that Germany needed strong
rule at any cost and backed Hitler. In fact, opposition came only from
the Social Democrats, who showed a certain courage merely in attend-
ing this Reichstag session. The Enabling Act was approved by the
comfortable margin of 441 votes to 94, whereupon the Nazi deputies
burst into the "Horst Wessel Lied." They had cause to celebrate. The
Enabling Act gave legal sanction to an absolute dictatorship. As dictator, Hitler would now reveal the sort of national revolution he intended
for Germany.

In 1922 Mussolini had embarked on a legal revolution by securing
extraordinary powers from the Italian Parliament. Yet, for two years,
the Duce had proceeded with circumspection. There was no such hesitation on the Führer's part; Hitler was simply more confident of himself and his political destiny than Mussolini. But also, Nazism's grass-
roots strength—a suspect factor in the case of Italian Fascism—made
possible an immediate and drastic reordering of German life. The
Nazis' own word for the process was *Gleichschaltung*, implying the co-

*Hitler and the family of Joseph Goebbels, Nazi propaganda minister,
listening to a recitation by one of the Goebbels's daughters. Nazi leaders
very easily became sentimental over little girls and pet animals.*

WIDE WORLD PHOTOS

ordination or leveling-out of all agencies public and private. It was a thoroughly totalitarian concept.

> Eventually no independent social groups were to exist. Wherever two or three were gathered, the Führer would also be present. Ultimately all society, in terms of human relationships, would cease to exist, or rather would exist in a new framework whereby each individual related not to his fellow men but only to the state and to the Nazi leader who became the personal embodiment of the state (W. S. Allen, *Nazi Seizure of Power* [1965]).

Within a year or so, *Gleichschaltung* had instilled Nazism in the German consciousness to a degree never approached by Fascism in Italy.

The federal system of states rights, which had afforded Hitler shelter in Bavaria, was now abolished. The states' popular assemblies and governments were dissolved, to be replaced by governors directly answerable to the Reich Ministry of the Interior. Parties other than the NSDAP were crushed; even Hitler's Nationalist allies found their party offices occupied by police and Nazi thugs. The Nationalists' *Stahlhelm* was forcibly integrated into the SA, and all other private armies were disbanded. On the tenth anniversary of Hitler's beer hall *Putsch*, a ceremony was held in Munich to mark the formal dissolution of the *Freikorps* and to assert the Nazis' claim to be their legatee. Independent trade unions were destroyed, the major blow falling on the morrow of May Day celebrations in 1933. All workers outside the civil service were ultimately made members of a new Labor Front. The intention behind this organization was plain from the outset; as director Hitler chose, not a figure from Nazism's socialist wing, but the drunkard Dr. Robert Ley who had long been an adversary of the Strasser brothers. The Labor Front was no substitute for the defunct trade unions; it was never properly concerned with labor conditions, only with propagandizing the work force.

No institution, however exalted, was immune from *Gleichschaltung*. The presidency itself supplied a classic instance of the Nazi policy of coordination. During 1933, Hindenburg's advancing senility facilitated the erosion of presidential power and, when the field marshal died the following August, Hitler announced that henceforth the two offices of chancellor and president were to be fused in his own person. Hindenburg's political testament, doctored to eradicate any reference to a monarchical restoration which had been the old man's dream, was produced and appeared to recommend the move. Then, in a plebiscite

—the standard electoral procedure in Nazi Germany—almost 90 percent endorsed Hitler's arrogation of supreme office. While the Duce had to tolerate Victor Emmanuel as his partner in a dyarchy, the Führer shared his sovereign position with no one.

Where Germany's conventional institutions were not wiped out or totally absorbed by Nazi-dominated organizations, they were neutralized by the creation of parallel offices. Thus, on top of the normal divisions of Germany into local administrative units was superimposed the Nazi distribution of the country into *Gaue* (districts), each presided over by a Nazi *Gauleiter* with considerable discretionary power. The legal system was similarly treated; alongside the regular courts was erected an array of special courts, staffed by Nazi-approved personnel, to try cases of treason and political offenses. These courts were serviced by a new political section created by Göring within the Prussian police department—the *Geheime Staatspolizei* (Secret State Police) or Gestapo. In due course, the Gestapo would operate all over Germany, and incarceration in a concentration camp would be possible by executive fiat without reference to any court of law at all. All this duplication of functions was, of course, expensive and wasteful, and produced chronic administrative confusion. The image of a superefficient monolithic Nazi state was always more myth than fact. Nevertheless, the confusion served a political purpose for, by sowing bewilderment among the citizenry, it kept up that sense of helplessness which had driven many Germans to accept Nazism in the first place. Never revealing where precise administrative jurisdiction lay was a classic totalitarian trick. Amid the Kafkaesque uncertainty and fear, there was only one voice of authority for the average man to turn to for security and refuge— that of the totalitarian leader mouthing his ideological certitudes.

The totalitarian bent of the Nazi regime was also evident in the way *Gleichschaltung* extended beyond public and prominent circles to every stratum of German life. Nazi purges reached down to the bottom echelons of the professions, particularly so in the vital areas of thought control—education and the mass media. Even in the most innocuous kinds of social activity, it was necessary to parade a conformity with Nazi principles. Local clubs ranging from football teams to beekeepers' associations added the initials NS for Nationalist Socialist to their titles. It has been suggested that in so large and complex a nation as Germany, no party or government could possibly hope to manipulate all popular activities. And it is true that everyday life, particularly in the countryside, went on undisturbed by Hitler's arrival in office. Nevertheless, after 1933, there hung over the whole of Germany a new awareness of the central authority in Berlin and an apprehension of Nazi power poised to intervene in any detail of national life whenever it was deemed necessary.

Twentieth-century totalitarian regimes have been remarkable in their claim to respond to a general will. Unlike old-fashioned Caesarian tyrannies, which imposed themselves on nations from above, totalitarian governments assertedly derived their authority from below, from the people. Nazi Germany provides a case in point. *Gleichschaltung* could not have been pushed as far as it was without the complicity of the majority of Germans. Some of this cooperation, naturally, was mere timeserving; as Nazism appeared the wave of the German future, many rushed opportunistically to join the NSDAP in the spring of 1933. They were dubbed the "March violets" in contrast to the *Alte Kämpfer* or old fighters, and in short order the qualifications for party membership had to be tightened to stem the influx. On the other hand, one cannot discount the sincerity of millions of Germans who welcomed *Gleichschaltung* as an exercise in national unity and discipline. As such, it was a preferable alternative to the pluralism and permissiveness of the discredited Weimar system. *Gleichschaltung* supplied the bureaucratic means for the inculcation of the sense of community (*Volksgemeinschaft*) which was Nazism's replacement for the libertarian democracy of November 1918. The yearning to belong ran deep in Germany, and it was to this need that the Nazis responded. Looking back after the Second World War, ordinary apolitical Germans fondly recalled for the American newspaperman, Milton Mayer, the *völkisch* democracy fostered by Hitler. Said a baker: "We simple working-class men stood side by side with learned men in the Labor Front." Added a teacher: "In the Labor Front we belonged to something together, we had something in common. We could know each other in those days. . . . there was a democracy in Nazism, and it was real. My— how shall I say it?—my inferiors accepted me."

The crucial importance of this spirit of confraternity emerged early in the Nazi era, as Hitler struggled to cope with economic problems. Between January 1933 and the end of 1934, the number of registered unemployed—the barometer of the Great Depression—dropped from 6 millions to 2.6 millions. This considerable achievement can be explained in various ways. Unemployment had been declining before Hitler became chancellor and so, to some extent, he merely rode the tide of economic recovery which was evident throughout the world.

Nonetheless, the German economic upswing in 1933–34 outpaced that of any other industrial country, which implies some special merit on the part of the Nazi government. One Hitlerian advantage was the absence of any doctrinaire attachment to laissez faire; therefore, the Führer felt free to embark on a series of public works schemes. All over Germany, federal money was made available in grants or low-interest loans for the repair and construction of roads (including the first *Autobahnen*) and parks, of single buildings and whole neighborhoods; a genuine boom in the building trades followed. Much of the work force for these projects was provided through the Labor Service which enrolled thousands of unemployed, at first on a voluntary basis and then compulsorily. A further governmental stimulus to economic activity came from the heightened tempo of secret rearmament after January 1933, enabling heavy industry to absorb a small number of unemployed. However, it would be quite wrong to suppose that Hitler consciously and consistently pursued a policy of pump priming to overcome the depression—Nazis were economic pragmatists, not Keynesians. Consequently, haphazard public works programs and modest rearmament accounted only in part for Germany's economic resurgence. In reality, the Nazi contribution was at least as much psychological as material. In the "battle for work," the Nazis' total propaganda talent was deployed—parades, demonstrations, bands, flags, radio speeches by Hitler—the objective being to convince every German that he was a direct participant in the national struggle. One unusually successful gimmick was "stew Sundays," on which families were expected to donate the money saved by not eating regular meals to Nazi welfare agencies. By this means it could be demonstrated that "all Germans are prepared to suffer together when the least of us suffers." In due course, the ambitious public relations campaign worked; a sense of united national purpose did develop, and with it came a revival of German self-confidence which, in turn, paved the way for the expansion of private investment and commerce.

In the opinion of most Germans, Hitler taught them how to pull together and how to escape the Great Depression. This was a blanket justification for the Nazi dictatorship. It is essential to realize that, by the mid-1930s, Hitler's government had made itself plainly acceptable to the German majority. Of course, the occasional plebiscites on specific topics, which replaced traditional elections, were rigged. Nevertheless, there must have been a solid plurality favoring official policies before terror and trickery intervened to inflate the majority to 98 or 99 percent. Nor should the internationally supervised Saar plebiscite in January 1935 be overlooked. By the Treaty of Versailles, this coal-rich area of the Rhineland had been detached from Germany for fifteen years; now, the inhabitants were invited to decide among reunion with Germany, incorporation into France, or continued administration by the League of Nations. No doubt, most Saarlanders would have chosen the German option regardless of the regime in Berlin, but the 90 percent vote to join Hitler's Reich, arising out of a perfectly fair poll, was something of a testimonial to Nazism's popularity with the average German.

At the same time that *Gleichschaltung* and economic success were rooting Nazism firmly in German society at large, Hitler moved to consolidate his own position in the narrower world of factional German politics. After the Enabling Act, pressure was put on the non-Nazis to leave the government; Hugenberg resigned in June 1933, and although Papen stayed on, it was made clear he did so on sufferance. In 1934 the precariousness of the old-guard politicians increased as a result of a crisis over the SA brown shirts.

Following Hitler's accession to office, new recruits swelled membership of the SA to a figure in the millions; many were ex-Communist street fighters now jocularly called beefsteaks—red inside and brown outside. But this paramilitary force, created to assist Nazism into power, lacked a raison d'être now that Hitler controlled the state. The assertive Ernst Röhm, leader of the SA, conceived two solutions to this dilemma. One idea was that the SA should be recognized as a regular military arm of the state. This implied either that the SA should supplant the *Reichswehr* or that the two armies should merge; on one occasion Röhm tried to persuade Hitler to give regular army commissions to several thousand SA officers. Röhm's other suggestion was for the SA to find its role in leading a "second revolution." Like the radical Italian Fascists from whom he borrowed the phrase, Röhm demanded a clean break with the old order; *Gleichschaltung* might be revolutionary, but it made no attack on the traditional privileges and class structure in German life. Röhm had always been on the left of the Nazi party; in 1934 he seemed to assume the mantle of the Strasser brothers. Naturally, the German aristocrats who had helped Hitler gain office were appalled by Röhm's proposals. Blomberg voiced the horror of the army officer corps at association with the SA, Papen was vehemently outspoken against any "second revolution," and both threatened to appeal to President Hindenburg. But Hindenburg's death was anticipated imminently, and Hitler planned to assume the presidency himself; to accomplish this, he needed the backing of the agitated conservatives. Hitler thus found himself squeezed between radical party elements and his traditionalist allies. For the sake of the latter, Röhm had to go; that was the first priority. However, to yield to one set of critics outright affronted Hitler's ego and undercut his political supremacy. All pretensions to bring pressure on the Führer had to be crushed. Hence, the purge which has gone down in history as the Night of the Long Knives extended far beyond Röhm and his associates; it engulfed other leading Nazis and also struck at the conservatives who had forced Hitler's hand in the first place.

The instrument chosen to execute the purge was the *Schutz Staffeln* (defense squads) or SS, originally formed as the Führer's personal bodyguard. Nominally part of Röhm's brown shirt army, the SS was distinguished not only by its sinister black uniform. Unlike the rowdy SA, the SS was a highly disciplined body sworn to absolute obedience to Hitler. The importance and independence of the SS increased rapidly after 1929 when it came under the direction of Heinrich Himmler, a totally humorless and unimaginative poultry farmer from Bavaria who had been jolted out of the common rut by war and depression. Although no more than conventionally anti-Semitic as a youth, he became a fanatical devotee of Nazi racial doctrines, and his utter dedication to Hitler carried him up the Nazi ladder. In addition to his SS post, Himmler was given charge of the Bavarian police, and on April 1, 1934, Göring made him head of the Prussian Gestapo. This sign of collusion between Göring and Himmler was an ominous portent for Röhm, since both were enemies of the SA chief, and together they did their best to convince Hitler that Röhm was planning a *Putsch*. No evidence was ever produced to substantiate this charge; nonetheless, the SS was told to be ready for action on the night of June 29–30.

As the SA was the prime target, Hitler had called a meeting of its top leaders at Bad Wiessee, near Munich. On the Führer's arrival in the small hours of Saturday, June 30, Röhm's companions were hauled from their beds and shot out of hand. Hitler himself confronted Röhm and ordered him taken to a Munich prison, where a pistol was placed in his cell as an invitation to suicide. But Röhm declined, trusting vainly in his long and close acquaintance with Hitler. On Sunday two SS officers entered his cell and shot him point-blank. Meanwhile, on June 30, Himmler and Göring in Berlin supervised the roundup and execution of other selected *Sturmgruppenführer*. It is impossible to say how many lives were taken during the Night of the Long Knives: some estimates have run into the thousands, but probably the figure announced at the time, eighty-three, is not far from the truth. Besides the SA officers, the most prominent victims consisted of men who had once associated with Hitler, only to drift away. Two such were Gustaf von Kahr, the old right-wing politician involved in the Munich beer hall *Putsch*, and Hitler's erstwhile party rival, Gregor Strasser. The former's body, hacked to pieces, was discovered in a swamp, and the latter was shot on Göring's express order. General von Schleicher, who had tried to make an alliance with the Nazis through Strasser in 1932, was visited by two SS men in plain-clothes. He was shot seven times in his own study; when his wife, whom he had recently married, rushed forward, she was shot too. Some killings were purely fortuitous. Dr. Willi Schmid, music critic of the *Münchener Neueste Nachrichten*, was playing the cello in his flat while his wife prepared dinner when the SS called and arrested him. Four days later, his body was returned in a coffin which his widow was warned not to open. Schmid had been mistaken for an SA officer of the same name! The SS graciously apologized and gave his family a sum of money in compensation. And then, inevitably, some Jews were murdered—just for sport.

Despite the extravagant violence, the purge never got out of hand, politically speaking. Of the two groups Hitler was determined to put down, the SA leadership was decimated. On the other hand, the conservative establishment was attacked more circumspectly, and its foremost spokesmen were not physically harmed. None of the army officers in Hindenburg's circle ran any danger, while Schleicher and his aides, who were hardly exemplary of the *Reichswehr*, perished. Similarly, Papen escaped, although two of his secretaries and the German leader of Catholic Action, all of whom had shared in Papen's campaign against a "second revolution," were shot. When Papen protested to Göring at the murder of his friends, the most he suffered was several days house arrest. Clearly, Hitler was still respectful of conservative strength. Loath to tackle the traditional potentates directly, his slaughter of secondary personnel was intended as a warning.

As it happened, the conservatives were more eager to be reassured than warned. For two weeks Goebbels prohibited any public comment on the purge; then, on July 13, Hitler gave his explanation to the Reichstag. Strategically, he concentrated on the execution of SA personnel. The shooting of Strasser and Schleicher was justified in passing by the assertion that they were implicated in Röhm's plots to make the

SA into the German army and to promote a "second revolution." What caught the headlines, however, was Hitler's furious denunciation of the homosexuality and general corruption of Röhm and his friends (although the homosexuality of the upper ranks of the SA had been common gossip since the early days of the Nazi movement). Germany's old guard, civilian and military, took its cue from Hitler's speech, rejoicing at the downfall of the SA and blithely ignoring the favors bestowed on the SS for its work on the Night of the Long Knives. The SS was now made an independent corps under Hitler's direct orders with Himmler as SS *Reichsführer;* thus, one private army was exchanged for another. In the long run, the disciplined, fanatical SS was to prove a much more formidable adversary to the army than the brawling SA had ever represented. Not only did the conservatives misconstrue the role of private armies under Nazism, but they also turned a blind eye to other aspects of the purge. They were unmoved by the brazen exhibition of Nazi viciousness and appeared unperturbed at the murder of respectable acquaintances. The German power structure drew no implications about its own security from the Night of the Long Knives. It was an attitude of monumental and incredible obtuseness.

Conservative complaisance toward Hitler extended to approval of his assumption of the presidency on Hindenburg's death in August—one of Hitler's objectives throughout the Röhm crisis. But although the merger of the offices of chancellor and president was a notable triumph of Nazi *Gleichschaltung,* Hitler was sensitive to the fact that he was somehow beholden to aristocrats and generals for the success. It rankled, as did the forced immunity of the Papens and the Blombergs on the Night of the Long Knives. So, for several years after 1934, Hitler continued the struggle to bring to heel those societal elements untouched in the early stages of *Gleichschaltung.*

One traditional force in German life to which the Führer now turned his attention was the churches. On becoming chancellor, Hitler, anxious to win conventional support, had announced his protection of Christianity, although he soon added that he meant "positive" or "German" Christianity. This reservation suited the Protestant or Evangelical churches, some of whose congregations were deeply imbued with *völkisch* prejudices, more than the Roman Catholic church. Notwithstanding, in July 1933, Papen had managed to negotiate a concordat between the papacy and Hitler's government, by which the former tolerated the extinction of the Catholic Center party in return for a guarantee of the free exercise of the Catholic religion in Nazi Germany. The Catholic church was an object of special concern to Hitler, not so much because of its record of political action since Bismarck, but because of its universality and timelessness. These attributes, Hitler —a lapsed Catholic like many leading Nazis—aspired to imitate by his supranational *Weltanschauung* based on race and by his "thousand-year Reich." The church and fascism alike coveted man's whole being and gave as much heed to his soul as his body. In sum, Hitler at once envied and feared Roman Catholicism as a rival.

Not surprisingly, the concordat of 1933 never functioned smoothly and, from the start, the Vatican had grounds for complaint about Nazi violations. However, it was not until after the Night of the Long Knives, during which Catholic Action was incidentally attacked, that the Nazi malice toward the Catholic church became evident. Catholic publications and schools were arbitrarily suppressed, and the Gestapo claimed to violate the privacy of the confessional. Charges of "currency smuggling" and "immorality" were used to dispatch an increasing number of priests and nuns to the concentration camps. The *Völkischer Beobachter* proclaimed: "The Catholic church is corrupt through and through, and must vanish." At last, in March 1937, the Vatican replied with the encyclical *Mit brennender Sorge*, roundly condemning Nazi breaches of the concordat and the worship of the false gods of race and state. Yet its theme, as in all papal pronouncements about Nazi Germany, centered on the question of the infringement of religious liberty and did not take issue with Nazi politics or government per se; it therefore constituted no clarion call to rebellion by German Catholics. Although Hitler was furious at the encyclical, it did not deflect him in the slightest from persecution of the Catholic church. On the contrary, the Vatican's reproof, guarded though it was, spurred the Nazis on to greater efforts. And by and large, the Catholic hierarchy in Germany acquiesced. To do otherwise would have required a challenge to Hitler's entire political system, and the Catholic church, at least in Germany, shrank from trespassing on Caesar's preserve.

From the Evangelical churches, too, came a flicker of defiance but not much more. In response to the excesses of the pro-Nazi wing of German Protestantism, a countervailing force sprang up under the name of the "Confessional church," with a Lutheran, Pastor Martin Niemöller, as its major spokesman. During World War I, Niemöller had commanded a U-boat, afterward he had been a *Freikorps* member and, in 1933, he had applauded Hitler's appointment as chancellor.

But soon he was expressing his disillusion openly. In 1937, a year which saw 800 clergy and laity of the Confessional church imprisoned, Niemöller was arrested for the first time. The following year, he was sent as Hitler's personal prisoner to detention camp, where he remained until 1945. Astonishingly, on the outbreak of the Second World War, Niemöller volunteered for military service in the Third Reich. Yet the gesture was typical of the Confessional church. Like the Catholics, the Protestants who crossed Hitler did so to preserve freedom of worship, not to oppose Nazism's secular rule. In other respects, they considered themselves obedient and patriotic subjects. In any event, the Confessional church was only a small minority among the Evangelical denominations. Most Protestant pastors were quite content with the Nazi regime, and expressed their satisfaction in 1938 by flocking in their thousands to subscribe to an oath of loyalty to the Führer.

It cannot be said that Hitler ever totally subjugated the German churches. Individual clergy of various faiths continued to preach sermons asserting the incompatibility of Christianity and Nazi ideology. If such clerics were important enough, the government tended to avoid disturbances by withholding its full punitive weight; for example, Niemöller's life even in captivity was never really threatened. On the other hand, the churches as institutions, especially the Evangelical churches which embraced the majority of the German population, accommodated themselves to Nazism. They did not bargain with the state on equal terms, as had the Vatican in the Lateran Accords. Also in contrast to the papacy in Fascist Italy, the German churches strenuously tried to stay out of politics and made a faint impression on the general public as a source of independent opinion.

Another section of the prefascist power structure which found it simpler to maintain an entrenched position in Mussolini's Italy than in Nazi Germany was the business community. Mussolini's corporative state offered no problem to Italian businessmen, who virtually took over the new agencies and made them responsive to capitalist pressures. German business interests expected to handle Hitler as easily. After all, they had dictated national economic policy in what they alleged to be the hostile environment of Weimar Germany. Why should they not anticipate holding the same sway under Hitler to whose rise they had contributed financially in 1932–33? At first, Hitler did nothing to disturb the businessmens' self-confidence. Not only were the German Socialist and Communist parties outlawed and their leadership scattered in exile and concentration camps, but a firm check was also put on the critics of capitalism within the Nazi party.

The Nazis, like other *völkisch* groups, looked back nostalgically to a Germany of small towns and villages. Their economic values were appropriately *bürgerlich*, and they were high in their praise of individual thrift and hard work. The Nazi economic constituency, then, resided in the small entrepreneurs and salaried workers whose savings and industriousness were dissipated in Weimar's capitalist vicissitudes. The Twenty-Five Points, Nazism's program of 1920, offered them protection within a *Ständestaat*. As chambers of professions or estates, *Stände* recalled the medieval guilds which, having once been an obstacle to the initial rise of capitalism, were proposed as a shield against exploitative capitalism in the twentieth century. The suggestion of a return to a preindustrial past was a typical *völkisch* flight of fancy, but at the same time it had an enormous appeal to the socially concerned elements in the Nazi party. An ideological mentor was Othmar Spann, a Viennese sociologist who devoted himself to updating *völkisch* theories of a *Ständestaat* for use in the modern world. During the 1920s, a regular clique of Nazi corporativists formed around the Strasser brothers, Gottfried Feder who first opened Hitler's eyes to "interest slavery," and Walther Darré whose anticapitalist bias was evident in the title of his book, *The Peasantry as the Life Source of the Nordic Race* (1929).

Unfortunately, Hitler himself never took these ideas seriously, finding them useful only as propaganda. Moreover, the legal and national revolution by which Nazism established itself required the cooperation of Germany's industrialists and bankers. As soon as Hitler became chancellor, therefore, the party word went out to stop the loose talk about breaking up the industrial cartels and department stores in favor of small businesses. A few months later the Führer laid it down: "We must not dismiss a businessman if he is a good businessman, even if he is not yet a National Socialist; and especially if the National Socialist who is to take his place knows nothing about business." Nor was a *Ständestaat* about to be created. Some idealists hoped that the Nazi Labor Front might be the cornerstone of a corporative edifice, but were disabused by Ley, the Front's narrow-minded director: "I feel called upon to take issue with the idea of organization by estates as it is found in Professor Spann's teachings, in the Italian corporative system, in the Austrian estates system, and in the demand for 'organic construction' found in the twenty-fifth point of the National Socialist program."

Simply put, the notion of a *Ständestaat*, in which the component estates enjoyed some autonomy, ran afoul of *Gleichschaltung* and the Nazi drive for totalitarian conformity. In consequence, the German corporativists went into speedy decline. Darré was made minister of agriculture in 1933, but he was never in Hitler's inner circle and was given no chance to implement his pet scheme for the reduction of interest on rural debts to 2 percent. Feder became an undersecretary in the Ministry of Economy and Trade, but was always firmly controlled by his superiors who were undisguised representatives of big business. And, of course, the blood purge of June 30, 1934, was aimed explicitly at any form of socioeconomic radicalism in the guise of a "second revolution." Then, in the next two years, Hitler stepped up the pace of German rearmament and, for this purpose, found the monopolistic structure of heavy industry a great convenience. Indeed, under Nazism, the German economy as a whole grew more rather than less centralized and restrictive. In 1937 a new law dissolved all corporations with capital under $40,000 and required capitalization of at least $2 million for the establishment of any corporation in the future. The small shopkeepers and honest artisans, who formerly aroused Nazi solicitude, were left materially worse off than ever. "Middle-class socialism" in Nazi Germany proved a mirage.

All this was highly satisfactory to Germany's big businessmen. On the other hand, they were shortly left in no doubt that their old authority in the national economy was finished. The test case involved rearmament and the role of Dr. Hjalmar Schacht, who was well qualified to speak for German financial and industrial interests. As president of the Reichsbank, he had been responsible for the stabilization of the German currency after the inflation of 1923, although he had resigned in 1930 in protest against the Young Plan. One of the businessmen who jumped on the Nazi bandwagon in 1931–32, he was rewarded in 1933 with the Reichsbank presidency again and, the next year, with the post of minister of economics. In the latter capacity, Schacht was charged specifically by Hitler with Germany's economic preparations for war. Schacht had no objection to rearmament, and devised a system of "Mefo" bills discounted by the Reichsbank expressly for the payment of the arms makers. But with Hitler's announcement of open rearmament in March 1935, Schacht, speaking on behalf of the German business community, remonstrated with increasing frequency at the distortions that rearmament was introducing into the economy. In particular, he decried the waste of Germany's foreign exchange resources and of raw materials at home; he was skeptical of Nazi dreams of using ersatz products and achieving national autarchy; and he forecast inflation and possibly state bankruptcy. Hitler's rejoinder was to appoint Göring, who was utterly ignorant of economic matters, plenipotentiary for a four-year plan which was to complete rearmament at any cost by 1940. For a time Schacht tried to cooperate with Göring, hoping that Göring might restrain Hitler, but it was a forlorn hope. By the end of 1937, Schacht insisted on resigning as minister of economics. Hitler was reluctant to let him go, for Schacht had won a reputation as the "economic wizard" behind German prosperity on two occasions—first in the Locarno era and then under Nazism itself. As replacement, Hitler chose another businessman who had supported him before 1933 —Walther Funk. But Göring continued to ride roughshod over all comers, and Funk's impotence was a token of the entire business community's subservience.

What the Schacht affair revealed was that Hitler was impervious to economic arguments. Ideology and politics were the only necessities he knew. His answer, such as it was, to Schacht's alarm was political— rearmament would pave the way for the acquisition of German *Lebensraum* which, in turn, would assure prosperity. German businessmen were required to set aside their principles of sound economic management and to trust in historical destiny as interpreted by the Führer. Regardless of their inner convictions, they felt compelled to obey lest Hitler take industrial and financial concerns out of private hands and break up the complex of monopolies. Thus, Hitler was enabled to establish what Franz Neumann has called a "command economy," reminiscent of Germany under blockade in World War I, by which the state assumed paramount jurisdiction over economic affairs.

In the final analysis, though, Hitler could not regard his mastery of the pre-1933 power brokers as complete without the submission of the army officer corps. By tradition, the military constituted the authentic voice of old-world German conservatism. Hitler had been forced to cultivate them in order to obtain the chancellorship, and he had appeased them further by destroying the SA in June 1934. His reward came in August when, on succeeding Hindenburg as German president, he also became the nation's supreme commander in chief. In addition, he was able to secure from all ranks of the *Reichswehr* an oath of allegiance, not to the state, but to himself personally: "I swear by God this holy oath: I will render unconditional obedience to the Führer of the German Reich and People (*Volk*), Adolf Hitler, the Supreme

Commander of the Armed Forces, and will be ready, as a brave soldier, to stake my life at any time for this oath." In 1935, soon after the announcement of conscription and general rearmament, Germany's armed services were designated the Wehrmacht. By this change the army was theoretically incorporated into a larger command under the Führer— a Hitlerian hint that a new era in German civil-military relations was in the offing. Yet the officer corps appeared oblivious of any threat to their prerogatives. They queried the efficacy of the Nazi rearmament plans and began to oppose Hitler's adventurous foreign policy on the grounds of Germany's continued military weakness. Like Schacht and the big businessmen, the generals conceived it their duty to interpose their experience and caution in the way of Nazism's madcap schemes.

Hitler delayed moving against the army until the new year 1938, either because he was daunted by the officer corps' prestige or else because a favorable moment did not present itself sooner. His opportunity finally arose out of Field Marshal von Blomberg's second marriage, a ceremony graced by the presence of Hitler and Göring. Immediately, rumors began to fly, and the Berlin police discovered a dossier proving that the bride had once been a registered prostitute and had been convicted of posing for pornographic photographs. Blomberg was apparently unaware of his new wife's background, but his indiscretion contravened the officers' code of honor. Hitler, embarrassed at having attended the wedding, was furious with the field marshal. Therefore, Blomberg had no choice but to resign. The important question now posed was who was to take his place, for Blomberg since 1935 had been both minister of war and commander in chief of the Wehrmacht, subordinate only to the Führer who was supreme commander. His natural successor was General Werner von Fritsch, commander in chief of the army and, much more than the pliant Blomberg, the true spokesman of the old, autonomous officer class. At this moment, Göring, who aspired to Blomberg's posts, and Himmler, whose hatred of the aristocratic army officers knew no bounds, came into the open. It is entirely possible they had been orchestrating the Blomberg affair all along; now, they produced evidence to suggest that Fritsch was homosexual. The allegation was quite false, being based on the perjury of a paid informer and the file of a retired cavalry officer with the analogous name of Frisch. But it served to force Fritsch's resignation and further enrage Hitler against the whole officer corps.

The outcome was that Hitler made a clean sweep of the troublesome generals. He himself assumed Blomberg's post of Wehrmacht commander in chief and abolished the office of war minister. Instead of the latter, he created a special High Command of the Armed Forces, *Oberkommando der Wehrmacht*, and as its chief of staff appointed one of the least independent and most sycophantic of army officers, General Wilhelm Keitel. In Fritsch's place as commander in chief of the army, Hitler chose Walther von Brauchitsch who was *persona grata* to the officer corps but not a strong character; also he was on the point of divorcing his wife which, after the Blomberg case, left him vulnerable to Nazi blackmail. Then, asserting himself still more, Hitler ordered the retirement of sixteen senior generals and transferred forty-four others to different commands. By no accident, these included the most outspoken and least Nazified officers. On top of everything, Göring, who was disappointed at not succeeding Blomberg, was compensated by promotion to field marshal with seniority over all other commanders in chief.

Faced with this assault, some of the military considered a *Putsch* against Hitler and looked to Fritsch for leadership. But Fritsch preferred to await the result of a court of inquiry into the homosexuality charge, which he and his fellow officers had demanded. He was duly exonerated, but by the time the court produced its verdict on March 18, 1938, Hitler had fabricated an Austro-German Anschluss. This raised the Führer's popularity to new heights, and the generals did not dare act. Several times in the next few years, the officer corps was to toy with the idea of using force to overthrow Hitler, but not until the tide turned against Germany in World War II would it be brought to make the actual attempt. In the meantime, the army chiefs were forced to keep their qualms about Nazism to themselves. In private, the professional military might continue to make snobbish jokes about Hitler's humble beginnings and to express indignation at the growing pretensions of the SS. But outwardly, they conformed to the Nazi pattern. After all, the officer corps were patriots and, by 1938, the only way to serve Germany apparently was to serve Hitler.

The taming of the army signified more than a Nazi victory over the generals. To begin with, it sealed Hitler's control over all of Germany's armed services, for both the navy and the air force, having been dismantled under the Treaty of Versailles, were rebuilt in the 1930s as Nazi creations. More important, Hitler recognized that the Blomberg-Fritsch scandals gave him the opportunity to move against the old conservative establishment in its civilian as well as its military guise. Consequently, at the cabinet meeting on February 4, 1938, when Hitler disclosed the new arrangements for the Wehrmacht following the resignations of Blomberg and Fritsch, he also announced the departure of several aristocratic career diplomats. Like the generals, Germany's foreign ministry officials in 1936–37 had begun to murmur at Hitler's hazardous diplomacy. The most eminent casualty was the foreign minister himself, Baron von Neurath, whom Hindenburg had imposed on Hitler in 1933 as a brake on Nazi impetuosity. His replacement was Joachim von Ribbentrop, a veteran of World War I and former wine salesman who had joined the Nazi party only in 1932, after which he had risen high in Hitler's esteem by slavishly copying the Führer's every prejudice. For some years before 1938, he had been intriguing to efface the German foreign ministry and oust Neurath. Another familiar conservative figure from the past affected by the attack on the diplomatic corps was Franz von Papen. After his narrow escape on the Night of the Long Knives, Papen had been sufficiently restored to Hitler's favor to be appointed to the sensitive position of German plenipotentiary in Vienna. Now, on February 4, he was recalled without explanation. Furthermore, the cabinet meeting which rubber-stamped all the resignations, dismissals, and reassignments turned out to be the last Hitler ever bothered to call.

February 4, 1938, marked the consummation of Hitler's thrust for unconditional dictatorial power. In just five years since taking office, Hitler had overcome in relentless sequence every potential and actual source of opposition. Politically, the presidential and parliamentary forms of the Weimar Republic were kept up, but were adapted to the dictatorship. The old balance between president and chancellor vanished with Hitler's occupancy of the two offices. The Reichstag met infrequently after 1933 and listened to Hitler's speeches instead of debating, while its main legislative function became to reconfirm every fourth year the Enabling Act which authorized Hitler to promulgate his own laws. By the Führer's fiat, Gleichschaltung produced administrative uniformity. Police power and terror destroyed the fragmented anti-Nazi Left, and the Röhm purge removed any challenge from within the Nazi party. Next, between 1936 and 1938, Hitler brought to heel the autonomous cliques and interest groups which had carried such weight in both Wilhelmine and Weimar Germany. Undeniably, some factions among the military and the clergy still harbored reservations about Nazism, but this was a trifling deficiency when set against the huge store of popularity among ordinary Germans that accrued to Hitler from his early triumphs over unemployment and in foreign affairs. Needless to say, the vast and expensive Nazi propaganda machine was adept at nurturing this groundswell of approval. And in the last resort, it was mass support which made the Nazi dictatorship unique, omnipotent, and the mirror of twentieth-century totalitarianism.

## Back to the *Volk*

Yet the cardinal question about Nazism remains to be answered: For what purpose was all this power amassed? In response, the historiography of Nazism has progressed gradually over two generations toward a broad consensus. Old interpretations of Nazism—as a tool of monopoly capitalism or as an embodiment of Prussian militarism or simply as a manifestation of Hitler's personal lust for power—have been, if not completely discredited, at least severely eroded. By and large, they were products of the passions of the Nazi era itself. In their place, during the last decade or so, has emerged a general recognition of Nazism as fundamentally a revulsion against the modern world coupled with a denial of all its values. A. J. Nicholls sums it up neatly: "The [Nazi] ideas amounted to a rejection of the Enlightenment of the eighteenth century on the political plane and the industrialization of the nineteenth century on the economic plane" ("Germany," in *European Fascism* [1968]). Gregor Strasser had once put it: "Nazism is the opposite of what exists today." This was the attitude of "cultural Luddites" (Fritz Stern's phrase). Hitler's intent was revolutionary but in a retrograde sense; he belonged in that lengthy procession of German romantics whose solution to current problems was to fly back to a Peter Pan age of lost innocence. The Nazis' ambition was nothing less than to bring back to life a golden era from the past, "which would rid them at one blow of all perplexities afflicting the modern world: capitalism, communism, liberalism, democracy, plutocracy, newspapers, elections, big-city life—the whole complex rigmarole of contemporary urban civilization" (G. Lichtheim, *The Concept of Ideology* [1967]). It was a dream culled right from Hitler's personal infantilism, but the infantilism was shared by myriad other Germans. Hitler was, in E. Nolte's words, "the medium who communicated to the masses their own deeply buried spirit."

In one respect, the search for a premodern Arcadia was over before it began. There was no going back on the industrialization of Germany. The Nazis regularly decried *die Landflucht* (flight from the land), but in reality the drift to the cities quickened after 1933. Moreover, we have seen how, once in power, the Nazis forgot their previous attachment to the antique principles of guild corporativism and a Ständestaat and how the small businessmen of the Mittelstand were sacrificed to Germany's industrial giants. The crux of the matter was that Hitler required a highly industrialized and urbanized society to sustain rearmament and an efficient war machine. Beyond Germany's frontiers it might be possible to implement some fantasies of village life, but to conquer territory for such experimentation, it was necessary for Germany to become more than ever a modern, mechanized power. Many high-ranking Nazis, it was observed, evinced a childlike fascination with the products of the assembly line—airplanes, cars, gadgets of all kinds. The possession of mechanical objects confirmed their power but signified no commitment to the spiritual values of technocracy.

Unable to take Germany out of the twentieth century materially, the Nazis concentrated instead on putting the clock back intellectually. "Those who see in National Socialism nothing more than a political movement," said Hitler, "know scarcely anything of it. It is more even than a religion: it is the will to create mankind anew." The very essence of Nazism resided in this objective of "a revolution of attitudes and feeling" ("Revolution der Gesinnung"). At the core of this revolution was a profound contempt for human intelligence. Of the search for truth by argument and counterargument, Hitler once remarked: "The intellectuals run this way and that, like hens in a poultry yard. With them it is impossible to make history." Significantly, none of Nazism's tame intellectuals, such as Rosenberg or Feder, was given much political power. The Nazi opinion of the spirit of free inquiry was further reflected in public book-burning ceremonies held throughout Germany after 1933.

In sum, the Nazis were determined to break with the tradition of scientific rationalism which had dominated most of Europe since the Renaissance or at least the eighteenth-century Enlightenment. Nolte uses the term "antitranscendental" to imply a repudiation of the very idea of progress. That man could achieve growth by application of his reasoning faculties was absolute anathema to the Nazis. In lieu of reason, they venerated instinct for, as Hitler said, "from instinct comes faith." For Nazis, as for religious saints, truth was an absolute to be perceived by revelation, a visceral not a cerebral experience. In a parody of Nietzsche, they claimed to be supermen whose instincts were in-

Nazism was dedicated to changing
Germany's whole cultural identity.
Hence, the refutation of humane and
rational values in the burning of "un-
German" books, 1933, (above). Decadent
modernist art, such as Paul Klee's Around
the Fish (below), was banned, its
place taken by Nazi-approved art—for
example, the statue erected in Berlin of
an Aryan hero slaying the dragon of
Judaism (left).

fallible. Many Nazis were well aware that by discarding intellectuality in favor of feeling they were reverting to a sort of animal primitivism. Hitler more than once was heard to glory in the reputation of barbarian. One Nazi who, in 1935, left the party when its primitive bias became too obvious to ignore was the conservative Hermann Rauschning. His discovery of the beast in Nazism made his published works by far the most perceptive contemporary analysis of the Nazi phenomenon. The titles of the American editions of his best-known books, *The Revolution of Nihilism* (1939) and *The Voice of Destruction* (1940), convey perfectly the sense of violently regressive anti-intellectualism which suffused Nazism.

The key to Nazism's revolution of the spirit was the *Volk*. While liberalism and socialism were products of the age of reason, the cult of the *Volk* came from the mainstream of irrational German romanticism. "The main plank in the National Socialist program," declaimed Hitler in 1937, "is to abolish the liberal concept of the individual and the Marxist concept of humanity, and to substitute for them the *Volk* community, rooted in the soil and united by the bond of its common blood." Hitler's ideal society owed nothing to intellectually conceived constitutions and man-made laws. The bond which held the *Volk* together was mystical, and the invocation of *Blut und Boden* (blood and soil) recalled the instinctual mores of the primeval tribe. To live in a *völkisch* society meant, in a phrase the Nazis took over from the Italian Gentile and popularized, "to think with the blood." The Nazis exploited the evocative connotations of the *Volk* to the utmost, making the word one of the commonest in their vocabulary. The Nazi newspaper was the *Völkischer Beobachter*, the court which dispensed Nazi justice the *Volksgericht*, and Nazi-approved culture *Volkkultur*. The Nazis liked to call their fellow Germans *Volksgenossen*, and when, in 1938, the state resolved to subsidize a cheap car for the ordinary German, it had to be christened a *Volkswagen*.

In Nazi theory, the *Volk*, until its cohesion was destroyed by the pursuit of commercial self-interest and the industrial class war, had led a contented existence. Of course, the historical idyll of *völkisch* bliss was a romantic myth, popularized by Wagnerian operas and Germanic sagas so admired by Hitler. However, as far as the Führer envisaged a definite bygone era to re-create, his preference seemed to be for feudal times. In *Mein Kampf* he wrote with reference to the Teutonic knights: "We take up where we broke off six centuries ago."

Later he caused himself to be painted in medieval knight's armor. The fanatical Himmler went one better by imagining himself to be the reincarnation of the tenth-century Saxon warrior king, Henry the Fowler. In an imaginative article, "Feudal Aspects of National Socialism," *American Political Science Review* (1960), Robert Koehl has compiled a whole series of resemblances between feudalism and the Nazi life style. For instance, he compares Hitler's control over the Nazi party bosses to that of a feudal monarch over his barons. In Nazism's administrative jungle, officeholders competed among themselves, each one trying to extend his own private fief, while the Führer's role was to adjudicate the disputes if they endangered the security of the Reich. Hitler's dispensation was obeyed blindly, not so much because of his constitutional position, but because of personal fealty. In Nazi Germany, as in feudal societies, great importance was attached to the taking of oaths, especially of personal allegiance to the leader. The bond thus created was not legal and artificial but deep and mysterious. This sort of relationship was epitomized in the motto of the SS: "Meine Ehre heisst Treue," literally "My honor is called loyalty." Indeed, the SS was the cynosure of Nazi neofeudalism. From its birth as the Führer's bodyguard, the SS was an elite body charged with tasks which required maximum dedication to the cause—most notoriously, running the concentration camps. Candidates for the SS had to meet strict eugenic standards, the corps being regarded as the flower of the *Volk*—the Nazi equivalent of medieval chivalry. Lastly, the Nazi party rallies—particularly those held each September in Nuremberg, a city heavy with medieval symbolism—recalled the meetings of feudal *comitati*. The staging seemed to owe a good deal to Wagner's celebration of ancient rites at his Bayreuth opera house. Waving banners, esoteric uniforms, torchlight processions produced the atmosphere of an antique barbarian ceremony. The party members drawn up in a solid mass on the floor of the arena constituted a physical expression of brotherhood. Only the Führer was spotlighted high above the throng, an overlord incarnate.

Nazi party membership was the badge of a new German aristocracy; the rest of the Germans existed on a lower plane. Yet the Nazi ideological revolution was intended to permeate all social strata. Whereas party members were deemed more or less secure in their beliefs, the German masses—for whom Hitler often evinced deep contempt—had to be indoctrinated continually through the mass media and occasionally subjected to brute force before seeing the light. Herein lay the reason for Hitler's accumulation of absolute power after 1933; it was in order to transform the mind of a whole people.

As far as the German working class was concerned, the Nazi revolution was the exact obverse of that proposed by the Marxists. While the Marxist demand was for an end to private property as a prerequisite to the moral reformation of society, the Nazis gave absolute priority to a spiritual revolution, after which economic problems would take care of themselves. Hitler, as we have already seen, had no interest in the redistribution of wealth for its own sake. In consequence, the German worker, although no longer haunted by unemployment under Nazism, was by no means materially well off. Between 1932 and 1938, the workers' share of the national income fell from 56.9 to 53.6 percent and, at the outbreak of World War II, his standard of living was substantially below that of his employed counterpart in Great Britain and North America. As a sop to the proletariat, an organization, Strength Through Joy, was created under the auspices of the Labor Front. Part of its function was to supply the workers with cheap day trips, bargain holidays and cruises, and cut-rate tickets for theaters and concerts. Actually, the workers paid for their pleasures through dues to the Labor Front, which never published its accounts and was burdened with a flock of sinecurists who grossly inflated administrative costs. Nonetheless, according to the eyewitness account of the American reporter, William Shirer, the ordinary German seemed to enjoy his regimented leisure. On the other hand, the circuses provided by Strength Through Joy were peripheral to its main object, which was to inculcate a *völkisch* spirit in the working class. "We had to divert the attention of the masses from material to moral values," Dr. Ley explained. "It is more important to feed the souls of men than their stomachs." Accordingly, the average German was encouraged to expect an egalitarian revolution, not in socialist terms, but in terms of the *Volk*. "Why need we trouble to socialize banks and factories?" asked Hitler. "We socialize human beings." As *Gleichschaltung* had indicated, Nazi equality resided in a common sense of identity and purpose. The notion is defined in David Schoenbaum's perceptive book, *Hitler's Social Revolution* (1966):

> With this went a campaign for egalitarianism intended not so much to change existing class relations, a function of profession and education, as to change status, the self-image, the state of mind. The employer was

to remain an employer, and the worker a worker. But these were intended
to be occupational designations and nothing more. Under National Socialism the basic determinant of status was common membership in the
German people or variously the German "race," not class, education, or
occupation. This was expressed in the concept of the *Volksgemeinschaft*
which transcended all social differences.

Vast energies and monies were expended on the task of *völkisch*
proselytization. Z. A. B. Zeman in his *Nazi Propaganda* (1964) has
catalogued the ramifications of Goebbels's vast propaganda empire. Of
all European fascists, the Nazis best appreciated the propaganda use to
which modern technology might be put. The airplane was still far
from a commonplace machine, and Hitler's arrival by plane at Nazi
meetings was calculated to lend an air of adventure and urgency to the
occasion. The Führer's voice, trained through years of public oratory,
was capable of transporting hearers, and it was discovered that the
charisma was not lost on the radio listener in his own living room.
Hitler believed that audience resistance was at its lowest after a day's
work and dinner, so he usually broadcast well on in the evening. Goebbels was intrigued by the persuasive possibilities of film, and German
studios were instructed to incorporate *völkisch* themes into their
movies. The popular historical film *Jew Suss*, released in 1940, was
compulsory viewing for German troops, and was known to provoke
adolescents to acts of anti-Semitic violence. Often, official intervention
gave rise to excruciatingly bad movies which were even hissed in the
cinema. But sometimes, when Goebbels secured the services of professional filmmakers to compose outright propaganda films, the outcome could be spectacular. The most famous achievements of this type
were Leni Riefenstahl's *Triumph of the Will*, shot mostly at the
Nuremberg party rally of 1934, and her *Olympiad*, based on the Olym-
pic Games in Berlin two years later. Seen today, these films still carry
a powerful emotional punch. The paradox in all this is that, while the
Nazis were exploiting the sophisticated apparatus of the modern mass
media, their message was of a reversion to *völkisch*, antimodern values.
   The Nazi aversion to modernity had some strange consequences in
the cultural field. Artistic self-indulgence was regarded as an offshoot
of the archenemy—individualistic liberalism. The Nazis were especially
withering about Germany's experimental writers, painters, architects,
and musicians who had flourished in Weimar's permissive atmosphere,
making Berlin the avant-garde capital of Europe. After 1933, of course,

their works were banned in Germany as a first shot in the war against "cultural bolshevism." But in 1937 in an interesting departure from censorship, the Nazi government tried to hold modern art up to public ridicule by mounting an Exhibition of Degenerate Art in Munich. Billed as a dire warning of Jewish subversion of time-honored artistic precepts, it featured the abstract and symbolic designs of such painters as Kandinsky and Kokoschka, Chagall and Mondrian. Thousands visited the display, but how many came to admire and how many to jeer will never be known. In reaction to the alleged decadence of modern art, Nazi taste gloried in the worst excesses of nineteenth-century bourgeois culture—in stiff, stylized representation, in the romantic heroic gesture, in the pretty and the sentimental. This last trait contrasted strangely with Nazi ruthlessness, but many Nazi leaders could and did grow quite maudlin over small children and pet animals.

Like everything else in Nazism, the cultural tone was set by the Führer. As an artist *manqué*, he devoted much of his time in the 1930s to supervising the nation's cultural diet. His attention turned increasingly to architecture. He greatly admired the work of Paul Troost whom he commissioned to build a ponderous, neoclassical House of German Art in Munich, where the Nazis displayed their Aryan answer to degenerate art. In the mid-thirties, Hitler made a special favorite of a rising architect, Albert Speer, with whom he drew up elaborate plans for rebuilding Germany's major cities; Linz, near his birthplace in Austria, was to become a model project. One of Hitler's main concerns, so Speer assures us in his *Inside the Third Reich* (1970), was that the buildings of the Third Reich be solid enough so that their ruins, like those of classical antiquity, would still be standing two millennia later. Hence, Nazi architecture was grandiose and substantial, typified by Speer's own brooding Reichschancellery in Berlin.

The other, prettified side of Nazi culture was mirrored in Hitler's personal life style in his mountaintop villa at Berchtesgaden. Before World War II, Hitler spent most of his leisure in the *ménage* he established there with his mistress, Eva Braun, an attractive but undistinguished blonde whose tastes ran to thick pile carpets and bowls of fresh flowers in every room, plenty of candy and whipped cream, and much reading of romantic novels. Hitler relished this small-minded existence, daydreamed as he gazed over the Alps, and sat up late listening to records of Viennese light operas or watching inferior Hollywood movies (many of which were banned in Germany) in his private cinema. The cultural stamp which Hitler placed on Nazism can be equated with middle-class Philistinism. The Führer found it easier to reward his supporters of the *Mittelstand* in cultural than in economic matters. In another sense, however, the banality and conservatism of Nazi culture must be regarded as aberrant traits, for they disguise— indeed they hid from many Germans at the time—the innate radical- ism in Nazism.

How successful, then, were the Nazis in converting all Germans to their way of thinking—or, more properly, feeling? It is difficult to gen- eralize, except perhaps on a comparative basis. The middle classes ap- peared to accept Nazism more wholeheartedly than the German proletariat, whose social democratic and communist memories were never completely swept away. It also seems safe to say that the impact of Nazi preaching was greatest among the younger generation. Elder and middle-aged Germans tended to welcome Nazism for the security it bestowed and for its restoration of familiar cultural values, but whether they really believed the full range of *völkisch* conceits that every Ger- man was expected to subscribe to must be doubted. By contrast, young Germany in large numbers was completely captivated. Germany's au- thoritarian educational system lent itself to the instillation of dogma, although, as in Fascist Italy, the major indoctrination occurred outside the schools.

Youth clubs were numerous in Germany long before Hitler. After 1933 they were gobbled up in the process of *Gleichschaltung*, to be re- placed by the different sections of the Hitler Youth movement, which catered to age groups from six to eighteen. The Hitler Youth was built up by Baldur von Schirach, a handsome and fervent younger Nazi with few brains but a good organizing sense. By the new year 1939, enrollment reached nearly eight million, about two-thirds of those eli- gible, and in March the government decreed conscription of all boys into the Hitler Youth. Between the ages of fourteen and eighteen, the training received in the Hitler Youth was intensive: constant in- struction in *völkisch* lore and world politics intermixed with bouts of camping and mock soldiering. The Hitler Youth included branches for girls, notably the League of German Maidens, where young women learned that their prime duty was to bear healthy children for the greater glory of the Reich. For the most part, this injunction was framed within the context of family life; the Nazis, reacting against Weimar's relaxed sexual morality, extolled the old-fashioned, patri- archal German family. Nevertheless, some of the more fanatical Nazis recommended breeding out of wedlock by eugenically sound partners

*The Pied Piper and his children. Hitler gained many fervent young disciples through the brainwashing administered in the Hitler Youth.*

PICTORIAL PARADE/EPA NEWSPHOTO

in order to multiply the *Volk* in a hurry. This was called "donating a child to the Führer," and Himmler created the *Lebensborn* (Spring of Life), a foundation to look after the unwed mothers of his SS progeny.

Membership in the Hitler Youth was prerequisite for entry into special educational programs designed for the Nazi elite. Alongside the regular gymnasia were established "napolas" (*Nationalpolitische-Erziehungsanstalten*), incubators for top-ranking government and army personnel, and Adolf Hitler-*Schule*, which were to nurture future political leaders. The ideal young Nazi did not go on to a university. After some years of labor, military, and party service, between the ages of twenty-five and thirty, he might be sent the rounds of four medieval-sounding *Ordensburgen* (castles of the knightly order), where he indulged in more war games and physical training in a brutalizing, narrowly masculine environment. In actual fact, not many reached the *Ordensburgen* which usually operated at two-thirds capacity. But equally, few of the rising generation were left untouched by the *Revolution der Gesinnung*.

Between 1933 and 1945, there was never a hint of German mass resistance to the Nazi government. After six years of Goebbels's propaganda, the Führer led the nation into a war which was decidedly unwelcome to the generation that remembered the privations of the First World War. Yet, for the remaining six years of the Third Reich, the German people sustained the war effort with uncomplaining obedience. In the field German forces fought to the end with typical Prussian discipline in the very suburbs of Berlin. Younger troops, militarized and brainwashed since their days in the Hitler Youth, fought with an extra frenzy for their secular religion. The Germans' record in following Hitler blindly to destruction stands in sharp contrast to the lackadaisical, token support Italians accorded Mussolini when the going got rough. Plainly, Nazism responded to something in the German psyche and sprang out of a long *völkisch* tradition; Italian Fascism, in comparison, always seemed a veneer plastered on society from the outside or above. When it came to totalitarian control of the masses, the Führer was in another league from the Duce.

In Hitler's own view, Nazi society was stratified into four levels. First there was the fanatical Nazi aristocracy whose members moved in Hitler's personal circle; then there was the elite made up of the rest of the party whose embrace of Nazism presumably also arose out of an inner faith; next came the German masses who were kept loyal by the greatest propaganda exercise in history; and finally there were those who either would not or could not accept the Nazi ideology at all. This last, outcast group was far from unimportant, however, for it was in dealing with its enemies that Nazism found its fulfillment—and also starkly and shockingly divulged its inner reality. Hitler's penal system became a microcosm of Nazism.

The first of the infamous concentration camps were established soon after Hitler's accession to office to house the straightforward opponents of Nazism—leftist politicians and trade union leaders, outspoken journalists and intellectuals, recalcitrant clerics and the whole body of Jehovah's Witnesses who refused to comply with the remilitarization of Germany. Because these people could be expected to obstruct

Hitler's policies by either word or deed, their incarceration by a cold-blooded, absolute dictatorship was explicable. But much more significant, and with the passage of time more numerous, were those prisoners who had never taken a stand against Nazism nor had any intention of ever doing so. Theirs was a deeper crime—that of being unable by their very nature to belong to the *Volk;* they were "objective criminals." The Nazis had a pathological obsession with contamination; Hitler was a faddist and a vegetarian, and made a fetish of changing his clothes and washing his hands at every possible opportunity. Projected in political terms, this meant the regeneration of Germany by removing all those impure elements which had been poisoning the race by intermarriage and ordinary social intercourse. And so, the Nazi revolution to restore the lost world of the *Volk* came down to a permanent purge of non-Aryans—"a matter," as one Nazi official put it, "of political hygiene."

Since, anthropologically speaking, the Aryan people do not exist, it was not easy to say who belonged to the *Volk.* In the popular mind, there was an image of the ideal Aryan as tall, athletic, and fair-haired. This was so at variance with the appearance of almost all the Nazi bosses that it gave rise to the sardonic joke that the perfect Nazi was as slim as Göring (who was fat), as stalwart as Goebbels (who was small and lame), and as blond as Hitler (who had dark brown hair). Nor was the Nazi leadership ethnically pure according to its own lights; it has been aptly compared to "the racially hybrid product of an Alpine province." The truth was that anyone or any group was Aryan if the Führer said so, and the exigencies of World War II would transform Italians and Japanese into honorary Aryans. Aryanism was another example of a Sorelian myth used to whip a whole nation into action. But even if the Aryan *Volk* was mythical, this did not hinder the Nazis from swallowing the ideology whole and acting out their faith. The problem of definition was met by defining the Aryan concept negatively—by designating those beyond the pale of the *Volk.* Given the Nazi preoccupation with health, Germany's mental defectives were inevitably singled out; as early as 1933, the Nazis enacted that mental patients should be sterilized. The regime's further proposal for euthanasia aroused vocal criticism by the churches. Nevertheless, between 1939 and 1941, under cover of war, thousands of alleged mental defectives in hospitals and prisons were to perish in the first Nazi experiment in mass killing by gas. The same fate would befall the Gypsies who were condemned not only as defectives but as possessors of mixed blood. But, of course, the group most clearly delineated as contaminators of the *Volk* were the Jews.

Jews numbered under 1 percent of the total German population. Most were patriots, having been well represented in the German trenches between 1914 and 1918. Comprising a productive segment of the German middle class, their days as moneylenders to the European governments lay in the past; instead, they had become prominent in certain professions and the arts. The Jews in the Weimar Republic had an exceptionally high profile in the publishing world where they were usually associated with liberal or socialist concerns. In this lay a cause of Jewish offense, for the German Jew of the twentieth century was the embodiment of those tendencies in the modern world which stemmed from the Enlightenment and the revolutionary turmoil begun in 1789. As a liberal, he reflected the fact that the Jews were new-comers to society who owed their standing to nineteenth-century constitutional law and artificial codes of civil rights. As a socialist, the Jew betrayed himself as an argumentative intellectual and an inquisitive, restless rationalist. The Jewish spirit appeared to be the very negation of that of the primeval, natural *Volk* worshiped by the Nazis. Moreover, there was a further dimension to Nazi anti-Semitism. To the devotees of *The Protocols of the Elders of Zion*, the Jews were a self-contained radical clique engaged in a dastardly conspiracy for world domination. Yet, substitute Aryan for Jew, and this was precisely the Nazi design; the exclusive *Volk* under Hitler's guidance would inherit the earth. Who can say whether the Nazis did not unconsciously sublimate their worst fears about Jewry into their own ambitions? At any rate, the Nazis perceived the Jews as their rivals in the game of spiritual *Weltpolitik*. The Jews in the Third Reich, then, were singled out on two counts—as purveyors of modern heresies and as ideological counterconspirators. Above all, they were persecuted not because they were mere convenient scapegoats for Nazi bestiality, but because they were the symbolic antithesis of the true *Volk*.

Germany's Jews were in trouble from the moment Hitler became chancellor. Nazi storm troopers immediately went on a rampage of Jew-baiting. But largely out of deference to the scruples of President Hindenburg and Hitler's other conservative allies, the initial persecution was unofficial and disorganized. After Hindenburg's death, however, came a new phase marked, in September 1935, by the Nuremberg Laws named after the party rally where they were announced. There were two laws. One, "for the protection of German blood and German

The Nazi ambition to create (or recapture) a homogenous folk
community spelled trouble for racial aliens, notably the Jews. Here is
an illustration of early Nazi anti-Semitism: Leipzig's Jews in 1933
are forced to scrub the walls clean of the slogans of Nazisms' electoral
opponents.

honor," made it a crime for a Jew and a non-Jew to marry or to have
sexual relations. The other deprived Jews of German citizenship, reducing them to German "subjects" without any civic rights whatsoever.
This latter law exposed them to arbitrary police action at almost the
same moment that the police of Nazi Germany assumed a more fear-
some aspect than ever by coming under Himmler's direction. In 1936
Germany was host to the Olympics (in which, unfortunately for the
Nazis, the star was Jesse Owens, a black American), and in order not
to upset the foreign tourists, a curb was placed on overt acts of anti-
Semitism. The Jews remained vulnerable though, as was devastatingly
revealed in November 1938. On November 7 the third secretary of
the German embassy in Paris was assassinated by a Jewish exile from
Germany. Forty-eight hours later occurred the reprisal of *Kristallnacht*,
so called for the broken glass from Jewish shopwindows all over Germany, smashed during the riotous night of November 9 by Nazi storm
troopers and the police themselves. But the pogrom did not stop with
looting; Jewish homes and synagogues were burned, an indeterminate
number of Jews killed, thousands beaten up and arrested, and in de-

fiance of the Nuremberg Laws there were several cases of rape. The Nazi authorities, having staged *Kristallnacht,* administered only the mildest penalties to a few of the vandals who had got out of hand. Rather, the government was concerned about insurance claims. This economic problem was solved by the state confiscating four-fifths of the insurance benefits and preventing a repetition of the situation by forbidding Jews to own stores or factories. After 1938 decrees segregating the Jews piled up: they were barred from the legal and medical professions, although, in fact, they had been informally excluded from the professions since 1933; they were banned from certain streets and concert halls, from park benches and public transport. By the end of 1941, the Jews were deprived of their surviving property and, in order to mark them off definitively from the rest of the German population, were compelled to wear the yellow Star of David in public.

This onslaught was deliberately calculated to force the Jews to leave Germany and, after 1938, Austria as well. Under Heydrich, Himmler's deputy, an SS Office for Jewish Emigration was set up and large sums for exit visas were extracted from wealthy Jews. By 1941, when emigration came to a halt, perhaps as many as half a million German and Austrian Jews had fled into exile. A high proportion were intellectuals and artists who, settling mostly in Great Britain and the United States, injected a new vitality into the academic and artistic life of those countries. Of the Jews who stayed behind, many were too poor to meet the Nazi price for an exit permit, while others simply failed to comprehend the full viciousness of Nazi anti-Semitism until too late. Succeeding only partially in "kicking the Jew out of Germany" (Heydrich's phrase), the Nazis cast about for other means of removing the Jewish "canker" from the *Volk.* The anti-Semitic legislation described above isolated the Jew but left his physical presence in society. Medieval ghettos, which many Nazis favored, were difficult to create in a modern city. By far the easiest thing was to pack the Jews off to the concentration camps. This is what happened increasingly after 1938; in the wake of *Kristallnacht* alone, 25,000 Jews were dispatched to the camps.

Ostensibly, the inmates of the concentration camps were engaged in hard labor, but the idea of securing a work load from the prisoners was always subservient to the task of degrading them. The most sadistic personnel of the SS were seconded to the *Totenkopfverbände* (Death's Head units) in charge of the camps in order to visit every conceivable humiliation and savagery on beings who were officially designated as inferior. Even among the despised, however, there were gradations:

the SS guards treated the common criminals least harshly; they vented more spite on the political prisoners; but their real venom was reserved for those incarcerated on racial grounds. As a result, the death rate among the Jews was always disproportionately high, arising out of starvation, brutality, and plain murder. Yet withal, before 1941, there were no Nazi death camps per se. Nor before that date is there any evidence that Hitler was *consciously* considering the systematic elimination of the Jews by genocide. On the other hand, human life was accounted so cheaply in the concentration camps from the start that mass murder was never an incredible prospect in that environment. Still more ominous was the fact that the anti-Semitism of Hitler and his Nazi toadies went beyond normal *völkisch* prejudice. Hitler was frighteningly sincere in his malevolent opinion of the Jew—"the ferment of decomposition in peoples" was his favorite phrase. Extermination of the Jews was implicit in his megalomania for racial purity. After all, Hitler was, in A. J. P. Taylor's words, "a great literalist." While other anti-Semites talked loosely about "elimination" and "eradication" of the Jews without ever contemplating the reality, Hitler, confident of his own predestination, was of a nature to turn the logic of his words into the act of genocide with scarcely a pause for reflection.

## Nazi-Fascist Distinctions

Racism and anti-Semitism were central to the Nazi *Weltanschauung*. More than anything else, these *völkisch* features set Nazism apart from Italian Fascism. The Fascists in Italy did not display the sort of commitment to an omniscient ideology that the Nazis gave to race. The differential in conviction goes some way toward explaining why and how Nazism was much more successful in building a genuinely totalitarian system. But this is not to say that Italian Fascism lacked any ideological content—far from it. Mussolini did arrive, albeit in halting fashion, at corporative economics as a theoretical guideline for reorganizing Italian society. Corporativism commended the Italian style of fascism to many idealists at home and abroad, and so came to serve as an adequate doctrine for Mussolini's regime. In ideological terms, corporativism was the rough Italian counterpart of Nazi racism. On the other hand, Nazism in its early days called itself corporativist, while Fascist Italy after the mid-1930s began to exhibit some racist traits. Nevertheless, a closer examination of Nazi corporativism and racism in

Fascist Italy, respectively, reveals more clearly than ever the great ideological divide between Hitler and Mussolini.

Nazi corporativism in its origins and nature was crucially different from the Mussolinian version. For the Nazis, corporativism was equated with a medieval *Ständestaat*, and thus represented another facet of that emotional Nazi hankering after a golden age long ago. In contrast, Fascist Italian corporativism owed much to syndicalist socialism of the late nineteenth century and something to modern Catholicism. Mussolini's corporativism was no reversion to a *völkisch* past, but rationally conceived as a novel answer to current problems. Then, it must be doubted whether Hitler himself was ever seriously attached to corporative ideals, even those derived from medieval guilds. He never made the slightest gesture toward implementing Nazi corporativism and, after January 1933, a *Ständestaat* quickly vanished from the realm of Nazi propaganda. On the other hand, in Fascist Italy a corporative state did come into existence, and although its institutions floundered amid corruption and ineptitude, corporative ideas remained official dogma to the end.

As for racism in Fascist Italy, we have seen earlier how domestic reform and corporativism ultimately had to take a back seat to the search for glory overseas. In this context, it might be suggested that in his drive for colonies Mussolini manifested his own form of racism with East Africa serving as Italy's *Lebensraum*. Undoubtedly, Fascist Italy's descent on Ethiopia in 1935 was motivated in part by a sense of racial superiority over the black African state. But, then, so was every European colonial conquest in the age of New Imperialism to which the Italo-Ethiopian quarrel belonged. Mussolini shared the general European arrogance toward the nonwhite world, but this was not at all the same thing as Hitler's singular racial dementia. Moreover, to rationalize Italy's foreign and colonial expansion in the 1930s, the Duce often invoked the model of the classical Roman Empire. Yet, this was a distinctly nonracial cosmopolitan ideal, and conjured up a society based on a strict legal code rather than a lawless totalitarian anarchy. "The swastika," as Nolte puts it, "did not, like the lictors' bundle, recall a remote but nevertheless still tangible historical era." The Third Rome and the Third Reich might be alike in nomenclature, but they differed fundamentally in their historical inspiration.

Mussolini appeared to take a more definite step back toward barbarism in 1938 when he introduced anti-Semitic legislation into Italy. Yet his pristine attitude to the *furor teutonicus* about the Jews had been one of derision. A typical remark was that made in 1934 to Rabbi Nahum Goldmann and recalled in his *Memories* (1969): "I know Herr Hitler. He is an idiot. . . . You are much stronger than Herr Hitler. When there's no trace left of Hitler, the Jews will still be a great people." The introduction of anti-Semitism into Italy, historically tolerant of Jews, came as a shock. Most Italians regarded it as completely out of character and as a reflection of Hitler's growing diplomatic domination of Mussolini. Once the Rome-Berlin Axis was invented and the Austro-German Anschluss put the Wehrmacht on Italy's northern frontier, Italian Fascism began to surrender to the baleful influence of Nazi Germany in domestic as well as foreign policy. It was a fate to be forced on several European fascist movements with the expansion of the Nazi empire during the Second World War. In the meantime the papacy protested Mussolini's anti-Semitic laws, and many Fascist officials, to their credit, executed them in a most perfunctory manner. The fate of Italy's Jewish population of some 50,000 became precarious but not yet intolerable. The situation is sensitively depicted in Giorgio Bassani's *Garden of the Finzi-Continis* (1965). In this novel the shrinking area of Jewish security is symbolized by the garden into which a well-to-do Jewish family retreats for comfort after 1938.

To summarize, Mussolinian anti-Semitism was a foreign element introduced into Italian Fascism from without and recognized as such by most Italians. It cannot be contended that the Duce was driven onward by diabolical visions of "secret enemies" within and Zionist plots for world domination. The only "conspiracy" he pledged himself to overthrow was a Freemasonic one. But merely to state Mussolini's animus against his one-time Masonic friends in the same breath as Hitler's frenzy against the Jews is to reveal the gulf between Duce and Führer. The Freemasons were chastised as old-fashioned, anticlerical liberals, not as an irreconcilably alien species. Until perverted by the pull of empire and too close an association with National Socialism, the indigenous and distinctive characteristic of Fascist Italy had been corporative. By hewing to a corporative line, Italian Fascism was enabled to keep up appearances as an enlightened movement, the heir to nineteenth-century tendencies. Indeed, the ties with the recent past were proudly admitted. As the Mussolini-Gentile definition of Fascism in the *Enciclopedia italiana* put it:

The Fascist negation of Socialism, Democracy, Liberalism should not, however, be interpreted as implying a desire to drive the world backwards to positions occupied prior to 1789.

Fascism uses in its construction whatever elements in the Liberal, Socialist, or Democratic doctrines still have a living value.

No doctrine has ever been born completely new, completely defined and owing nothing to the past; no doctrine can boast a character of complete originality; it must always derive, if only historically, from the doctrines that have preceded it and develop into further doctrines which will follow.

Such a statement could never have been made by Hitler. His mania for a racially pure, *völkisch* community divorced him from the dominant values of modern Europe and the mainstream of recent European thought. Nazi Germany was intended to be a throwback to legendary feudal or prefeudal times. Where Mussolini might exhort his countrymen to emulate the deeds of the ancient Romans, the Nazi revolution of the spirit aimed at inciting the Germans, not only to do what the distant Teutonic giants had done, but also *to be* those same tribal heroes reincarnated in the twentieth century.

# 4

# The Spread
# of Fascism

## Fascism—Progressive and Regressive

In the previous chapter a basic contrast between the Italian and German varieties of fascism has been developed. On the one hand, Mussolini's movement for all its brutality and tawdriness, by clinging doctrinally to corporativism, disclosed a residual faith in human reason, perhaps even in the Enlightenment vision of the perfectibility of man. On the other, Nazism consciously derided man's intelligence and proffered as substitute a cult of primitive, racial feeling. The question to be faced now is how these two movements, both styling themselves fascist and springing analogously out of the breakdown of liberal systems, arrived at such diverse prescriptions to fulfill the goal they held in common—that of restoring social harmony.

Since the end of the Second World War, scholars and publicists have been fascinated by the abnormal ferocity and extremism of German National Socialism. They have customarily and properly sought an explanation in the extraordinary dislocation produced in German life by the technological advances of the period 1871–1933—advances that occurred so swiftly that social patterns and culture were left hopelessly in arrears. The patriarchal German family and the autocratic

German educational system, to cite just two examples, lived on anachronistically into the freewheeling era of capitalism and urbanization. In historical perspective, the failure of the Weimar Republic to produce the expected and urgent social transformation of Germany was shattering. Thus, Schoenbaum writes:

> What complicated solution in Germany was not a failure to recognize the structural inadequacies of industrial society, but rather a failure to find an alternative social model adequate to correct them. Advancing literacy, urbanization, industrialization, and the development of overseas agriculture all pointed to the liberal society envisaged by the Weimar Convention. But the main currents of social thought since at least the constitution of the [Bismarckian] *Reich* pointed away from it.

And in the same vein, the German sociologist, Ralf Dahrendorf:

> But the parties of the Weimar coalition did not want the social transformation that they needed. . . . Insofar as the Weimar parties had ideas of social reform at all, these were largely directed at the transformation of the authoritarian welfare state into its republican version.

In other words, the clash between the material conditions of modern industrial Germany and the social mores of much of the nation set up an unbearable tension. Nazism was its outlet. Because in Germany the problem was one of maladjustment to the modern world, fascism there took the form of a blind, nihilistic fury directed against modernism in nearly all its forms.

By 1933 Germany had experienced a full measure of industrialization, whereupon the Nazis in a fit of destructive rage used the tools of a technological age to attack the very society which modern science had created. But in 1922 Italy was, by comparison, an industrially underdeveloped country. It is difficult to fix upon exact criteria to distinguish between advanced and backward nations. A. F. K. Organski suggests two tests for an economically developed community: either that at least 50 percent of working males be occupied in nonagricultural pursuits, or that a somewhat lower proportion of the entire labor force be engaged in the provision of services. On both counts Italy was not a modern state economically when Mussolini came to power; 55 percent of male laborers still worked on the land and only about 20 percent of the work force was employed in services. W. W. Rostow, on the other hand, prefers to use the annual rate of increase in net investment as a criterion, a minimum of 10 percent marking "the takeoff into self-sustained growth" of a modern state. In the pre-1914 era, the Italian rate exceeded 11 percent, although it fell off after the war. But, as Rostow is quick to point out, investment and the question of economic growth at large cannot be discussed solely in material terms; the psychological factor is vital. Similarly, C. E. Black refers to modernization, not just as economic and social transformation, but as an "intellectual" and a "psychological" phenomenon. It is in precisely this sense that Italy's backwardness can be most readily appreciated; the mental image and a consciousness of national retardation was as important as the economic reality itself. Whatever objective statistic of growth might be attained, many Italians early in the twentieth century were convinced that their country was not an advanced one. In a way this was recognition of the tremendous drag on Italian progress exerted by the backward south. It was the Italian Nationalists who coined the phrase a "proletarian nation," meaning a have-not state lacking the raw materials and economic resources to compete with the major powers. At the end of World War I, Italian patriots in general took up the cry that Italy was a "proletarian nation" as a means of staking out a claim for vast colonial acquisitions; but the campaign was successful only in displaying a far-ranging feeling of national economic inadequacy.

Thus, the crisis of Italy's liberal society was the precise opposite of that in Germany. The Italian national trauma was caused not by an excess of modernity but by its apparent lack. Fascists in Italy, therefore, promised to do what the liberals had failed to do—drag Italy into the twentieth century. We have seen how Mussolini, in his drive for power, appealed to the Italian school of "productivism." Of course, Fascism promised to modernize Italy without certain consequences attendant on economic advance elsewhere: individualistic liberalism, so characteristic of the nineteenth-century industrial revolution in western Europe, was to be suppressed, and so too was the chief heresy of Western progress, Marxian socialism. In this manner, the traditional elites were reassured that, whatever the need for a new managerial aristocracy, their old social privileges would be preserved. This modus vivendi with the *ancien regime* was the essence of what Organski calls a "syncratic" fascist regime: "Syncratic governments have typically come to power at a time when the country was not yet industrial and the industrial élite was still weaker than the agricultural élite" (*Stages of Political Development* [1965]). At this stage, writes Organski elsewhere, "such

major contradictory patterns as the attempt to permit the nation to be
both modern and non-modern, to modernize economically without
the sociopolitical consequences of such modernization, are characteristic
of fascism" ("Fascism and Modernization," in *Nature of Fascism*
[1968]). Corporativism was an ideal formula for the "syncratic" fascist
situation; it did not overthrow the principle of private property and, by
ending the class war, it was supposed to exorcise the bolshevik threat. And
at the same time, corporativism was expected to pave the way for a vast
increase in productivity. Once all this was accomplished, a "spontaneous and inevitable movement of Italy in the twentieth century," in
Mussolini's words, would occur. The Italian people would be seen to
be "rising again after many centuries of abasement and foreign servi-
tude." The shame of the "mutilated victory" at the close of the First
World War would be removed. In the final analysis, however, this and
every aspiration of Mussolini's Italy turned on Fascism's success—or
failure—in modernizing the country. Hitler, significantly, with a modern nation-state at his disposal from the start, was less concerned with
Germany's place among the powers (which was assured despite the defeat of 1918) than he was with realizing his supranational racial phan-
tasmagoria.

A further distinction between fascism in an advanced country and
fascism in a relatively backward one is suggested by the social scientific
concept of "mobilization"—mobilization, that is, in the sense of engaging the political enthusiasm of normally apolitical segments of the
population. Obviously, both the NSDAP and the PNF succeeded in
rallying the disillusioned and the discontented. However, G. Germani
in a suggestive essay, "Fascism and Class" (*Nature of Fascism*), has
argued credibly that the social groups mobilized by fascism varied according to the degree of modernity of the nation in question. In industrialized Germany Hitler's mass following, if one excepts the "youth
cohort," came from those who before 1918 had been more or less
comfortably integrated into the German political scene. Their disenchantment arose out of military defeat, revolution, and economic depression. Having once belonged, so to speak, their sense of atomization
was particularly acute. When they were remobilized by Nazism, they
readily joined in an attack on the modern liberal world in which, between 1918 and 1933, they had felt completely rootless. In Italy, too,
some who followed Mussolini belonged once to the Italian political
class only to become estranged from the parliamentary system by the

events of 1918–22; they were reinspired politically by Fascism. On the other hand, it was a characteristic of pre-Fascist Italy that much of the populace was untouched by the political process. This was due partly to general economic backwardness, especially rural isolation and illiteracy, and partly to political corruption in Rome which bred widespread cynicism. Insofar as Fascism overcame this alienation, it represented a primary mobilization of a great number of Italians. Participating, at least mentally, for the first time in national politics, these Fascist sympathizers had no inclination to pull down the modern nation-state but rather intended to build a viable Italian one by Fascist methods.

At this point, let us recapitulate the argument so far. The fundamental problem of the historian of fascism has been to embrace within that concept two contradictory expectations of the fascists themselves, "some envisaging a return to a sort of Jeffersonian golden age, while others wanted to forge ahead, through revolution, to a new collectivist social order" (Eugen Weber, *Varieties of Fascism* [1964]). The prototype of a fascist movement craving to retreat to a mythical past was found in Nazi Germany; the prototype of modern, corporative fascism was Mussolini's Italy. German fascism in its search for social cohesion adopted a backward-looking stance because Germany was already an advanced society, in which it was possible to contrive a secondary political mobilization of those disenchanted with modernity. In contrast, the Italian variety of fascism, before it succumbed to Nazi influence after 1938, was forward-looking in a modern idiom as befitted a relatively backward state where political mobilization tended to be a primary experience. The yardstick of a modern nation was in the first instance economic—industrialization and technological progress; but national psychology also played a part. It was the German sense of an oppressive, confusing modern world and the Italian feeling of material inferiority which produced the two respective brands of fascism. If the German and Italian cases were typical, then the following hypothesis might be suggested: Where fascism sprang up in advanced societies, its predominant traits tended to be nihilistic, racist, and regressive. Where it appeared in areas economically and emotionally backward, fascism normally promoted itself as an agent of modernization along progressive, corporativist lines. The remainder of this chapter will be devoted to a survey of fascist movements outside Germany and Italy to test the validity of this analysis.

## Backward Nations: The Iberian Peninsula;
## Central and Eastern Europe

SPAIN

In the early 1930s Mussolini's prestige was at its zenith, due in large measure to the Italian church-state reconciliation in the Lateran Accords of 1929 and to the hopes raised by the corporative state still in process of construction. Understandably, Fascist Italy's apparent success in these fields invited imitation. Hence, there appeared the so-called clerico-corporative fascist regimes. These took root in several of the more stagnant European states where preindustrial elites, in which the Catholic church figured prominently, still held sway. Although perhaps not the most exemplary case of clerico-corporative fascism we shall meet, the Spanish experience fits well enough into this category.

Spanish fascism arose out of the situation created by the proclamation of a Spanish republic in 1931. Actually, long before this date, political and social unrest had been in the air in Spain. The small minority of wealthy aristocrats who dominated Spain through the monarchy were shaken by defeat in the Spanish-American War of 1898. Within a few years, Barcelona became a center of working-class and anticlerical agitation and of Catalonian separatist sentiment. Another foreign defeat, this time by Arab forces in Spanish Morocco, spelled danger to the reactionary monarchical regime in the early 1920s. However, in 1923, a group of military conservatives, headed by General Miguel Primo de Rivera, stepped in and persuaded King Alfonso XIII to suspend the Spanish constitution. The king welcomed Primo de Rivera as a savior, rather in the way King Victor Emmanuel had accepted Mussolini a year earlier. Indeed, Mussolini at first imagined Primo de Rivera to be a Spanish replica of himself. But the general was no fascist; he was a blunt spokesman for Spanish ultraconservatism. Moreover, he was too much of a hedonist—he was a prodigious drinker—to be a really serious politician, and his lax dictatorship drifted without policy. In 1930 King Alfonso dismissed Primo de Rivera who, in failing health, died some weeks later in Paris. Discontent, which mounted as the Great Depression swiftly affected Spain, was now directed at the king himself. In a gesture of pacification, Alfonso restored the constitution, only to find a series of local elections in 1931 turned into a sort of referendum on the monarchy. Although the countryside remained loyal to monarchism, republican candidates swept the board in the major cities, including Madrid and Barcelona. Shaken, King Alfonso abdicated, and on April 14 a Spanish republic came bloodlessly into existence.

The problem was to determine who would rule the new republic. Initially, the government consisted of a coalition of moderates under Manuel Azaña. Azaña addressed himself more to liberal constitutional reform than to material questions of land tenure and labor conditions. It was probably this lack of practical radicalism which, in the elections at the end of 1933, cost Azaña his majority in the Cortes, the Spanish parliament. As a result, the republic was turned over to its enemies— irreconcilable monarchists, clericals incensed by the republican constitution's separation of church and state, and those members of the military upset by Azaña's army reforms. The "bienio negro" was ushered in, the black two years of the republic, when the conservatives tried to reverse the liberal tendencies of the Azaña period. In October 1934 the miners of Asturias rose in revolt, and there were sympathetic uprisings in Madrid and Barcelona. These outbursts were put down with considerable brutality, but the turmoil in the streets and the political polarization recalled Italy before 1922 and Germany before 1933. But where the Left in Italy and Germany, when threatened, had remained uncoordinated and supine, the Spanish Left resolved to mount a counterattack. For the general election of February 1936, a wide range of left-wing groups formed a popular front which won 258 seats out of 473 in the Cortes.

Although the leadership of the Popular Front was plainly more reformist than revolutionary (Azaña, soon to be elected president of the republic, was its guiding spirit), the coalition included the socialists and, always a factor in Spanish politics, the anarchists. During the spring, these far-left elements took matters into their own hands, fomenting strikes, land seizures, outrages against churches and clergy, and even political assassination. The conservatives seized on all this as justification for rebellion, and from the moment the Popular Front won the elections, right-wing plots were being hatched. Most involved the Spanish army which, like the German Reichswehr, was often regarded as the voice of national conservatism. On July 18, 1936, a call to take up arms against the republic was issued by General Francisco Franco who, after participating in the suppression of the Asturian miners, had been made chief of the general staff only to be dismissed when the Popular Front took office. Swiftly, the various groups on the Spanish Right—

landowners and industrialists, bishops and monarchists, many members of the frightened middle class and of a backward superstitious peasantry —rallied to the generals. A Junta of National Defense, representative of these factions, was formed. On October 1 it accepted Franco as *generalísimo* of the rebel forces and also *Caudillo* or head of state. Meanwhile, the parties loyal to the republic armed themselves, and so the civil war between Nationalists and Loyalists was joined.

Although the Franco-led revolt was the backlash of Spanish reaction, it had been dawning on many conservatives that it was not enough simply to put the clock back. The military-monarchical dictatorship of the 1920s having been completely discredited, it was necessary to offer a fresh vision of society, which would counter the attractions of left-wing radicalism and reconcile all Spaniards to the perpetuation of the existing class structure. The formula increasingly advanced was a corporative one. Catholic politicians rediscovered the organic view of society, conveniently reaffirmed in the Vatican's *Quadragesimo Anno* of 1931. Foremost among the propagators of Christian corporative ideas was José María Gil Robles, who enjoyed widespread influence through his role as architect of the conservative coalition, the *Confederación Española de Derechas Autónomas* (CEDA), which ruled Spain during the "bienio negro." But by the 1930s, the achievement of national harmony and socioeconomic justice through corporativism inevitably suggested fascism. José Calvo Sotelo, the monarchist orator, recognized this when he addressed the Cortes in June 1936:

> Against this sterile [republican] state, I am proposing the integrated state, which will bring economic justice, and which will say with due authority "no more strikes, no more lockouts, no more usury, no more capitalist abuses, no more political salaries gained by a happy accident, no more anarchic liberty, no more criminal conspiracies against full production!" The national production will be for the benefit of all classes, all parties, all interests. This state many may call fascist; if this be indeed the fascist state, then I, who believe in it, proudly declare myself a fascist!

The Spanish ruling classes not only embraced fascist ideas, but like their counterparts in Italy and Germany, many were prepared to use the fascists themselves who, until the conservatives sponsored them, were a marginal force in Spanish politics. In 1931 amid the turbulence engendered by the downfall of the monarchy, two young men, Ramiro Ledesma Ramos and Onésimo Redondo Ortega, joined together to found the *Juntas de Ofensiva Nacional-Sindicalista*. JONS, as it was referred to, was the first avowed fascist movement in Spain. Both Ledesma and Redondo were admirers of Hitler, nationalists, anti-Marxists, and anti-Semites. On the other hand, the economic program of JONS was more like Mussolini's corporativism and derived from syndicalist socialism. JONS won a student following, but its radicalism prevented much headway among the population at large: at its maximum, membership never exceeded several hundred. Not until the national syndicalism of JONS was wedded to a more conservative type of corporativism would Spanish fascism blossom. Hitler's appointment as German chancellor may have helped to convince the Spanish landowners, industrialists, clericals, and CEDA politicians of fascism's validity. At any rate, it was in 1933 that they began a serious search for a congenial Spanish fascism.

One man who commended himself to Spain's conservatives as the ideal fascist leader was José Antonio Primo de Rivera, son of the late military dictator. Born in 1903, José Antonio was deeply hurt by his father's fall. The political career he fashioned for himself in the 1930s was intended to be a vindication of General Miguel Primo de Rivera, while avoiding his mistakes. In particular, José Antonio was scornful of the aristocrats who had deserted his father in 1930. To prevent any repetition, he was determined that his own political movement should have a wide base, and he dreamed of calling into play the idealism of an entire younger generation. Despite his readiness to indulge in mass politics, José Antonio was no democrat. He possessed none of the earthiness of his father. He had received an aristocratic upbringing, and his refinement and upper-class sense of probity made him one of the more attractive spokesmen of European fascism—a point granted even by his political opponents. An avid reader of Ortega y Gasset, he was a confirmed elitist. His ideal state, therefore, might be an integrated one, but it would also retain social distinctions. It was, of course, this part of José Antonio's philosophy which attracted the Spanish Right.

An important link between José Antonio and the conservatives was Julio Ruiz de Alda, a renowned aviator with a taste for reactionary politics and good organizing ability. Together, Primo de Rivera and Ruiz de Alda, early in 1933, launched a new party and newspaper with the initials FE. These letters could be taken to stand for "Fascismo Español," but the word fascism was deliberately foresworn lest it incite the republicans to crush the movement before it was really started. Moreover, José Antonio was reluctant to call himself a fascist as this implied imitation of foreign models which affronted his patriotism. For the same reason he refused to attend the Fascist International at Montreux in 1934, although he always kept a picture of Mussolini on his desk. The formal interpretation of FE was finally given as "Falange Española" (Spanish Phalanx). On October 29, 1933, the campaign to win mass support for the Falange began with a public meeting in Madrid attended by 2,000, who were well-dressed and appeared to be drawn largely from the propertied classes. The meeting was to allow José Antonio to offer a definitive and inspirational statement of Falangist aims. Liberalism was denounced as the enemy and held responsible for materialism and the class war. To overthrow liberalism's false gods, violence would be needed, and a national regeneration would be accomplished by totalitarian means. Whatever José Antonio might like to call himself, the tenor of his message was thoroughly fascist.

Among those present at this first Falangist rally was Ledesma, and José Antonio in his general references to economics seemed to be in tune with the syndicalism of the JONS: "We are all born members of a family; we are all citizens of a municipality; we all work at a job. These are our natural units: the family, the municipality, and the profession; and if these are the realities of our lives, what need have we for the intermediate, pernicious instrument of political parties which, in order to unite us in artificial groups, start by disuniting us in our genuine realities?" Indeed, the Falange shortly came out in favor of a system of national syndicalism, although José Antonio, anxious as ever to avoid the stigma of foreign imitation, insisted on "vertical" in preference to Mussolini's "parallel" syndicates of employers and workers.

Nonetheless, the acceptance of corporative economics was clear, and it provided common ground between the Falange and JONS. In February 1934 the two movements fused under the grandiloquent title of *Falange Española de las Juntas de Ofensiva Nacional-Sindicalista*. The new Falange then drew up a program of twenty-seven points, in which the national-syndicalist state figured prominently both as preserver of private property and preventer of capitalist exploitation. National syndicalism was also billed as the means of bringing the working class "into direct participation in fulfilling the great task of the national state." This task ultimately lay abroad: "We have the determination to build an empire. We affirm that Spain's historic fulfillment lies in empire. We claim for Spain a pre-eminent position in Europe." (Although it was not spelled out, many Falangists dreamed of the reannexation of Portugal.) Except for an injunction to respect the Catholic church, the Falange's Twenty-Seven Points duplicated Mussolini's prescription in 1922: political dictatorship and corporative economic reorganization at home in order to sustain a nationalistic foreign policy.

For a year the Falange was run by a triumvirate of Ledesma, Primo de Rivera, and Ruiz de Alda. However, José Antonio had always entertained doubts about the ability of the Falange to overcome the socialists without the help of the traditional Spanish Right. The prospect of any such alliance alienated the more radical Ledesma. In the struggle that developed between the two men, José Antonio was narrowly elected *Jefe Nacional* (national leader); then in 1935 he secured Ledesma's expulsion from the Falange. Due partly to this internal dissension, the Falange made only modest progress during its first two years. The movement was also held back by its leader's scruples and humanity; unlike Mussolini and Hitler, José Antonio Primo de Rivera could never muster an all-consuming hatred for his enemies. Consequently, although the blue-shirted Falangist militia were constantly engaged in street brawls with the anarcho-socialists, the Falange's efforts lacked a final touch of ruthless determination at the top. In addition, the anticipated mass following was slow to materialize. By the time of the crucial elections for the Cortes in February 1936, the Falange numbered at most 25,000, of whom the majority were under twenty-one years of age, while ordinary laborers were conspicuous by their paucity. The Falange participated in the February elections but polled only 40,000 votes. Not a single Falangist was elected, and José Antonio, who received 7,000 votes in Cadiz, lost the seat he had held in the Cortes since 1933.

Yet, in spite of this mediocre electoral performance, the Falange was swept up in the maelstrom created by the Popular Front victory. The Spanish Right, as it began to contemplate armed insurrection, felt the need for a paramilitary force. A sometimes unruly conservative youth section, *Juventud de Acción Nacional*, already existed, but the Right looked with growing appreciation at the Falangist militia. The main overture was made in April when Ramón Serrano Suñer, secretary of Catholic Youth, brought his movement into a loose alliance with the Falange. In the meantime, the Popular Front government, alarmed at the Blue Shirts rioting in the streets, banned the Falange and arrested José Antonio, which action pushed the Falange further into the arms of the conservatives. In June José Antonio, although in prison, conveyed secretly the Falange's endorsement of the generals' plot to overthrow the republic which, the following month, sparked the Spanish Civil War. This development was to elevate the Falange into a major political force within a spectacularly short time; but it also marked the beginning of the end of the Falange's independence.

Naturally, the extremist parties gained from the polarization of Spanish politics induced by the civil war. The ranks of the Communists and the Falange, hitherto fringe groups, were swelled with recruits from the Left and Right. By the end of 1936, the Falange was estimated to number a million. However, if it increased its numbers dramatically, its casualty rate in the fighting was higher than that of any other faction. To a degree, this was inevitable because the Falange's appeal to student youth meant that an unusually large percentage of its members were of an age to be military combatants. Moreover, the Loyalists, recalling that it was fascists who had overthrown democratic government in Italy and Germany, regarded the Falange as their mortal enemy and went out of their way to direct their heaviest attacks against the Falangists. The viciousness with which the Spanish Civil War was fought hurt the Falange in another way. Within the first half year of war, each side meted out summary justice to any enemy leaders who fell into its hands. In this way the Popular Front disposed of practically every potential rival to Franco in the Nationalist camp; Calvo Sotelo and Gil Robles, for instance, were both executed. More to the point, the entire leadership of the Falange, past and present, was decimated— Ledesma, Redondo, Ruiz de Alda were all seized by the Loyalists and killed. José Antonio Primo de Rivera, who had been imprisoned since March 1936, was tried by a people's court for complicity in the military's antirepublican plot, found guilty, and shot by firing squad on November 20.

In the months before his death, José Antonio from his prison cell managed to communicate his advice and opinions to the Falange. Although he never backed away from support of the Nationalist cause, he several times warned of the danger that the Falange might be totally swallowed up by Franco's coalition. His warning was justified but hardly heeded. Beginning in the summer of 1936, the Falangists allowed themselves to be used by the Right to ferret out suspected left-wingers in the areas of Spain controlled by the Nationalists. In Hugh Thomas's phrase, they "acted more as political police than as a political party." However, it was not until after José Antonio's execution that the Falange really forfeited its identity, for José Antonio was the movement's one unmistakably charismatic figure, able to articulate ideals, supply inspiration, and offer a focal point of loyalty. Even from prison, his presence was felt; he became "the hero in the empty room." There was no substitute, and without José Antonio Primo de Rivera, the Falange would be hard put to forestall Franco's domination. As an Italian diplomat in Spain observed: "Franco is a leader without a party, and the Falange a party without a leader."

The crisis arrived in the spring of 1937 in the form of a scheme to merge the Falange with the branch of the monarchists known as the Carlists. For military reasons, it was desirable to coordinate the activities of the Falangist Blue Shirts and the Carlists' shock troops, the requetés. From the vital political angle, the destruction of the autonomy of the Falange and the Carlists at one blow was designed to bring under Franco's firm control the two most turbulent segments of his following. The man chosen to bring the Falange to heel was Serrano Suñer, the Catholic conservative politician and brother-in-law of Franco who, early in 1937, escaped from a republican prison. Suñer skillfully exploited the struggle in the upper echelons of the Falange to succeed Primo de Rivera. The spokesman for an independent Falange was Manuel Hedilla, in character the very reverse of José Antonio. A semiliterate proletarian, he still dreamed of making the Falange a vehicle of working-class politics, and hence vehemently opposed Suñer's designs. But Suñer outmaneuvered him utterly and won over sufficient Falangists to enable the statute of merger with the Carlists to be promulgated in April. As a mark that the Falange was now fully integrated into the conservative milieu, the word tradicionalista was added to its official title. Suñer himself became secretary general of the Falange Española Tradicionalista (FET). Hedilla, who continued to balk at these dispensations, found himself in one of Franco's jails.

Generalissimo Franco was never a fascist, nor was he ever to become one. Nevertheless, he found it expedient, at least for a time, to give a fascist gloss to his regime. Thus, in 1937, the FET was proclaimed the sole and official party of the "new state" which Franco was pledged to create. The Nationalists often employed the Falangist emblem of five intersecting arrows with a yoke superimposed, which conveniently also had monarchist overtones. And they invoked regularly, if cavalierly, the name of José Antonio Primo de Rivera as one of their martyrs. All this was obvious strategy to retain the sympathy of that constituency, mostly youthful, first mobilized by the Falange. But in addition, Franco's fascistic gestures between 1936 and 1939 were a response to the international situation, for the Spanish conflict was a civil war in name only.

Fascist Italy and Nazi Germany joined in the fray on the Nationalists' behalf to the tune of 50,000 and 10,000 men, respectively. Both powers had realpolitik reasons: Mussolini thought of building a western Mediterranean empire with Spain an Italian puppet state; Hitler's main concern was to keep the Spanish Civil War going as long as possible to distract the western powers from Germany's revisionist activity in central and eastern Europe. However, beyond these specific motives, German and Italian intervention was prompted by ideology, in at least a negative sense. Franco had taken up arms against the liberal parliamentarianism of the republic and against the socialism of Azaña's

*Right to left, Mussolini, Generalissimo Franco, and Ramón Serrano Suñer, Franco's brother-in-law who in 1937 became secretary-general of the Falange, Spain's fascist party. During the Spanish Civil War (1936–39), Franco was glad to accept help from both foreign and domestic fascism, thus creating the erroneous impression that he himself was a fascist.*

ACME PHOTO

Popular Front. To rescue Europe from decadent liberalism and combative Marxism was precisely the self-justification advanced by Duce and Führer. It was a short step from the identification of common enemies to the assumption that Mussolini, Hitler, and Franco shared the same positive political philosophy. The wily Franco, to insure continued Italian and German war supplies, did nothing to disabuse Nazis and Fascists of this belief. Serrano Suñer proved of great assistance in the charade. Since helping to form the FET, Suñer had turned into a keen Falangist. By making him his counselor-in-chief, Franco deliberately created an impression of a fascist-dominated administration. Suñer mixed well with the German and Italian envoys to Nationalist headquarters. He was usually more at ease with Italian Fascists than with Nazis whose virulent anti-Semitism was seldom imitated in Falangist circles. Fortunately, it was Mussolini and Ciano who most wanted assurances that foreign aid to Franco was building in Spain a duplicate of the Fascist Italian dictatorship—assurances that Suñer was always graciously prepared to give.

Given the presence of Nazis and Italian Fascists in Spain and the quasifascist posturings of Franco, it was little wonder that many assumed an international fascist conspiracy to be afoot in Spain. It was primarily this conviction which made the Spanish Civil War into the great *crise de conscience* of the 1930s. For years, the fascists and the Marxists had cornered the market in political enthusiasm; liberals and social democrats tended to disillusion and apathy in the face of war and depression. But in Spain the latter found a cause to rekindle their lost idealism. Under the umbrella of the Spanish Popular Front, heterogeneous groups could forget their own differences and unite against the fascism they all feared and hated. This rediscovered sense of purpose brought a stream of volunteers to Spain to fight for the republic—mostly young, often intellectuals, all politically fervent. They numbered about 40,000, although probably no more than 10,000 foreigners served in the republican army at any given moment. Many were exiles from fascism elsewhere; particularly noteworthy was the Italian contingent of *fuorusciti* under the leadership of the Communist Luigi Longo. In addition, there were "international brigades" from the democratic world—from the United States, Canada, Great Britain, France.

Of course, these volunteers could not counterbalance the military help given Franco by Nazi Germany and Fascist Italy. Tragically, this forced the Spanish republicans into the clutches of the only government prepared to intervene on the Loyalist side—the Soviet Union. The logistics involved in sending military supplies from Russia to Spain were stupendous. The Soviets, therefore, had an excuse for making their main contribution in the form of politico-military advisors. These excellently trained administrators brought some much-needed discipline and tactical planning to the Loyalist war effort. However, they were also under orders to transform the Spanish Popular Front into a thoroughly communist operation, which they proceeded to do relentlessly, using intrigue and the firing squad, while Barcelona even witnessed three days of internecine street-fighting among republican factions. The non-Marxist elements in the Loyalist camp found themselves trapped between the equal ferocity of Generalissimo Franco and of Moscow's henchmen. By the end of 1937, the Soviet Union had its way; the Spanish Republic was firmly in the communist grip. For most who served in the international brigades, this was a heinous betrayal of their dreams, and some—George Orwell, Arthur Koestler, Hugh Garner, for example—expressed their bitterness in literary form.

Thus, international intervention on both sides in Spain gave rise to the picture of two supranational ideologies, fascism and communism, locked in combat. This, indeed, corresponded to the scenario of the future envisaged by fascists and Marxists themselves: a struggle to the death between two world forces with no place for compromise or third parties. But the situation within Spain belied the simplistic appearance. While the republicans succumbed to Moscow, Franco never became the puppet of Rome and Berlin. With the gradual construction of a Nationalist state in the areas of Spain conquered by his forces, Franco revealed that his movement remained what it had always been—an expression of military, clerical, and propertied conservatism, which was unchanged by its absorption of the Falange and acceptance of outside fascist help. Franco's first cabinet in January 1938 contained ten members, of which four were military men and four were monarchists; the only Falangist was Serrano Suñer. In like manner, a National Council, forty-eight strong, included representatives from all parts of the traditional power spectrum. The assembly was a far cry from Mussolini's single-party Grand Council of Fascism, with which it was sometimes compared. The two traditionalist forces with the most pervasive influence in the new Francoist state were the monarchists and the church. As for the monarchy, Franco merely promised its future restoration, without specifying a date, a constitutional format, or even which branch of the royal family he preferred. Franco's shrewd procrastination was notorious; a German envoy, asked how he found the new Spain,

replied: "When I find it, I shall tell you." Nonetheless, the promise to
the monarchists was taken seriously, and it formed a cornerstone of
the Nationalist regime. The church also enjoyed Franco's favor. The
omnipresent Suñer helped to arrange a Spanish counterpart to the
Lateran Accords, although the Catholic church in Spain won many
more privileges. In one important gesture, the Jesuits, who had been
expelled from Spain after the founding of the republic, were allowed
to return.

The monarchy and the church were also the two institutions of the
old order most successful in retaining their integrity in Fascist Italy.
What differentiated Franco from Mussolini was the former's exclusive
reliance on the conservative establishment and his aversion to mass
politics. Despite Franco's loose talk to his foreign fascist allies about his
totalitarianism, he showed little interest in mobilizing the population
at large. Despite its status as official party, the FET, which might have
served as an agency for whipping up popular enthusiasm, was never
given a free hand to do so. The Spanish generals, whenever they
thought of the Falange operating politically among the masses, also
imagined the Falangist Blue Shirts developing into Mussolini's
*squadristi* or Hitler's SA. They would tolerate no private armies in
Spain to challenge their own military prerogatives. Franco's regime,
then, did not go beyond a centralized dictatorship, content with the
outward conformity of Spaniards, its authority rooted not in the masses
but in the historical Spanish elites.

Furthermore, the fascist component of Franco's regime was likely to
grow more subservient to the conservative elements with time. In 1938
the Soviet Union decided that the republican cause in Spain was a
losing one and cut off military aid. The result was that in the first
months of 1939 the urban centers of Spanish republicanism, Barcelona
and Madrid, fell to Franco. After 600,000 casualties and manifold
atrocities (the *Luftwaffe's* bombing of the Basque town of Guernica
gave rise to Picasso's great antiwar painting), the Spanish Civil War
ended in total victory for the Nationalists. Since such fascist leanings
as Franco had exhibited stemmed in the main from the exigencies
of war, the role of the Falange in Franco's peacetime state was surrounded by doubt. What happened, in Stanley Payne's appraisal, was
that Franco found it convenient to retain of Spanish fascism "much
of the form . . . but little of the content."

But one Falangist legacy which Franco inherited and chose to implement, albeit formally rather than substantively, must be acknowl-

edged. This was an economic arrangement based on those national-syndicalist principles which had run like a thread through the history of Spanish fascism from the founding of JONS to the FET. On March 9, 1938, the Nationalist authorities published their Labor Charter. The document began with a deferential reference to "the Catholic tradition of social justice," then went on to lay down general prescriptions regarding minimum wages and working conditions in factories, as well as tenant rights and peasant landholding in the countryside. These rules were to be administered, as José Antonio Primo de Rivera had recommended, through a series of "vertical" syndicates: "The vertical guild is a corporation by public law, which is formed by combining into one single organism all elements that devote themselves to fulfilling the economic process within a certain service or branch of production, arranged in order of rank, under the direction of the state." In due course a hierarchy of syndical assemblies was created, rising from local corporations to five national chambers for agriculture, shipping, industry and commerce, public and national service, and culture. At the pinnacle was a national corporative assembly. Positions in this national-syndicalist network were reserved at first for members of the FET. Nevertheless, some old Falangists were displeased, arguing that the Labor Charter and its concomitant syndicalist organization were too paternalistic and regulatory, and insufficiently revolutionary. They were right to be skeptical. Like Mussolini's corporative state which it closely resembled, Franco's national-syndicalist system promised more than it delivered. In practice, the rights of workers remained paper guarantees; the rights of property holders, also recognized in the Labor Charter, were scrupulously enforced. Here was another example of the triumph of Spain's *ancien régime* over the radical, upstart Falange.

Yet, however partial and impaired its application, national syndicalism was of crucial importance to Franco's government. Even if the *Caudillo* made no totalitarian appeal to the masses, he still had to make some gestures of propitiation to the lower classes. National syndicalism was Franco's token gesture. In his own way, he proved the truth of what the Falange had preached all along: that a corporative economic program could be used to reconcile the masses to an elitist society. S. Payne in his authoritative *Falange: A History of Spanish Fascism* (1961) sums it up:

> It is not simply by chance, however, that the Right hung on to the Falange and made it the *partido del Estado*. In the Western world, some

sort of corporatism has become a logical response whenever the revolutionary demands of workers cannot be resolved by ordinary economic means. Something very similar to national syndicalism was the only device that could be used to harness the Spanish working class after the outbreak of war in 1936. This was the indispensable contribution of *falangismo* to the Franco regime. To be sure, the syndical system was organized entirely as the government saw fit, but it was vital nevertheless.

In backward Spain, then, corporativism was the dominant fascist trait, and as in Italy, it began as a reformist movement aimed at bringing the nation up to date. Quoting Payne once more: "To create a nationalist, élitist culture based on modernized Spanish values, harmonizing tradition with the revolutionary demands of the twentieth century"—this was the prime objective of the Falange. But corporativism in Spain, even more emphatically than in Mussolini's Italy, was turned into a device for propping up the traditional social structure. Moreover, elsewhere in the Iberian peninsula, corporativism was prominent and functioned in much the same way. Portugal in the 1930s was ruled by a conservative, corporativist government. Because of this combination of authoritarian politics and corporative economics, Portugal has sometimes been regarded as a fascist state.

PORTUGAL

One can trace generically fascist ideas in Portugal back to the period before the First World War. In 1910 the monarchy was overthrown and replaced by an anticlerical republic. As in Spain a generation later, a republican upheaval generated a counterreaction. The first antirepublican wave in Portugal saw the founding in 1914 of a journal and movement called *Integralismo Lusitano*. As the name implies, this was an integral nationalist movement whose recommendation for the restoration of shattered national unity was to cultivate traditional values and practices. It abominated the nineteenth century and all its works, appraising faith and feeling above science and reason. The integralists' ideal was a precapitalist world of local communities and guilds. Their nationalism was narrowly conceived, excluding certain "internal foreigners" such as the Jews. In fact, *Integralismo Lusitano* in its racism and extravagant love for the distant past recalled a German *völkisch* society. Its membership was largely upper class and relied heavily on the university community. Among the students influenced by integralist notions was António de Oliveira Salazar. On the other hand, while

Salazar's conservatism and nationalism owed something to his integralist youth, the dictatorship which he was to fasten on Portugal in the 1930s did not rest on an indiscriminate and racist worship of an idyllic past characteristic of *Integralismo Lusitano*.

In May 1926 a military revolt, very similar to General Franco's later uprising in Spain, toppled the existing government and abolished parliament, parties, and trade unions. After suppressing a liberal counterattack the next year, the military dictatorship dug in under the presidency of General Carmona. The general sought an economic expert to bring order to the unstable national finances which had burdened the liberal regimes between 1910 and 1926. He chose Salazar, professor of economics at Coimbra University, to be Portugal's minister of finance. On accepting office, Salazar demanded and received extraordinary powers. So armed, he succeeded in raising appreciably the level of efficiency and honesty within his ministry, but apart from his bookkeeping reforms, it is questionable whether his economic policies benefited the average Portuguese much. Nonetheless, it was Salazar's outward success at the Ministry of Finance which provided the springboard for his rise to supreme power. In 1930 he founded the National Union party and persuaded the government to recognize his party as the only legitimate one in Portugal. Although this was a sign of Salazar's growing political stature, the National Union made no pretense of being a mass party like the Italian PNF or German NSDAP. It did not hold a national congress until 1934, and the austere Salazar, who never wore a uniform, was anything but a messianic leader of the Mussolini-Hitler stamp. The National Union had little to do with Salazar's appointment by President Carmona as premier in 1932. This was a crucial date, however, for it marked the end of a purely military dictatorship. Henceforth, there would never be a hint of Salazar's removal as premier; for all practical purposes he was dictator of Portugal.

Between 1932 and 1934 Salazar was engaged in laying the legal foundations of his "Estado Novo" (new state), the inspiration for which came overwhelmingly from Catholic sources, particularly the papal reaffirmations during the nineteenth and early twentieth centuries of Christian corporative theology. Salazar's corporativism had nothing in common with the syndicalist socialism which informed the corporativism of the Spanish JONS and early Italian Fascism. The foreign counterpart of Salazar was Gil Robles, spokesman of the Spanish Catholic Right. It was, therefore, a highly traditionalist document that Salazar proudly announced on February 22, 1933, as "the first corporative constitution in the world." (He was able to stake the claim to novelty because, although Mussolini's corporate state had been spelled out on paper, Fascist Italy's mixed corporations of employers and employees did not materialize until 1934.) Portugal's new corporativism was manifested in two bodies—the National Assembly and the Corporative Chamber. The former was to be chosen half by economic corporations and half by certain educated heads of families on a geographical basis. The latter was to contain representatives not only of vocational groups but also of "moral" and "cultural" sectors of society. Complementing this corporative institutionalization was the Statute of National Labor promulgated in September 1933. Besides setting out broad guidelines for capital and labor, the statute created machinery in the form of industrial *sindicatos* and labor courts to resolve the class war. But, as in Italy and Spain, the propertied classes dominated the corporative system, running it at best paternalistically and at worst in their own selfish interests. In addition, neither the National Assembly nor the Corporative Chamber had much influence on governmental decision-making.

In other words, despite its corporative façade and its name, Salazar's *Estado Novo* was a fairly old-fashioned dictatorship that survived primarily because of its close cooperation with the army, and more important, the Catholic church. Given Salazar's deep Christian convictions, it was not surprising that the church in Portugal came to enjoy wider power and privileges than in either Mussolini's Italy or Franco's Spain. In sum, there was really little about this clerico-corporative regime to suggest fascism—until 1936.

Portugal was historically sensitive to events across the frontier in Spain, and the outbreak of the Spanish Civil War in July 1936 began a new era in Salazar's Portugal. From the start, Salazar's government openly sympathized with Franco's insurgents, and until 1937, when British diplomatic pressure became too strong to ignore, Portugal was a main route by which foreign supplies reached the Spanish Nationalists. Patently, Salazar felt Portugal had a vested interest in the outcome of the neighboring civil war. As the Spanish conflict became increasingly polarized between the fascist Right and the Marxist Left, Salazar hastened to align his country with the former cause. So began the "fascistization" of Portugal—a concerted effort to mobilize the populace, in particular the younger generation, using the gimmicks of uniforms, salutes, and slogans culled from Fascist Italy. In this endeavor the National Union party was of some use but of less prominence than

*Swimming with the fascist tide in the late 1930s, Salazar's Portuguese regime adopted certain fascist trappings: as shown here, a uniformed youth movement which saluted with a characteristic fascist gesture.*

WIDE WORLD PHOTOS

some new organizations. The *Legião Portuguesa* (Portuguese Legion) was a militia of 20,000 men over the age of eighteen. It was to be a shield "in defense of the corporative order," lest the Spanish Civil War spill over the border. Another innovation was the green-shirted *Mocidade Portuguesa*, a state youth movement for both boys and girls. At first, participation was compulsory for the entire school and university population; later, it was compulsory only between the ages of seven and fourteen. Membership in the *Mocidade* or the *Legião* proved to be of enormous advantage in pursuing a career in government service and moderately valuable in other professions. Teachers and civil servants were required to take oaths of loyalty to the regime and its corporative principles. To deal with recalcitrant Portuguese, a plethora of secret police forces were formed, of which the most notorious, and a match for Mussolini's OVRA in brutality, was the International Police for the Defense of the State (PIDE).

By the close of the Spanish Civil War in 1939, most of the trappings of a fascist regime were present in Portugal. In its excursions into thought control, Salazar's government seemed to have totalitarian ambitions. Yet, when all is said, doubt about the sincerity of Salazar's conversion to fascism—after he was already in power—must persist. Like Franco's embrace of the Falange, it smacked of opportunism and the calculation that fascism was the wave of the future. If the prognostication was wrong, would the appreciation of fascism survive hard times? Furthermore, there was a lack in Salazar's Portugal, even after 1936, of the frenzy and idealism which accompanied the rise of the PNF and the Falange. It was as though the authorities were determined not to let things get out of hand. Indeed, despite the "fascistization" of 1936–39, not much was changed beneath the surface. The old power structure remained potent. Symptomatically, in May 1940 a concordat with the papacy restored some of the Catholic church's status lost in the early days of the republic. In Portugal, even more than in Franco's Spain, the enduring forces of conservatism held the incipient radicalism of fascism firmly in check.

All in all, it may be stretching the definition of fascism to apply the word to Salazar's Portugal. On the other hand, the Portuguese experience fits into the pattern common to the Latin nations of the Mediterranean. In Italy, Spain, and Portugal, fascist regimes or else rightist governments which cloaked themselves in a fascist garb held out corporativism as a means of national advancement. Moreover, the pattern extended to the Latin world outside Europe. Although strictly speaking beyond the scope of this book, it is noteworthy that another version of Latin corporative fascism occurred in Argentina between 1946 and 1955. Here, corporative ideas took the title of *Justicialismo*, which the dictator Juan Perón liked to describe as the Third Position, a compromise between individualism and collectivism. *Justicialismo* served Perón as a somewhat imprecise "national doctrine," ideally suited to weld together the heterogeneous coalition of social forces on which his power rested. Also, like European corporativism, Argentine *Justicialismo* held out the prospect of reform and progress in a recognizably fascist style.

All these Latin examples of fascism or quasi-fascism were nationalistic; occasionally they were moved by memories of historic imperial splendor; there were traces of anti-Semitism. But in no case was any of these movements inspired by a racial vision of the past, nor did any seek refuge in mythology as did German Nazism. The explanation would seem to lie in the underindustrialized condition of these Latin states; Spain and Portugal were decidedly rural, while Italy in 1922 and Argentina in 1946 had reached no further than the threshold of an industrial age. For such countries, the nihilistic, backward-looking fascism of a modern nation like Germany was wholly unsuitable to their needs and aspirations.

### AUSTRIA

Yet another country whose economic status fell short of modernity was post-World War I Austria. Created out of the collapse of the Hapsburg Empire, the Austrian republic was a rump state of six and a half million German-speaking people. An industrial revolution had started in the Hapsburg Empire toward the close of the nineteenth century, but what was left in 1918 was a huge industrialized Vienna, with over a quarter of the Austrian republic's population, while the rest of the nation was made up of small towns and pastoral villages. The Austrian countryside hardly provided a sufficient market for Viennese industry. The problem was compounded because the Danube Valley, Vienna's natural commercial hinterland, was now cut off as the successor states to the Hapsburg Empire erected tariff barriers almost as a matter of pride. One measure of Austrian economic weakness concerned reparations imposed on the new republic, as they were on the German Weimar Republic, in the postwar peace settlement. But while the victorious

Allies made determined efforts to force Germany to pay, they quickly realized that the chance of extracting reparations from Austria was virtually nil. On the contrary, beginning in the early 1920s, a series of international loans were made available to Austria through the League of Nations, and it was only through these "rehabilitation loans" that the Austrian state was kept solvent. Here, then, was a scarcely viable, backward nation, whose people could hardly forget they had recently been a premier nationality in the vast, quite prosperous Hapsburg Empire. In other words, there was in Austria a distinct national consciousness of having been pushed out of the modern economic mainstream.

The postwar political situation in Austria was novel, too. The Austrian republic, like the Weimar Republic in Germany, was a pristine experiment in liberal parliamentarianism. Its chief backers were the Viennese Social Democrats, but its standing among Austrians at large was dubious. Should the liberal regime falter, it would create a situation ripe for exploitation by the fascist antithesis of liberalism. The interesting question, however, was whether a fascist reaction against the Austrian liberal republic would follow the pattern of Nazi racism or the Italian corporative model. Of course, Austria was a hotbed of Pan-Germanism; it was in Vienna that Hitler had received his political education. Hence, any fascist group in Austria was bound to indulge in racist nationalism to some extent. Also, it will be remembered, the first party in Europe to call itself National Socialist was born in the Hapsburg Empire in 1904. With the breakup of the empire, this party was split into its Austrian, Czech, and Polish wings. The Austrian Nazi party, starting out on its own in 1918 under the chairmanship of Dr. Riehl, was very influential in *völkisch* circles for several years; Hitler, for one, was indebted to Riehl for some of his tactics. From the outset, the Austrian Nazis were eager to work with like-minded groups in southern Germany, and along with the Bavarian Pan-Germans came into Hitler's orbit. Although cooperating with the Munich Nazis, Riehl's followers maintained a nominal independence until after Hitler's emergence from Landsberg prison. Then, in 1926, at a conference in Munich chaired by Hitler, all Austria's Nazis—the main body as well as splinter groups—agreed unconditionally to accept Hitler as Führer and the Twenty-Five Points as their program. Henceforth, Nazism in Austria would be at least as much a German as an Austrian phenomenon.

Since Austrian Nazism quickly turned into a replica of the German kind, another indigenous brand of Austrian fascism was given a chance to flourish. It began with the proliferation of still more Pan-German groups in the aftermath of the First World War. Fearful that the republic might embark on a Marxist course and that foreign enemies might exploit Austria's parlous condition, various reactionary and ultra-nationalist associations adopted the name of *Heimwehr* or home guard. They were strongest in the south whence invasion from Yugoslavia was anticipated. At first, the *Heimwehr* consisted of nothing more than disoriented demobilized soldiers, typical of paramilitary units all over Europe at the war's end. Like the German *Freikorps*, they had little coherent political philosophy beyond vague right-wing prejudices. But the *Heimwehr* prospered and, within a few years, gained status as a permanent political force in Austrian life, a development that was due to encouragement from two quarters.

The coalition ministries of the Austrian republic, again paralleling the Weimar experience, came to be dominated by conservative elements. Monsignor Ignaz Seipel, leader of the Christian Socials, the Catholic and rural party, was chancellor from 1922 to 1924 and again from 1926 to 1929. Seipel lived in mortal terror lest Marxist socialism spread from its base in "red Vienna" over the whole of Austria, and he thought the *Heimwehr* a useful antidote. As a result, the organization's brawling activities were treated with the utmost tolerance by the authorities, both national and local. Official connivance with the *Heimwehr* became pronounced after 1927. In July of that year, street demonstrations in Vienna resulted in the burning of the Palace of Justice. The Socialists, in response to police brutality, called a general strike, whereupon the Seipel government called on *Heimwehr* units to smash the strike by force.

The other source of comfort for the *Heimwehr* lay outside Austria. In the second half of the 1920s, after Mussolini had secured his position within Italy, he was able to devote more attention to foreign affairs. Austria, as a buffer state between latently powerful Germany and Italy's German minority in the Alto Adige, automatically engaged the Duce's interest. One means he conceived to give Italy a stake in Austria's fortunes was to assist the Austrian fascists. He was urged to do this by the ultraconservative Hungarian premier, Count Bethlen, another politician agitated by the Marxist threat in the heartland of the former Hapsburg Empire. Partly on Bethlen's prompting, Mussolini sent the *Heimwehr* supplies of money and arms, although the importation of arms into Austria was expressly prohibited by the postwar peace treaty. In return, the *Heimwehr* were expected to serve as a bulwark not only against socialism but against the Pan-German menace from the north as well. On one occasion, Rome even extracted from the Heimwehr a recognition of Italian sovereignty over the Alto Adige.

Thus encouraged from within and without the Austrian republic, the Heimwehr gradually changed from a purely paramilitary formation into what its nominal leader, Dr. Richard Steidle, called "a state-political organization." An important step in this process was the taking of an oath by several hundred Heimwehr leaders at Korneuburg in May 1930. The Korneuburg Oath involved a distinctly fascist-style party program to which all Heimwehr members were required to subscribe in the following months. Condemning "western democratic parliamentarianism and the party state," it called instead for "a strong national leadership." There was the ritual obeisance of a Teutonic group to the needs of the Volk, but then, too, the corporative style of fascism was prominently represented in the demands for "the self-government of estates" and the "development of the economy on a corporative basis." This seemed to reflect the example of Mussolini who, at this juncture, was endeavoring to project an intellectual and reformist image. Similarly, Austria's fledgling fascists tried to harness the teaching of such Viennese theorists of Catholic corporativism as the economist Karl von Vogelsang and the sociologist Othmar Spann. However, if the Heimwehr was making progress in formulating a coherent program, the movement still remained administratively disorganized and torn by internal factionalism. In September 1930 Steidle was ousted and replaced by Prince Ernst Rüdiger Starhemberg, who had begun his political career in the German Freikorps and had even marched with Hitler in Munich in 1923. He was better known, though, as the scion of a distinguished aristocratic family and a symbol of old-fashioned Austrian conservatism. From then on, Starhemberg was to be the acknowledged and colorful leader of the Heimwehr, but he was always something of a playboy in politics, and never provided the firm command of a Hitler or even a Mussolini.

Starhemberg, in fact, was soon engaged in acrimonious quarrels with his Heimwehr lieutenants, most notably Dr. Walter Pfrimer, over the issue of cooperation with the government of the day. This, it must be said, was no empty dispute in the fluid Austrian situation of 1930. On the one hand, the Great Depression afflicted Austria as swiftly and devastatingly as it did Germany, and although the populace gave fewer signs of psychological disorientation in Austria than in Germany, misery and uncertainty nevertheless afforded a suitable climate for a possible

*Heimwehr Putsch.* On the other hand, the growing difficulty of finding a reliable majority in the Austrian Parliament (*Nationalrat*) to sustain a ministry produced a constitutional crisis which opened up the prospect of the *Heimwehr* obtaining power legally. In September a stopgap government, pending the outcome of new elections, was created under presidential authority, and included Starhemberg as minister of the interior and another *Heimwehr* officer as minister of justice. Encouraged, Starhemberg chose to enter the *Heimwehr* in the upcoming elections, not as in the past as a partner in a Christian Social coalition, but as the nucleus of a new independent party, the *Heimatbloc*. The strategy misfired. In the elections of November 9, 1930—the last free election to be held in Austria between the wars—the *Heimatbloc* won only 6 percent of the votes and eight seats in the *Nationalrat*, apparently at the expense of the Christian Socials who, with 36 percent of the vote, lost seven seats. The Social Democrats emerged as the largest single party in Parliament, gaining 41 percent of the vote, although they were not strong enough to form a government. On balance, however, the election amounted to a decided setback for both the *Heimwehr* and the orthodox conservatives, and a victory for the democratic Left.

The election result might well have been the signal for the *Heimwehr* to switch its tactics to a *Putsch*, which had been talked about and threatened for several years. Indeed, Starhemberg more than once appeared on the verge of precipitating a *Putsch* but always drew back. Plainly, he still perceived hope for his own ambitions in the constitutional process. The electoral swing to the left, albeit clear, had not been exorbitant; unlike the German experience in the depression, the Communist vote in Austria remained miniscule. The new coalition ministry, although it excluded the *Heimwehr*, was dominated by the Christian Social elements which, throughout the 1920s, had proved most accommodating to the organization. And in the final analysis, the *Heimwehr* was too internally disunited to contemplate a *Putsch* with absolute confidence.

Meanwhile, Austria's economic condition worsened, unemployment rising by 30 percent and exports dropping by 15 percent during 1930. The gravity of the situation was such that it seemed to justify a joint Austro-German proposal for a customs union. This, of course, could be interpreted as a prelude to a political Anschluss, forbidden by the postwar peace treaties. So the French chose to regard the scheme, and raised loud objections. Not even the spectacular collapse in May 1931 of the *Kreditanstalt*, for generations Vienna's leading commercial bank, served to shake French opposition. On September 3 the Austrian government announced that, in view of international protests, it was dropping the customs union proposal. Just over a week later, one *Heimwehr* faction erupted in Styria, and under Pfrimer's command, occupied several towns including Graz, the provincial capital. But the expected march on Vienna never began, chiefly because Starhemberg refused to commit the rest of the *Heimwehr* to the escapade. The authorities waited for the *Putschists* to disperse peaceably, which they did. Pfrimer at first fled to Yugoslavia but returned a few weeks later to face trial in Graz for high treason. He and seven other ringleaders were acquitted by unanimous verdict of the jury.

Despite its anticlimactic ending, the Pfrimer *Putsch* shaped the *Heimwehr*'s future in two very distinct ways. First, by leaving Pfrimer in the lurch, the *Heimwehr* turned its back on the violent overthrow of the Austrian republic and committed itself to working within the existing political system. In turn, this implied further cultivation of the friendship of traditional conservatives—the fascist stratagem pioneered by Mussolini and being practiced concurrently by Hitler. Secondly, Pfrimer's group now broke with the *Heimwehr* and, because they were characterized by fanatical Pan-German racism, quickly found their way into the Nazi camp—a development that served to clarify the differences between the *Heimwehr* and Austria's Nazi party. Hitherto, Starhemberg had been quite willing to form a coalition provided the *Heimwehr* was given the upper hand. But with the loss of its extreme Pan-German wing, the *Heimwehr* was free to move—indeed was compelled to move—in a corporative direction in imitation of the Italian rather than the German version of fascism. The *Heimwehr* never ceased to be something of a *völkisch* movement, but increasingly after 1931, Austria's fervent anti-Semites and racists tended to join the Nazis.

Both of these *Heimwehr* mutations—into a more traditionalist and into a more corporative force—were aided by the coincident advent on the Austrian political scene of Engelbert Dollfuss. Dollfuss was the embodiment of those rural values which predominated everywhere in the Austrian republic save Vienna. He was orderly, hard-working, pious, and reverent of prescriptive rights; his aim was to mold an Austria expressive of these virtues. He relished the nickname of "milli-Metternich," which testified not only to his small stature (under five feet tall), but also to his aspiration to be the savior of Austria. Coming from a family of independent farmers, he made his way through various civil service posts until becoming minister of agriculture in 1931. Still relatively unknown and not a member of parliament, he was invited, in May 1932, to form a cabinet. Dollfuss became chancellor as a consequence of one of Austria's endemic parliamentary crises, although significantly the spring crisis of 1932 was engendered by a new and ominous problem. In local elections the Austrian Nazis had come from electoral insignificance two years earlier to make sweeping gains in Lower Austria, Salzburg, and even Vienna. The cause was not far to seek. Across the German frontier, Hitler's mounting strength had just been demonstrated in the presidential elections. The fortunes of the Austrian Nazis followed in the wake of those of their German brethren. Faced with the prospect of a Nazi Germany, numerous Pan-Germans in Austria rallied to the Nazi cause and furiously escalated the demand for an Anschluss. Thus, Dollfuss's efforts to restructure and reinvigorate an independent Austria were bedeviled from the start by foreign influences.

Not surprising, the appointment of Hitler as German chancellor in January 1933 had immediate repercussions in Austria. Rumors of a Nazi *Putsch* in Vienna proliferated. The Socialists countered by putting their own defense force, the *Schutzbund*, on the alert. Efforts to bring the Christian Socials and the Social Democrats together in a grand coalition to save Austria seemed to be getting nowhere. It was against this backdrop of brooding civil unrest and political deadlock that Dollfuss struck out on the road to dictatorship. On March 7, taking advantage of a procedural impasse in the *Nationalrat*, he invoked the War Emergency Powers Act of 1917 to suspend parliament, institute press censorship, and prohibit public meetings and parades.

Dollfuss took this excursion into authoritarianism convinced that he could generate enough popular enthusiasm, without either the Socialists or the Nazis, for a truly national movement. In May he announced the formation of the Fatherland Front, which proved to be a brave rather than an effectual gesture. The Fatherland Front was never much more than the old Christian Social bloc under a new name; as such, it represented a substantial segment of Austrian political opinion, but it was hardly a dynamic national consensus. Furthermore, the Fatherland Front failed to transform the *Heimwehr* into a tame government supporter, mainly because the *Heimwehr* refused to join the front on the grounds it was insufficiently fascist. In spite of this rebuff, Dollfuss recast his ministry to make it even more "*Heimwehr*-heavy." The most significant change was the elevation of Major Emil Fey, the devious and sinister chief of the Viennese *Heimwehr*, from "state secretary" in charge of public security to full-fledged minister of public security.

The truth of the matter was that Dollfuss did not dare break with the *Heimwehr*. It was not only that an alienated *Heimwehr* would be a disruptive force within Austria, but that behind the *Heimwehr* stood Fascist Italy. On Hitler's accession to power, Mussolini became more than ever concerned with propping up Austria as a barrier to German expansion in the direction of the Alto Adige. The *Heimwehr*, long accustomed to look to Italy for supplies, now became a lever to force Dollfuss's government to play Mussolini's game. What the Italian Duce demanded, in brief, was the admission of still more *Heimwehr* luminaries (Starhemberg and Steidle especially) to the Austrian cabinet and the transformation of Austria into a fascist state along Italian lines. Once given this token of Austrian friendship, Mussolini offered in return an Italo-Austro-Hungarian alignment which would provide economic favors and protection against a German attack. On several visits to Italy, the Austrian leader was harried to accept this proposal, and at Riccione in August 1933 Dollfuss and Mussolini came to an informal understanding. Dollfuss yielded reluctantly, but fear of Nazism thrust him into Mussolini's arms. Some years later, Starhemberg produced a memoir of these events whose contents were tendentious in the extreme but whose title, *Between Hitler and Mussolini* (1942), summed up perfectly the dilemma of Dollfuss's Austria.

Admittedly, Dollfuss had no love for liberal parliamentarianism or for socialism of any kind. Therefore, it cannot be pretended that the extirpation of these elements from the Austrian political scene, as predicated under the Riccione formula, was exactly uncongenial to him. On the other hand, there can be little doubt but that in the final showdown with the Social Democrats, Dollfuss's hand was forced. In the new year 1934, the *Heimwehr*, patently at Mussolini's instigation, embarked on a round of provocative gestures—noisy parades, flamboyant speeches, hints of a *Putsch*. Moreover, Fey, as minister of public security, stepped up his harassment of the Socialists, organizing searches for Socialist arsenals, arresting *Schutzbund* members, and so on. Overall, the aim was to incite the Socialists to some violence or illegality which would justify drastic suppressive action by the government.

On February 12 the Social Democrats in Linz fell into the trap by mobilizing the local *Schutzbund* units. For the sake of workers' solidarity, the Socialist leaders in Vienna backed their colleagues in Linz, proclaiming a general strike and calling out the *Schutzbund* on a national basis. In effect, this amounted to a leftist bid to capture the state. It was launched with a minimum of planning and never came close to success. The strike was honored only in part by the workers, and the *Schutzbund* failed to occupy the administrative center of Vienna. All the Socialists did was to afford their enemies a glorious excuse to wreak vengeance. From February 12 to 15, the police and the army, aided by *Heimwehr* units, conducted a full-scale military operation against Socialist strongholds in the huge blocks of workers' flats which dotted the capital's poorer districts. These dwellings, it was rumored, had been erected by the postwar Socialist city council of Vienna to serve as proletarian fortresses when the class war took to the streets. Although the suspicion was unfounded, the workers' flats did prove ideal defensive positions, and the authorities had recourse to artillery to compel surrender. The bitterest fighting raged about the Karl Marx Hof, a block over half a mile long and more than 100 yards wide, containing 1,400 apartments. Civilian casualties were inevitable, although exact figures can never be established; the official tally of those killed all over Austria in the four-day civil war was 314, but the Social Democrats estimated their own dead in the Battle of Karl Marx Hof alone at several times that figure.

The events of February 12–15, 1934, crushed the Austrian Socialists utterly; their leadership mostly fled into exile and their party was banned by law. As the Social Democrats had been the main proponents of the *Nationalrat*, their demise guaranteed there would be no return to the former parliamentary system. Now, Dollfuss was free to transform Austria into a legal despotism with fascist overtones—the price required by Mussolini and his *Heimwehr* clients to support Austria's international integrity. On the other hand, with the annihilation of the Austrian Socialist movement, Dollfuss lost potentially his firmest ally in his struggle to ward off Nazi Germany. During the 1920s, many of Austria's Socialists had been ardent advocates of Austrian union with the democratic Weimar Republic. But immediately after Hitler took power in Berlin, Austrian Socialists almost to a man became adamant opponents of Anschluss. It remained to be seen whether, in sacrificing the Social Democrats to the fascists, Dollfuss had made a wise bargain.

On May 1, 1934, Dollfuss announced a new Austrian constitution. The *Nationalrat* was abolished and replaced by a complicated legislative apparatus. There were to be four advisory councils: one was a council of state made up of prominent citizens nominated by the president, another was a body composed of provincial officials and mayors, while the remaining two councils were corporative in that they contained representatives of, respectively, various cultural organizations and seven vocations designated in the constitution. All four councils meeting together comprised a federal assembly, and each council elected members to sit in a fifty-nine-man federal diet, which was the only body empowered to make laws. In reality, power was centralized in the hands of the chancellor, whose lack of responsibility to any representative assembly was emphasized in his additional title of "leader" of the federal government. This leader-chancellor would owe his position to approval of the Fatherland Front, Dollfuss's loose coalition of patriotic groups which was now expected to serve as something akin to a totalitarian party. The sole safeguard in the constitutional document against a personal or one-party dictatorship was the largely corporative representation in the advisory councils. As in Italian Fascist theory, the central authority and the corporative delegates were supposed to balance each other.

With the constitution of May 1, 1934, what has been termed "Austro-fascism" reached full flower. Yet the architect of the constitution, Dollfuss, was not, strictly speaking, a fascist—a point made emphatically in his somewhat hagiographic English-language biography by Gordon Brook-Shepherd. Both his authoritarianism and his corporative beliefs were rooted in a profound Christian conscience. As a boy, Dollfuss had once trained for the priesthood, and he claimed his constitutional law of May 1934 to be the realization of the ideals of the papal encyclical, *Quadragesimo Anno*, which called for social and economic justice in a paternalistic setting. His faith was expressed in the constitution's preamble: "In the name of God, the Almighty, from Whom all justice derives, the Austrian people receive this constitution for their Christian, German federal state on a corporative basis." What Dollfuss hoped to inaugurate in 1934 was a clerico-corporative regime similar to Salazar's government in Portugal. But in Austria the Catholic conservatives were uncertain masters of the situation. The *Heimwehr* expected its share of power under the new constitutional system, which it greeted as a giant step toward fascism, and it was not disappointed. Coincident with the promulgation of the constitution, Starhemberg was made deputy leader of the Fatherland Front and vice-chancellor in the federal administration; he was now manifestly second-in-command to Dollfuss. The new regime in Vienna, then, rested on a coalition of Austrian traditionalists and *Heimwehr* fascists. Its philosophy of Austro-fascism appeared a blend of modern Christian doctrine and Mussolinian practice adopted by the *Heimwehr*.

If Dollfuss imagined that his introduction of a quasi-fascist regime and his alliance with the *Heimwehr* (and by extension with Mussolini) would deter the Nazis, he was gravely mistaken. Rather, the reverse was the case; the Nazis were driven into action to forestall Dollfuss's schemes to build up the Austrian will to resist Anschluss. In consequence, the long-feared Nazi *Putsch* was planned for July 25, 1934. How closely Hitler supervised the plot is obscure; its actual details were organized by a Nazi official in Munich, Theo Habicht. But unquestionably, the Führer inspired and approved the *Putsch*. As for the Austrian National Socialists, they counted heavily on German intervention to insure success. About 1:00 P.M. on July 25, about 150 members of the Viennese Nazi SS invaded the Chancellery, expecting to capture the entire Austrian cabinet in session. However, news of the *Putsch* had leaked out, and the cabinet had already dispersed. The chancellor himself, on the other hand, was still in the building and unprotected. The Chancellery guard was a ceremonial one without ammunition, and the police units which had been summoned failed to arrive in time, possibly due to Nazi sabotage in the police network. The SS were thus able to hunt down Dollfuss in his office, where they shot him twice. With their usual callousness, the Nazis refused Dollfuss medical aid, and he bled to death painfully by midafternoon.

Notwithstanding this tragedy, Dollfuss proved to be the posthumous victor in the immediate crisis. For two years, Dollfuss had struggled to develop a sense of Austrian patriotism, principally through his Fatherland Front. On July 25, 1934, this policy seemed to be vindicated when, despite Dollfuss's death, not many Austrians harkened to the Nazi call to Anschluss. The army and the police remained loyal to the existing Austrian government. A few *Heimwehr* figures were implicated in the *Putsch*. Dr. Anton Rintelen, a former minister of education whom the Nazis hoped to install as a puppet chancellor, was the most seriously compromised and attempted suicide; Major Fey played an ambiguous role and was certainly guilty of delay in alerting Dollfuss about the *Putsch*. But the *Heimwehr* as a body held firm against the Nazis. Indeed, it was an ultimatum from Starhemberg to evacuate the Chancellery that convinced the *Putschists*, in the evening of July 25, of their isolation. Within a few hours of Dollfuss's murder, then, the *Putsch* fizzled out in the face of Austrian antipathy.

The Nazi *Putsch* might still have been carried to success if Hitler had sent military reinforcements, but at this moment, Dollfuss's complementary strategy of enlisting Mussolini in Austria's defense paid a dividend. On March 17, 1934, as reward for Dollfuss's suppression of Viennese Marxism, Fascist Italy had concluded with both Austria and Hungary the Rome Protocols. Overtly economic agreements, in political terms they made Fascist Italy the protector of the weaker partners. In accord with the spirit of the Rome Protocols, Mussolini, in July 1934, ordered partial Italian mobilization on the Brenner and dispatched thinly veiled warnings to Berlin. Were Hitler contemplating an invasion of Austria, the Duce's attitude was sufficient to deter him, at least for the time being.

With the failure of the Nazi *Putsch*, Austria continued ostensibly on the course charted by Dollfuss. The constitution of May 1, 1934, still provided the legal framework, with actual power shared between Catholic conservatives and the *Heimwehr*. The division of authority was neatly symbolized by the respective positions of Starhemberg and Kurt von Schuschnigg, a confidant of Dollfuss and his minister of justice; the former now became leader of the Fatherland Front while remaining federal vice-chancellor, the latter was the new chancellor but only deputy leader of the front. Schuschnigg, a distinguished lawyer, was, like Dollfuss, a devout Catholic. He lacked, however, Dollfuss's personal magnetism, and for this reason, perhaps, he was less inclined than his dead mentor to take a firm stand against Anschluss, inclining rather to avert the danger by negotiation. The unpleasant truth was that the Nazi threat to Austrian independence was as great as ever, the collapse of the July *Putsch* and consequent execution of Dollfuss's assassins notwithstanding. In other words, Austria won a battle against Pan-Germanism in 1934, but the war was far from over.

The preoccupation of the Austrian government with the chronic Nazi problem crippled the development of Austro-fascism. The corporative reorganization of Austrian life proceeded slowly. For the most part, corporative officials were appointed by the government rather than, as planned, elected by occupational constituents. Out of frustration and in the hope of gaining some breathing space to pursue his Christian-corporative designs, Schuschnigg sought a modus vivendi with the Nazis through negotiation with the German minister in Vienna, Franz von Papen. Papen, having narrowly escaped liquidation in the Röhm purge, was immediately restored to Hitler's favor and sent to Vienna in July 1934. In view of his failure to bring about an Anschluss by violence, Hitler determined to try a more subtle, "evolutionary" approach. Papen, whose aristocratic and Catholic connections commended him to the Austrian power structure, was an admirable choice to beguile the pliant Schuschnigg into compromising Austria's sovereignty. From Papen's labors emerged, on July 11, 1936, an Austro-German accord incongruously called the "Gentlemen's Agreement." Superficially, the agreement met Austria's pressing need; each party pledged noninterference in the other's internal affairs, but on the other hand, Schuschnigg made significant concessions to the principle of Pan-Germanism. In the diplomatic area, he promised that Austria henceforth would conduct her foreign policy "in accord with the fact that she recognizes herself to be a German state." More important, in an unpublished codicil to the agreement, Schuschnigg agreed to take into his cabinet two members of the "National Opposition." This euphemism was used to designate the Nazis, whose party was officially proscribed in Austria, as well as other Pan-Germans acceptable to the Nazis. In due course, two representatives of the latter group, General Glaise-Horstenau and Guido Schmidt, entered Schuschnigg's ministry. In 1933 Mussolini had forced his *Heimwehr* protégés into the Austrian government in order to manipulate Dollfuss; three years later, Hitler was applying exactly the same tactic with Schuschnigg.

To be fair to Schuschnigg, his attempt to appease Hitler was prompted in great measure by the disappearance of other options. Specifically, the policy established by Dollfuss of looking to Fascist Italy was fast losing credibility. In 1935 Mussolini relinquished his "watch on the Brenner" for the sake of imperial conquest in Ethiopia and, a year later, he committed his country to the Spanish Civil War. As we have already seen, these adventures drove a wedge between Italy and the western democracies and, by late 1936, led to Mussolini's enunciation of the Rome-Berlin Axis. Schuschnigg, who like many Austrian patriots had always felt uneasy in partnership with the traditional Italian enemy, was swift to perceive in the blossoming Mussolini-Hitler friendship the portent of Italy's desertion of Austria. Not only did he adjust Austria's policy to the new reality by seeking an accommodation with the Nazis, but he also turned against the *Heimwehr* whose role as bridge to Fascist Italy was almost played out. In May 1936 as a prelude to the upcoming Gentlemen's Agreement, Schuschnigg dismissed Starhemberg as both vice-chancellor and head of the Fatherland Front. (To add insult to injury, Starhemberg was then named patron of the front's "Mothers' Protection" branch; the prince being a ladies' man, his new post was the cause of much ribaldry.) After the signing of the Gentlemen's Agreement, Schuschnigg moved even more decisively against the *Heimwehr*. Taking advantage of a squabble between Starhemberg and Fey, he decreed the dissolution of all private armies in Austria, the *Heimwehr* in particular, and their merger into a *Front-Miliz*.

After 1936 Austro-fascism, reflecting the waning influence of the *Heimwehr* and of Fascist Italy, went into eclipse, and in its place the German type of racial fascism flooded Austria. In the spring of 1937, Schuschnigg was constrained to incorporate the "moderate" Nazi wing into the Fatherland Front. Yet the chancellor remained under constant pressure to swim further with the rising tide of Pan-Germanism. Much of this pressure was exerted by Artur Seyss-Inquart who presumed to act as middleman between Vienna and Berlin. Seyss-Inquart, like Schuschnigg, was an Austrian Catholic lawyer, and although not a Nazi, he believed, as did Glaise-Horstenau and Schmidt, in the historic need for a special Austro-German association. These Pan-German Austrian patriots flirted perpetually with Anschluss without definitively embracing it.

It is a moot point whether Hitler consciously decided in the new year 1938 to abandon the evolutionary road to Anschluss. Some circumstantial evidence suggests that he did. Only a few months earlier, he had learned that Mussolini would probably not duplicate his 1934 obstructionism, and in November 1937, Hitler had briefed his generals on the possibility of German expansion in central Europe. Then, the following January, the Viennese police uncovered plans for a Nazi *Putsch* to be sprung in April, although no documentary proof has ever been adduced to implicate the Führer directly in the plot. Furthermore, at this time all Hitler's energies seemed to be absorbed by his purge of the last independent conservatives within the German civil and military administration—a side consequence of which was the recall from Vienna of Papen, the chief exponent of an evolutionary Anschluss. What is beyond doubt is that, no matter how premeditated his general policy might have been, Hitler was lightning quick to exploit the opportunity to strike which Schuschnigg unwittingly gave him. For some time the idea of a Schuschnigg-Hitler meeting to review the creaking Gentlemen's Agreement of 1936 had been in the air, and the discovery of precise plans for a Viennese Nazi uprising made such a meeting more than ever desirable. Papen's final action in Vienna was to arrange for Schuschnigg to visit Hitler's aerie at Berchtesgaden. Of and by itself, a Schuschnigg-Hitler encounter was innocuous. However, in the weeks before the meeting, Schuschnigg saw fit to make concessions to what Seyss-Inquart coyly termed his "Little Program." Austrian press criticism of Nazism was muffled, members of the crypto-Nazi "National Opposition" were given a role in Austria's youth organization, and there was even a hint of a "National Opposition" presence in the cabinet. Schuschnigg intended these moves as a gesture of good will; to Hitler, though, they were signs of weakness and a standing invitation to raise the most extravagant demands at Berchtesgaden.

On February 12 Schuschnigg crossed the German frontier to find himself immediately in an atmosphere of coercion. The Berchtesgaden area had been transformed into an armed camp, and Hitler was accompanied by his military commanders in chief. Once closeted with Hitler, the Austrian chancellor was treated to one of the Führer's histrionic exhibitions which alternated between maudlin self-pity and bombastic ranting. After this performance, Ribbentrop presented Schuschnigg with an ultimatum: as guarantees of the future Germanic nature of Austria, Seyss-Inquart was to be made minister of public security in charge of the police, Austrian Nazis were to be allowed to engage in "legal activity" within the framework of the Fatherland Front, and a hundred German officers were to be detailed for duty with the Austrian army. Failing compliance within three days, German forces would march on Vienna. To back up this threat, Hitler at one point summoned General Keitel to the conference. By evening, a weary and cowed Schuschnigg signed the document.

The Berchtesgaden agreement was implemented. Meanwhile, Schuschnigg, in desperation, cast about for new ways to rally Austrian patriotism. In one direction, he made overtures to the residual Austrian socialists; in another, he broached an old personal dream of a Hapsburg restoration. But his most dramatic gesture was to schedule a plebiscite on Austria's independence for March 13. With control of the organs of state propaganda, he felt he could count on about a 70 percent majority in favor of "an Austria free and German, independent and social, Christian and united." Unfortunately, Schuschnigg had once more played into Hitler's hands; the Nazis were able to claim that the plebiscite would be a violation of the Berchtesgaden agreement, which perhaps it was in spirit although certainly not in a legal sense. At any rate, such was the pretext for more ultimatums. First, Schuschnigg was warned to call off his plebiscite. Then, when he promised to do so, Göring phoned Seyss-Inquart to demand Schuschnigg's replacement as chancellor by Seyss-Inquart himself. There was no help for Austria forthcoming from Fascist Italy; Mussolini was conveniently "unavailable" to telephone calls from Vienna. The rest of the international community were inclined to regard an Anschluss as inevitable and even justifiable by national self-determination. On March 11, 1938, the isolated Schuschnigg gave way to Seyss-Inquart, who now informed Berlin there was no longer any need for a German invasion of his country. He was bluntly told that the Wehrmacht was already under orders to march and that it was too late to draw back. The Nazi propaganda machine informed the world that German troops were entering Austria at the request of Chancellor Seyss-Inquart.

On March 12, while the Wehrmacht completed the Austrian occupation, Hitler began a leisurely tour of his childhood haunts—his birthplace at Braunau and Linz, the site of his schooling—before proceeding on to a swastika-festooned Vienna. On the 13th the Austrian authorities were presented with a "Law for the Reunification of Austria with the German Reich." The Austrian president, Wihelm Miklas, refused to countenance it, and transferred his functions to Seyss-Inquart, whereupon the latter committed his final treason and gave it his signature. The Anschluss law provided that the Austrians would participate in a plebiscite after all. On April 10, the populace was required to answer the question: "Do you acknowledge Adolf Hitler as our Führer and the reunion of Austria with the German Reich effected on March 13, 1938?" In view of the delirious reception Hitler had recently received in Linz and Vienna, the result was a foregone conclusion. Many Austrians who had no discernible Nazi sympathies were nevertheless proud of their fellow countryman who had risen from obscurity to dominate powerful Germany. Hitler's record since 1933, especially in overcoming the depression, had caused his popularity to soar among Germans and Austrians alike. Moreover, important segments of the Austrian power structure rallied to Hitler after March 11. A prominent part was played by the Catholic primate of Austria, Cardinal Innitzer who, having once enthusiastically backed Schuschnigg, executed a quick turnabout and ordered church bells to be rung in celebration of the Anschluss. Under Innitzer's guidance, the church left no doubt in the minds of the Catholic peasantry how they should vote: "On the day of the plebiscite, it is the obvious national duty of us bishops to declare ourselves as Germans for the German Reich, and we expect of all faithful Christians that they know what their duty is to the people (*Volk*)." More surprising was the similar if more restrained advice given the workers by some socialist leaders, although Gestapo blackmail was probably operative here. In the final analysis, of course, Austrians were being asked to vote on a *fait accompli* which seemed to have been predetermined for a long time—maybe since the dismemberment of the Hapsburg Empire in 1918. A negative vote was a patent denial of history. On April 10, 1938, out of four and a half million votes cast, 99.73 percent said *ja* to the Anschluss.

The new Austrian province of the Third Reich was treated to a swift dose of *Gleichschaltung*. The Catholic church, because of its puissant status in Austria, was brought into line with exceptional ruthlessness; even Cardinal Innitzer on one occasion was taken into protective custody

The shift from Austro-fascism to Nazism was vast; the Nazis, having murdered Mussolini's protégé, Dollfuss, in 1934, now tried to destroy his memory (picture shows his statue about to be torn down).

WIDE WORLD PHOTOS

to save him from a Nazi mob. The Nazi regime in Austria was remarkable for its egregious anti-Semitism. The tone was set in the days
following the Anschluss when Vienna's Jews were forced into the
streets to scrub the walls and pavements of the capital clean of pro-
Schuschnigg slogans. Thousands of Jews fled into exile while there was
still time, among them the venerable Sigmund Freud. The emphatic
assertion of anti-Semitism symbolized the final victory of the German
racial kind of fascism over Austro-fascism. The triumphant Nazis showed
no sympathy for Austria's indigenous fascists. The Fatherland Front
was summarily dissolved and its leadership hounded. Major Fey together with his family, and even his dog, was killed. Starhemberg
found opportune refuge in Switzerland. In contrast, Schuschnigg sto-
ically refused to run, and spent the next seven years in Nazi prisons and
concentration camps.

Yet, in spite of their ultimate failure, Dollfuss and Schuschnigg, and
the Heimwehr too, proved one thing—that Austria's fascist reaction to
liberalism and social democracy was different from Germany's. Although Pan-German and anti-Semitic traits were present in Austro-
fascism, they never formed its leitmotif as they did in Nazism. Instead,
out of Austria's Catholic, conservative heritage and the example of
Fascist Italy emerged the corporative constitution of May 1, 1934. Given
Hitler's looming presence across the frontier and his built-in Pan-German
appeal, the very birth and survival for four years of Austro-fascism
should be cause for surprise. The explanation can be found partly in the
vagaries of the international situation. But it must also be acknowledged
that Austro-fascism lived for awhile because it was an authentic Austrian
voice and because its clerico-corporative mode of fascism answered to
the rural and premodern condition of much of the nation.

Nevertheless, the Anschluss of 1938 was a sure indicator that corporative fascism, no matter how congenial it might be economically and
socially to a small, backward Danubian state, was always liable to be
swamped by the chronic racism of the area. As a general rule, the further
one traveled along the Landstrasse, the famous highway running east
from Vienna, the more probable was such an eventuality; Hungary and
Rumania will illustrate this. Race-thinking, it bears repeating, gave rise
to primitive, instinctual ideologies wholly at variance with the rationalist
premises of socioeconomic corporativism. In the underdeveloped Latin
nations, the virtual absence of racism left the field free for corporative
fascism to flourish. In sparsely industrialized eastern Europe, the fascist

movements likewise embraced corporative theory as a means of national modernization, sometimes in direct imitation of Mussolini's Italy. But where race consciousness antedated the growth of fascism, the longing to return to a mythical past of racial purity—akin to German *völkisch* reveries—tended in the long run to predominate, shaping native fascisms into a Nazi mold. Due to the racial factor, then, in eastern Europe the correspondence between economically retarded communities and corporative fascism grew blurred, in places almost to the point of disappearance.

### HUNGARY

Hungary, like Austria, came out of the breakup of the Hapsburg Empire in 1918 geographically truncated and economically beggared. While national self-determination drove Austrians to consider union with Germany, this sentiment directed Hungary's gaze to those Magyar pockets in the areas of mixed population just across her postwar borders; in the period between the two world wars, nearly all Hungarians were zealous irredentists. After World War I, the Allies intended to exact reparations from Hungary but, as in Austria, economic realities made this impossible, and during the 1920s, international rehabilitation loans barely kept the Hungarian economy on an even keel. In 1919 Hungary shared with the rest of central Europe the problem of constructing a viable political system in the midst of revolutionary turmoil. In Budapest the confrontation between the *ancien régime* and the revolutionaries became stark and violent with traumatic consequences.

In March 1919 a liberal government, crippled by its inability to prevent Allied depredations on Hungarian territory, was supplanted by a coalition of communists and socialists under Béla Kun. The Béla Kun regime tried to establish its control by terrorist methods, and its bolshevik program sent a shock wave across Europe. In August, Rumanian troops, on behalf of the Allies, invaded Hungary and expelled the left-wing government. The Béla Kun episode, brief though it was, conditioned Hungarian attitudes for the next quarter of a century and gave rise to a blind hatred of all left-wing politics; liberals and social democrats were lumped together with genuine Marxists in a general anathema. Against this background it was impossible to erect a democratic parliamentary system comparable to those set up in Berlin and Vienna. Moreover, because many of Béla Kun's lieutenants were Jewish, the indiscriminate backlash took on an ugly anti-Semitic tone. Hungarian anti-Semitism before 1918 had been relatively restrained. Jews numbered about 5 percent of Hungary's population but, being prominent in the arts, the professions, and the business world, were a very visible minority. The postwar situation in Hungary was a replica of that in Bavaria out of which Hitler sprang. In each place a large section of public opinion held that the national interest was being subverted by racially foreign, leftist traitors.

The Hungarian center of antibolshevism was Szeged, where a committee was formed under the leadership of Admiral Miklós Horthy. After the Rumanians had driven Béla Kun out of Budapest, the Szeged committee became the effective Hungarian government. It immediately launched a counterrevolutionary terror in which "order detachments" assaulted and slaughtered thousands of liberals and Jews on the pretext of cleansing the country of bolshevism. The regime which got its start in the Szeged committee and the white terror rested on the support of the so-called "historic classes"—landowners, bishops, generals, and the like, who had comprised Hungary's rigid and aristocratic power structure under the Hapsburgs. To emphasize the continuity with the imperial past, Horthy assumed as head of state the title of regent—an epithet that did not betoken any intention to restore the Hapsburgs, for whom there was limited sympathy among the historic classes. Horthy conceived it his duty to preserve the prewar social, not constitutional, order. In this, he was remarkably successful for twenty-five years.

During the first decade of Horthy's regency, the most conspicuous ministerial figure was Count István Bethlen, who served as premier from 1921 to 1931. In 1919 Bethlen had founded the Christian National party which, a few years later, fused with the Smallholders party to produce the Unified party. This Unified party constituted the preponderant bloc in the Hungarian parliament, although the party was totally subservient to Bethlen and Horthy, and parliament mostly a rubber stamp for the government. We have previously seen Bethlen, in collusion with Mussolini, encouraging the Austrian *Heimwehr*, but this was done with an eye to international revisionism. Bethlen, in no way a fascist, was a solid Christian conservative who, despite his own Calvinism, relied heavily on the backing of the Catholic church. His social policy was mildly paternalistic in the towns, but he made no real effort to allay distress in the countryside lest it upset the vested interests of the historic classes. The policy of sustaining Hungarian feudalism followed an untroubled course until 1929, when the Great Depression caused a fall in agrarian prices which discredited Bethlen. The depression, in fact, created just enough discontent in Hungary to persuade Horthy to broaden the base of the government.

It is customary to interpret Hungary between the wars in terms of two sorts of political Right: the historic Right of Horthy and Bethlen, and the radical, fascistic Right. The latter drew its recruits primarily from the younger generation—junior officers and students—who, inflamed by the events of 1919, strove to keep alive the passions and prejudices of that year. In doctrinaire fashion, they denounced the Horthy regime because it tolerated the shadow of a parliament in Budapest and practiced informal instead of legal anti-Semitism. Their program was to sweep away feudalism and capitalism, as well as all the privileges of the historic classes which divided Hungarians among themselves. National unity was the prerequisite to national regeneration after the defeat of 1918, and to recovery of lands lost in the peace settlement. As a focal point of unity, Hungary's fascist Right conjured up a racial identity derived from romantic legend. Hungarian racial fantasies centered on a group of Turanian tribes who, in time immemorial, reputedly crossed the Carpathian Mountains from the east and founded the modern Hungarian people. Some Hungarian racists insisted that the Magyars were of Near Eastern descent and that Jesus himself was a Turanian, although this did not deter them from reviving the worship of Hardúr, the pagan war god of the ancient Magyars, in the same manner that *völkisch* Germans cultivated the memory of the Nordic Wotan. The new Turanians formed themselves into secret societies, sometimes termed hunting clubs, which adopted all manner of strange tribal symbols. Because much of their membership was military, many of these societies had a paramilitary arm. Amid the dislocations caused by the Great Depression, Horthy's concern was with violence, not so much from a working-class movement, but from Hungary's militant racists.

Horthy's tactic was to mollify this radical Right by an accommodation with one of its luminaries, General Julius Gömbös. Gömbös, like many of his fellows among the highly politicized Hungarian officer class, came from Magyarized Swabian stock and, despite this Germanic background, subscribed heartily to Turanian mysticism. First achieving prominence in the antibolshevik and anti-Semitic pogrom of 1919, he served briefly as minister of defense. At this time, he called himself a national socialist, long before the designation was widely known in Germany. Four years later, Gömbös formed a Party of Racial Defense, but his political career limped along until 1929 when he was reappointed defense minister. It was not until 1932 that he was made premier.

Although Horthy accepted Gömbös under the combined pressure of the depression and the fascist Right, he also shrewdly judged that the general could be tamed. Since 1928, Gömbös's ideological allegiance had been gradually shifting from German National Socialism to the Italian brand of fascism. Bethlen's revisionist association with Mussolini suggested to Gömbös parallels between Hungary and Italy, and he cast himself in the role of the Magyar Duce. Such was his pose on becoming premier. Immediately afterward, he organized a giant demonstration of his followers whom he addressed from a balcony in the middle of Budapest; they responded with the rhythmic chant: "Long live our Leader!" It was a second-rate rerun of Mussolini's reception of his Black Shirts at the close of the March on Rome. In 1934 Gömbös seized the chance to place Hungary alongside Dollfuss's Austria in Fascist Italy's diplomatic camp by signing the Rome Protocols. At home Gömbös promised a one-party state and corporative institutions, but these were empty words; he did not even come close to abolishing Hungary's ineffectual parliament. Gömbös always accorded the regent much more respect than Mussolini did King Victor Emmanuel. During his entire premiership, which lasted until his death in October 1936, he was content with the flashy superficialities of power. His constant and often ridiculous mimicry of Mussolini could not hide the reality that authority in Hungary still lay with the historic classes.

If the vainglorious and malleable Gömbös lived up—or maybe down —to Horthy's expectations, he grievously disappointed his confreres of the fascist Right. Not only did the latter resent Gömbös's subservience to Hungary's traditionalists but also his adulation of Mussolini. Italian Fascism before 1938 being minimally racist, Gömbös could hardly pretend to be the Italian Duce's disciple and at the same time keep up his anti-Semitism. So, to accord with his Mussolinian image, Gömbös became, by Hungarian standards, a racial moderate. In addition, by his token embrace of modern corporative doctrine, he cut himself off spiritually from those Hungarian mystics for whom, in István Deák's words, "the future spelled the decline of urban civilization and the country's return to the 'blessed, eternal Hungarian soil.' " The radical Right, therefore, came to be counted among the opponents of the Gömbös government, and the struggle was resumed to establish a mass fascist party with a racist philosophy, of the sort Gömbös had once promised but failed to deliver.

Hungary's racists were encouraged to agitate against the Horthy-Gömbös regime by the German Nazis. Hungary's position vis-à-vis

Hitler's Germany was not dissimilar to that of Austria. In both countries Berlin was prepared to whip up the local national socialists as a means of forcing the Hungarian and Austrian governments to align themselves diplomatically with Germany and even to recast their domestic institutions in line with the ideology of the Third Reich. A year before his death, in fact, Gömbös—his emulation of Fascist Italy notwithstanding —visited Berlin and felt constrained to conclude with Göring a secret pact providing for the introduction of national socialist practices into the Hungarian administration. It was Hungary's counterpart to the more celebrated Austro-German Gentlemen's Agreement signed the following year. In any event, Horthy, who was not consulted in the negotiations of the Gömbös-Göring deal, had no intention of allowing it to be implemented. Nonetheless, the episode signaled the growing foreign pressure behind the development of Hungarian fascism in the 1930s.

The conjunction of economic depression, Gömbös's inconstancy, and the proximity of Nazi Germany spawned a swarm of Hungarian fascist sects. One such was the Scythe Cross founded in 1931. Taking its cue from the antimodernist program of German Nazism, this movement attracted mostly poverty-stricken and landless peasants who were persuaded all their woes were caused by cosmopolitan Jews and urban communists. In 1936 the Scythe Cross reached its climax when several thousand peasants marched on "sinful" Budapest, the symbol of all they feared and hated, but the government had no difficulty in putting down the uprising, and the Scythe Cross was never again a significant force to be reckoned with. Another fascist group, which came into existence in 1932, went by the name of the Hungarian National Socialist Agricultural Laborers' and Workers' party. This was more of a parliamentary movement and pledged its loyalty to Horthy. The pristine Nazi influence was obvious, however, in the wearing of a brown shirt and the swastika, emblems which were shortly replaced by a green shirt and a badge of crossed arrows. The green shirt and arrow cross were used by more than one Hungarian fascist faction, but only became truly famous when they were adopted by the Party of National Will which, in 1937, changed its name to the Arrow Cross party. The Arrow Cross swiftly came to dominate the Hungarian fascist scene and later, during the Second World War, to absorb all other fascist groups.

The inspiration behind the Arrow Cross was Major Ferenc Szálasi, a sincere, fervid, and compelling figure of mixed Armenian, Hungarian, and Slovak stock. The son of a noncommissioned officer in the Hapsburg army, Szálasi was in the midst of a successful military career when, in 1934, he resigned from the Hungarian army to found his own political movement. Yet he never divorced himself completely from his military upbringing. His political ambition became the realization of the wilder fantasies of the Hungarian officer corps. He wanted not merely to assure the Turanian character of Hungary but to fulfill the imperatives of "Hungarism" by territorial expansion. This expansionist scenario did not stop with simple revisionism which would restore Hungary's pre-1918 borders, but envisaged a "Carpatho-Danubian Great Fatherland" —a huge swathe of southeastern Europe to be ruled by Magyars by right of biological superiority as, it was claimed, they had so ruled the region a thousand years earlier. And it was the army, on whose general staff Szálasi had served, that was designated to point the way to this goal.

Even more important than his attractiveness to idealist officers, however, was Szálasi's talent for mobilizing the Hungarian workers in town and country alike. His economic proposals were radical in that they included land redistribution, bank nationalization, and a national council of corporations. On the other hand, he had no very coherent economic policy simply because he was more interested in social integration than in social justice. Szálasi's strong suit with the proletariat was his personal charisma, established as the result of regular visits to working-class districts. His tactics paid off; sometimes even the outlawed Hungarian Communist party instructed its followers to support the Arrow Cross because it appeared the most radical party in sight. The addition of proletarian recruits to the lower-middle class anti-Semites and conservative nationalists normally found in a fascist movement transformed the Arrow Cross into Hungary's first and only mass fascist party.

In 1938 the government, in alarm, imprisoned Szálasi on a charge of unconstitutional activity. In Szálasi's absence, Horthy tried to buy off the fascist Right by appointing Béla Imrédy, leader of a minor national socialist group, premier. Imrédy was, in some ways, an even more ferocious racist than Szálasi. The Horthy conservatives accepted Imrédy's extension of legal race discrimination, but balked at his plans for a one-party fascist state. In January 1939 Horthy dismissed him. Meanwhile, Szálasi, as a martyr figure in jail, continued to inspire widespread devotion. In May the true strength of Arrow Cross fascism was revealed in the first Hungarian elections to be held by secret ballot; out of two million votes cast, the Arrow Cross polled three quarters of a million, and in Budapest ran a strong second behind the governmental Unified party, surpassing the Social Democrats and showing strength particularly in slum districts. The recent work by N. M. Nagy-Talavera, *The Green Shirts and Others* (1970), demonstrates conclusively the working-class base of Arrow Cross support.

By 1939 the popularity of the Arrow Cross could not be denied; junior army officers showed rising sympathy, while the formidable weight of Nazi Germany was brought to bear on Horthy to cooperate with Hungarian fascism. Horthy and his new premier from the historic Right, Count Teleki, were faced with a problem which could not be settled by repression alone. They decided to mix severity with concessions. Hence, Teleki kept Szálasi in prison as long as he dared in the hope of expediting some fragmentation of the Arrow Cross. On the other hand, the olive branch was extended in the form of the appointment to secondary offices of state of sundry racist politicians and "Hungarist" military men congenial to the Arrow Cross. A modest program of land reform was a conciliatory gesture to the Arrow Cross's economic radicalism. Abroad, the close alignment with Nazi Germany which the Horthy-Teleki regime perforce had to accept was applauded by most Hungarian fascists, albeit some reacted patriotically against German arrogance. Finally, as a result of the German-Hungarian alliance, Teleki was compelled to release Szálasi in September 1940. On the whole, though, the flexible policy of Horthy and Teleki was a success. Despite demonstrating its electoral prowess, the Arrow Cross made no immediate push for power. Although Szálasi was never domesticated to the extent that Gömbös had been, the historic classes managed to contain the Arrow Cross without seriously distorting Hungary's traditional social framework. Not until Nazi German troops invaded Hungarian soil in 1944 and stirred the Arrow Cross to a state of frenzy was the grip of the regent and the historic classes broken.

Although Hungarian fascism failed to gain power by its own efforts, it left its imprint on the country. Principally, it was the propagator of race consciousness in the areas of domestic anti-Semitism and imperialism abroad. Furthermore, in the absence of a viable communist party, Hungarian fascism provided a vehicle for the expression of radical socioeconomic opinion. Much the same picture can be drawn of fascism in Rumania. Before German intervention in World War II, Rumanian fascists were unable or unwilling to topple the conventional power structure. Nevertheless, in the interwar period, fascist ideas even more radical and racially bizarre than those in Hungary were rampant and helped to shape Rumanian society.

## RUMANIA

Rumania fought on the winning side in the First World War and made substantial territorial gains in the peace settlement. National instability in Rumania did not stem—as it did in Germany, Austria, and Hungary—from humiliation at the hands of external enemies, but rather from a consciousness of enemies within. By her postwar acquisitions in Bessarabia, Bucovina, and Transylvania, Rumania brought within her borders thousands of Ukrainians, Magyars, and Germans. In addition, these new Rumanian lands also contained a formidable proportion of Yiddish-speaking, unassimilated Jews. The net result was that the population of interwar Rumania was barely 70 percent Rumanian. The country suffered from a severe identity crisis.

The Jews were not Rumania's largest minority; they were less than a million in number and constituted 5 percent of the total population. Nevertheless, they were singled out as the main obstacle to national harmony. Of all the countries examined so far in this book, Rumania had perhaps the longest and strongest tradition of anti-Semitism. Rumania's economy, having remained for the most part rural, had not developed a solid middle class, and retail trade and finance rested heavily in the hands of Jews who were popularly suspected of gouging the peasants at every turn. After 1917, on the other hand—their capitalist activities notwithstanding—Rumania's Jews were often accused of being agents of the Russian Bolshevik regime across the frontier. As in German *völkisch* thought, the Jew was identified with the modern city vices of usurious exploitation and proletarian unrest. He thus appeared a clear and present danger to the healthy and time-honored values of a racially homogeneous Rumanian peasantry.

A strong streak of anti-Semitism existed in Rumanian academic circles, particularly among those university students who came from a rural background. The mentor of these youthful anti-Semites was Professor A. C. Cuza who, when not ranting against the Jewish threat to the purity of Christian girls, taught political economy at the University of Jassy. One of his most ardent disciples was Corneliu Zelea Codreanu, destined to be the founder and mouthpiece of Rumanian fascism. Codreanu's character was shaped early by his strong-willed family. His parents, naturalized Rumanians of Polish and German backgrounds, had been baptized into the Orthodox church as adults. On both counts they displayed all the zeal of the recently converted; from them the young Codreanu received his first taste of the fiery patriotism and religious mysticism which informed his later fascism. Codreanu's father, a secondary school teacher, won a reputation before the First World War in Moldavian local politics as an anti-Semitic and nationalist spokesman. He made certain that his son was thoroughly grounded in patriotic Rumanian folklore and sent him to a military academy before the university. At Jassy, in the postwar years, the young Codreanu was in perpetual trouble with university authorities because of his part in violent forays against Jews and those he alleged were communists and traitors. In 1923 all resident Jews were granted full Rumanian citizenship, which infuriated the professional anti-Semites. The Codreanus, father and son, joined with Cuza in founding the League of Christian and National Defense. An embryonic fascist movement—anticapitalist, antiparty, and antiparliamentary (although it won ten seats in the national assembly)—the League sported the anti-Semitic swastika, and its branch in Bucharest called itself a *fascio*. In a few years, however, the Codreanus and Cuza split up. The League lost its parlia-

"The Captain" of Rumanian fascism. The mystic C.Z. Codreanu who founded the Legion of the Archangel Michael after receiving a celestial vision.

UNITED PRESS INTERNATIONAL PHOTO

mentary representation in the elections of 1927 and went out of existence. The younger Codreanu thereupon set out to build his own fascist movement.

In 1923, by his own account, Codreanu was vouchsafed a vision of Saint Michael who urged him to dedicate his life to the salvation of Rumania. Four years later, he founded the Legion of the Archangel Michael. Like early Italian Fascism, the Legion deliberately eschewed a set policy: "The country is dying for lack of men, not programs." What Codreanu had in mind almost defied definition; national revival was to be a mystical experience, a resurrection of an ancient communion based on shared religion and race. This was a replica of the Nazi conceit that the bond between blood and soil created the spiritual essence of a people which was best sublimated in a natural or pastoral environment. Codreanu was fascinated by the historical survival of the *razasi*, a species of self-governing Rumanian village. The most fanatical legionaries, to indicate their attachment to the land, wore around their necks a small pouch of Rumanian soil often dug from the site of an ancient battlefield. Yet, the Legion's ideal past of rustic and racial serenity was fictional. Writes Z. Barbu:

> Codreanu identified himself with the "people," an idealized community which he never defined save in vague and abstract terms such as "unity," "purity," "Christianity." It was an unhistorical entity including all Rumanians who had existed in the past and would exist in the future. . . . The reference group of the legionaries, of the intellectuals in particular, was an imaginary one. It was an ideal society in which the legend of an old traditional Rumanian community loomed large. ("Rumania" in *European Fascism*)

The practical twentieth-century demonstration of this "mystic nationalism" was a ferocious anti-Semitism. Significantly, Codreanu's closest companion in the Legion was Ion Mota, translator of the *Protocols of Zion* into Rumanian and spokesman for the racist wing of *universalfascismo* at the Montreux Conference, whose pathological anti-Semitism has been compared to Hitler's.

Lacking any precise policy, the Legion sought to convey its beliefs through ritual and symbol. The movement was organized into conspiratorial "nests." Meetings were likely to open with incantatory song and dance, and all proceedings, often reminiscent of African tribal ceremonies, were calculated to emphasize the sense of a blood brotherhood.

By far the most striking feature of the legionaries was their total dedication to Codreanu as leader and to the cause. The Legion was a chiliastic movement, and the religious fervor of its members was in no way better exemplified than in their eagerness to kill and die for principle. Rumanian public affairs were frequently conducted with gratuitous violence; for example, Codreanu himself was once arrested arbitrarily by the authorities, tied up, and dragged bodily through the streets. But the Legion elevated violence to a new status, employing a select "death squad" to murder Jews and their bourgeois protectors, and to execute vengeance on legionary traitors. At times, the Legion appeared to delight in the shedding of blood for its own sake, as though it was a primeval act of purification. Such fanaticism was not for the common herd, and the Legion, in fact, operated on narrow elitist assumptions. Codreanu rigorously weeded out anyone whose faith and obedience were suspect in the slightest. He counted on finding enough pure spirits among Rumania's youthful intelligentsia, and the Legion concentrated on developing "brotherhoods of the cross" in high schools and universities.

Rumania, then, was to be redeemed from modernist corruption through the energy and inspiration of a legionary elect. Because of its selectivity, the Legion never aspired to be a mass movement and held aloof from Rumanian party politics. However, in 1930, spurred by the crisis of the Great Depression, Codreanu judged the moment opportune to carry his message to the people. For this purpose he created the Iron Guard, which espoused the same ideas as the Legion of the Archangel, although in somewhat less messianic form. The Legion remained intact as a sort of brains trust and leadership cadre within the Iron Guard, the Guard being simply a device to mobilize the masses and mount a challenge to the status quo.

The political system of Rumania was a parliamentary one, although it scarcely represented many shades of opinion. The dominant interwar party was called Liberal, but its members were quite different from the liberals whom Mussolini and Hitler swept aside. The Rumanian Liberal party, standing for entrenched privilege, had more in common with Hungary's historic classes. Periodically, a self-styled reformist faction won control of the government—in 1926, the Popular party and, in 1928, the National Peasant party. But once in office, these "reformers" turned out to be almost as timeserving as the liberals. All Rumanian ministries of whatever complexion ended up in league with an establishment of landed aristocrats and urban millionaires. Official tolerance of radical dissent was minimal. Although legionary economic policies were vague, the denunciation of Jewish capitalism and the populist appeal to the peasantry smacked of an attack on private property. Consequently, Codreanu's movement, despite its antibolshevism, was labeled subversive by Rumanian authorities who tried to stamp it out by force and intimidation. Given the Legion's own predilection for terror tactics, a veritable civil war developed between legionaries and police. The quarrel escalated with Codreanu's effort to disseminate his ideas far and wide through the Iron Guard, and consequently in 1931, the National Peasant government banned the Legion and the Guard. Indeed, during the 1930s, the pair of organizations were proscribed several times. But it was to no avail; the Legion always operated as a semisecret society, while the Iron Guard continued to function under assumed names like the "C. Z. Codreanu Group" or "All for the Fatherland." In 1932 the Iron Guard, having been restored to legitimacy by a friendly court, won 73,000 votes and five seats in Parliament. From this point, Rumanian fascism really started to grow apace.

But parliament remained peripheral to the Guard's main thrust. Codreanu's philosophy idealized the Rumanian peasant as the inheritor of true native values, and his priority in the mid-thirties was to establish a foothold in the villages. So thousands of green-shirted legionaries fanned out over the countryside, moving usually on foot from hamlet to hamlet. Where a legionary band stopped, its members would devote themselves to manual labor, helping in the fields or repairing roads, cottages, and churches. Unremitting hard work and Spartan living close to the blessed Rumanian soil, they explained, was spiritually uplifting. In the evenings they arranged village gatherings where Rumanian folk tales and songs were rehearsed and icons of "the captain," Codreanu, handed out. The legionaries' selfless discipline and their dedication to their puritan ideal were enormously attractive to the peasantry, while their persecution by the police won them the automatic sympathy of the downtrodden.

What Codreanu termed his "holy crusade" to the rural masses met with such success that it aroused the grudging envy of Rumania's power brokers. They needed a means such as Codreanu had found of communicating with the lower classes disoriented by the Great Depression. Between 1931 and 1939, real wages in Rumania fell by some 20 percent, and social unrest bubbled beneath the surface. As a countermeasure, some businessmen began to consider the anticommunist Iron Guard as a possible ally. They were encouraged in this dream by the Guard's nominal adoption of the economic ideas of Mihail Manoilescu, a former neoliberal economist and cabinet minister. In his best-known work, *Theory of Protection and International Trade* (London, 1931), Manoilescu argued that a backward agricultural country like Rumania was hurt by liberal economic practices in a highly competitive world. Such a nation could only industrialize and prosper with a guided and sheltered national economy, and this required an authoritarian government and a corporative economic structure. It was exactly the same line of reasoning advanced by Italy's "productivists" and corporativists, who were concerned with overcoming their nation's economic retardation. When, after 1934, Fascist Italy largely deserted corporativism on the home front for the sake of empire and glory overseas, Manoilescu became Europe's leading corporative theoretician. In fact, his reputation outside Rumania was probably greater than within his own country, for the Iron Guard merely adopted his corporative economics as a convenient party platform. Apart from some fascist idealists in the academies, most legionaries could not be bothered with anything so mundane as a consistent economic policy. Nevertheless, Manoilescu's loose association with the Iron Guard gave the movement a touch of sane respectability which commended it to the business community.

Of much greater importance to the Iron Guard's standing, however, was the favor of the Rumanian monarchy. The ambitious and rapacious King Carol II was inspired to emulation by the rise of authoritarian regimes elsewhere. Although no fascist himself, he aimed at the destruction of Rumania's creaking and corrupt parliamentary system. And he was acute enough to recognize that in the modern age he needed a popular base for his projected autocracy. He hoped to enlist Codreanu's youthful legionaries on his side and to use them as a link with the people. Once the king's good will to the Iron Guard became known, the police vendetta died down and several helpful doors were opened. For the first time, money from propertied interests and even government officials began to reach Codreanu, and two Bucharest newspapers offered to promote legionary views.

The combination of royal benevolence and legionary tactics at the village level produced some spectacular triumphs for the Iron Guard. By 1937 it was estimated that 34,000 "nests" existed in Rumania, and through a Legionary Workers' Corps the Guard was now making converts among the Bucharest proletariat as well as villagers. In the elections at the end of the year, the Iron Guard won 16 percent of the vote

Alarmed at the growing popularity of the Iron Guard, King Carol of
Rumania tried to destroy the movement in a bloodbath. Then, in 1939,
the king founded his own national party with some fascist overtones. Here,
Carol wears his party uniform and gives the party salute.

and sixty-six seats in the chamber of deputies to become the third
largest parliamentary party. In his "Men of the Archangel" (*Journal of
Contemporary History* [1966]), E. Weber has dissected the legionary
poll to discover that while it was, as usual, heavy in anti-Semitic coun-
ties in the north, the most striking gains were made in southern areas
where rural poverty rather than racism seemed the conditioning factor.
In short, the Iron Guard proved itself the most authentic and dynamic

voice of Rumanian radicalism. Yet, at the very moment that Codreanu's movement seemed poised to sweep to supreme power, it lost royal patronage and suffered a drastic reversal of fortune.

There were several reasons for King Carol's volte-face. Foreign policy was one consideration. The followers of the Archangel Michael, in their simplistic, apocalyptic way, construed international affairs as a struggle between universal fascism and world communism. Such was their view of the Spanish Civil War, and a token legionary detachment was sent to fight for Franco; its leader, Mota, was one of the first casualties. In the same vein, after his electoral success of December 1937, Codreanu openly urged Rumania's alignment with the Axis powers, thus contradicting King Carol who wanted desperately to keep open a line to the west in order to avert German tutelage. On internal matters, the Legion kept up its strident anti-Semitism and, tactlessly oblivious to royal feelings, persistently cited the case of Carol's Jewish mistress as proof of Jewish intrigue in high and secret places. But, above all, the king was surprised and alarmed at the election figures; the Iron Guard was much more popular than he had guessed, and it loomed as a Frankenstein's monster about to turn on its would-be royal master. In truth, Codreanu was quite sincere when he protested that he had no thought of using the Iron Guard in a coup against the king. In February 1938, when Carol moved to establish his personal dictatorship and abolished the parliamentary constitution, Codreanu acquiesced and voluntarily dissolved the Guard. But the king was taking no chances. Codreanu was arrested and sentenced to ten years hard labor on a charge of conspiring to take over the state. Hundreds of other legionaries were thrown into concentration camps.

The men of the Archangel responded to persecution as they had been trained to do—by violence against the Jews for supposedly manipulating the royal government against the Legion, and by assassination of public officials for protecting the Jews. The new round of legionary terrorism was directed mostly by Horia Sima, a provincial schoolteacher who tried to fill the captain's shoes. Codreanu himself disapproved, feeling that time was on the Legion's side and that his own life was being jeopardized by Sima's tactics. But, in prison, Codreanu was powerless to arrest the flow of blood. In November 1938 legionaries killed the rector of the University of Cluj, whereupon the government resolved on savage deterrent action. Codreanu and thirteen legionaries convicted of murder were taken from prison by truck, and on a deserted stretch of road, they were strangled with ropes and then shot in the back. This barbarity was

laid at the door of Armand Călinescu, the strong and ruthless chief
minister in King Carol's authoritarian government. The Legion vowed
to exact vengeance. During the next ten months, the police unearthed
innumerable plots, and scores of legionary assassins were caught, tor-
tured, and executed. But at last, in September 1939, a group of six
succeeded in ambushing Călinescu and shooting him dead; they then
occupied a radio station long enough to broadcast that Codreanu's mur-
derer had been punished. Călinescu was the second premier the legionaries had killed (the Liberal Ion Duca being the other). The royal
government now indulged in wider reprisals against the Legion than
ever before. In addition to the execution of Calinescu's assassins on the
spot of their crime, the prefect of every district was instructed to designate three local legionaries for immediate execution. For good measure,
the legionary corpses were strung up publicly all over Rumania.

The grotesque violence and slaughter of 1938–39 resembled the sort
of ritual purification by bloodshed that Codreanu had all along suggested was necessary for national regeneration. In the short run, however, the atrocities served only to perpetuate the old order in the guise
of King Carol's dictatorship. True, the royal regime tried to give itself
a radical image and, in doing so, often copied the Legion of the Archangel. There were speeches extolling work and self-discipline, Christianity and a racist patriotism. Lip service was paid to Manoilescu's
corporative theories. A royal youth movement, Strajeri (Watch), was
set up, and an all-embracing organization called the Front of National
Revival superseded the defunct political parties. Yet withal, Carol's
regime was never more than a narrow autocracy which aped the superficialities of the mass fascist movements.

In the meantime, the Legion went underground, its strength impaired but certainly not destroyed. For example, many instructors in
Strajeri were secret legionaries. Other legionaries, including Sima, found
asylum in Nazi Germany. In fact, after Codreanu's death the Legion
fell increasingly under Nazi sway. With the outbreak of the Second
World War, its leaders bided their time until German domination of
Rumania gave them a chance to resume the legionary assault in their
homeland. This new political tie matched the ideological affinity that
had always been present between legionary fascism and Nazism. Fundamentally, Codreanu's inspiration and goal was the same as Hitler's—a
spiritual revolution which would resurrect a glorious, golden past. Of
course, this is merely to say that Rumania affords the extreme example
of the fascist pattern we have observed at large in the Danube Valley.

Despite the region's need to modernize in accord with rationalist precepts, the Danubian fascist movements were, in Nagy-Talavera's words, "imbued with a desperate, infantile romanticism," and their absorption of racist traditions generated hysterical, backward-looking visions in the paradigm of German National Socialism.

### FINLAND

Before leaving eastern Europe, one other national experience of fascism warrants passing treatment. This concerns the growth of fascist societies in Finland, significant in their own right, and in some ways reflective of the generic model of eastern European fascism. Until 1917 the Duchy of Finland was an integral part of the Russian empire. Only after the defeat of czarist Russia by Germany in the midst of the First World War did an independent Finnish state emerge. The question was, what political character would the new Finland assume? The extreme Left naturally hoped that, as czarist autocracy in St. Petersburg had been supplanted by a bolshevik regime, the same thing would happen in Helsinki. From the opposite end of the political spectrum, Finnish conservatives accused the Left of subversion, not only because of its economic radicalism but because it looked now for help to Russia, the Finns' traditional oppressor. In the winter of 1917–18, a bitter civil war broke out between Reds and Whites. Atrocities were frequent on both sides until Field Marshal Mannerheim, a former czarist officer but also a Finnish patriot, accepted German military help and led the Right to victory. Although the fighting lasted only a few months, this Red-White clash in Finland, like the similar civil disturbances in Bavaria and Hungary, cast a long shadow over the interwar era.

After the turbulence of the civil war, Finland adopted a republican and parliamentary constitution. The Right chafed at this liberal experiment, contending that the regime was too feeble to protect Finland from her enemies. For one thing, the Finnish Communists, despite their defeat on the battlefield, remained strong. During the 1920s, they polled between 10 and 15 percent in elections, and gained a foothold in the trade unions. Meanwhile, in 1920, Finland signed a treaty with Russia which affronted the nationalist Right's concept of a Greater Finland (*Suur-Suomi*); especially resented was the failure to obtain Eastern Karelia. The most vociferous critics of the parliamentary regime's leniency to the Soviets at the negotiating table and to Russian communism at home came from the adolescent "war generation."

During the First World War, two thousand young Finns had fled to Germany and fought in the *Jäger* battalion against Russia on the eastern front. On their return home, the *Jägers* brought with them an adulation of the German military values of order, authority, and patriotism. Their influence was great in the army, where *Jägers* formed the nucleus of the officer corps, and among the student population, too. The *Jäger* spirit impelled many student activists into the Civil Guards, a 100,000-strong paramilitary organization similar to the German *Freikorps*, which devolved from Mannerheim's antibolshevik coalition of 1918. Many Civil Guards in 1921–22 crossed into Eastern Karelia where they joined White forces still fighting against the Soviets. When the Finnish minister of the interior closed the border, he was assassinated. Out of this ambience of youthful, militant anticommunism and nationalism sprang Finland's first quasi-fascist group.

In 1922 three young soldiers returned from Eastern Karelia to found the Academic Karelia Society. Organized on military hierarchical lines, the society despised rational debate and demanded a blind faith from its members. Its raison d'être was the cultivation of Finnish national consciousness through emphasis on the Finnish language at home and *Suur-Suomi* abroad. Moreover, the nationalism of the Academic Karelia Society had a distinct racist tinge. The society reversed the usual racialistic argument and claimed that peoples of mixed stock (the Finns being a combination of Balts and Scandinavians) were biologically superior to those of a single ethnic strain. Needless to say, no more scientific evidence existed for this racial position than for the contradictory Nazi one. It was sufficient that race consciousness was a weapon to use against alien forces—namely, the hated Russian Slavs and, even more, the Swedes who comprised 11 percent of Finland's population. There was a good deal of jealousy over Swedish preponderance in the professions and business; the Swedes in Finland were thus cast in somewhat the same role as the Jews in the Danube Valley. During its career, which lasted until 1944, the Academic Karelia Society wielded a certain influence, mostly in intellectual circles, but it never sought political power for itself, and took pride in restricting its membership to an elite of two or three thousand. A mass fascist movement was not attempted in Finland until the Great Depression arrived to serve, as it did in so many countries, as a catalyst.

Already in the elections of 1929, before the full fury of the depression struck, the Finnish Communist party had made modest but significant gains, and the deteriorating economic situation threatened to play further into the hands of the extreme Left. The Great Depression, then, stirred up the passions of the civil war a decade earlier and, in particular, the pervasive fear of bolshevism. In November 1929, in the small village of Lapua, Civil Guards and local farmers interrupted a Communist youth meeting and severely manhandled the participants. This incident gave its name to the Lapua Movement, a sudden upsurge of popular political feeling. The movement's first and foremost aim was the outlawing of the Finnish Communist party. To the argument that such an action would be unconstitutional, the movement responded with the so-called Law of Lapua—a rough synonym for Finland's ineffable historical destiny which overrode all artificial legal barriers. From its start, the Lapua Movement backed up its demands with violence—against the Communists themselves and against the authorities. On one occasion, 13,000 armed Lapua members and Civil Guards demonstrated in downtown Helsinki. On another, a former Finnish president known as a moderate was kidnapped by *Jägers*. Communist deputies were attacked within the precincts of parliament, and elsewhere Communist press and trade union offices were ransacked. The antibolshevik scare sown by the Lapua Movement bore fruit in new elections in October 1930 which saw a swing to the right. Parliament was now sufficiently conservative to provide a two-thirds majority for constitutional changes banning the Communist party. Not until 1944 would Finnish Communists again enjoy legal status.

But despite the achievement of its original purpose, the Lapua Movement did not cease agitating. Its leader, Vihtori Kosola, began to see himself as the Finnish Mussolini, and to call for the suppression of the Social Democrats and the overthrow of the parliamentary system itself. By February 1932 the Lapua Movement was poised for a coup. An ultimatum was issued for the cabinet's resignation and replacement by one "free from party aims and depending . . . on the support of the nation's patriotic elements." But spasmodic but persistent terrorism had by now alienated much of the bourgeoisie. More important, Finland's grandees of the Right under the leadership of President Svinhufvud, who had connived at Lapuan violence in order to destroy the Communists, turned against the movement. Svinhufvud, who enjoyed among Finns the status of Hindenburg among Germans, made a personal appeal to the populace to stay loyal to the constitution and declared a state of national emergency. In face of this resoluteness, the Lapua revolt fizzled out before it got started. Soon after, the Lapua Movement was declared an illegal organization, ironically under the same law used against the Communists.

But Finnish fascism was not dead. In April 1932 the People's Patriotic Movement rose out of the ashes of the Lapua coup. The new organization fused Lapua's obsessive anticommunism to Academic Karelia's racial nationalism directed against the Swedish minority and their language. The People's Patriotic Movement, or IKL as it was usually known, was encouraged by the rise of fascism across Europe, deliberately copying the successful foreign models. In deference to Italian Fascism, an elaborate design for a corporative structure in lieu of the Finnish parliament was drawn up. But Hitler's Germany was the chief exemplar of political authoritarianism and race-thinking; as watchwords, IKL adopted *johtajaperiaate* and *kansakonaisuus*, ungainly but literal translations of Nazi *Führerprinzip* and *Volksgemeinschaft*. Again in imitation of Hitler, the movement set great store by the cultivation of an adolescent constituency and establishment of youth cadres, often overlapping the activity of the longstanding Academic Karelia Society.

The youthful orientation of IKL, however, contributed to the organization's basic weakness—its failure to restore fully the fascist alliance of 1930 with the elderly, traditional Finnish Right. Indeed, the very choice of colors and uniform—a blue tie on a black shirt—was a symbolic affirmation of the new fascist party's distinction from the old order:

> The People's Patriotic Movement represents not only new colors; it represents a new conception of the world, it heralds the new in place of the old. . . . Blue-Black is something other than White. It is more than White. White has a glorious past, the most glorious to be found in Finland's history. An even more glorious future belongs to Blue-Black. Namely, Blue-Black will finish that which was left half finished in 1918. We believe that, just as White raised half our nation from a state of humiliation sixteen years ago, Blue-Black will yet raise our entire nation with the exception of those few who have sold their souls to Marx.

Between 1932 and 1935, IKL and the traditional conservatives maintained a loose parliamentary understanding, but this collapsed before the elections of 1936 won by the democratic Left. IKL polled over 8 percent of the vote, but this turned out to be a peak, for three years later electoral support dropped by one fifth. In the early 1930s, Finnish fascism in tandem with the old conservatives had threatened the existence of the liberal state; by the end of the decade, the fascists, operating alone, were largely a spent force. As in Hungary and Rumania, it was the historic Right which could make or break a fascist movement.

Fascism in Finland was not nearly so virulent as it was in the Danube Valley, but there were resemblances. After all, the key to every fascist movement in eastern Europe was Soviet Russia. It was no coincidence that Finnish fascism originated on the Karelian border, that Rumanian fascism was born not far from the Russian frontier at Jassy, and that Hungarian fascism was a backlash against Béla Kun's bolshevik interlude. Nor was this sensitivity to Russia's proximity and spell simply a matter of anticommunism. Significantly, not one of the three eastern European states in which fascism reached meaningful proportions between the wars belonged to the Slavic family of nations. In other words, Russia was seen and feared in Finland, Hungary, and Rumania as racially as well as politically alien. Undoubtedly, this helped to raise the racial quotient of fascist nationalism in each case. Instinctual race-thinking was, indeed, a vital factor common to all fascisms in eastern Europe. Faced with the general backwardness of the area, the fascists there fled from modern reality and took refuge in romantic racial dreams—Magyar Turanianism and Hungarism, Rumanian Christian mysticism, and the Finns' peculiar brand of Nordic racism. In day-to-day practice, they found a scapegoat for current ills in their own racial minorities—Jews, Slavs, and Swedes. And so, eastern European fascism, through its fixation on race, was rendered a regressive, highly irrational phenomenon.

## The Advanced Nations of Western Europe

In its escapist racism, east European fascism conformed to the Nazi stereotype. But the present on which the fascists in eastern Europe tried to turn their backs was very different from that which the German National Socialists abhorred. Fascists on the Danube and in Finland reacted against the auguries of an alien, urban modernity, the Nazis against the actuality. For a true parallel with Germany's fascist experience, therefore, we must turn to the advanced states of northwestern Europe—France, the Low Countries, and Great Britain. It is in this context that we may best examine the proposition that fascism, wherever it appeared in a modern setting, expressed an emotional longing to call up a golden age from the past.

France early in this century was not a fully modernized country, economically speaking. Roughly half the population lived in hamlets or towns of 20,000 or less. Agriculture still employed almost as many as industry, and many factory workers added to agrarian produce from market gardens in their spare time. The Industrial Revolution had transformed parts of France, notably in the north, yet only some 150 factories had a labor force over 1,000, while the national average per establishment was six. Industrialization and urbanization remained regional phenomena.

On the other hand, in intellectual terms and national mentality, the French were a thoroughly modern community. The value system of nineteenth- and twentieth-century liberalism was rooted in the Enlightenment of the eighteenth century which, insofar as it was tied to any one country at all, had its spiritual home in France. Moreover, out of the eighteenth-century Age of Reason sprang the French Revolution— the mightiest political inspiration of modern liberalism. The successive Parisian uprisings of 1830, 1848, and 1871 were all, after their different fashions, efforts to fulfill the promise of the *philosophes* and the revolutionaries of 1789. Given the dominance of Paris over the rest of the country, it followed that, by the close of the nineteenth century, France was a nation shot through with the presumptions of modern social thought, and no Frenchman could remain unaffected, however subconsciously. It has already been observed that Italians after World War I were convinced their country was stagnant regardless of the recent industrialization of the north, thus creating a national sense of backwardness. Likewise, in France it was the psychological climate that mattered. In spite of France's inability to keep pace economically with Germany and Great Britain, her intellectual environment was a progressive one. For several generations, Frenchmen had felt themselves to be foremost among western European innovators in politics, culture, and social mores. It was as a recoil against this modernist image that French fascism evolved.

One stumbling block in dealing with fascism in France should be mentioned at the outset: that is, the French never developed a single comprehensive fascist party comparable to the PNF or the NSDAP on which to focus analysis. French fascist groups were numerous enough, especially in the 1930s when the Great Depression and a Marxist scare supplied the usual fertile breeding ground; but these factions could not or would not amalgamate, and none alone managed to pose a deadly threat to the liberal regime. French fascism, however, was much more than the sum of these splinter groups. For instead of centering in one party, fascist notions became diffused throughout the right wing of the political spectrum. One popular analogy is to compare fascism to a fever which infected the French body politic. Or, in the words of Robert Brasillach, one of a coterie of fascistically inclined French intellectuals in the thirties: "Fascism is for us no political or economic doctrine. . . . But fascism is a mood, an anticonformist spirit, antibourgeois in the first place, and irreverent." Such a humor is not easy to capture in print, yet it could be enormously contagious in social reality.

If French fascism was a fever of ideas and attitudes, from whence did it emanate? By common consent, the force which was first chronologically and foremost influentially in directing French conservative opinion into fascist channels was the Action Française. Ernst Nolte in his important book, *Three Faces of Fascism* (1966), places Action Française alongside German National Socialism and Italian Fascism. Nolte is careful to point out that Action Française was never a full-blown fascist movement, but at best a "protofascist" one. Nevertheless, he is right to include Action Française in his trio of exemplary fascisms, for the social and political philosophy it disseminated for almost half a century bore a distinct resemblance to the *völkisch Weltanschauung* of Nazi Germany.

Action Française was an offshoot of the Dreyfus affair. In 1894 Captain Alfred Dreyfus, who had served on the French general staff, was convicted by a military court of spying for the Germans and transported to Devil's Island. Gradually over the next few years, it became apparent that Dreyfus had been framed, chosen as a convenient scapegoat partly because he was Jewish, partly because he hailed from the province of Alsace which, since 1871, had been ruled by Germany. The question of whether the Dreyfus case should or should not be reopened tore French society apart and rocked the state itself. On one side, it was contended that military justice should not be challenged for fear that the army, as the guardian of French national honor, be held up to scorn. On the other, the argument concentrated on the right of every citizen to fair and equal treatment before the law. Justice for the individual, *raison d'état* notwithstanding, was the quintessence of atomic liberalism and of its practical manifestation in the Third French Republic. In this way, Dreyfus tested the validity of the entire French political system.

France's liberal republic always found difficulty in mobilizing popular support. It had been adopted piecemeal in the 1870s on the negative

grounds of "the form of government which divided Frenchmen least."
In the ensuing years, the republic's reputation was further tarnished by
a series of scandals, which revealed a close and sometimes unsavory
nexus between big business and republican politicians who were derisively termed "Opportunists." In one instance, the son-in-law of the
president was discovered to be selling national awards and decorations
(including the prestigious Legion of Honor, so it was rumored) to the
highest bidder. In another, political chicanery kept the frailty of the
French Panama Canal Company from the investing public long after
the company was, in reality, bankrupt. In lack of principle and materialism, political circles in the Third Republic fell not far short of Italy's
transformist politicos of the same era. Just as the sickness of the Italian
liberal regime encouraged the Right to provoke the constitutional crisis
of 1898–1900, so antiliberal elements in France saw their opportunity
in republican corruption.

In the Dreyfus affair, the French Right, seizing on the clear-cut issue
of national interest versus individual rights, believed its moment had
come. Monarchists, aristocrats, the higher clergy, nationalists, and anti-
Semites, all joined with the army officers in a formidable anti-Dreyfusard
and antirepublican coalition. More important, they enjoyed wide sympathy in all strata of society. However, this muster on the right was
matched by a countervailing force. Again as in Italy at the turn of the
century, the prospect of a rightist coup produced a rallying to the liberal
cause by many figures of note—intellectuals and artists, radicals and
socialists—who had been hitherto alienated by the daily conduct of
liberal politicians. Faced with this stiffening of the republican backbone
and the possibility of civil war, the French Right shrank back. In
September 1899 Dreyfus was granted a new court-martial which recon-
victed him of treason, but "with extenuating circumstances." Whereupon, the president of the republic pardoned Dreyfus, although it
would be 1906 before the guilty verdict was reversed. But in the meantime, the Third Republic had survived its sternest trial to date.

In April 1898 a *Comité de l'Action Française* was founded by Henri
Vaugeois, a schoolmaster, and Maurice Pujo, a hack journalist, but this
was only one of myriad rightist leagues spawned at the height of the
Dreyfus affair. It was a year later before the Action Française organization which would survive to shape the thinking of two generations of
French conservatives was born. In May 1899 Vaugeois, abetted by a
young writer from southern France by the name of Charles Maurras,
reused the former nomenclature and established the Action Française

Society. Thus, Action Française, properly speaking, was launched toward the close of the Dreyfus affair, when it was becoming clear that the republic was not about to fall. Action Française reflected the bitterness of the Right's impending defeat; its function was to keep alive and give doctrinal form to those reactionary attitudes which had peaked in the Dreyfus years.

Like every French political faction, Action Française based its creed on an interpretation of the events of 1789. To Action Française, naturally, the great revolution was an unmitigated catastrophe and the source of all France's ailments. Two Jacobin evils were selected for special denunciation—egalitarianism and centralization. Egalitarian politics not only upset the "natural" social hierarchy so beloved by conservatives, but also granted civic rights to those on the fringe of the French national community such as resident foreigners, derisively termed *métèques*, and, above all, the Jews. "The only one to whom the Revolution was profitable was the Jew," wrote Edouard Drumont in *La France Juive* (1886), and the Dreyfusard victory was testament to Jewish legal equality won as a result of 1789. Racial hatred of the Jews in France was on the upsurge in the last decades of the nineteenth century, fomented by professional anti-Semites like Drumont who were wont to attribute the venality of the Third Republic to Jewish finance. Action Française absorbed this anti-Semitism and, like the German *Volkists*, fixed on the Jew as a detested symbol of the bourgeois and egalitarian features of modern France.

The centralization of French administration, which Action Française unhistorically imputed to the French Revolution, was condemned because it exalted the values of the capital at the expense of rural ones. The sound traditions and certitudes of old France were held to reside in the countryside, while Paris, in contrast, was the haunt of sharp businessmen, intellectual freethinkers, and upstart cosmopolites. Revolutions always began in Paris, and Paris stood for experimentation and change. Maurras, who from the start was the high priest of Action Française, had come to Paris in 1885 at the age of seventeen and been shocked to the core by what he regarded as the city's licentiousness. Maurras's youthful revulsion on discovering Paris has been compared to that of the young Hitler on reaching Vienna. Each man in due course built his political movement around an aversion to big-city life and morals.

The kernel of Action Française philosophy was contained in a metaphor which Maurras appropriated from the French royalists and then popularized. This said that, at least since 1789, two Frances had existed side by side—one, a *pays légal*, and the other, the *pays réel*. The former was the institutional state fabricated of man-made laws, the product of intelligent but artificial contrivance. The Third Republic was such a regime. On the other hand, the "true nation" of the French Right was an organic community with deep roots in the French past and soil. The object of Action Française was to make the *pays légal* correspond again to the *pays réel*, entailing, in Maurras's view, a return to "the permanencies of the past." Consequently, he advocated the revival of the historic orders of aristocracy, church, and monarchy, although he appreciated more the social functions these institutions might perform than the institutions themselves. Maurras personally was a bourgeois, his father having been a tax collector, while in religious matters he was a professed atheist. And as a royalist, Maurras was no absolutist; his "positivist" monarchy, while offering a focal point of loyalties, was intended to preside over a decentralized system. In the ideal Maurrassian state, regions were to be self-governing and villages self-supportive as far as possible. Economic activity was to be regulated, not by the interplay of big business and big government on a national scale, but by local, autonomous guilds. Yet, despite demanding this fragmentation of French life, Maurras's Action Française had in mind a society of exceptional order and unity. Once released from "the anarchy of the Rights of Man," Frenchmen would naturally defer to the prescriptive rights of ancient authorities. Capitalism's class war and other internal divisions would vanish. Each citizen, secure in his appointed station, would feel himself a vital, composite part of the organic national body. In this way, Action Française, like the later fascist movements, tried to combine social elitism with a sense of community; its philosophy was an early attempt to solve the riddle by propounding integral nationalism.

The Maurrassian dream, it is clear, rested on a glamorized interpretation of prerevolutionary France. Indeed, Maurras's *pays réel* seemed to go back several centuries and to rest on medieval concepts. Certainly, the combination of a hierarchical social structure and political decentralization recalled the Middle Ages. So, too, did his corporative economic notions which, in contradistinction to Mussolinian corporativism, owed nothing to modern syndicalist socialism and everything to Catholic social writers such as the Comte de Mun and the Marquis La Tour du Pin, who idealized medieval Christianity. To Action Française, the most venerated figure in French history was Joan of Arc. Of course, the *pays réel* no more existed in historical fact than did the Teutonic Valhalla and Wagnerian Rhine idyll. Nonetheless, visions of the past can be the more potent for being mythical; it makes it simpler to invest the halcyon age with the requisite virtues. Thus, Maurras pretended that in his antique utopia something he never defined but called "Latin culture" had reigned supreme, deliberately creating the impression of a simple, homogeneous community as yet untainted by foreign influences. In truth, Action Française evinced much the same preoccupation with lost innocence and purity as Hitler's Nazis. Connotations of a tribal racism were never far away. The fellowship of the *pays réel*, rooted in instinctive ties of nature, was the French equivalent of the German *Volksgemeinschaft*.

Many of these ideas were conventional staples of French reactionary thought, but the Maurrassian synthesis was original and virile, and found a ready audience among the antirepublican Right in France between 1900 and 1914. Although the Third Republic appeared to have emerged from the Dreyfus affair purged and strengthened by the danger it had run, the regime was still very vulnerable. The lofty resolution of the liberal politicians to elevate their conduct in the new century faded with time. The situation matched that in Giolittian Italy where hopes of a brave new liberal start after a crisis surmounted were dashed in the years before the First World War. In France, republican ministries became embroiled in bitter quarrels with the military and the church as they sought to get even with these anti-Dreyfusard stalwarts. A witch hunt was set afoot to weed out antirepublican officers, under cover of which many private scores were settled. Moreover, the length of time young conscripts were subjected to the possibly antirepublican influence of professional officers was reduced from three years to two. Similarly, another campaign was launched to reduce the role of the Catholic church in the sensitive area of education. The upshot in 1905 was the breach of France's concordat with the papacy, which went back to 1802, and the separation of state and church. This vindictive attitude toward both army and church was perhaps understandable in the wake of the Dreyfus affair, but, in practical terms, it enabled the officers and the clergy—and by extension French conservatives at large—to pose and win sympathy as victims of unfair persecution. Meanwhile, at the other end of the political spectrum, a rising tide of strikes after 1906, including syndicalist efforts to organize a general strike, suggested that the Left's rallying to the republic in the Dreyfus affair had been a temporary phenomenon. In brief, many Frenchmen remained apathetic or openly hostile to the liberal parliamentary system. Action Française's prosperity was one measure of disgruntlement with the Third Republic.

Not until March 1905 was Action Française rated significant enough to appear in police dossiers on reactionary activity. However, by May of the following year, police reports recognized Action Française as the pacesetter among potentially subversive right-wing groups. This reflected the inauguration in 1905 of the League of the Action Française, an open declaration that the movement was determined to emphasize political action. The fresh orientation brought in recruits, and within a few years, Action Française's membership topped thirty thousand. With funds becoming more plentiful, the publication *Action Française* was transformed in 1908 into a daily paper and a prime example of scurrilous yellow journalism. Its new editor was Léon Daudet, son of the famous novelist and literary *bon vivant* about Paris. He was to become the second most influential figure in Action Française after Maurras. Also in 1908 the *Camelots du Roi* (hawkers for the king) made their appearance. Originally teen-agers who sold *Action Française* and royalist tracts on the streets, they soon came to form the private army of Action Française. One of their first escapades was to disrupt a series of lectures at the Sorbonne which were mildly critical of Joan of Arc. The *Camelots du Roi* were the forerunners of the nationalist gangs which would plague Italy and Germany after the First World War.

Yet for all its increase and bravura, Action Française was always a circumscribed movement. Its leaders were literary men and artists *manqués* who trafficked in ideas rather than hard political realities. E. R. Tannenbaum sums them up as "café intellectuals." Their invocation of a legendary past appealed to the déclassé nobility and pretentious, *bien-pensant* bourgeoisie who comprised the bulk of Action Française members. The movement also offered novelty and excitement to the bored middle-class youth who enrolled in the *Camelots du Roi*. On the other hand, great difficulty was experienced in attracting mass support. This shortcoming was epitomized by Maurras himself, whose personality did not fit him to be the dynamic leader of a populist movement. He was rather scrawny in appearance and afflicted with deafness from childhood. Despite his romanticization of the past, he affected to be a cold positivist intellectual who despised "sentimental" appeals to the public. The total impression was of a crabbed, bookish bachelor with no talent at all for communication with the masses.

Action Française did make one concrete endeavor to build a bridge to the working class with the formation in 1911 of the *Cercle Proudhon*, a discussion group of intellectuals drawn from the socially concerned fringe of Action Française and a branch of the syndicalist socialists under the political philosopher, Georges Sorel. It was hoped that the two factions would find grounds for cooperation in their joint admiration for the family as the ideal social unit and in their common antipathy to the bourgeois Third Republic. It represented one of the few serious attempts before 1914 to make socialism and nationalism coexist within a single political framework, but the experiment failed. Sorel himself was skeptical all along, while the impetus within Action Française came, not from an unenthusiastic Maurras, but from an ex-revolutionary intellectual, Georges Valois. So the popular image of Action Française continued unchanged. Because of its veneration of traditional monarchy and aristocracy, the workers by and large dismissed Maurras's organization as a party of privilege. It was this failure to establish a mass base which, more than anything else, prevented Action Française from flowering into a genuine fascist movement.

The Great War of 1914 was a blow to Action Française. In the first place, all French factions joined together behind the existing republican regime in a patriotic *union sacrée*. For the time being, the alleged gulf between the *pays légal* and the *pays réel* ceased to exist. Moreover, in the postwar struggle over the peace treaties and German reparations, the Third Republic continued as the champion of French nationalism, thus cutting into Action Française's patriotic market. In the meantime, the youthful membership of Action Française had been decimated on the western front. This is not to say that the movement declined drastically in numbers; in 1925–26 the circulation of the daily and Sunday editions of *Action Française* reached a peak. But by now, Action Française had lost much of its earlier vitality, and seemed tacitly content to play the role of a pressure group within the established order. One indication was the movement's failure to take inspiration from Mussolini's March on Rome. So upset was the former syndicalist Valois that, in 1925, he left Action Française to found his own *Faisceau* organization patterned blatantly on Italian Fascism. *Faisceau* members wore blue shirts and subscribed to the doctrines of syndical corporativism, but in the well-being and euphoria of the Locarno era, *Faisceau* made little headway and, in three years, was virtually defunct. Nevertheless, the departure of Valois was a loss Action Française could ill afford, for it meant the end to any pretense that the movement could speak to the workers. Next, Action Française suffered a defeat on its right flank.

In 1926 Maurras's dogmatic integral nationalism clashed with the Catholic church's insistence on man's spiritual freedom within the secular state. The Vatican was persuaded to condemn Action Française and all its works. In sum, the status of Action Française was on the decline between the world wars. Ironically, the process was accelerated after February 6, 1934, the events of which raised anew the question of the Third Republic's viability.

In the decade after World War I, a republican synthesis seemed to have matured. By eschewing attacks on vested interests and catering to the wishes of France's numerous rentiers and small property-holding classes, the republic tapped a vein of popular support. It was hardly a dynamic political constituency; Stanley Hoffmann has aptly termed it "the stalemate society." In an era of stability, the regime's caution was welcome or tolerable to all but the extreme antirepublicans; in the depression-ridden 1930s, however, it was a different story. The impact of the Great Depression on France was a delayed one, but by 1932 economic distress demanded strong government action which was not forthcoming. In little more than a year, four cabinets came and went. Then, in the new year 1934, a stock manipulator, Sacha Stavisky, who was under investigation for fraud, committed suicide. The case was rumored to involve political personages and revived memories of the Panama Canal scandal of 1892. In the hope of unlocking the stalemate, as it were, both the far Right and the far Left resolved to exploit the prevailing atmosphere compounded of economic crisis and shady politico-financial dealing. It was the rightist press which called for direct action on February 6, but communists as well as student elements from right-wing leagues made up the mobs which tried repeatedly to storm the Chamber of Deputies on that day. By midnight, they were finally dispersed by police use of small arms and fire hoses; there were twenty-one dead and 1,600 other casualties. The Third Republic was saved once more.

Yet, republicans had to be apprehensive in view of the manifest temper of their enemies, particularly on the right where February 6 marked the passing of the torch from Action Française to the fascist leagues. The Camelots du Roi were to the fore in the rioting—two out of three casualties among the leagues came from Action Française—but the leadership discredited itself. At the height of the disturbances, Maurras and Daudet repaired to their offices to write the morrow's scathing editorials, thereby confirming the suspicion they were more concerned to tilt at the republic with words than to topple it with deeds. Action

Française, it was said, had forfeited its name; as a longstanding foe of the Third Republic, it had been expected to direct the attack of February 6. The abdication of this responsibility left the way clear for newer, more activist groups to step into the spotlight. The "proto-fascist" Action Française was pushed aside by the "parafascist" leagues.

Some of the organizations customarily included in the category of French fascist leagues long antedated 1934. For example, the ultrana-tionalistic *Jeunesses Patriotes* was founded by the right-wing deputy Pierre Taittinger as early as 1924. A more important movement, the *Croix de Feu*, began somewhat obscurely in 1928 as a reunion of war veterans, but with financial help from François Coty, the perfume manufacturer whose money was available for all manner of antirepub-lican intrigues, it grew into a threatening force. Coty's favorite was a Colonel de La Rocque who, assuming the presidency of *Croix de Feu* in 1931, made it into a mass movement. In 1934 the police estimated its numbers at 180,000. In 1938, by which time the movement had been made over into a full-fledged political party, De La Rocque boasted of three million followers. Obviously, the latter figure was inflated, but it does give some indication why many people at the time saw in *Croix de Feu* a French counterpart to the Italian and German fascist parties. This impression was misleading, however. De La Rocque was an uncomplicated, soldierly type who hated liberals and communists, Jews and foreigners, and of course the Third Republic. His dislikes were those of France's upper *bourgeoisie*, the same constituency to which Action Française appealed. But apart from its middle-class prej-udices, *Croix de Feu* had no doctrine to compare with Maurras's *re-cherche du temps perdu*. Class consciousness was no substitute for a positive ideology, without which *Croix de Feu* fell short of being a real national or fascist force. The problem of ideology beset other self-styled fascist leagues in France, although in an opposite fashion. The *Fran-cistes* and *Solidarité Française*, both established in the train of Hitler's arrival in power, had no trouble in stating their beliefs; they took them directly from Berlin. But because they were so consciously imitative, these neonazis hardly staked a claim to represent native French fascism, and accordingly won only limited support among the enemies of the Third Republic.

The riots of February 6, 1934, had demonstrated the trouble these noisy factions could cause, but they had also clearly shown their limita-tions. As the official parliamentary inquiry into February 6 remarked under the heading, "Fascist Organizations":

There does not exist in France at this time any political group having a military or semimilitary character in the sense that it is actively preparing for military action or war. Groups do exist, however, which by their authoritarian organization, their discipline, their orientation, and by the virtual absolute power of their leaders, constitute powerful organs which through politically-oriented manifestations in the street, can endanger public order.

The evolution of a broader, more serious fascist opposition to the liberal republic awaited further stimulus.

This was provided by the elections of May 1936. As the depression bit deeper into French life, Radicals, Socialists, and Communists agreed on a common platform and won striking gains at the polls. In consequence, a Popular Front ministry based on all these parties (albeit the Communists did not sit in the cabinet) took office with the premiership going to a Socialist, Léon Blum. To big business led by the "two hundred families" who reputedly controlled the Bank of France and by the *Comité des Forges* (the heavy industry lobby), bolshevism had arrived. Worse still, Blum, the personification of the red menace, was Jewish. Whereas French conservatives had been accustomed to talk in terms of "better Hitler than Stalin," now "better Hitler than Blum" was heard.

The Popular Front government was well aware of the danger of creeping fascism. One of its first actions was to ban all political leagues lest one succeed in becoming the engine of French fascism, but the measure was only partially effective. Some leagues simply changed their titles and carried on with little inconvenience. *Croix de Feu*, for instance, was reborn as the *Parti Social Français* (PSF). Other groups sprang up which were avowedly conspiratorial. The press made much of the sinister-sounding *Cagoulards* (the hooded ones). Created by a former *Camelot du Roi*, Eugène Deloncle, the *Cagoule's* ostensible purpose was to root out communists from the army. In practice, it was a well-armed terrorist society which plotted sabotage, the seizure of Popular Front ministers as hostages, and ultimately the violent capture of the state. Its most notorious feat, before being uncovered and broken up by the police, was to oblige Mussolini by murdering the Italian antifascist Rosselli brothers when they were holidaying in Normandy. The *Cagoule*, dangerous though it was, remained far too narrow in its activities and personnel to be called a political movement, fascist or otherwise.

By far the most significant fascist response to Blum's appointment came not from the right but from Jacques Doriot, an archetypal man of the people. Son of a blacksmith and in his youth himself a metal-worker, Doriot rose to prominence as a Communist until he left the party in 1934. But he retained a foothold in proletarian politics as he was reelected mayor of the Parisian working-class municipality of Saint Denis. Doriot had once advocated a popular antifascist front but soured on the idea after breaking with the Communists. Within weeks of Blum's electoral victory in 1936, he formed his *Parti Populaire Français* (PPF). In true fascist style, the PPF threatened to mobilize both political extremes against the liberal center. On the left, the PPF was the only French fascistic movement to make a valid appeal to the masses. Its emphasis was anti-big business rather than anti-Semitic, although its specific program did not go much beyond decentralization of a few monopolies in favor of small private enterprise. The credibility of the PPF with the workers rested largely on Doriot's personal popularity, which was nevertheless enough to give the party a wide advantage over the class-ridden leagues. On the other hand, the Right was wooed by Doriot's fierce anticommunism, such as can only be displayed by a backslider from the faith. Moreover, Doriot was not averse to recommending a return to old patterns in the manner of Action Française: "A nationalism understands itself only if it looks for its sources in the old traditions of the French provinces." The strength of the PPF, then, lay in mirroring a cross section of French society. By 1937, of 137,000 members it was believed two-thirds came from the working class. At the same time, the movement attracted such well-known intellectuals as Bertrand de Jouvenel and Pierre Drieu la Rochelle. However, it was not long before Doriot began to experience the same problem of fascist leaders everywhere—that of keeping all the contradictory elements within the movement happy. By the end of 1938, there were distinct signs of proletarian discontent in the PPF with the financial subsidies from big business that Doriot was eagerly accepting. On the outbreak of war, in September 1939, the likeliest fascist movement to arise in France was unmistakably on the wane.

Since 1934, a *Front National* had been in existence, promising to unite the French fascistic movements. However, it did not include all germane factions, and the cooperation it produced was not great. French fascism, in effect, remained fragmented throughout the 1930s, as the discontented flitted from one organization to another seeking the best means of breaking up the republican synthesis. Although the

Great Depression and the Popular Front constituted an incitement to fascism, the Third Republic managed to skirt any climactic provocation which might have pushed the fascist leagues and parties into one huge coalition. Perhaps the corner was turned in July 1936, soon after the opening of the Spanish Civil War. The new Popular Front ministers in Paris were sorely tempted to go to the aid of their confreres of the Spanish Popular Front. But, in that eventuality, several French rightist groups promised civil war in France. Blum, for one, took the threat seriously. Arguing that his political mandate was for domestic reform and not foreign adventure, he defused the issue by adopting nonintervention in the "Spanish cockpit." Then, the following April, the French Popular Front split up, although not before it was able to obtain through the Matignon agreement with employers across-the-board wage increases and other worker benefits which took some edge off the depression. The Popular Front was succeeded by a more conservative government under Edouard Daladier, which made a much less inviting target for the PSF, the PPF, and similar parties. Daladier, in fact, felt himself sufficiently secure to deal in quite an authoritarian manner with the fascist street rallies which had been such a feature of the Parisian scene in the middle thirties. Obviously, the Third Republic, for all its faults, was not yet completely bankrupt. In the public eye, party and ministerial fluctuations suggested confusion at the center; but, behind the façade, bureaucratic continuity provided the regime with some hidden strength.

Meanwhile, in a larger perspective, another factor, soon to overshadow all others, militated against French fascism. After 1936, the international situation made it increasingly difficult in France to be at one and the same time a fascist and a nationalist. To call oneself a fascist anywhere in Europe in the late thirties implied some sympathy for the regimes in Germany and Italy. Yet, in March 1936, Nazi Germany's remilitarization of the Rhineland demolished French guarantees of security won at Locarno, and at the same time Hitler was well on his way to dismantling France's network of alliances in eastern Europe. Also in 1936, Mussolini joined Hitler in the Rome-Berlin Axis and shortly began to demand the French territories of Nice, Corsica, and Tunisia. With each passing year, the fascist partners of the Axis revealed themselves to be France's mortal enemies. For French fascists who, like all fascists, were ipso facto nationalists, this posed an indissoluble dilemma. Many forgot their nationalism so far as to tolerate appeasement of Hitler and Mussolini. Maurras, Daudet, and Doriot all applauded the Munich Conference of 1938 because, as they freely admitted, they had no relish for fighting on the side of liberals and communists. This, however, did not stop them from calling Munich a French defeat and proof of the republic's incapacity. On the other hand, many Frenchmen, who might otherwise have enlisted in a French fascist cause, must have held back for fear of playing into the hands of France's enemies in Berlin and Rome. They put patriotism ahead of fascist ideology, albeit at the cost of supporting and prolonging the life of the hated Third Republic.

The problem of a relationship with foreign fascisms was to assume an acute form after the fall of France in 1940. Then, it became a matter of collaboration with the Nazi occupation forces, and the fascist leagues of the 1930s proved the most abundant source of collaborators. But collaborationism was not the only avenue opened to French fascists during World War II. At Vichy, the attempt was made to construct an indigenous French alternative to liberal republicanism. Here, inspiration was drawn not so much from the frenetic movements of the 1930s but from the older, more intellectualized Action Française. The Action Française movement itself had fallen into eclipse after 1934 when, rebuffed by the church and even the royalist pretender, the league of the Action Française and the *Camelots du Roi* had been proscribed by the Popular Front government, and Maurras himself had spent nine months in jail. But its doctrines had survived as an active bacillus of France's fascist fever. As we shall see in the next chapter, it was, above all, Maurras's backward-looking ideal of the *pays réel* which was taken out of storage to serve as the dogma of Vichy France.

### THE LOW COUNTRIES

Another western European area to exhibit fascist tendencies was the Low Countries—Belgium and Holland. The former, especially, was the scene of substantial fascist activity. Divided more or less equally between the French-speaking Walloons and the Flemings who in language and culture were akin to the Dutch, Belgium produced two brands of fascism corresponding to each ethnic community. Ever since the union of Walloons and Flemings in 1830, the former had been the dominant partner; Walloons by and large formed Belgium's plutocracy and occupied most of the pivotal administrative and professional posts in the state. The nationalist grievance of the Flemings at this situation emerged into plain view during the First World War. In the occupied portion of Belgium, the Germans actively encouraged Flemish nationalism, and some Flemings collaborated with the Germans to obtain revenge on the Walloons. Simultaneously, in the Belgian army, which fought on the Allied side, a movement sprang up among the Flemish rank and file who resented their French-speaking officers. This was in no way a pro-German revolt, but it did express a rejection of the Belgian status quo. After the war, the Flemish nationalist elements fused together in the *Vlaamsch Front* (Flemish Front) whose political party in the 1920s regularly won several seats in the Belgian Parliament. Their program called for Flemish self-government either within a loose Belgian federation or outside Belgium altogether.

It was out of this wartime and postwar nationalist agitation that Flemish fascism grew. One ex-soldier who became a parliamentary deputy for the *Vlaamsch Front* was Joris van Severen. Born into the Flemish middle class and university educated, Van Severen appealed especially to the student wing of Flemish nationalism. He was captivated by the idealism of early fascism, but mainly because the *Vlaamsch Front* was critical of Mussolini, Van Severen broke away in 1929 to form his own green-shirted militia. Two years later, he established a more ambitious organization, the *Verbond van Dietsche Nationaal-Solidaristen* (League of Netherlands National Solidarists), *Verdinaso* for short. From its beginning, *Verdinaso* was a putative fascist movement run in military hierarchical style with absolute obedience due the leader. Van Severen, a devout Catholic, provided his movement with a body of Christian corporative beliefs. *Verdinaso* was, predictably, antiparliamentary and also vehemently anti-Semitic, but the most striking feature of *Verdinaso* doctrine lay in its proposed realization of Flemish nationalism. In Van Severen's eyes, the problem of Flanders originated in the sixteenth century when the artificial division of the Netherlands was enforced. Therefore, he proposed the reunion of the Dutch and the Flemings in a new *Dietschland*. In this, to be sure, Van Severen was not much out of step with most Flemish nationalists. However, in 1934, he altered his views and, to the consternation of some of his followers, revived a historical precedent which encompassed the Walloons. His new vision postulated the reunification of the seventeen ancient provinces of the Netherlands, which comprised modern Holland, both Flemish and Walloon Belgium, and Luxembourg. They were to be loosely federated with assurances of provincial autonomy along medieval lines. The rationale behind such a proposition was that the population of the fresh *Dietsche Rijk* would all derive from Frankish stock.

This nostalgia for a decentralized but biologically uniform ideal was pure Maurrassianism. Indeed, Van Severen was deeply influenced by the doyen of Action Française. *Verdinaso* also copied Action Française in that it always remained an intellectualized operation, attractive to students above all, but never presumptive of the standing of a mass movement by contesting elections. *Verdinaso* was more influential than its small membership suggested because it concentrated on converting the Flemish elite—a tactic that also left plenty of room for an alternative Flemish fascist party on a mass basis. Such was the *Vlaamsch Nationaal Verbond* (VNV), established in 1933 under the leadership of Staf de Clercq who, like Van Severen, had begun his political career in the postwar *Vlaamsch Front*.

The VNV subscribed to much the same doctrines as *Verdinaso*, although, in truth, Staf de Clercq was always less concerned with the ideological message than with recruitment to the cause. Less centralized than *Verdinaso*, the VNV permitted its regional branches freedom to adjust to local conditions in an endeavor to win the maximum number of adherents. A modest reward was forthcoming in the parliamentary elections of 1936 and 1939, which saw the VNV capture 12 percent of the Flemish vote. In its drive to become a mass party, Staf de Clercq's organization tried to emulate the successful NSDAP across the border, but admiration of the Nazis turned undiscriminating, and in the late 1930s, the VNV was justifiably accused of being a mouthpiece for German propaganda. At the same time that Van Severen was proposing Flemish-Walloon cooperation in a Frankish *Dietsche Rijk* as a bulwark against Germany, the official VNV newspaper was stating: "As Germanics we Flemings belong to the spiritual Germanic front in the west. . . . If we do not want to be annihilated by the French robbers of land, we must, in our centuries-old struggle, more than ever seek the support of Germany."

The VNV was not alone among Dutch-speaking fascists to succumb to the lure of nearby Nazi Germany. This was the fate of Anton Mussert's National Socialist movement in Holland itself. Begun mainly in imitation of Italian Fascism—Mussert even looked like Mussolini—the National Socialist movement of the Netherlands became, by 1939, a pale replica of German Nazism. Because of this, Mussert progressively lost popular support in the pre-World War II years until his party was left with only four seats in Parliament, thus reducing his role in Holland to a minor one before the German occupation of 1940. Mussert, however, proved an encouragement to Flemish nationalism for he, too, dreamed of reuniting Holland and Flanders in a Greater Netherlands. Consequently, he was cultivated by both the *Verdinaso* and the VNV.

All these fascist recommendations to solve the Flemish national problem were conceived in almost racial terms as Flemings were urged to join with their kith and kin either in Holland or Germany, or else within a conceptualized Frankish empire. Invariably, such notions drew sustenance from a historical or legendary example. This preoccupation with a national minority problem and the resultant shaping of local fascisms into an ethnic, backward-harking formula recalls what has already been observed of Danubian fascism. Moreover, just as racist fascism in southeastern Europe sprang out of a backward environment, so also Flemish fascism with its racial overtones was a phenomenon of the more backward part of Belgium. This was singularly true of the mass movement VNV which was exclusively Flemish and garnered by far its strongest backing in the rural areas of Flanders.

It follows, therefore, that in order to appraise Belgian fascism as a specimen of modern western European politics, we must turn to the fascist movement nurtured by the Walloons. It was not just that the Walloons constituted a more commercialized and industrialized community than the Flemings. Culturally, they were an appendage of French civilization, and so lived in the milieu of intellectual and social modernity engendered by the Enlightenment and the French Revolution.

Typically, French influence was paramount in molding the character of the creator of Walloon fascism, Léon Degrelle. Born into a family of Luxembourg brewers, Degrelle was educated by Jesuits who were ardent admirers of the Action Française movement. Every evening the students read Maurras's newspaper, and when Degrelle moved on to the University of Louvain, he mixed in similar Catholic circles where the secular bible was *Action Française*. In 1926, when the papacy imposed its anathema on Action Française, Degrelle dutifully complied. Nonetheless, Maurras's ideas stuck, as was apparent ten years later when Degrelle founded his own political party. Meanwhile, he took up a journalistic career with Belgian Catholic Action which resulted in his being appointed director, in 1931, of that organization's new publishing house dedicated to *Christus Rex*. The next year, Degrelle became editor of a monthly journal simply entitled *Rex*. His editorial staples were anticommunism and the need for a Christian renewal of

Belgian society. But, gradually, Degrelle became more and more anti-capitalist—a shift that was not so much a response to the Great Depression as it was a growing awareness of the ties between business and government revealed in several Belgian scandals similar to the Stavisky affair in France. In November 1935 Degrelle and some followers disrupted a meeting of Belgium's Catholic party and, seizing the podium, he denounced the delegates as corrupt. His career in Catholic politics and journalism came to an abrupt end. For some time Degrelle, who never lacked self-confidence, had been picturing himself as Belgium's savior. Now, still not yet thirty, he launched his own Rexist movement.

The new party's platform, ready by February 1936, expressed more what Rex was against than what it was for. First and foremost, it opposed the dictatorship of supercapitalism in Belgium and the Congo, and then went on to dismiss Belgian parties and the parliamentary system itself as mere extensions of the rotten business world. Rex was, in fact, a reaction against the entire modern bourgeois complex. Degrelle summed up all his movement's hatreds in a pun on the word *pourris*, meaning "the corrupt." But *pourris* also signified the brooms with which Rex promised to sweep away the old gang of politicians and businessmen. Rexists liked to appear wherever the regular parties held a meeting and symbolically sweep the street in front of the building. However, it was left rather vague as to what kind of regime would replace that of the decadent *pourris*. Banks were to be controlled in an unspecified way and unemployment solved by some sort of national planning. Workers were to be protected by a corporative system "based on the solidarity of the classes," and Rexist confederations were formulated on paper for trade, industry, agriculture, the artisans, the professions, and even the Belgian Congo. Yet, much of the old order would remain; there was room for the monarchy, and even Parliament in truncated form would share legislative authority with the corporations. On the surface, Rex's program was hardly a totalitarian one.

On the other hand, Degrelle's ultimate purpose was extreme. Like the German *Volkists* and the French Maurrassians, he yearned to return to a pastoral, idyllic utopia. Not for nothing was the official Rexist newspaper called *Pays Réel*. The *pourris* were abominated because their wealth came from commerce and manufacturing, but Rexist propaganda made no comparable attack on landed property, for in the countryside and its traditional patterns lay the best hope of national regeneration. The masses were urged to go back to the land where they would be "deproletarianized" and exposed to "true democracy" within the framework of a "popular community." Although the popular community presupposed a natural homogeneity of society, it was not an overtly racial idea and anti-Semitism was assumed more than advertised in the Rexist message. Rather, the popular community, "established on elementary and moral foundations accepted by all," was set against the "concept of the individual which forms the erroneous philosophical foundation of the present regime, and which was born of the catastrophic ideologies of the seventeenth and eighteenth centuries." Degrelle's historical paragon was his ancestral homeland of Burgundy, and his oft-stated goal was to resuscitate the ancient Burgundian kingdom. Here again, loathing of the present led straight to an idolization of the past.

Rex declared its intention to become a mass movement by participating in the parliamentary elections of May 1936, only a few months after the party's birth. Ostensibly, the omens for a Rexist success were not good. In particular, 1935 had been a year of strong economic recovery from the depression. What Rex had to depend on was Degrelle's political sixth sense. An avowed admirer of the Hitlerian techniques of manipulating the masses, and himself possessed of a biting invective, Degrelle was a superb propagandist. Hence, Rexist rallies were staged in the flamboyant style of the German Nazis; bands and uniforms created an intoxicating aura, while searchlights played on speakers and on massed banners which exploited the same striking combination of black and red used by the Nazis. Degrelle was tireless in organizing and addressing monster meetings, and his example fired the enthusiasm of the younger Rexists, who worked feverishly to set up a party branch in every corner of Belgium. All this energy paid off, for in the elections Rex won 11.5 percent of the vote and 21 seats in a Parliament of 202.

For an infant party these results were spectacular. Degrelle informed King Leopold III that he wanted "power, all power, and not just a ministerial post," exactly the same demand made by Mussolini of King Victor Emmanuel and by Hitler of President Hindenburg. Degrelle's peremptory request was refused, but his slogan, "Rex vaincra" ("Rex will conquer"), carried conviction. There were flaws in Rex's position, however. The elections had disclosed that the movement's following was concentrated in certain segments of the Belgian population. Rex won its share of votes in all classes in the countryside, but in the towns support came predominantly from the Catholic petty bourgeoisie. But Rex made little impact on the urban proletariat, which upset Degrelle, who sincerely believed fascism should be a worker's movement. "Either you have the people with you, or you have nothing with you," he remarked. Consequently, in a great strike by miners in the fall of 1936, Rex intervened actively on the strikers' side; its principal gesture was to lodge thousands of miners' children with Rexist families for as long as their fathers were out of work. Needless to say, this stance alarmed some of the staid middle class who had recently voted Rexist on anti-communist grounds. Another area to which Degrelle felt compelled to pay attention was Flanders. Despite the presence of a Flemish organization within Rex, the *Rex-Vlaanderen*, the movement had polled only 7 percent in the Flemish provinces. To offset this, Degrelle in October 1936 reached a working agreement with Staf de Clercq's VNV. However, the partnership did not last beyond the following summer, and in the meantime, Degrelle came under attack for selling out to Flemish separatism.

Nevertheless, Rex continued to draw huge crowds to its rallies. In the spring of 1937, hoping to force the government to call new elections, Degrelle optimistically engineered a referendum on his movement. A proper plebiscite being constitutionally impossible, Degrelle instructed a Rexist deputy for a Brussels suburb to resign his parliamentary seat, and he put himself forward as a candidate in the ensuing by-election. The three conventional parties—Catholic, Liberal, and Socialist—accepted the challenge and joined together behind Paul van Zeeland, the current premier, who agreed to run against Degrelle. It was a straightforward battle between the establishment of the *pourris* and Rex as a radical fascist alternative. On April 11, 1937, Van Zeeland received 275,000 votes, 80 percent of the total; Degrelle 69,000 or 20 percent. Moreover, 6 percent of the electorate were Flemings, and their vote was delivered to Degrelle *en bloc* by the VNV. Put another way, Rex captured under 14 percent of the Walloon vote, significantly less than in the general election just eleven months earlier.

Rex never recovered from this setback. The whole Rexist enterprise had been conducted in a state of euphoria induced by a dynamic leader who seemed capable of delivering instant success. With Van Zeeland's victory, the spell was broken; Degrelle, "the master deceiver" in Jean Stenger's phrase, found his bluff called. Intrinsic weaknesses in Rex quickly made themselves evident: there was no solid party organization to fall back on nor, after Degrelle, was much political talent unearthed in Rexist ranks. Now, Rex proceeded to sink almost as rapidly as it had risen. Degrelle, to keep his movement afloat, relied increasingly on money and newsprint supplied by Hitler and Mussolini. In April 1939 the Belgian people pronounced on this performance in new elections; Rex was accorded a mere 4 percent of the poll and four parliamentary seats. At the opening of the Second World War, Degrelle's depreciated status was comparable to Mussert's in Holland. Like Mussert, too, Degrelle would discover future political notoriety only in collaboration with the Nazi invaders of his country.

However briefly the Rexist meteor flared, it still seems tenable to claim Rex as the authentic voice of Belgian fascism. The Flemish fascist groups, although longer-standing than Rex, arrived at their fascist beliefs indirectly, through the nationality question. This suggested that Verdinaso and, even more, the VNV adopted the fascist alternative to liberalism mainly because, in Belgium, liberal politics were intimately associated with the Walloon hegemony. In contrast, for Rexists, liberalism itself was the prime enemy; political philosophy, not some incidental grievance, dictated fascism to Degrelle. Rex was a revulsion against the pervasive materialism of twentieth-century western Europe. And fascism in this modernist mise en scène followed its customary path—back to a past seen through rose-tinted spectacles, to a more primitive value system, and to an instinctual, antirational version of the political process.

### GREAT BRITAIN

In the final analysis, of course, the touchstone of the technologically developed nations of western Europe must be Great Britain. If fascism in advanced communities did indeed take on the form of a complete, nihilistic rejection of modernity, then this should certainly have been evident in Britain, the home of the first industrial revolution and mother of liberal parliamentarianism.

Set against Britain's liberal tradition, though, was a centuries-old record of imperialism redolent of theories of race supremacy and the subjugation of inferior peoples by force. After World War I, British policy in Ireland, still technically part of the British Empire, was executed by the Black and Tans, a paramilitary force of a piece with the German Freikorps. Out of the imperial background sprang the only significant British fascist movement of the 1920s. Arnold Leese was a veteran of the colonial service in India and Africa. During most of the twenties, he collaborated nominally with upper-middle-class cliques who played at imitating Mussolini, especially by denouncing "red" trade unionism in the general strike of 1926. But in 1929 Leese struck out alone with his Imperial Fascist League. This group adopted the German Nazi black shirt and as insignia placed first the fasces and later the swastika in a white circle in the middle of the Union Jack. The Imperial Fascist League was obsessively anti-Semitic; Leese, a veterinarian by profession, concocted pseudomedical theories to account for the Jews' alleged iniquity, going so far as to measure the craniums of his followers for signs of Jewish ancestry. The league was also bitterly antiparliamentary, as was shown in the slogan: "Boycott the ballot box!" Leese's movement never enrolled more than two hundred active members. But it indicated the path that fascism in Britain would take in the succeeding decade.

British fascism, properly speaking, was the product of the Great Depression and, like Belgium's Rex, the personal creation of one man. Oswald Mosley, one of the rare fascist leaders to hail from his country's historic ruling class, was born into a family of Staffordshire gentry whose lineage was traceable for four hundred years. In 1928, on his father's death, he succeeded to a baronetcy and became Sir Oswald Mosley. Like all of his generation, his life was decisively shaped by the Great War; what impressed him most was, first, the camaraderie among the common soldiers in the trenches, and then, the awesome capacity of the wartime "interventionist state" to get things done. After the war, Mosley entered politics hoping to see state power now used to realize the promise of a brave new world for the returning troops. He called his political creed "Socialist Imperialism," thus foretelling his later merger of nationalism and socialism in the typical fascist synthesis. Entering Parliament as an independent Conservative, he switched to the Labour party in 1924. In the Labour government of 1929, he was given a junior ministerial post, and was tipped as a potential premier in the making.

The Great Depression overwhelmed the Labour ministry. As a minority government, it lacked the strength to embark on drastic remedies, nor for that matter were its leaders, Ramsay MacDonald and Philip Snowden, temperamentally inclined to radical policies. The Conservatives were too tied to tradition to advance novel solutions, and so a deadlock ensued which, as the dole queues lengthened, drove the idealistic and impatient Mosley to distraction. All around him he saw nothing but "indecision, compromise, and blether." In March 1931 he broke with Labour and founded his New party. Its proposals to overcome the depression involved a mixture of governmental investment on

French fascist ideas were perhaps best articulated by Charles Maurras, leader of the Action Française (right). Ineffectual as a practical politician, he never overcame his image of a desiccated desk politician. More flamboyant and personally attractive was the British Fascist chief, Sir Oswald Mosley, seen here inspecting his Black Shirts (below). But the BUF was never more than a marginal force in British life in the 1930s.

WIDE WORLD PHOTOS

the lines of Keynesian pump priming and protectionist measures within an imperial framework such as many Tories from Joseph Chamberlain onward had advocated. But Mosley was less anxious to offer a specific program than to "unfreeze" the party political situation. The New party was intended to be a centrist alternative to the two major parties, Conservative and Labour, and it succeeded in drawing recruits from both left and right. Among several intellectual socialists who were attracted, John Strachey stood out, while William Morris, later Lord Nuffield, of Morris Motors contributed funds in the hope of wooing the New party to a conservative position.

The New party was in no real sense a fascist movement; nevertheless, it provided a bridge by which Mosley crossed to fascism. The charge of anachronism leveled at both conservatives and socialists and the attempt to construct a movement obliterating right-left divisions were standard fascist strategies. Moreover, as the depression obstinately refused to recede, Mosley began to veer toward corporative economic views. When a New party meeting in Glasgow was disrupted by communist hecklers, Mosley spoke in polarized terms of either fascism or communism. The most sinister development, however, concerned the New party's youth movement. It was quite appropriate that an enterprise geared to cut "like a sword through the knot of the past to the winning of the modern state" should have made a special plea to the rising generation. In view of the mounting turbulence of the New party's public rallies, some younger followers were enlisted as stewards and trained by a Jewish boxer, "Kid" Lewis, to use violence on hecklers; the press christened them "the biff boys." The paramilitary image was heightened when it was resolved to give the New party youth corps a uniform although, in an exquisite British compromise, the choice was not for an outright black shirt but a gray one. Professor C. E. M. Joad was only one who discerned "the cloven hoof of fascism," and hastily left the party. By October 1931, when a general election was held, many other intellectuals, Strachey included, had deserted.

The New party failed to win a single seat. To all intents, the party was now finished, although it lingered on for some months. In the new year 1932, Mosley, accompanied by Harold Nicolson, the editor of the New party's magazine, set out on a visit to Italy and Germany. Nicolson was appalled at the adulation of Mussolini in the state-controlled Italian press, quarreled with Mosley, and left the trip in Rome. Mosley, on the other hand, enjoyed a very cordial interview with the Duce, and was in general attracted by what he saw of Fascism in Italy. It was the quintessence of a "modern movement," he concluded. Ironically, Mussolini, in 1932, was just about to abandon the corporative modernization of Italy and turn to imperialism in Africa, but Mosley perceived nothing of this. Fascism became his immediate inspiration, and on his return to England, he embarked on construction of a real fascist movement which, unlike the elitist and intellectualized New party, would attract the workers. Mosley was able to gather in recruits from the minor fascist groups, although Leese's Imperial Fascist League remained aloof. On October 1, 1932, the British Union of Fascists (BUF) was formally inaugurated.

There can be no doubt what sort of fascism Mosley had in mind in 1932. He envisaged a sane, progressive phenomenon. All his political attitudes hitherto had been rationally conceived; Revolution by Reason (1925), a work which Mosley had helped Strachey to write, was no empty title. And in his own Greater Britain, which appeared the same day as the BUF was launched, Mosley reaffirmed his faith in human intelligence. After his visit to Italy, he openly combined his advocacy of Keynesian national planning with promotion of a corporate state "based on teamwork." Corporative theory, the intellectual side of Fascist Italy, appealed to Mosley; the Nazis' emotional attachment to bygone times seemed to have no attraction for him at this juncture. The term which more than any other Mosley liked to apply to his policies was the adjective "modern," and he employed it still on turning Fascist. He wanted to come to grips with the twentieth century, not to retreat from it. In the tradition of the Enlightenment, he was confident of man's ability to master his environment. By his own intelligence and commitment to progress through reason, Mosley appeared the most able and attractive leader to grace the fascist scene.

On the other hand, once he became a Fascist, Mosley found himself gathering adherents who were neither modern nor intellectual in outlook. There was the country gentry crowd who thought the BUF was somehow a way back to a simple, rural Merrie England. A. K. Chesterton, a gifted writer like his famous novelist brother, has been described as seeing in Mosley "the man who would remove the stains of industrialism from England's green and pleasant land." Then, in January 1934 the press baron Lord Rothermere started extolling the BUF in his newspapers. Rothermere, however, a shallow politico who never understood Mosley properly, backed the BUF simply because it was anticommunist. But the most serious threat to Mosley's idealism came from the recruits who congregated at BUF headquarters, the barrackslike Black House in Chelsea, London. These were tough young men whose chief excitement was to go on a Fascist street march into "red" working-class districts. They implanted in the BUF a spirit of brutality and ruthlessness, typified in the person of William Joyce. A British superpatriot who by birth was Irish-American, Joyce was a brilliant but warped personality. His hardness was emphasized by a facial scar from a razor slash received when stewarding a political meeting in 1924. He became propaganda officer in the BUF, and he would die on the gallows after World War II for his role as "Lord Haw-Haw" in broadcasting German propaganda to Great Britain.

The question was how long Mosley could resist the brutalizing influences within his own organization. The answer came in the middle of 1934. During the spring of that year, Mosley, with Rothermere's help, staged several huge rallies which suggested that British Fascism was on the rise. This prospect alarmed the Marxist Left which took to heckling Mosley whenever he spoke in public; inevitably, skirmishes with black-shirted stewards erupted. A climax was reached on July 7 at London's Olympia where fifteen thousand persons, including many of social and political prominence, assembled. The Black Shirts, determined to show their efficiency in keeping order, treated interrupters with a viciousness that shocked many present and the British public at large. A few weeks later occurred the Nazi Night of the Long Knives which the BUF endorsed on the grounds of Röhm's homosexuality and his disloyalty to Hitler. Together, the Olympia brawl and the approval of the Röhm purge stamped the BUF henceforth in the popular mind as a party of violence. Yet violence had accompanied Mosley's politics since 1931 and had always hovered about the BUF; its prominence in 1934 was at best a change of degree.

More important was an almost simultaneous change in kind— Mosley's formal adoption of anti-Semitism. Nothing in his background foretold this step, since he had mixed easily with Jewish intellectuals when a member of the Labour party. Most of the Black House gang of the BUF were anti-Semites and writhed under Leese's odious taunt that they were "Kosher Fascists"—to which Mosley replied that "national pride has no need of the delirium of race." But, grudgingly, he gave way. Beginning in 1933, no Jews were admitted to the BUF and the few already enrolled, including "Kid" Lewis, were eased out. In July 1934 Rothermere detected a rising note of anti-Semitism in the organization, which was one reason for his withdrawal of support. Mosley, however, did not openly attack the Jews until October when

he started to accuse his leftist hecklers of being Jewish. Next, in another
monster rally, this one in London's Albert Hall, he introduced into his
speech the theme of a secret Jewish conspiracy:

> I find that as I have proceeded in Fascism, I have encountered forces
> which I did not dream existed in Britain. . . . One of them is the power
> of organized Jewry which is today mobilized against fascism. . . . We
> declare that we will not tolerate an organized community within the state
> which owes allegiance not to Britain but to another race in foreign
> countries.

On this occasion, Mosley was unusually eloquent and his tall, athletic
figure exceptionally spellbinding. When he finished, the Black Shirts
chanted "Hail Mosley" over and over, while the audience, on its feet,
gave him a fifteen-minute ovation. It was a crucial moment for, in embracing anti-Semitism, Mosley totally and irrevocably changed the
nature of the BUF.

Why, then, did Mosley put anti-Semitism in the forefront of his
program? In his autobiography, *My Life* (1968), he is not very enlight-
ening, insisting that the Jews attacked the Fascists first. One turns
necessarily to conjecture. A possible relevant factor in Mosley's personal
background was the tragically early death in 1933 of his wife who, as
the daughter of Lord Curzon, had provided him with a tangible link
to the old English establishment. Mosley sought natural solace in his
political career and in the company of his new political colleagues.
Gratitude to his friends of the BUF in time of need seems to have
extended to espousal of their anti-Semitism. Such is one explanation
offered by Colin Cross in *The Fascists in Britain* (1961).

Cross goes on to remark, however, that Mosley felt the need to
personalize the enemy to win adherents. "A dynamic creed such as
Fascism," Mosley is quoted as saying, "cannot flourish unless it has a
scapegoat to hit out at, such as Jewry." In other words, anti-Semitism
was a tactical move. In over two years of existence, the BUF had
attracted eccentrics and a measure of sympathy from the young and
the propertied classes, but hints of lower-class support were few and far
between. Meanwhile, the British establishment showed every sign of
surmounting the crisis of the Great Depression as the Conservatives and
the official wing of the Labour party united behind the National coalition government. By 1934 Britain's economy was marginally on the
upswing, and the BUF was in danger of being relegated, like the New
party before it, to the role of a ginger group on the flank of the conven-

tional parties. For the ambitious Mosley this was not enough. His anti-Semitic call was a desperate attempt before it was too late to make contact with the urban masses. For there was, indeed, a strong vein of anti-Semitism among the British working class, deriving not so much from imperial race-thinking, whence came the anti-Semitism of Mosley's bourgeois followers, as from the memory of the immigration of east European Jews about the turn of the century. Many trade unionists before 1914 held that cheap Jewish labor undercut the position of the British workingman, while Jews who tried to rise in the social hierarchy, often through retail trade, were resented for their initiative. And in the event, it was only after Mosley took up anti-Semitism that he made an impact in certain working-class districts.

This tactical maneuver must also be interpreted in a more philosophical fashion. Anti-Semitism, an emotional and fundamentally irrational credo, was a denial of Mosley's own intellectual antecedents and of the rational tradition of recent British liberalism. By choosing anti-Semitism, Mosley turned his back on his vaunted "modern" policies in favor of a primitive approach. It was rather as though, in 1934, he came to the subconscious realization that for a Fascist movement to take root in twentieth-century industrial Britain, it would have to capitalize on popular revulsion against the current environment of the depression by pitting itself unreservedly against the modern world and all its spiritual values. Mosley, in brief, seemingly felt the need to radicalize himself and his movement totally. "In this way," writes Robert Skidelsky, "radical ideas which in themselves offer no threat to civilized political behaviour become attached to social forces and methods which do. A perfectly reputable case against international finance degenerates into an antisemitic one, a nationalist case into a racialist one, and so on" ("The Problem of Mosley," *Encounter* [1969]). By capitulating to violence and racism, Mosley gave a token of his conversion to an antimodernist and antitranscendental position. Thus, in Great Britain, too, we may perceive the emergence of a regressive variety of fascism in an advanced economic and intellectual milieu.

After the adoption of anti-Semitism, Mosley's Fascism imitated German Nazism more and more. The huge and colorful rallies sparked by Mosley's magnetic personality assumed Hitlerian proportions. A new Fascist uniform was modeled on that of the SS, complete with peaked cap and jackboots. When Mosley remarried, and because of his notoriety required privacy, a secret ceremony was held in Berlin; Goebbels was present, and Hitler attended the reception afterward. In early 1936

Mosley's movement enlarged its title to the British Union of Fascists and National Socialists; henceforth, it was known simply as the British Union. In October the British Union organized a march into Jewish districts in London's East End. In spite of the presence of 6,000 police, the ensuing fracas almost escalated into a pitched battle between Fascists and leftists. The government thereupon determined to clamp down and passed the Public Order Act which came into force on New Year's Day 1937. The act banned uniforms, forbade the use of stewards at open-air meetings, and gave the police discretion to prohibit any demonstration likely to cause a breach of the peace. Mosley, who insisted on reaching power legally, acquiesced.

Amid all this excitement, the active membership of the BUF and the British Union remained fairly steady at approximately 6,000. But many came and went quickly, and it has been estimated that up to 100,000 individuals passed through Mosley's organizations between 1933 and 1938. Caught unawares by the sudden announcement of a general election in 1935, the Fascists ran no candidates. A year later, Mosley became very exercised over the abdication crisis, for he pictured Edward VIII as the ideal monarch to work with a Fascist grand council. Disappointed at Edward's refusal to stay and fight it out, the British Union, in 1937, threw all its energies into the London County Council elections in three East End constituencies where Jewish immigrants had congregated two generations earlier. The stratagem paid off: British Union came in second in one constituency, and overall polled an average of nearly 20 percent. It was the high-water mark of British Fascism in vote-getting terms, yet it was also a very modest success. The British Union could not repeat its East End performance in other municipal elections, and made no advance at all in national politics, lack of funds being a chronic difficulty. Since power remained as elusive as ever, petty jealousies within the movement surfaced. For instance, William Joyce and John Beckett, who ran practically all British Union propaganda, were both purged in 1937 and went off to found their own ineffectual national socialist group.

On top of everything, Mosley found himself caught, like the fascists in France and the Low Countries, in the foreign policy trap. With tension mounting between the western democracies and the Rome-Berlin Axis, his ideological admiration of the fascist powers clashed with an ingrained patriotism. The British Union took refuge in appeasement. The last and largest of British Union rallies, held in London's Earl's Court in July 1939, was preoccupied with the shadow of war.

The hall was festooned with banners announcing "Britons fight for Britain only," "Fight to live, not live to fight," and "Mind Britain's business." The audience of 15,000 heard Mosley in his peroration appeal to the sanctities of blood and soil in the veritable manner of a *völkisch* fascist:

> We are going, if the power lies within us—and it lies within us because within us is the spirit of the English—to say that our generation and our children shall not die like rats in Polish holes. They shall not die but they shall live to breathe the good English air, to love the fair English countryside, to see above them the English sky, and to feel beneath their feet the English soil.
> This heritage of England, by our struggle and our sacrifice, again we shall give to our children. And with that sacred gift, we tell them that they come from that stock of men who went out from this small island in frail craft across the storm-tossed seas to take in their brave hands the greatest Empire that man has ever seen.

On the actual outbreak of the Second World War, the British Union instructed its members to obey official orders, but it deplored "this Jewish war" and hoped for a negotiated peace. In the spring of 1940, the British Union contested three by-elections on a peace platform. The party secured between 1 and 3 percent of the poll, depending on whether or not it had to share the peace vote with a Communist candidate. This revelation of impotence was the end of the road for Mosley's Fascism.

Sir Oswald Mosley embodied pretty much the whole of British fascism as a political force. Fascist groups other than the BUF and the British Union were minor affairs. But in addition to the formal fascist movements, there was on the part of some of the British intelligentsia a vague sympathy for fascistic notions, rather like the French fascist "fever." One remembers Muriel Spark's splendid novel, *The Prime of Miss Jean Brodie* (1961), whose central character reacts against the conventionalities of her Scottish background by instilling in her pupils a romantic distaste for materialist values together with an appreciation of Mussolini, Hitler, and Franco. Also, when the Spanish Civil War polarized London's artistic world between Right and Left, several traditionalists of the Wyndham Lewis school flirted with fascism for anticommunist reasons. And it was the South African poet, Roy Campbell, who embraced fascism and fought for Franco in order to oppose "MacSpaunday," a delicious composite he made out of the names of the leading Anglo-American leftist writers—MacNeice, Spender, Auden, and Day Lewis.

In the last resort, however, neither political nor literary fascism made serious inroads in liberal Britain. The absence of a tangible communist threat within Britain itself enabled the bulk of the population to stay loyal to the national traditions of individual rights and representative government. The innate strength of British liberalism first impelled the local Fascists, in their search for a radical alternative, to renounce Mosley's original progressive vision and to adopt the anti-intellectual posture of fascisms in other modern nations. Ultimately, by 1940, the liberal system emerged the clear victor over Fascism in Britain, setting the stage for Britain's role in the war against European fascism at large.

## Summary

The foregoing has been a rather hectic tour of ten national experiences of fascism between the world wars. Yet these examples, albeit the most significant, do not begin to exhaust the myriad European groups which employed the term fascist; for instance, a recent volume entitled *Native Fascism in the Successor States* (1971) includes essays on Czechoslovakia and Yugoslavia. In both these countries fascism was indissolubly mixed with the internal nationality problem. In Czechoslovakia Monsignor Hlinka built up a clerico-corporative party which claimed to speak for backward Slovakia, while in the Sudetenland Konrad Henlein became the Nazi voice of the German minority. Henlein's Sudeten German Homeland Front and Hlinka's Slovak Peoples party helped Hitler enormously in gobbling up the Czech state in 1938–39. The most important Yugoslav fascist group was the Croatian separatist *Ustaši* under Ante Pavelić. The *Ustaši* gained stature in the 1930s chiefly because they were backed by Mussolini, who hoped to use the organization as a lever to break up the Yugoslav union. Among other fringe fascisms there was even a Russian variety. As early as 1905, an anti-Semitic, radical right-wing Union of Russian People was formed; some of its younger members wore yellow shirts, others called themselves the Legion of the Archangel Michael. After the Bolshevik Revolution of 1917, the Russian fascist tradition was carried on by émigrés in China and the United States. Elsewhere, in western Europe, Hitler's advance to power in the period 1930–33 instigated other national socialist movements. In 1933 the Norwegian Vidkun Quisling founded a

National Unity party based on the myth of Nordic racism and the social vision of "a simple association of peasant farmers." The German-speaking cantons of Switzerland saw several fascistic "fronts" band together in a small but noisy national organization. Also in the mid-thirties, there flourished briefly in Ireland an ex-servicemen's league, the Blueshirts, whose trimmings if not beliefs recalled continental fascism. All of these movements fell within a broad definition of fascism, although none could be counted a major fascist force, at least before 1938.

Then, there were those regimes which assumed certain fascist characteristics to suit the times—a practice that was particularly prevalent in eastern Europe. Thus, Poland, after 1926, lived under a virtual military dictatorship established initially by a coup modeled on Mussolini's March on Rome. After the death in 1935 of Marshal Pilsudski, the military strongman, the Polish government drifted further toward authoritarianism of a militarist sort and practiced anti-Semitism and discrimination against the 30 percent of the population who were not Polish. This policy, with which the formal parliamentary opposition substantively concurred, stole the thunder of the Polish fascists, the *Falanga*, who as a result constituted a small group. In the Balkans, pro-Axis monarchical dictatorships were set up in Bulgaria and Greece. Between 1935 and 1938, King Boris III of Bulgaria ruled without a parliament, contending that his hand-picked cabinet stood above party and represented the national will in a vaguely fascistic way. In Greece, the royal favorite, General Metaxas, was given autocratic power in 1936, and in imitation of nearby Italy, he introduced a fascist salute, youth organizations, censorship, and token corporativism. Nevertheless, the governments in Warsaw, Sofia, and Athens remained at heart old-fashioned, conservative dictatorships and their fascism merely skin-deep.

To chronicle and appraise every faction, regime, or climate of opinion in interwar Europe which might be designated fascist would be a laborious and often repetitive process. Hopefully though, the fascist cases recounted in the body of this chapter have provided an ample cross section. It seems worth recapitulating that our survey saw the principal fascist movements fall into three geographical groups. First, the relatively underdeveloped Latin countries all gave birth to the clerico-corporative variety of fascism. Fascist Italy served as the prototype to which the Spanish Falange, especially after its incorporation into Franco's coalition, and Salazar's Portugal conformed. Second, the mostly rural nations of central and eastern Europe also showed a tendency to regard fascist corporativism as the road to modernization. But here, sooner or later, fascism was forced by local race-consciousness and the proximity of Nazi Germany into a more savage and antirational cast. Thus, in Austria the corporativism of Dollfuss and the *Heimwehr* gave way to Pan-Germanism and Anschluss, and in Hungary the Mussolinian Gömbös was followed by the national socialists, Szálasi and Imrédy. Further east, the fascist groups in Rumania and Finland were unreservedly racist from the start. Third, fascism in modern, industrialized western Europe resembled German Nazism in its nihilistic rejection of the twentieth century. This was apparent in Maurras's cult of the *pays réel* which was the germ of the French fascist "fever," in the Belgian Rexists' onslaught on the *pourris*, and in the British Union of Fascists' obeisance to anti-Semitism.

From these illustrations, what may be deduced about the congruence of fascist types with their social and economic settings? Plainly, the hypothesis of a rational, corporative fascism catering to the needs of backward communities and of visceral, racial fascism attuned to the inner urges of advanced societies cannot be taken as an absolute rule. There are the obvious exceptions of irrational, racist fascism in the backward Danube Valley and also in rural Flanders in western Europe. Yet, once one has allowed for the possibility of strong historic racial and national minority feelings upsetting the norm, the theoretical construct would appear to hold good. The ubiquity of a progressive, comparatively enlightened version of fascism in the underindustrialized and socially retarded states of Italy, Spain, Portugal, and, for a time, Austria and Hungary, was no coincidence. Neither was the prevalence of backward-looking, anti-intellectual fascism amid the pluralistic complexities of truly modern societies in Germany, France, the Low Countries, and Great Britain. Out of these affinities emerges a loose but visible pattern.

**THE AXIS—Rise and Fall**

- Allied powers
- Axis powers
- Axis allies
- Neutral countries
- Areas annexed by Russia, 1940
- German diplomatic gains, 1936–1939
- Areas occupied by Germany
- Areas controlled by Vichy France

*ATLANTIC OCEAN*

NORWAY

Oslo

SWEDEN

*BALTIC SEA*

Stockholm

*FINLAND*

Helsinki

Leningrad

*RUSSIA*

Moscow

ESTONIA

IRELAND

UNITED

KINGDOM

*NORTH SEA*

DENMARK

Copenhagen

Memel

LATVIA

LITHUANIA

Danzig

Rastenburg

Smolensk

Byelorussia

German front,
Nov., 1942

London

Rotterdam

NETH.

Berlin

GERMANY

Dresden

Warsaw

POLAND

Kiev

German front,
Dec., 1941

Stalingrad

Dunkirk

BEL.

Brussels

EAST PRUSSIA

Auschwitz

Paris

Ardennes Mts.

Nurnberg

SUDETENLAND

Prague

CZECHOSLOVAKIA

UKRAINE

Maginot Line

FRANCE

Munich

Vienna

Danube

Lake Garda

Lake Como

SWITZ.

AUSTRIA

HUNGARY

Budapest

BESSARABIA

CAUCASUS

Vichy

River Po

Venice

Belgrade

Bucharest

RUMANIA

*BLACK SEA*

SPAIN

Madrid

CORSICA

ITALY

Rome

YUGOSLAVIA

BULGARIA

Sofia

TURKEY

SARDINIA

ALBANIA

Taranto

GREECE

*GULF
OF
TARANTO*

Athens

SYRIA

Algiers

Tunis

SICILY

CYPRUS

CRETE

LEBANON

ALGERIA

TUNISIA

Tripoli

*MEDITERRANEAN SEA*

PALESTINE

*Suez
Canal*

El Alamein

LIBYA

EGYPT

Cairo

# 5

# The Culmination of Fascism— World War II

Fascism's association with the Second World War was twofold. In the first place, there is the matter of fascism's responsibility for the outbreak of war. Specifically, it is often said that it was Hitler's war that began in 1939. And secondly, in the course of World War II, Nazi Germany came to control, directly or indirectly, almost the entire European continent—a development that put most of the native fascist movements in harness with German Nazism, and inextricably linked their fate with the fortunes of the Nazi Führer. These two issues—the blame to be attached to fascism for the onset of war and the vicissitudes of fascism in a wartime Europe dominated by Hitler—will be examined in turn in this chapter.

## Hitler's War?

By its very nature, fascism was a threat to international peace. Since the prime objective of all fascists was a renewal of national harmony, one self-evident way to group unity was through hatred of

264

the stranger, both within and without the nation. Tolerance of foreigners smacked of despised liberal pluralism. Moreover, fascists could not abide uncertainty; they were the new dogmatists who followed blindly the laws of history. In particular, they subscribed to hoary nineteenth-century Social Darwinism whereby the nations, or races, of the world were doomed to struggle endlessly one against the other. Every fascist naturally assumed that his movement and his ideology was the tide of the immediate future; in Hitler's case the future was predicted for a thousand years. And perhaps most important, fascism exalted action and adventure over reflective thought. As Mussolini had to acknowledge by marching on Ethiopia, fascists expected to act out their beliefs through fighting in a Darwinian struggle for survival. Although fascists had no monopoly on international aggressiveness, their taste for violence, their worship of physical strength, and their ideological self-confidence predisposed them to diplomatic risk-taking and to resolution on the battlefield. In this sense, the mere presence in Europe of fascist regimes and influential fascist parties contributed to the international tension of the 1930s.

When this generic fascist belligerence was combined with nationalist grievances deriving from the settlements at the end of World War I, a real witches' brew was produced. A good example was supplied by the Hungarian fascists who reflected the vengeful and implacable resentment of patriots whose country, after the defeat of 1918, had been drastically abridged. Significantly, Hungary's two most prominent fascists, Gömbös and Szálasi, were military men, for the recovery of lost Magyar lands would require armed force. Similarly, Finland's fascists fixed their eyes on Eastern Karelia and looked to the military *Jägers* to seize the territory when the moment was ripe. In Italy, too, despite membership in the victorious coalition of 1918, Fascism and nationalist discontent worked in tandem. One important reason why Mussolini won power was that he convinced Italians that he would make their nation strong enough to bargain with Great Britain and France on equal terms; he would remove the stain of the "mutilated victory." Hence, Fascist Italy was always a volatile member of the family of nations. The search to sublimate Italian national pride was pursued by violence or the threat of violence—in Corfu, Fiume, Albania, and ultimately with stupendous consequences, in Ethiopia.

But by far the most potent compound of fascism and embittered nationalism was found in Germany. Hardly any German mentally accepted the Versailles *Diktat*. Despite Stresemann's partial fulfillment of the postwar settlement at Locarno, Germany remained unequivocally a revisionist power. Given Germany's economic and military potential and central position in the European continent, Berlin was bound to be the linchpin of any concerted attack on the status quo established in 1919. Mussolini recognized this as early as 1923 when, seeking outlets for disaffected Italian nationalism, he made contact with the super-patriots of the German Right, and probably even helped secret German rearmament. From the start, the Duce's favorite German nationalist was Hitler, not because he called himself a fascist but because he was the only German revisionist who recognized the Alto Adige as Italian. But Hitler was a special sort of revisionist in a more fundamental respect; he was no more inclined to go back to 1914 in international affairs than he was in German domestic politics. He followed in the footsteps of the "annexationists" who had framed Germany's First World War aims, and achieved them in the Treaty of Brest-Litovsk which brought all of Poland and much of Byelorussia and the Ukraine under temporary German control. In *Mein Kampf* Hitler extolled Brest-Litovsk as simple recognition of Germany's legitimate interests. The borderlands of Europe and Asia were predestined to be German by right of biological superiority; the native populations, being for the most part Slavs with Jews a sizable minority group, were lesser breeds designed to serve the Aryan conquerors. Emperor William II had claimed Germany's "place in the sun" in the colonial world outside Europe; for the Nazi Führer *Lebensraum* resided closer to home—in European Russia and the Eastern Marches, the ancient battleground of the Teutonic knights. Although Hitler shared and fostered German revulsion against Versailles, his goal far exceeded mere revisionism: his racial imperatives dictated that the bounds of the Third Reich should outstrip those of the Second German Empire. It was this vaulting ambition which lay at the root of the conflict of 1939.

In 1945–46, at Nuremberg, the principal Nazis who survived World War II were indicted, and some were convicted, of "crimes against peace." No matter how inadvertently, the Nuremberg verdict made it seem that the war of 1939 had a conspiratorial origin; a small band of demonic Germans had apparently willed war. It was to refute this simplistic moral, which has been widely drawn from the Nuremberg trials, that A. J. P. Taylor wrote his celebrated if controversial *Origins of the Second World War* (1961). Taylor contends that the great majority of Germans backed Hitler's foreign policy before 1939 to the full; therefore, war guilt should be placed not on Hitler and his lieutenants alone, but also on the mass of Germans. Unfortunately, this perfectly tenable position is obscured in Taylor's book for, in urging the point that Hitler tried to deliver abroad what the German people wanted, Taylor stretches his argument so far as to portray the Führer as just another conventional statesman. The perversity of this view of the megalomaniacal Hitler merits the abundant criticism it has attracted. Yet withal, Taylor's aversion to the misconceptions born at Nuremberg is shared by most scholars.

In emphasizing the guilt of a few Nazis at the expense of collective German responsibility, the Nuremberg trials managed also to create the impression of "planned aggression." According to this popular scenario, Hitler in *Mein Kampf* revealed his expansionist determination more frankly than any other politician before or since. It seemed as if the Führer himself believed his autobiography might alert the world to his intentions for he refused to authorize an English-language translation (although he could not prevent pirated editions from appearing abroad). Once in power, so this conspiracy theory runs, Hitler immediately began to lay the groundwork for future German expansion: first, in 1933, withdrawal from the League of Nations in protest at the failure of the other powers to grant Germany parity in armaments; then, in March 1935, the introduction of conscription and the announcement of an already extant German air force (*Luftwaffe*); and one year later, in the midst of a French cabinet crisis, the re-militarization of the Rhineland.

This last coup locked Nazi Germany's back door, leaving Hitler free to work his wiles in central and eastern Europe. It was during the winter of 1937 that Hitler allegedly decided on action beyond Germany's frontiers. The key piece of evidence produced at Nuremberg to support this charge was the Hossbach memorandum, a record made by Colonel Hossbach of a meeting in the Reichschancellery to which Hitler summoned a select group of his ministers and military chiefs on November 5, 1937. The Führer discoursed, at his customary length, about the need for acceleration of rearmament to enable Germany to take advantage of any shift in the international scene, and pronounced his long-term strategy to be, initially, the incorporation of all Germans (that is, those in Czechoslovakia and Austria) into the Third Reich, and later, German expansion eastward. There was nothing too remarkable about this message. Hitler had spelled it all out previously, although perhaps less explicitly than on November 5, 1937. The importance of the Hossbach memorandum, to the prosecution at Nuremberg anyway, lay as much in the date it bore as in its substance. It could be represented as a blueprint for the crises which soon followed: *Anschluss* in March 1938, Munich in September 1938, Prague in March 1939, and Danzig in September 1939. This sequence of crises at regular six-month intervals, culminating in World War II, appeared to betoken a systematic plan of Nazi German aggression.

Yet, if anything, the Hossbach memorandum pointed not toward but away from a second world war. Prominent in Hitler's audience on November 5, 1937, were the German generals who had begun to express alarm lest the Führer's revisionism and quest for *Lebensraum* lead to conflict with France and Great Britain; they repeated these fears at the Reichschancellery session. These were the cautious military voices that were to be silenced by the Blomberg-Fritsch purge early in 1938. In the meantime, Hitler sought to mollify the generals by asserting that France and Britain would not move to save Czechoslovakia or Austria. Should such a contingency loom, he promised to tread warily. Hitler would countenance a general European war only in the most advantageous circumstances. One *sine qua non* mentioned was that Fascist Italy would fight alongside Nazi Germany and neutralize Anglo-French forces in the Mediterranean. But in no event, Hitler reassured his listeners, would he allow Germany to become embroiled in a major conflict before 1943–44, the date at which German rearmament would peak.

In all probability, Hitler was sincere in his determination to avoid an immediate showdown with the western powers. On several occasions, he insisted that Germany could not be fully prepared before 1943–44. Moreover, later research has shown that in Nazi Germany before 1939 neither economic planning nor strategic military directives made any provision for total war. In short, Hitler expected little wars and easy victories. The Hossbach memorandum reveals him confident that German rearmament had given him the advantage in central Europe— with the inclination to use it in the near future. Foreign conquest, in Hitler's eyes, was a simple way out of the problem of monetary inflation just beginning to appear in Nazi Germany. Furthermore, the removal of the old German conservatives, civilian and military, from positions of influence in February 1938 lifted an important brake on Hitler's actions. In particular, Ribbentrop, ever the optimistic advocate of adventures abroad, now took charge of the foreign ministry and had Hitler's ear. Out of these changes inside Nazi Germany and Hitler's increasingly impatient ambition sprang the succession of Nazi international coups in 1938–39, but there was never a precise timetable for German expansion. Above all, the war of 1939 was neither planned nor wanted by Hitler.

The truth of the matter, as Taylor suggests, was that Hitler was seduced into overreaching himself by the western policy of appeasement. In the interwar years, appeasement—the word being used synonymously with international conciliation—arose out of a revulsion against war as manifested in the trenches of 1914–18. As a specific policy to be applied to Germany, appeasement was reinforced by the revisionist historiography of the 1920s. Broadly speaking, this held that Germany had been unfairly saddled with exclusive blame for the outbreak of war in 1914 and that the peace settlement, resting on this moral fallacy, was unfair to Germany. Notably, it was recalled that while the map of Europe was supposedly redrawn according to the principle of national self-determination, substantial Germanic populations were put outside Germany's frontiers. Appeasement, then, amounted to recognition of Germany's moral arguments for the revision of Versailles. Sympathy for Germany was strongest in the English-speaking world where international conciliation, having been a commodity pushed mostly by the Wilsonians and the Left in the 1920s, was bought in the form of appeasement by the British Conservatives in the thirties.

The French, on the other hand, after agreeing to conciliate Weimar Germany at Locarno in 1925, viewed the rise of the militant Third Reich with understandable suspicion and hostility. However, the French were in no position to take a firm stand against Nazi Germany. As 1870 and 1914 had demonstrated, France by herself was no match for German might, and in the 1930s the French continental alliance system crumbled away. In January 1934 Poland signed a ten-year non-aggression pact with Germany. France's endeavor to replace Poland by the Soviet Union was half-hearted, and the hope of using Fascist Italy against Germany disappeared in the Ethiopian affair. French isolation and weakness were dramatically exposed on March 7, 1936, when Nazi troops, unmolested, reoccupied the demilitarized Rhineland. Now, even the paper promises of French security won at Locarno had vanished. After 1936 France, torn internally by the polarization between the extreme Left and the fascistic Right, crouched fearful and passive behind the fortifications of the Maginot Line along the Franco-German border. Perforce, France turned to Great Britain, where appeasement of Germany was the order of the day; between 1936 and 1940, the general shape of western policy toward Germany was set in London.

This proved to be crucial because of the manner in which appeasement came to be interpreted in the British capital. In the mid-1930s, British appeasement could be equated with isolationism. Thus, the national government under the Conservative Stanley Baldwin eagerly liquidated British involvement in the Ethiopian crisis once lip service had been paid to the League of Nations, and from the start of the Spanish Civil War ostentatiously pursued a noninterventionist policy. Faced with German open rearmament and the Rhineland remilitarization, the Baldwin government, although verbally deploring unilateral revisionism, ruled out any retaliatory action. But then, in May 1937, Neville Chamberlain succeeded Baldwin, and brought with him into office the firm intention to pursue an activist foreign policy. Chamberlain subscribed wholeheartedly to the notion that Germany possessed legitimate grievances, but rather than wait for issues to escalate into dangerous international crises, he preferred to bring the matter of German national rights in Austria, Czechoslovakia, and Poland out into the open and to a quick solution. Here was "positive appeasement" in contrast to Baldwin's negative policy of drift.

In November 1937 Lord Halifax, undersecretary for foreign affairs and soon to become foreign secretary, visited Berchtesgaden. In conversation with Hitler, he referred to the frontiers in central and eastern Europe where "possible alterations might be destined to come about with the passage of time." Britain "would not block reasonable settlements . . . reached with the free assent and goodwill of those primarily concerned." Nevile Henderson, the British ambassador in Berlin and a close collaborator with Chamberlain, continually spoke in the same vein. All this was supplemented by overtures for trade and colonial pacts—"economic appeasement" which, it was vainly hoped, might strengthen the moderate elements in the Third Reich. Chamberlain's policy for general European pacification was an ambitious—some have said arrogant—dream, but it was not ignoble and, in the abstract, it made sense to anticipate problems. The flaw was that Chamberlain chose the worst possible subject on which to practice positive appeasement. Hitler, encouraged by the Chamberlainites to raise and negotiate German grievances, proceeded to do so impetuously, stridently, and uncompromisingly. At last, overestimating even British conciliation, he stumbled into the Second World War.

The first of the four international crises leading up to World War II saw the end of Austrian independence described in the previous chapter. Since 1933 Hitler's agents in Munich had connived with certain Austrian Pan-Germans to bring about an Anschluss. After the unsuccessful Viennese *Putsch* of July 1934, it was understood that Anschluss would be an evolutionary process, but, in the new year 1938, Hitler embarked on a more forward Austrian policy. Either, as charged at Nuremberg, the Nazis were now ready to implement an aggressive program sketched in the Reichschancellery on November 5, 1937, or else Hitler, without much prior scheming, seized opportunistically on the deteriorating situation within Austria and on the openings fortuitously presented by Chancellor Schuschnigg. Most likely for a combination of these reasons, Hitler was able to consummate Austro-German union on March 13, 1938. Internationally, the Anschluss was of most concern among the major powers to Fascist Italy, but the Rome-Berlin Axis insured Mussolini's approval. If Italy raised no objection to Anschluss in 1938, as she had in 1934, Great Britain and France were not going to pull her chestnuts out of the fire. The subsequent plebiscite in which over 99 percent of Austrians voting endorsed the Anschluss gave assurances to London and Paris that the "free assent and goodwill of those primarily concerned" was taken into account. National self-determination was vindicated in the Anschluss. The colloquialism coined to explain away the Rhineland remilitarization two years earlier could be applied again: Hitler was only "working in his own backyard."

The Anschluss whetted Hitler's appetite, and he turned his attention to the Czech Sudetenland, where the situation provided enough parallels with Austria to suggest a repetition of tactics. Like the six and a half million Germans in Austria, the more than three million Germans who made up a majority of the Sudeten population constituted a problem bequeathed by the breakup of the Hapsburg Empire. Both groups were prevented in the post-World War I peace treaties from joining Germany. Frustrated Pan-German sentiment could be used to violate the integrity of Czechoslovakia just as Hitler had used it to destroy the Austrian republic. Among the Sudeten Germans, there was even a National Socialist workers tradition going back to 1904. Sudeten Nazism languished during the years of Locarno prosperity, but it came back into prominence with the Great Depression. The Sudetenland, a heavily industrialized area, was one of the hardest hit by the depression in all Europe. Unemployment was a chronic problem throughout the 1930s, especially among German workers who tended to be the last hired and the first fired by the Czech managerial class. Discrimination against the Germans in Czechoslovakia was never as bad as Nazi propaganda pictured it, but there was just enough to permit the Nazis to pose as guardians of threatened minority rights. After 1933 the Sudeten German Homeland Front, like equivalent Pan-German organizations in Austria, received generous financial help from Berlin, becoming progressively more Nazified and a tool of German foreign policy.

In the wake of the Anschluss, Konrad Henlein, the Nazi leader who was to play in the Sudetenland the role that Seyss-Inquart had played in Austria, received his orders from Hitler. These were always to ask for more by way of special status for the German minority than the Czech government offered. Henlein acted at once by demanding at his party's congress that the Sudeten Germans be recognized as a "legal entity" with freedom to profess Pan-German opinions. This outburst alarmed the authorities in Prague, who were very conscious that their strongly fortified Sudeten frontier with Germany had been turned now that the Wehrmacht was camped on the comparably undefended Austro-Czech border. Czech edginess was manifested over the weekend of May 20, 1938, when the movement of Austro-German troops around the Czechoslovak frontiers caused Prague to mobilize. It was a false alarm. The Wehrmacht activity was routine, for Hitler had not yet perfected military plans against Czechoslovakia. However, the Czech show of resistance angered the Führer who, on May 30, revealed his determination to "smash Czechoslovakia" by signing a military directive for invasion (Operation Green) to be executed no later than October 1, 1938.

At the same time, this *furor teutonicus* was encouraged by some classic positive appeasement. The western powers, taking Sudeten German grievances at face value, exerted by Lord Halifax's own admission the "greatest possible pressure" on Prague to make concessions to Henlein. After the May 20 scare, these efforts were redoubled. By July 1938 the Czech president, Eduard Beneš, was reluctantly brought to accept a supposedly independent British mediator, Lord Runciman, a well-to-do, flinty businessman whose experience of central European diplomacy was nil. In August he visited Prague and the Sudetenland where Czech officials greeted him with glacial formality. Runciman thereupon spent his weekends in the country homes of Sudeten Germans who plied him with hospitality and memoranda. In his reports to London, he laid the blame for Sudeten tension squarely on Czech shoulders. Early in September, Beneš, realizing how bereft was his nation, agreed to meet Henlein's demands which added up to autonomy for the Sudeten Germans.

This was the signal for the Nazis to lift the level of their expectations. On September 12 Henlein demanded what he termed the Sudetenland's "return to the Reich." Meanwhile, clashes between the nationalities in the Sudetenland requiring police action were translated into Czech atrocities by Goebbels's propaganda ministry. In an address to the party faithful assembled in the Nuremberg stadium and broadcast by radio around the world, Hitler let loose a torrent of fulminations: "The misery of the Sudeten Germans is intolerable. It is sought to annihilate them. . . . If these tormented creatures can of themselves find no justice and no help, they will get both from us." Faced with this clear threat of war, Chamberlain resolved on his boldest piece of appeasement yet. Obtaining an audience with Hitler, he flew to Berchtesgaden. There, on September 15, he assured the Führer that "personally he recognized the principle of the detachment of the Sudeten areas." Certain niceties needed to be observed; plebiscites would have to be held and consultations with interested parties taken. But, in effect, Chamberlain promised Hitler the Sudetenland.

During the ensuing week, Chamberlain wrung acceptance of his scheme from the British cabinet, from the French who had had a military pact with Czechoslovakia since 1924, and even from Beneš. On September 22, Chamberlain returned to Germany to seal the bargain with Hitler at Bad Godesberg. To his consternation, Hitler, in a much sourer mood than at Berchtesgaden, turned him down flat. Chamberlain's project for the transfer of the Sudetenland was too slow; it must be accomplished before the Wehrmacht's military deadline of October 1 ran out, and without the delay of plebiscites in pockets of mixed population. Moreover, Polish and Hungarian claims on Czech territory had to be met. Considering what Chamberlain offered Hitler without firing a shot, these were puny objections. The Führer at Godesberg appeared at his most demonic, seeking war for its own sake. It may be that Hitler was bluffing, probing how far he could push the appeasers—for future reference, as it were. But it seems more probable that he had set his heart on the utter destruction of Czechoslovakia, perhaps testing the new German army in the process, and had no wish to be deflected by a Chamberlainite compromise. It must be remembered that multinational Czechoslovakia was a microcosm of the Hapsburg Empire which Hitler had learned to despise in his youth. Furthermore, of all the successor states, Czechoslovakia was the most democratic, industrialized, and up-to-date; in central Europe she stood as a symbol of that modernity Nazi Germany was pledged to extirpate. Toward Czechoslovakia, Hitler's attitudes were formed not so much by realpolitik as by his deeply felt, unreasoning *Weltanschauung*.

Chamberlain, more to save face than out of principle, rejected Hitler's Godesberg ultimatum. In the closing days of September 1938, Europe teetered on the edge of war, not over whether the Sudetenland should be German or not but whether the transfer should be measured and decorous or quick and brutal. A few of the German military, principally General Ludwig Beck who had recently resigned as chief of the general staff, perceived that Hitler might be leading Germany to ruin. Beck urged Chamberlain to stand fast, and promised a coup to remove Hitler if war should come; but no feasible plans had been drawn up by the conspirators. Chamberlain, unconvinced, pushed for further diplomatic negotiations. At the last minute, Hitler, affecting to be moved by a plea from his friend Mussolini, offered one more round of talks. Chamberlain and Daladier, the French premier, grasped at this straw and flew to Munich to confer with the two fascist dictators.

The Munich Conference of September 29 handed down a settlement scarcely less vindictive than that demanded by Hitler a week earlier. The Sudetenland was to be occupied by German troops during the first ten days of October; a boundary commission was to supervise plebiscites if and where necessary although, in fact, no plebiscites were ever held; and machinery was established to meet Polish and Hungarian revisionist claims. The Czechs were not consulted, simply compelled to  acquiesce under pain of being left to Hitler's tender mercies. Nevertheless, Munich appeared less than total capitulation because a façade of negotiation had been preserved. This was vital to Chamberlain who sincerely believed that peace depended on the ability of London and Berlin to communicate. The morning after the conference, Chamberlain paid a private visit to Hitler's Munich apartment and invited the Führer to sign an agreement "that the method of consultation shall be the method adopted to deal with any other questions that may concern our two countries, . . . and to continue our efforts to remove possible sources of difference and thus to contribute to assure the peace of Europe." Hitler responded testily; he was already feeling cheated out of the annihilation of Czechoslovakia, and anyway was not used to doing business before noon. Nevertheless, he signed the document. It was this scrap of paper that Chamberlain waved before cheering London crowds on his return when he announced: "It is peace for our time."

Chamberlain gambled that Hitler's word was as good as that of the reliable Birmingham iron manufacturers among whom he had been brought up. Yet, even if Hitler had been the man of bourgeois probity Chamberlain hoped, it is doubtful that the Munich settlement could have lasted. As in any heterogeneous state, the grant of independence to one national group aroused the separatist tendencies of the others. Czechoslovakia had begun with six nationalities, and after the departure of most of the German minority, it was the turn of two million Slovaks to agitate for their freedom. In October 1938 Prague tried to ward off trouble by granting Slovakia a degree of autonomy and by accepting as Slovak premier Monsignor Tiso who had succeeded to the leadership of the Catholic, fascistic Slovak Peoples Party. Tiso was to follow in the footsteps of Seyss-Inquart and Henlein. Egged on by Germany, he intrigued for more Slovakian special rights until, on March 9, 1939, Prague dismissed Tiso for subversion and proclaimed martial law in Slovakia. Tiso looked to Berlin and was told to declare Slovakian independence. Tiso hesitatingly persuaded the Slovakian diet to do so, and Hitler now had another excuse to intervene in Czechoslovakia under cover of national self-determination. On the same grounds he urged the Hungarians to press their ethnic claims to the Czech province of Ruthenia; Horthy leaped eagerly into action. Whereupon, the Czech president, Emil Hácha (Beneš had resigned after Munich) decided, like Schuschnigg and Chamberlain before him, to appeal to Hitler face to face.

In Berlin Hácha found Hitler full of venom against all that Czechoslovakia represented. The Führer ranted about the havoc the *Wehrmacht* and *Luftwaffe* were about to wreak on the "ungrateful" Czechs. When he finished, Göring and Ribbentrop took up the browbeating. Twice the aged Hácha fainted. Finally, to save his country from physical destruction, the Czech president signed the document the Nazis kept thrusting at him. It provided for German annexation of the main Czech provinces of Bohemia and Moravia, with the promise of autonomy if the Czechs cooperated with the German occupiers. On March 15 German troops entered Prague and the Hungarians occupied Ruthenia; the next day, Tiso invited Nazi Germany to assume a protectorate over "independent" Slovakia. Beyond question, the liquidation of Czechoslovakia had been orchestrated by Hitler. On the other hand, Czechoslovakia was bound to crumble away after September 1938; Hitler merely had to pick up the pieces. Prague was the natural conclusion of what had been done at Munich.

This logic was somewhat lost on London, however. By no stretch of the imagination could Nazi stormtroopers in the Czech capital be explained away in terms of "Hitler's own backyard." Chamberlain was pushed by sentiment in the British press and in Parliament to issue veiled warnings to Hitler. The British government announced guarantees of the integrity of those states deemed to be threatened by the Axis powers—Poland, Rumania, Greece, and Turkey. On the surface, these guarantees appeared to be incompatible with further appeasement and to signal a dramatic turnabout in British foreign policy. But although a change was brewing, it had not yet taken place. Throughout the summer of 1939, Britain strove energetically for accommodation with Germany. Plans were broached for a worldwide Anglo-German trade pact, and there was still a lot of loose talk about satisfying Germany's legitimate interests in eastern Europe. On the periphery of British official circles, aristocratic conservatives continued to speak admiringly of Hitler as the man of order who had saved central Europe from bolshevism. The German ambassador in London cautioned against setting too much store by gossip and stressed instead the rising anti-German temper of mass British opinion. Hitler and Ribbentrop, however, made a habit of dismissing the pessimism of Germany's career diplomats and old-line military alike; they were relics of traditional Germany and out of place in the Nazi new order. Furthermore, in Berlin it was hard to conceive that the liberal western powers, having sold out Czechoslovakia, would fight for a small power further east. Geography and logistics aside, Czechoslovakia was an industrialized democracy in the western sense, while Poland and Rumania were backward, autocratic, anti-Semitic countries of dubious military prowess. All in all, the Nazis had every reason to believe that warnings from Chamberlainite Britain were bluff and that appeasement was still in vogue.

So the Führer turned to Poland, spurred by the momentum of his successes in Austria and Czechoslovakia. Having gained these territories, neither of which had ever before belonged to Germany, he was driven irresistibly to deal with the Polish Corridor dividing East from West Prussia, a region which, until 1918, had been an integral part of the

German state. The corridor was an area of mixed population, and Nazi propaganda fixed its sights on the German majority in the port city of Danzig. Yet Danzig was a red herring. A free city under League of Nations jurisdiction, its municipal council had had a Nazi majority since 1933. The agitation over Danzig, then, was just a token of Hitler's desire for the entire Polish Corridor. Since 1934 the colonels' regime in Warsaw had aligned itself diplomatically with Nazi Germany and had joined in the despoliation of Czechoslovakia. There is evidence that, as late as the new year 1939, Hitler hoped to retain Poland as an ally in an upcoming drive on the Ukraine, although with the proviso of prior German satisfaction in the corridor. However, the Polish government, its sense of military honor aroused, refused to adopt the supine role that Czechoslovakia had played. It categorically ruled out any discussion of German extraterritorial privileges in the corridor or any derogation of Polish sovereignty there. By April Hitler, concluding that Poland would have to be dealt with by force, issued a directive for Operation White, an invasion of Poland "any time as from September 1st."

During the summer of 1939, Nazi Germany acquired two allies whose support, Hitler assumed, would diminish the western powers' frail intent to oppose his Polish designs. First, Italy was brought securely into the fold. Mussolini, on several visits he exchanged with Hitler, was dazzled by the aura of power and success surrounding the Führer. Immediately after the Anschluss placed Italy at the mercy of German troops poised on the Brenner, a formal Italo-German treaty was drawn up. But signature was delayed for a year by the Germans, who hoped for a tripartite pact including Japan. The Japanese were prepared to make an agreement aimed at the Soviet Union, but when, in the spring of 1939, Hitler made it clear that his immediate target was Poland not the U.S.S.R., Japan backed off. Thereupon, Germany accepted Mussolini's overture for a bilateral treaty.

Some German diplomats feared lest Mussolini embroil Hitler in his own foreign adventures. To keep pace with his fellow dictator, the Duce in the wake of Hitler's Prague coup sent Italian troops into Albania, although that poor and mountainous country had been a virtual protectorate of Italy for over a decade. While the Führer pressed Germany's claims to Polish territory, Mussolini kept up a steady clamor for the French possessions of Nice, Corsica, and Tunisia. In reality, though, Berlin would be bound to set the pace in any Nazi-Fascist partnership, as was foreshadowed in the drafting of the

Italo-German treaty which Mussolini, with startling insouciance, left entirely to the Germans. Ribbentrop produced a document without the conventional diplomatic safeguards. It was to be a blanket offensive pact; if either party became involved in war for whatever cause, the other would lend support "with all its military forces on land, on sea, and in the air." "I have never seen such a pact," wrote Ciano in his diary. "It contains some real dynamite." But Ciano was too much his master's voice to object openly, for the Duce was so convinced of the common destiny of Italy and Germany that he saw nothing wrong in Ribbentrop's proposal. On visiting Berlin to conclude the accord, Ciano informed the Nazi foreign minister that Italy would not be ready for war before 1943. Ribbentrop replied that Germany, too, had no wish to provoke a conflict before that date. With this private understanding, the alliance was signed on May 22, 1939. Mussolini at first wanted to call it the Pact of Blood but settled for the Pact of Steel.

The Italian alliance was a comfort to Hitler, but Russian friendship was a necessity. One eventuality above all others might have transformed Great Britain's guarantee to the eastern European states into a credible deterrent in Hitler's eyes—an alliance between the western powers and the Soviet Union. This would have threatened Germany with war on two fronts, a repetition of 1914. And presumably, it would have exploded the interpretation which Hitler, and indeed most Germans, placed on appeasement; namely, that so long as the west itself was left inviolate, Germany had a green light to move east in order to crush the bolshevik threat.

Since 1935 France had had a treaty of mutual assistance with the Soviets, although no arrangements for military cooperation had been made. But in view of London's diplomatic primacy in the western camp by 1939, it behooved Great Britain to try to build a rapport with Russia. Despite the urgency of doing so after the guarantee to Poland, Chamberlain acted with a show of the utmost reluctance. It was August before a British negotiating team set out for Moscow; moreover, it was a low-level delegation with no plenipotentiary authority and, in contrast to Chamberlain's frantic scurrying by plane in the Munich crisis, traveled by leisurely passenger-cargo boat through the Baltic. In the actual negotiations, the British were unable to meet the price the Soviets demanded in the event of war with Germany—passage of Russian troops through Poland and Rumania, and the establishment of Russian bases around the Gulf of Finland. For his part, Stalin had even less faith in the British than they had in him. Understandably, the Soviet leader viewed appeasement as a capitalist plot against communist Russia. It was a natural riposte to side with one enemy faction against the other, thus expediting the split in the capitalist world predicted by the Marxian dialectic. If Stalin could not make a deal with the victors of 1918, he would turn to revisionist Germany; after all, the Soviet Union herself was a revisionist power.

The possibility of a Russo-German rapprochement, flagrant ideological antipathy notwithstanding, appeared after the Munich Conference from which the Soviets were pointedly excluded. "My poor friend, what have you done?" inquired a Russian foreign ministry official of the French ambassador. "As for us I see no other outcome than a fourth partition of Poland." Yet it took almost a year for this logic to work itself out. After the failure of the Anglo-Russian talks confirmed Stalin's impression of western ambiguity, Moscow accorded Hitler and Ribbentrop what they had been angling for throughout the summer of 1939. On August 23 Ribbentrop and his Soviet counterpart, Molotov, signed a nonaggression pact which was to apply in the case of defensive or offensive war. By a secret protocol, whose existence was widely rumored, Germany and Russia anticipated "a territorial and political transformation" in Poland and the Baltic states, and carved out their respective zones of influence ahead of time.

The Nazi-Soviet pact was a superb piece of opportunism by Hitler. It cleared the way for his onslaught on Poland, while seeming to rule out a second world war. The ability of the west to save Poland from her predatory neighbors, never very strong, vanished completely with Germany and Russia in collusion. By any realpolitik standard it would now be the height of folly for the British to honor their commitment to Poland's integrity. So Hitler reasoned and advanced the date of the projected attack on Poland from September 1 to August 26. But in the midst of the Führer's jubilation occurred the first indications that the characters in the drama might not play the roles allotted to them by Hitler. Mussolini, taken aback by the Nazi-Soviet pact, was swiftly persuaded by his military advisors of Italy's absolute unpreparedness for an approaching war. In lieu of a plain statement of Italy's intended neutrality, the Italian ambassador in Berlin, on August 25, presented a list of supplies—sixteen million tons of both raw materials and finished products—which his country required of Germany in order to fulfill the Pact of Steel. "Enough to kill a bull, if a bull could read," Ciano jested. There was never any question of the Germans complying with Italy's impossible demands. More important than Mussolini's desertion, however, was the simultaneous news that, at long last, a formal Anglo-Polish treaty was about to be ratified. Did this mean that Great Britain would make the quixotic gesture of fighting for Poland after all? Hitler, shaken, put back the date of the Polish invasion to September 1, which pleased his generals who held any earlier date to be impractical anyway.

The last days of August 1939 brought some reassurance to Hitler that his original prognostications might yet be borne out. It was common knowledge that Poland was now under relentless pressure from London and Paris to seek a compromise with Hitler on Danzig and the corridor. The spirit of Munich was clearly alive in the west. But the Nazis also knew, having broken the telegraphic cipher used by the Polish foreign ministry, that although the Poles might go through the motions of negotiation to gratify Britain, they had no intention of conceding anything to Germany. From this information two conclusions could be drawn. First, that if Hitler wanted the Polish Corridor, he was going to have to make war on Poland. Second, that when he did so, there was still a fair chance of the appeasement mentality keeping Britain and France out of the conflict. In addition, Hitler might no longer have been wholly averse to a showdown with the western powers. His victories in Austria and Czechoslovakia had fed his self-assurance to the point of recklessness. Already by 1939, the tendency was growing in the Third Reich to subordinate decision-making to what its Führer termed fate. If World War II was preordained for 1939, Hitler half welcomed it, confident that his own star was on the rise.

At dawn on September 1, 1939, German troops crossed the Polish border. The Nazi hope that Britain and France might condone this aggression proved not totally unfounded. For two days Chamberlain and Daladier vacillated, promising conferences, negotiations, and more pressure on the Poles to satisfy Germany's interests, if only the Wehrmacht withdrew from Polish soil. Hitler, however, was not impressed by a mere repetition of what the British had been offering all summer, and so German penetration of Poland continued. On September 3 at 11:00 A.M., Chamberlain, responding to British public opinion, announced that a state of war existed with Germany; a few hours later the French followed suit. Hitler, Ribbentrop, Göring, and Goebbels were gathered in the Reichschancellery when news of Britain's declaration of war arrived. Christopher Thorne in his *Approach of War 1938–39* (1967) presents the scene and the issues in a nutshell:

They read, and there was silence; then, with a savage look at Ribben-trop, Hitler asked: "What now?" Outside the room Goering muttered: "If we lose this war, then God have mercy on us." Goebbels stood alone in a corner; he looked downcast and absorbed with his thoughts. Between them, these men, their movement, and the nation which had spawned and followed them had brought war to an unhealthy Europe. The timing and circumstances had been to a certain extent fortuitous. The responsibility was not.

Hitler's war though it might have been, the Second World War was not in the first instance an ideological battle for and against Nazism. It started, if for any clear reason, for the European balance of power. But with the Nazi military advance across Europe, almost all the fascist movements became enrolled under Hitler's banner. Conversely, the war saw the gradual evolution of a gigantic anti-Nazi coalition ranging from conservatives to communists whose common bond was opposition to fascism of every denomination. In this way the entire struggle ultimately polarized around the issue of fascism.

## Fascism in Hitler's Europe

GERMAN CONQUEST EAST AND WEST

Poland's fate was quickly sealed. By the end of September 1939, the country was divided between Germany and Russia. The U.S.S.R. then moved to establish bases in the Baltic states. Finland, however, tried to resist, and the bitter winter war of 1939–40 ensued. The Finnish fascists of the IKL, hoping to ride a wave of anticommunism, were badly discomforted when Hitler, in the spirit of the Nazi-Soviet non-aggression pact, left Stalin carte blanche in the Gulf of Finland. The Finns' opposition to the Soviets in this instance was inspired by democratic, not fascist, motives. But the western democracies could bring little beyond moral support to Finland, and by March 1940, Mannerheim's forces had been overwhelmed by superior Soviet numbers.

Meanwhile, the war in the west hung fire. German inaction was a sign that Hitler had not planned to fight Great Britain and France so soon. In the spring of 1940, however, the "twilight war" gave way to the real one. In April Hitler, anticipating an Anglo-French venture into Norwegian waters to cut vital German supplies of iron ore from northern Sweden, ordered the occupation of Denmark and Norway, which was accomplished with bewildering speed. This cleared the way for a larger enterprise—an all-out lightning attack (blitzkrieg) on France which came in May via neutral Belgium and Holland, thus outflanking the French Maginot line. The Dutch, stunned by an aerial blitz on Rotterdam, surrendered on the fifteenth, and the Belgians followed suit on the twenty-eighth. By this time German armored (Panzer) divisions, starting from the hinge of the Franco-Belgian frontier, had driven clear to the English Channel. Hitler left it to the *Luftwaffe* rather than his tanks to finish off over 300,000 Anglo-French forces trapped to the north of the German thrust; this proved a mistake as the bulk of the Allied troops, if not their equipment, were rescued from Dunkirk.

Now France lay open to Hitler. Statistically, the French were not outmanned or outgunned by the Wehrmacht. Rather, they suffered from a lack of military imagination, especially in the deployment of mechanized forces, and more crucially still, from a crisis of morale. The conquests of Poland, Denmark, Norway, and the Low Countries in little more than six months convinced many Frenchmen that the German advance was irresistible. Nazi threats of a rain of terror from the skies seemed all too credible after Guernica, Warsaw, and Rotterdam, persuading thousands to become refugees who clogged the roads of northern France and played havoc with French military logistics. While the German nation had been uniting under Hitler since 1933, Frenchmen in the wake of February 6, 1934, had grown increasingly divided. Rumors flew about a French fifth column. (The phrase had been coined in the Spanish Civil War when General Mola, one of Franco's commanders, remarked, while marching on Madrid with four columns, that he also relied on a fifth column of sympathizers within the capital.) Actually, France in the summer of 1940 was not so much harmed by sabotage and active support for Nazism as by passive defeatism; the nation was beaten psychologically before she was overrun militarily. The "stalemate society" and the Third Republic, adopted out of convenience in the 1870s, could mount no spirited defiance of Nazi Germany either in ideology or on the battlefield. On June 16 with Paris already occupied, the French cabinet resolved to sue for an armistice. The armistice was signed in Hitler's presence on the twenty-second; the location was the very railway car in the forest of Compiègne used for the German capitulation in November 1918. From Compiègne Hitler went on to view the architectural sights of Paris; accompanied by Speer, he looked for ideas to incorporate in the rebuilding of Berlin.

COLLABORATIONISM AND VICHY

The German sweep through western Europe brought within Hitler's purview several indigenous fascist movements. From their ranks came the most notorious collaborators with the Nazi occupiers. One was Vidkun Quisling whose Norwegian racist party, after its rise in the Great Depression, had been fading since 1937. Because he was one of the first, Quisling's name was used for all collaborators. Yet Mussert of Holland or Degrelle of Belgium (although not Van Severen who was killed by French troops in May 1940) might equally well have supplied a cognomen. The collaborators were flattered to participate in the making of Hitler's new world order. At the same time, most of them unrealistically expected to enjoy considerable independence within the German orbit. The Nazis were always lavish with promises of noninterference, but in practice the quislings were puppets who danced to Berlin's measure.

Quisling himself was accepted by the Germans, then deposed, and finally reinstated as Norwegian minister-president. His regime was feeble and constantly torn between the moderates and those who advocated Norway's total integration into the Third Reich. In Holland Anton Mussert by 1942 managed to persuade Hitler to recognize him as *Leider* (Führer) of the Netherlands; but his new title cut no ice with the domineering Seyss-Inquart, German Reich commissioner for the Netherlands, who regarded Mussert's movement mostly as a useful source of Dutch recruits for the SS. Similarly, in Belgium the Germans treated their fascist collaborators cavalierly. Léon Degrelle, for instance, was forced to fuse his Rexists with the Flemish VNV which, for racial reasons, was favored by the occupation authorities. Many of these western European fascists hoped, by their collaboration, to protect their fellow countrymen from the full fury of the Hitlerian dictatorship. It was a vain hope; nowhere in Europe, west or east, were the Nazis deflected from looting the conquered nations of supplies and manpower for the German war effort.

An interesting variation on the general theme of collaborationism occurred in France. Notwithstanding the French capitulation of June 1940, it remained open to doubt whether the French Mediterranean fleet and North African colonies would abide by the decision of the metropolitan government or side with the British who were still fighting. To prevent the latter, Hitler, who subjectively despised the French as a non-Aryan people, deemed it politic to treat France with relative and unexpected leniency. Hence, Germany occupied only two-thirds of

France, including the northern industrial regions, Paris, and the Atlantic coastline. The rest was to be a semisovereign French state whose officials would even have a little authority in the German-occupied zone. This rump French state was expected to cooperate closely with Nazi Germany; for example, an exceptionally odious clause in the armistice of June 22 provided for the handing over to the Gestapo of refugees from Nazism living anywhere in French territory. Nonetheless, the shape of society and politics in southern France was, in the main, left to Frenchmen to determine. The regime which took its name from Vichy, the capital of unoccupied France, far from being imposed by the Germans, was propelled into being by powerful currents in modern French history.

All the longstanding reservations about the Third Republic came to a head in the defeat of 1940. At Vichy a national assembly composed of former deputies and senators, the spokesmen of the political class which had sustained the republic for almost seventy years, responded to the promptings of former republican premier, Pierre Laval, and authorized Marshal Philippe Pétain to promulgate a new constitution. Pétain at once assumed the title of chief of state, eliminating the word "republic" and the constitution of 1875, and for "liberty, equality, and fraternity" substituted "work, family, country." The military hero of Verdun in 1916, Pétain was an authentic voice of old France, a French equivalent of the German Hindenburg. The Vichy regime under his tutelage drew its inspiration more from conservatism than from fascism. On the other hand, during the 1930s "a part of the classic Right," in René Rémond's authoritative words, "let itself be won over by the vocabulary and taken in by the propaganda of fascism." It was this conservatism, deeply infected by the fascist fever, which prevailed at Vichy.

Pétain's rule was predictably authoritarian. The former republican civil liberties were abrogated as was representative government. Ministers were appointed by and responsible solely to the marshal and, on the whole, were less influential at Vichy than France's senior civil servants. But there was more to Vichy than mere autocracy. A "national revolution" was projected on the basis of definite sociopolitical principles. In all his speeches Pétain reminded his countrymen of the ancient values of the soil, countryside, and family. In true conservative fashion he wanted to revivify the natural bonds which had originally brought Frenchmen together. Instead of modern centralization, Vichy stressed the cultural autonomy of the traditional provinces, the distinctions of an old-fashioned social hierarchy, and in the economic sphere

Marshal Pétain and Pierre Laval, French collaborators with the Nazi
occupiers. Although the architects of the generically fascist regime at Vichy,
their collaborationism arose less from ideology than from a patriotic hope
of carving out an independent French sphere in Hitler's "new order."
WIDE WORLD PHOTOS

the independence of medieval-style corporations. The ties binding these
elements together were not artificial and legal but organic and instinctive. The ideal has been properly called a "société communautaire."
The intellectuals of Vichy interpreted this reversion to premodernity
as a revolt against the rationalism of the Enlightenment. Thus, Pierre
Drieu la Rochelle: "France was destroyed by the rationalism to which
her genius had been reduced. Today, rationalism is dead and buried.
We can only rejoice at its demise. The destruction of the monster
that had been gnawing away at the very soul of France was the *sine qua
non* of her revival." And Gustave Thibon celebrated this move away

from a supposedly sterile intellectualism in a book entitled *Retour au réel* (1943).

Vichy's national revolution was almost a spiritual one in which the *pays légal* would be dissolved in the mystical *pays réel*. It was what Action Française had been advocating for forty years. Action Française, however, even under Vichy, never quite recovered from its post-1934 slump. The movement had grown too attached to the Parisian salons and newspaper offices to function effectively in provincial Vichy; so much for the decentralization Action Française preached. Age and poor health prevented Maurras himself from playing an active political role, but he enjoyed some Vichy lionizing, the sales of his writings went up, and many of his disciples served as officials in Pétain's administration. All his life Maurras had been a monarchist, although his movement in 1937 had been repudiated by the French royal pretender. In 1940 Maurras found in Marshal Pétain a vicarious king, and he heartily endorsed Vichy's endeavor to restore the age of the Bourbons in all but royal name.

The realization of Maurrassian ideas proved difficult, though. As a step to curbing cosmopolitanism in France, Vichy in October 1940 adopted anti-Semitic legislation sometimes compared to Nazi Germany's Nuremberg Laws, although it was implemented, at least at first, more in the lax fashion of Fascist Italy's anti-Semitism. A marginal effort was made to inculcate right thinking in the rising generation by state-sponsored youth cadres and a militia. A charter of labor was drawn up which defined the status of workers within a corporative system. Vichy's philosophy found an echo in the countryside where Pétain's eulogies of the family bond corresponded to the paternalistic social structure. However, the nebulous concept of the *pays réel* seemed to have little relevance amid the marketplace realities of the urban centers, and consequently made little impact there. Hitler had failed to check *Landflucht* and discovered that he could not dismantle Germany's industrial complex, despite its anti-*völkisch* connotations, without crippling his country. In like manner, Pétain found that Maurrassian ideology alone was powerless to change the face of modern France. Perhaps the only way in which Vichy might have come close to imposing its revolution on the nation was through a tight, centripetal dictatorship, but this was ruled out by the Maurrassian hatred of centralization as a modern Jacobin vice. In any case, the aged Pétain was no Führer or even Duce to direct a ruthless, totalitarian experiment. Maurrassianism thus remained a promise that was mostly unfulfilled.

Broadly speaking, two forms of collaboration existed in Vichy France. On the one hand, the Vichy conservatives hoped to save *la patrie* by dealing with Germany on the basis of independent nation-states; these could be termed collaborators. On the other, French national socialists looked for integration of their country in a supranational Hitlerian new order based on race; these were the collaborationists. Between 1940 and 1942, the former were in the ascendancy at Vichy, but inadvertently they provided a bridge by which the more unscrupulous and intemperate elements of French fascism reached power.

This transition was personified in the fortunes of Pierre Laval. As G. Warner's recent biography demonstrates, Laval was by inclination a collaborator rather than a collaborationist, but circumstances and his well-developed sense of opportunism pushed him into an ever-closer alignment with the fanatical French nazis and their German masters. In October 1940 he stage-managed a meeting of Pétain and Hitler at Montoire whence emerged a communiqué promising Franco-German cooperation and a mutual "interest in seeing Britain defeated as soon as possible." In December, however, Pétain took a firm stand against the German transfer of population from Alsace-Lorraine, and replaced Laval with the reputedly less collaborationist Admiral Darlan. Laval moved to Paris where he mingled with the French national socialists congregated there and intrigued with the Germans to force his return to an influential post in Vichy. Indeed, with the passage of time German pressure on Vichy grew greater and Pétain's position weaker. The Vichy regime certainly did not improve its image during 1941–42 when its most notable political act was to prosecute at Riom Léon Blum, along with other politicians and generals of the Third Republic, on a charge of responsibility for the French defeat in 1940. The Riom trials of February 1942 backfired to the discredit of Vichy, for Blum defended himself with great eloquence and the proceedings were suspended on German orders. This ignominy paved the way for further erosion of Vichy's integrity. In April, Otto Abetz, the German ambassador to France, forced Pétain to take back Laval and grant him "effective direction of internal and foreign policy." Henceforth, Pétain became increasingly a figurehead devoid of influence.

In November 1942 the Allies landed in Morocco and Algeria. Since Hitler's tolerance of a semiautonomous Vichy government was largely a tactical maneuver to keep French North Africa neutral, there was now no further reason for the Germans to hold back from the occupation of all France. Laval, self-confidently negotiating on Vichy's behalf, won a temporary victory in the battle to achieve preference for France in Hitler's new order. Specifically, French industry was allowed to contribute to the German war effort by operating independently under the direction of Jean Bichelonne, Vichy's highly competent minister of industrial production. Successful though this scheme was, Hitler tired of it and, without regard for French production, ordered a million French workers to be conscripted for labor in Germany in 1944. Furthermore, under total German occupation, Laval found his own style of collaboration was insufficient to satisfy the fanatical ideologues who became more and more prominent at Vichy. The ex-communist and PPF leader, Jacques Doriot, was now a thoroughgoing nazi. Another heretical socialist, Marcel Déat, was the guiding spirit behind the *Rassemblement National Populaire*, which was designed to be the single party in an idealized totalitarian state. Under such influences Vichy's racism turned more vicious; *Je Suis Partout*, long the most strident of French anti-Semitic journals, became almost required reading for officials. The agency through which the extremists worked was Joseph Darnand's *Milice*, which served as an auxiliary of the Gestapo and, in its satanic mixture of fervor and sadism, rivaled the German archetype.

All this subservience to the flattery of the Germans was too much for the patriotic Maurras and other Action Française elements. Although most of them never broke formally with Pétain and Laval, they tended to drift away from Vichy. Yet, in essence, the change at Vichy from Maurrassianism to an uninhibited national socialism was more one of degree than of kind. Both creeds purposed the overthrow of twentieth-century society in favor of a romantic ideal from the past. Maurras, as we have seen, was in love with the Middle Ages. So, too, the neonazi Déat conceived his movement in terms of an abstemious medieval order: "People might ask whether we want to create an Order—the word does not frighten me. . . . And if the future members of the One Party took the oath of poverty on joining it, it would not be a bad idea. . . . We live in times when exemplary behaviour is essential, especially in those who want to reform." And for Déat, reformation meant the weeding out of alien strains: "The defense of the French ethnic community against unassimilable or noxious racial elements by measures of psychological, economic, and political protection, and its regeneration by ambitious policies for Youth, Sport, Public Health, and the Family." The sentiments could have appeared in any *Action Française* editorial. In the end, what distinguished the French nazis was an extra dimension of brutality and a taste for centralized dictatorship in the execution of the national revolution.

MUSSOLINI'S PARALLEL WAR

The French surrender in 1940 and Vichy's subsequent collaboration had ramifications far beyond France. Italy was deeply affected. Although, on the outbreak of World War II, Mussolini had been persuaded to stay out, he resented his country's neutral stance which recalled liberal Italy's neutrality in 1914. Fascist Italy was supposed to have left behind such inglorious postures, and Mussolini spoke not of neutrality but of "nonbelligerency." Some time in the new year 1940, he resolved to intervene in the war at the earliest advantageous moment, refusing to be deflected by the voices of caution which came from many quarters—the Vatican, King Victor Emmanuel, and even Ciano who, since Nazi deviousness in the Danzig crisis, was convinced that the German alliance would lead Italy to perdition. Hitler's blitzkrieg in western Europe was Mussolini's cue. Having designs on French territory, Fascist Italy needed to be in at the kill. Therefore on June 10 the Duce announced from the balcony of the Palazzo Venezia:

> We are entering the lists against the plutocratic and reactionary democracies of the west, which have always hindered the advance and often plotted against the very existence of the Italian people. . . . According to the laws of Fascist morality, when one has a friend, one goes with him to the very end. We have done this and will do this with Germany, with her people, with her victorious armed forces.

In the brief fighting in the Alps before the Franco-German armistice brought hostilities to an end, the Italians were able to push only a few yards into France. It was an unimpressive military performance with which to bargain, and Hitler was hardly inclined to alienate the complaisant Vichy government by consigning large tracts of French territory to Italy. In fact, all that Mussolini gained from intervention was a few square miles of Alpine land and the demilitarization of the Franco-Italian frontier.

Mussolini had been heard to complain that whenever Hitler made a major diplomatic move, he sent him a telegram about it. Now the Duce determined to repay his fascist partner in kind. Thwarted in the west, Fascist Italy, from its Albanian protectorate, launched an attack on Greece on October 28, 1940. Hitler had been informed of Mussolini's intent to invade Greece but not the date of the attack. The Führer was due to visit Italy and, alighting from his railway sleeper in Florence on the morning of the twenty-eighth, he was greeted by Mussolini bubbling over with the news that he had already embarked on his Balkan adventure. From the start, however, Mussolini's enterprise did not go well, and within days Italian troops were in retreat from Greece. Hitler was not pleased; the Italian gesture promised to offer the British, so soon after Dunkirk, a foothold on the Continent. But with typical opportunism he made the best of the situation. The Wehrmacht not only moved into Greece to uphold Axis prestige, but also Hitler seized his chance to subordinate Italy completely to the German war strategy. Italian compliance was rendered all the more necessary by Hitler's failure to lure Franco's Spain into the war.

On the fall of France, Generalissimo Franco was disposed to align himself with the two fascist dictators, thus continuing his policy during the Spanish Civil War. But second thoughts developed in Franco's mind as Britain kept on fighting. For the same reason Hitler needed Spain. Unable or unwilling to invade Britain, he sought to cut her imperial lifeline by encouraging Spain to take Gibraltar. With this idea in mind, the Führer, in October 1940, journeyed to Hendaye on the Franco-Spanish border to meet Franco. The encounter was a fiasco. Franco arrived deliberately late; as his price for entering the war, he suggested stretches of French North Africa which, if conceded by Hitler, would have undermined his policy of securing Vichy's collaboration; and overall, Franco was irritatingly vague about future commitments. Hitler was not used to such treatment, and afterward remarked ruefully that, sooner than repeat his Hendaye experience, he "would prefer to have three or four teeth extracted." Franco held the whip hand, though, and knew it. Even Hitler would not dare to dragoon Spain by force so long as the war with Britain continued; and anyway his thoughts were already turning to Russia. So Franco remained cautious and neutral. His cold-blooded, realpolitik attitude contrasted sharply with the doctrinaire fanaticism which, by now, infused Fascist Italian diplomacy. In truth, the choices made in the latter half of 1940 in Madrid and Rome, respectively, settled the fate of two dictators. The nationalist Franco would survive in neutrality; in contrast, Mussolini, by tying himself to Hitler, was doomed.

Because he came away empty-handed from Hendaye, Hitler had to turn to Italy for his entrée to the Mediterranean. During the winter of 1940–41, a horde of German officials, military and civilian, descended on Italy to supervise supplies and plot strategy. The *Luftwaffe*, operating from Sicilian airfields, cut the Mediterranean in two. General Erwin Rommel took over the North African campaign when the Italians were driven back from Egypt by the British. Even in the

Balkans, where Mussolini had hoped to pursue his own "parallel war," the same German dominance prevailed. Early in 1941, the Wehrmacht prepared a crushing attack on Greece which depended on the transport of men and matériel through Yugoslavia. The royal dictatorship in Belgrade was willing to oblige, but a nationalist uprising, in which the military were prominent, overthrew the monarchy on account of its supine attitude to Hitler. Therefore, the Nazi onslaught was hurled at both Yugoslavia and Greece and, in a brilliant blitzkrieg exhibition, the campaign was completed by the end of April 1941. Yugoslavia, Greece, and the island of Crete were all occupied, although guerrilla resistance soon sprang up in the mountains.

For over a decade, Mussolini had labeled Yugoslavia, more than Greece, a mortal foe of Italy, and he had intrigued with separatist elements there to destroy the South Slav state. Now, the dream could be realized. An autonomous Croatian state was set up under Italian tutelage and its government entrusted to the local fascist chief, Ante Pavelić. In the event, Pavelić's *Ustaši* movement showed itself less interested in creating a fascist society than in murdering as many Serbs as possible, and untold thousands of the latter were driven from their homes. Perhaps because this persecution of an ethnic group was more in Hitler's line than Mussolini's, Pavelić found it more congenial to deal with the Nazis than with the Italians. The *Ustaši* took to describing the Croats as a "Gothic people." The result was that Croatia, regardless of its designation as an Italian zone of influence, soon came to be ruled in effect by directives conceived in Berlin. In sum, wherever the Axis partners joined forces after 1940, Hitler alone called the tune.

LURE OF THE EAST

The extension of the Nazi empire in southern Europe was accomplished at the precise juncture that Hitler's plans were maturing for the climactic episode of the Third Reich—the invasion of the Soviet Union. Contrary to popular belief, however, the foray into Greece and Yugoslavia did not seriously incommode the larger Nazi enterprise. Only a limited quantity of troops and supplies were diverted south and a three-week delay at most incurred in the opening of an eastern front which was scheduled for the summer of 1941.

Hitler had never wavered in his conviction that the true Nazi empire would be established in the east at Russia's expense. The Nazi-Soviet pact of August 1939 was only a parenthesis in the Führer's grand design and the war in the west a distraction. After the elimination of Poland in the autumn of 1939 and again after the fall of France in June 1940, Hitler expected to negotiate an armistice with Great Britain; the latter would be given a free hand outside Europe, in exchange for the Third Reich being left unchallenged on the Continent—a genuinely Napoleonic contemplation. On the British side, so long as the Chamberlain cabinet continued in office, the chance of London's accepting such a bargain was always present. The possibility of a negotiated peace evaporated, however, once the obdurate Winston Churchill became prime minister in May 1940 and began to establish a special rapport with the U.S. president, Franklin Roosevelt. In view of the fading hopes of an armistice with Britain, most of Hitler's military advisors recommended an amphibious invasion before the British could recover from the Dunkirk evacuation. They were, indeed, authorized to proceed with Operation Sealion. But the German invasion of Britain never materialized, ostensibly because the *Luftwaffe* could not clear air space over the Channel long enough for the troop barges to cross. But just as important, Hitler displayed a marked lack of enthusiasm for Operation Sealion. For one thing, it did not appeal to his blitzkrieg mentality which had accustomed him to project quick victories won by armored columns. Additionally and significantly, however, by the end of July 1940, Hitler was already talking about the Soviets: "Russia's destruction must therefore be made a part of this struggle. . . . The sooner Russia is crushed, the better. The attack will achieve its purpose only if the Russian state can be shattered to its roots with one blow. . . . If we start in May 1941, we will have five months in which to finish the job." The first directives for an eastern campaign were issued in August 1940. Operation Sealion was pushed into the background almost as soon as it was enunciated. It was left to Göring's *Luftwaffe* to bomb the British into submission—if it could. If not, Hitler was ready to do what in *Mein Kampf* he had denied he would ever do—repeat the folly of 1914 and embroil Germany in a serious two-front war.

In the diplomatic arena German preparations for the war against the Soviets were carefully made. In September 1940 Hitler and Ribbentrop finally succeeded in bringing Japan as well as Italy within Germany's orbit in the Tripartite Pact. The agreement was based on recognition of the parties' spheres of influence, and in the succeeding weeks negotiations were set afoot to extend the pact to the Soviet Union by recognizing Russia's special interests in eastern Europe. On

Germany's part, this was mere dissimulation which ceased when the last Soviet *démarche* in November went unanswered by Berlin. Hitler's real concentration was on bringing the small states of eastern Europe into his fold. The Winter War and Russia's subsequent annexation of Baltic states in the summer of 1940 gave Finland solid reason to fight at Nazi Germany's side. Amid rumors of war against Russia, the old pro-German *Jägers* reemerged and enjoyed fresh influence in Helsinki. In January 1941 the fascist IKL also came out of eclipse and joined a coalition government—a sure sign that the Finns were thinking in terms of an anticommunist front. Hungary and Rumania, too, were easily enlisted in the anti-Soviet cause, although interestingly in neither case did Hitler count much on the local fascists. Admiral Horthy, the wily Hungarian regent, had aligned his nation with the Third Reich in world affairs ever since the Munich crisis of 1938. In return, Hitler had been niggardly in his support of the Arrow Cross and other Hungarian fascist groups, which enabled Horthy and his fellow conservatives to hold them at arm's length. There was no change in this pattern in 1941 as the Horthy-Hitler understanding blossomed.

The situation in Rumania was more complicated. During the summer of 1940, Rumania had suffered a sequence of blows. Moscow took advantage of Hitler's preoccupation in western Europe to wrest Bessarabia and northern Bucovina from Rumania under threat of war; and not to be outdone, Hungary and Bulgaria with Axis blessing forced Bucharest to disgorge half of Transylvania and the southern Dobruja. King Carol could not survive these humiliations and abdicated in favor of his son, Prince Michael. But real power passed into the hands of General Ion Antonescu, a favorite of the fascist Iron Guard, who styled himself *Conducator* (leader) and wore in public the green shirt of Rumanian fascism. In cooperation with Horia Sima, now returned to Rumania from his exile in Nazi Germany, Antonescu proclaimed a "legionary state" which suggested a racist, totalitarian regime such as the Legion of the Archangel Michael advocated. It was certainly a large step beyond King Carol's corporative dictatorship in the direction of national socialism. Yet, fundamentally, Antonescu was a spokesman of Rumanian conservatism and, before the end of 1940, found himself quarreling with Sima over legionary violence and murder that swept the country and struck at Jews, foreigners, capitalists, and intellectuals. In January 1941 the dispute escalated into a three-day civil war, which resulted in the army's total suppression of the Iron Guard and drove Sima back to his German refuge. Strange to relate, the key to Antonescu's victory was the encouragement he received from Hitler. So long as Antonescu put Rumanian oil wells at Germany's disposal and stood ready to join in the projected attack on the Soviet Union, he could rely on Nazi backing—even to the extent of the virtual annihilation of Rumanian fascism.

Hitler's preference for the Horthys and Antonescus of eastern Europe's historic classes paralleled his collusion with the German conservatives on his march to power. In each case anti-Marxism provided the meeting-ground. The Nazi attack on Soviet Russia was, at long last, to be the fulfillment of that antibolshevik crusade that had been bruited about Europe since 1917, and it enrolled professional anticommunists everywhere. Mussolini, as usual, was informed of Hitler's Russian plans at the last moment, but in due course he was to scrape together an Italian expeditionary force to perish in the snows of Russia. Even the cautious Franco could not forego a gesture of support for the anticommunist champion and would send eighteen thousand volunteers, the "blue division," to the Russian front.

But, for Nazi Germany, the impending war against the U.S.S.R. was motivated by much more than simple anticommunism. The destruction of Soviet Russia, "that degenerate Jewish sponge-fungus" in Hitler's words, was to be the sublimation of the Nazis' most cherished racial ideals. "The conception of the nation," Hitler once said, "has become meaningless. We have to get rid of this false conception and set in its place the conception of race. The New Order cannot be conceived in terms of the national boundaries of the peoples with an historic past, but in terms of race that transcend these boundaries." Symbolically, the plan of attack on Russia was labeled Operation Barbarossa. The nickname "redbeard" recalled a mythical Teutonic giant whose lair was conveniently situated near Berchtesgaden and who was supposed to reappear whenever Germany was threatened. One reincarnation of Barbarossa was believed to be the medieval Hohenstaufen warrior king, Frederick I. Now, in 1941, his spirit was conjured up again, and so the new Teutonic knights were impelled eastward by memories of a *völkisch* legend.

The prospective Russian campaign generated great enthusiasm in Nazism's upper echelons. But on the eve of Operation Barbarossa, one top Nazi at least was looking west rather than east. Rudolf Hess, although officially a deputy of the Führer and in direct line of succession after Göring, had been pushed out of the limelight by Hitler's personal secretary, Martin Bormann. To recoup his waning influence,

Hess decided, on his own initiative, to try to bring off the peace settlement with Great Britain which had evaded Hitler. Hess made three abortive efforts to reach Britain before May 10, 1941, when, in one of the most bizarre incidents of the war, he parachuted into Scotland. On being arrested, he asked to speak to the Duke of Hamilton. As the duke was of no political consequence, Hess's request spoke volumes about Nazi fantasies regarding the British aristocracy and the political process. The British soon spotted the mental instability of Hess and wasted little time with him. Concurrently, Hitler disavowed his deputy, giving Bormann his party posts, and ordering that Hess be shot if he returned to Germany. But if the Hess mission was a chimera, it nonetheless pointed to the risk Hitler was about to run by launching Operation Barbarossa while Britain was still in the field.

At first, though, the warning expressed by the flight of Hess seemed unnecessary. When the Wehrmacht moved on June 22, 1941, it brushed aside the Red Army which was scandalously unprepared. Although the German generals preferred a concentrated thrust on Moscow, Hitler insisted on fanning out south and north. In September Kiev fell and German troops were fighting in the suburbs of Leningrad. At this point, all available Panzer divisions were thrown into the drive on Moscow, and early in December, a few advanced units gained a glimpse of the Russian capital. There, they ground to a halt in the face of a Soviet counterattack using troops brought from the Far East. Now, German troops faced the Russian winter with totally inadequate clothing. Hitler had optimistically calculated that Moscow would be taken before winter began in earnest. In addition, Hitler's disregard of the Russian climate probably owed something to his espousal of the strange scientific theories of Hans Hörbiger. According to these, the universe was controlled by the struggle between fire and ice, with the former destined to triumph over the latter with the coming of a new race of Nordic supermen. Out of such cosmic fantasies grew the inadequacies of Operation Barbarossa.

In the meantime, however, the German armies were exhausted; over a quarter of the invading forces and a higher proportion of tanks had been lost. The army general staff, which all along had been dubious about advancing through the November snows, now counseled a strategic retreat. But Hitler, obsessed as ever by the psychological angle, feared that a retreat would suggest Napoleon's disaster of 1812 and ruin German morale. Therefore, he categorically forbade any withdrawal; officers who disobeyed were court-martialed, several generals were dismissed, and the commander in chief, Field Marshal von Brauchitsch, resigned. This quarrel with the army officer corps brought to the surface all the Führer's contempt for the "gentlemen" who wrote "von" before their names and had never fought in the trenches. Brauchitsch was a "vain, cowardly wretch who could not even appraise the situation, let alone master it." Instead of appointing a new commander in chief, Hitler himself assumed command of the troops in the field, which marked a further step in the denigration of the professional military begun in the Fritsch-Blomberg affair four years earlier.

Notwithstanding this internal bickering and the German check before Moscow, the prospect of a total Nazi victory in Russia in the spring of 1942 appeared bright enough. Soviet losses had far outstripped German—2.5 million men killed, wounded, or captured, and practically the entire tank force of 15,000 wiped out. Moreover, the German line before Moscow bent in places but did not give way. Amid unbelievable privations, the morale of the German army, under Hitler's skillful manipulation, did not erode. The magic of the infallible, totalitarian Führer over the Germans at the front and at home was unbroken, and the failure to take Moscow conveniently laid at the door of obstreperous generals with insufficient faith in National Socialism. Meanwhile, German arms by the end of 1941 had secured *Lebensraum* enough to serve as a laboratory for the application of those *völkisch* precepts which comprised the *ultima ratio* of Nazism.

ZENITH OF RACIST IDEOLOGY

The perfect *völkisch* society was by definition a rural one. Only where the bulk of the population were farmers and craftsmen living in villages or at most small towns could the bond of blood and soil, the sense of racial solidarity, the virtues of manual labor and family discipline—all the shibboleths of Nazi belief—truly flourish. It was impossible to make modern Germany revert from an industrial state to a primitive, agrarian one, but in the underindustrialized east of Europe and steppes of European Russia, the Nazis perceived a much more congenial setting for their ideal *völkisch* community. For this reason, the return to the past was to be pursued more eagerly in occupied Poland and Russia than in the German homeland itself.

Inexorably, then, the Nazi German state was drawn by the force of its own convictions first to conquer, then to reshape the east. Not surprisingly, there was a scramble among the Nazi bosses to participate in the grand ideological experiment, and in typical Nazi totalitarian manner, a series of overlapping jurisdictions sprang up. Already a callous Nazi bureaucrat, Hans Frank, administered the "General Government" in those areas of western Poland not directly annexed to Germany in 1939. In addition, Alfred Rosenberg, the German Balt and Nazi ideologue, was elevated from semiobscurity to the post of Reich commissioner for the eastern territories. But his authority was immediately challenged by Göring who demanded and obtained a say in economic policy in the east. Most important of all, however, was the role assigned to the SS under Himmler:

> In the area of operations, the *Reichsführer* SS is entrusted, on behalf of the Führer, with special tasks for the preparation of the political administration, tasks which result from the struggle which has to be carried out between two opposing political systems. Within the scope of these tasks, the *Reichsführer* SS shall act independently and under his own responsibility.

Since 1935 a Race and Settlement Office had existed within the SS and, since October 1939, Himmler had presided over a Reich Commissariat for the strengthening of Germandom (RKFVD). These agencies, especially the latter, were geared to administer population resettlement in the east.

Very simply, Nazi plans called for Aryan colonization on a massive scale. Because Germany was considered overpopulated, it was hoped that many of the fatherland's inhabitants would of their own accord seize the chance to move into the occupied territories. More direct encouragement to migrate was applied by the RKFVD to the *Volksdeutsche*, ethnic Germans living as minority groups throughout southern and eastern Europe. After screening and indoctrination in Germany, they were offered material inducements to join the great trek eastward. The first region to be designated for German settlement comprised the Polish provinces annexed to the Third Reich. Over a million Poles were forcibly expelled from these lands and crowded into Hans Frank's General Government to the south. Their property was expropriated by the RKFVD and some of it turned over to the German colonists. By 1943 close to a million Aryans of one sort and another had been settled, mostly on farms, in former Polish territories. After the Wehrmacht's advance in 1941, Himmler produced General Plan East which envisioned German colonization of European Russia from the Baltic states to the Crimea. The Crimean peninsula had a strange fascination for Nazi planners who proposed that it be annexed out-right and linked to Berlin by autobahn. But elsewhere in Russia, settlement would take the form of "frontier marches," fortified centers astride the main communications routes, a defensive scheme made necessary by the presence of a hostile population and the proximity of the military frontier of the *völkisch* domain. In other words, the colonization of European Russia would be a hazardous occupation as long as the Russo-German war lasted. In fact, apart from a few settlements on the Baltic where the *Volksdeutsche* had roots and in the Ukraine, the colonization of Soviet territory remained largely a program on paper.

Because of the war's inhibition of actual colonization, the thrust of Hitler's *Ostpolitik* came to be fixed on the treatment meted out to the vanquished populations. For the minority, "Germanization" was possible—that is, designation as racially akin to Aryans and the prospect of assimilation into the *Herrenvolk* or master race. This concept was tailored to fit such western European peoples as the Dutch, Flemings, and Norwegians. But even among the inferior races in the east, it was deemed modestly applicable. For example, Himmler's chief lieutenant, Heydrich, considered half the Czechs fit for Germanization. In Poland perhaps as many as ten thousand children "of Nordic appearance" were rounded up and sent for proper upbringing with German, usually SS, families. Hitler, on the basis of a visit to the Ukraine where the folk costume of the peasant girls reminded him of his native Austria, fostered a scheme to bring Ukrainian girls to Germany as domestic servants in the hope they would marry Aryan husbands. Needless to say, there were no objective criteria of a "racially valuable" individual or social group. Chance and expediency reigned, just as on the diplomatic plane Italy and Japan were accorded honorary Aryan status.

The fate of the bulk of the subject peoples, on the other hand, was the very opposite of Germanization; they were to be removed from their homelands in order to make room for German settlers. The Polish General Government was intended to be only a temporary dumping ground for displaced Poles. Ultimately, they, together with millions from all over European Russia, were to be transported east of the Urals and to the Arctic. But like German colonization itself, mass expulsions had to await the end of the war. In the interim, eastern Slavs would provide menial labor for their conquerors, either in the occupied territories or as slave labor in German camps and factories. Since these Slavic *Untermenschen* or subhumans (the word did not really become popular in the Nazi vocabulary until 1941) had no stake in the future *völkisch* utopia, they could be treated as nonpersons; their property was to be taken for the German war effort while nothing that might detract from the needs of the war was to be expended on their upkeep. In the Führer's own words: "As for the ridiculous hundred million Slavs, we will mold the best of them to the shape that suits us, and we will isolate the rest of them in their own pigsties; and anyone who talks about cherishing the local inhabitant and civilizing him goes straight off to a concentration camp!"

Starvation of the subject peoples was not ruled out, but rather welcomed. As so often, it was Göring's brutal tongue which expressed most plainly the malignancy of Nazi policy. Even before Operation Barbarossa was launched, a directive was issued by Göring's office in charge of economic policy in the east reading:

The German administration in these territories may well attempt to mitigate the consequences of the famine which will undoubtedly take place, and to accelerate the return to primitive agricultural conditions. . . . However, these measures will not avert famine. Many tens of millions of people in the industrial areas will become redundant and will either die or have to emigrate to Siberia. Any attempt to save the population there from death by starvation by importing surpluses from the Black Soil Zone would be at the expense of supplies to Europe. It would reduce Germany's staying power in the war, and would undermine Germany's and Europe's power to resist the blockade. This must be clearly and absolutely understood.

A year later, Göring observed: "In the old days, the rule was plunder. Now, outward forms have become more humane. Nevertheless, I intend to plunder and plunder copiously." Himmler did not mince words either and instructed his SS in ruthlessness: "How the Russians or the Czechs fare is absolutely immaterial to me. . . . Whether nations live in prosperity or starve to death interests me only insofar as we need them as slaves for our culture."

It was not a large step from tolerance of death by starvation to more direct forms of slaughter. Already in 1939, SS *Einsatzgruppen* (action teams) had followed the German army into Poland, systematically murdering civilian officials, Jews, and others who might form the core of a future resistance. After June 1941, the *Einsatzgruppen* were expanded and operated more intensively than ever on Soviet soil. One of four main groups of *Einsatzkommandos* reported 90,000 Russian victims in the first year; another later claimed 135,000 in four months. It was, of course, the "war of extermination," as Hitler called his Russian campaign, which brought into the open the genocidal tendencies in Nazism. The enemy in the east, Hitler told the Wehrmacht, "consists not of soldiers but to a large extent only of beasts." Goebbels called the Russians "a conglomeration of animals." Therefore, Soviet prisoners of war were herded into open compounds in the middle of the Russian winter, and then shipped off to labor camps in Germany where food and shelter teetered on the edge of subsistence. Of five million Soviet soldiers and three million civilians deported westward, about two-thirds never returned.

But although regarded as inferior, the Slavs did not occupy the bottom rung of Nazism's biological ladder. This had been reserved, since the earliest days in Munich, for the Jews. Yet, it was only on moving east that Hitler and his gang came face to face with the "Jewish problem" in its full magnitude. Germany possessed some 600,000 Jews, and the Nazi blitzkrieg in western Europe brought another half million under German rule. However, the combination of Germany's conquest of Poland and advance into the U.S.S.R. placed a further five million Jews within the Nazi grasp. Overall, Operation Barbarossa heightened the racial sensitivity of the Third Reich's leaders. The ideological euphoria of *Ostpolitik* provided the stimulus to embark on the "final solution" of the Jewish question; by this most notorious euphemism was meant the annihilation of European Jewry. Nazi administrators in the east often spoke of the choice between deporting and exterminating the subhumans; obviously, the more extermination was used, the less need there would be for costly and complicated deportations from the Germanized zones. The Jews, already condemned as the worst polluters of *völkisch* purity, were inevitably selected for Nazism's first conscious essay in genocide. "The Jew must clear out of Europe," said Hitler simply in January 1942. "Otherwise no understanding will be possible among Europeans. It is the Jew who prevents everything."

As early as July 1941, Göring had instructed Heydrich of the SS to prepare a plan for the elimination of the Jews. By the time a program was presented and accepted at an interdepartmental conference in the Berlin suburb of Wannsee in January 1942, it was already being implemented. Mobile gas vans were in use in the Polish General Government, suggesting an alternative means of execution to the firing squads of the *Einsatzkommandos*. Under construction were several death

Jews formed a much higher proportion of the population in eastern Europe than in Germany itself. And it was in connection with the drive for Lebensraum in the east that the Nazis consciously adopted genocide as the "final solution" to the Jewish problem. Here, terrified Jews rounded up in Warsaw, 1943.

camps, while Auschwitz in Silesia, destined to become the most sinister name in the entire program, was converted from a concentration to an extermination camp. These centers were designed to manufacture death on the assembly line: a railroad terminal to receive the cattle trucks crammed with victims; Spartan barracks to accommodate them for a few days; the gas chambers mocked up to look like communal shower baths, the largest capable of holding two thousand, into which prisoners of both sexes were herded naked; and finally, the crematoria for the corpses tended by the few permanent inmates of the camp. Under this system, Auschwitz reached a destruction rate of 6,000 a day. Exact figures of the slaughter will never be known. Probably 7 or 8 million souls passed through Nazi concentration and death camps, of which some 5 million perished. Of these, 3 million or so were Jews, and up to another 2 million were liquidated, mostly by *Einsatzgruppen*, outside the camps. By the end of World War II, only one Jew in six living in Nazi Europe in 1941 had escaped the holocaust.

Throughout Europe, Jewish elders were compelled to provide lists of names for successive consignments of victims. This procedure gave rise to some ghoulish haggling as the SS allowed the richer Jews to buy a temporary stay of execution or inveigled the elders to cooperate in the destruction of their coreligionists with hints of exit permits from Nazi Europe or incarceration at Theresienstadt, the Prague ghetto for favored Jewish prisoners. The non-Jewish peoples of the occupied countries reacted variously. The Danes managed to hide all of their small Jewish minority and smuggled many to safety in neutral Sweden. The Dutch supplied countless cases of Gentile self-sacrifice in trying to shelter their country's Jews; Anne Frank's moving and deservedly famous *Diary of a Young Girl* (1952) has immortalized a characteristic episode. Tragically, the relentless zeal of the SS, coupled with the presence of a nucleus of local collaborators, usually overwhelmed the heroics of individual humanists, not only in Holland but throughout western Europe. In eastern Europe, where anti-Semitism had a long history, there was more general approbation of Nazi Jew-baiting. Many Poles, although themselves Slavic *Untermenschen* in the Nazi canon, willingly participated in rounding up Jews for the final solution. The regimes of both Antonescu in Rumania and Horthy in Hungary were officially anti-Semitic and were constrained by the Nazi hegemony to become more extreme. However, to some extent, these traditionalist governments were repelled by the Nazis' racial frenzy. Antonescu sanctioned pogroms in Bessarabia and Bucovina, where perhaps as many as a hundred thousand perished, on the pretext that the Jews there were pro-Russian, but he stood firmly in the way of wholesale SS deportations of Rumanian Jewry. Horthy and his wartime premier, Miklós Kállay, were even more obdurate toward Himmler's emissaries, and not until the closing stages of the Second World War were the Jews of Budapest subjected to outright slaughter.

Understandably, in many quarters during the war there was a reluctance to believe that the Nazis were actually engaged in genocide. Evidence of the enormity of the final solution reached the Vatican through the testimony of concerned German and Austrian priests. But Pope Pius XII chose not to speak out openly calculating, with some justification, that no verbal condemnation could deflect Hitler, but might rather impede the papacy's efforts to help those Jews within its orbit in Italy. By its silence, on the other hand, the papacy left itself open to retrospective criticism that it abnegated a moral responsibility because a preoccupation with bolshevism blinded it to the utter evil of Nazism. Such a view gained wide exposure when it was presented on the stage in 1963 in Rolf Hochhuth's bitter play, *Der Stellvertreter* (*The Deputy*). Like the Vatican, the wartime Allied governments have been accused of keeping an unnecessary silence on what they were aware was happening in nazified Europe. In particular, the U.S. State Department, it has been suggested, was laggard in not exploring all the possibilities of evacuating Europe's Jewry.

But among observers on the sidelines, so to speak, by far the most vulnerable to criticism were the German people themselves. Of them it has been asked, over and over, did they know what their leaders and elite were perpetrating? After 1945, it became a sick German joke that no one had known. Yet, in a literal sense, the majority of Germans did remain ignorant of the real horror in their midst. It was not that there were no indicators—the sudden disappearance of neighbors, the mysterious boxcars on railway sidings, the unavoidable rumors—but that the Germans closed their minds to the implications. For almost a decade, the German populace had been trained to suspend judgment and to trust in an omniscient Führer. Nazi brainwashing guaranteed that the Germans would not want to be aware of the dark underside of Hitler's regime.

The Germans' lack of curiosity was a function of the totalitarian society in which they lived. In other ways, too, the final solution provided the cynosure of Nazi totalitarianism. The entire exercise was conceived in impersonal, bureaucratic terms. Although there were sadists and degenerates aplenty in charge of the actual camps, the supervisors and organizers of genocide were faceless civil servants who led humdrum, law-abiding lives. Their concern, as revealed by their interoffice memoranda, was with the mechanics of the final solution—how to transport huge masses of humanity or how to dispose of the bodies after extermination. They evinced no thrill or *Schadenfreude* in their gruesome work, nor any feeling of remorse. These were, in Riesman's phrase, "other-directed men," who had long since freed themselves from the anguish of conscience and discovered serenity in complete submission to the ideology of the totalitarian movement. Aryanism dictated the destruction of the Jews, and the "Schreibtischtaeter" (desk criminals) obeyed mindlessly. It was fitting that the final solution should have been presided over by Himmler. Of all the top Nazis, Himmler was the least charismatic; his somewhat waxen face and rimless glasses suggested a bourgeois clerk; and his exaggerated sense of *Treue* (loyalty) found expression in a single-mindedness unique even among Nazis. Speer summed up Himmler's pedantic, dogmatic personality as "half schoolmaster, half crank." Or an even better example of the totalitarian bureaucrat might be Adolf Eichmann, executed by the Israelis in 1962. Working closely with Himmler, although without the publicity lavished on the *Reichsführer* SS, Eichmann handled in impeccable fashion the administration and paperwork of the final solution. One is reminded of Goethe's words: "I would sooner commit an injustice than endure disorder." The pedestrian nature of this dedicated civil servant is caught in the subtitle of Hannah Arendt's commentary on his trial, *Eichmann in Jerusalem: A Report on the Banality of Evil* (1963). The book raises the question of whether such an automated character can be properly judged by the standards of western humanism and law.

In the last resort, of course, the ultimate in depersonalization took place in the Nazi prison and death camps. It was not just a matter of the degradation of the inmates which, during the war, extended to their use as human guinea pigs. (None of the genetic experiments or tests of the human body's reaction to variations of altitude, pressure, and temperature proved of any medical value.) In addition, the behavior of the prisoners themselves in the extermination camps has occasioned doleful speculations. It has often been remarked that hardly any prisoner revolts occurred at Auschwitz, Treblinka, and similar camps. On arrival, the victims could hardly doubt what was in store for them, notwithstanding the façade of gay Viennese waltzes played over loudspeakers and the distribution of picture postcards to be sent to friends and relatives left behind. The stench of burning corpses, which hung over all the death camps, was an unmistakable, telltale clue. To storm en masse the barbed wire fences was to invite being cut down by SS machine guns on the watchtowers, with the chance of maybe one prisoner in a thousand breaking out. On the other hand, to walk passively into the gas chambers was to renounce that one-in-a-thousand opportunity for survival. Yet the millions, Jew and non-Jew, gave their SS captors little trouble as they were shepherded to their doom. The supreme test of a totalitarian regime, supposedly, is so to "atomize" society that the very outcasts, the "objective criminals," acquiesce in their own annihilation. Nazi Germany may have achieved just this in the death camps.

From the beginning in 1933, Nazi policy had been shaped by ideology. By the winter of 1941–42, the Nazi leaders were more than ever convinced that a racial tide of history was flowing in their favor. This arrogant certitude lay behind the lurch toward the final solution, and also behind the German response to Pearl Harbor on December 7, 1941. Under the Tripartite Accord of September 1940, there was no obligation on Berlin's part to go to Japan's aid against the United States, nor had Japan joined Nazi Germany in the attack on the Soviet Union. Nevertheless, Hitler brushed aside these considerations, which were indeed voiced by Ribbentrop, and, on December 11, announced war with the U.S.A. Mussolini, the dutiful lackey, stifled his own qualms and followed suit. In rationalizing the declaration of war, the Führer argued that Japan, potentially a useful German ally, needed to be saved from the United States, and that American aid to Britain was going to force Washington into World War II sooner or later anyway. But his true motive was not rational but ideological; as a mélange of races, the "mongrel" United States could not conceivably mount a war effort to halt the onward march of the *Herrenvolk*. The Nazi star was plainly in the ascendant, and Hitler's mind was running to thoughts of the inevitable death-struggle between *Weltanschauungen* in which, naturally, his own cause was preordained to triumph. As he proudly declared on December 11:

I can only be grateful to Providence that it has entrusted me with the leadership in the historic struggle which, for the next five hundred or a thousand years, will be described as decisive, not only for the history of Germany but for the whole of Europe and indeed the whole world.

. . . A historical revision on a unique scale has been imposed on us by
the Creator.

Hitler's incursion into Russia followed by his gratuitous declaration
of war on America, both while Britain and the Commonwealth were
undefeated, seems in retrospect an invitation to disaster. At the time,
however, Nazi Germany looked invincible. Before 1942 the German
economy was barely extended; the lightning victories of the first
two years of war had been won with improvised economic arrangements. In January 1942 Hitler issued a decree for a stepped-up
arms program, which brought to the fore two successive Nazi ministers
of armaments and munitions of exceptional administrative talent.
Fritz Todt, before his death in an air crash in February 1942, laid the
organizational groundwork on which Albert Speer, the former architect, proceeded to build. Within a year of Speer's appointment, German
munitions production more than tripled—yet this did not indicate an
all-out economic war effort. In several ways Speer and his technocrats
were frustrated by the "revolutionary" wing of the Nazi party under
Bormann, who objected to working with Germany's old industrial elite
and put ideology in the way of practical solutions. Efficiency dictated
that the raw materials and labor of the occupied countries be exploited
in factories on the spot, but, over Speer's protests, their resources were
carried off to Germany with considerable expense and waste. By 1943
the "revolutionary" Fritz Sauckel had supervised the deportation of
some six million foreign workers to the Reich. Then, there was the
question of the squandering of valuable labor in the death camps. It
was only a token recognition of this drain to designate some of the
healthier prisoners to be "worked to death" instead of gassed. The
infamous Auschwitz possessed an adjacent labor camp for precisely
this self-defeating purpose. Furthermore, Bormann and his fellow
ideologues were able to persuade Hitler that the German people should
not run short of consumer goods, even at the cost of war production;
in 1942 and 1943, the level of civilian consumption hardly dropped at
all. Nazi planning at the midpoint of World War II, then, could not
and did not aim at competing with the enemy powers in mass production; it was assumed to be enough to win the battle of quality. Indeed,
not until the desperate days of 1944 would German economic policy
become geared to anything like total war.

At the apex of Nazi success early in 1942, the even tenor of German
life had been little disturbed outwardly. The victories abroad had been

won cheaply; only scattered air raids had hit the fatherland; and the German populace lived high off the fruits of the conquered territories. There was no certain knowledge of what the Nazi leaders were preparing by way of a terminal resolution of the Jewish problem to disturb the ordinary citizen's sleep. The main signs of war on the home front were a proliferation of uniforms and official propaganda. The Führer was less visible now, for he spent almost all his days at the austere "mixture of cloister and concentration camp" which was his military headquarters, *Wolfsschanze* (Wolf's Lair), near Rastenburg in East Prussia. His absorption in his life's mission in the east left him scant time for a private life or for the intoxicating public speeches of yesteryear. All in all, though, there was nothing to alert the German people to the turn of the tide which was to occur within twelve months.

TURNING POINTS AND TWO JULYS

The swing began on the battlefield. During the campaign of 1942, Hitler decided to forego further attack on Moscow, which naturally the Russians had heavily fortified over the previous winter, in favor of a major push south toward the oil-rich Caucasus. At the same time, Rommel, in command of an Italo-German army, the nucleus of which was the famed *Afrika Korps*, was to drive east from Libya to take Cairo and Suez. The two pincers, if extended, would have completed the Nazi encirclement of the geopolitical "heartland," roughly Suez and the Straits plus the Ukraine and the lower Danube. In control of the heartland lay the key to world dominion, so taught one geopolitical school founded by a British geographer after the First World War. Between the wars, a German military scholar, Colonel Haushofer, became the high priest of geopolitics and, under Nazi auspices, built up a famous *Institut für Geopolitik* in Munich. The definitiveness of geopolitics appealed to the Nazi taste for grandiose simplicities, and it was from the geopoliticians that Hitler picked up such concepts as *Lebensraum* and autarchy. On the other hand, there is no evidence that the Führer consciously chose his military strategy to suit geopolitical theories. Nevertheless, the Nazi thrust for world empire in 1942 assumed, by remarkable coincidence, a geopolitical form. And it was on the fringes of the heartland that the Nazi tide was stemmed.

In Russia, the Wehrmacht, bolstered by contingents from Rumania, Hungary, and other Nazi satellites, reached the outskirts of Stalingrad. But in the process, the German front was pushed out in a dangerously exposed salient. When the professional military led by the chief of staff, General Halder, expostulated, Hitler turned a deaf ear and fired Halder. "You and I have been suffering from nerves," the Führer told him. "Half of my nervous exhaustion is due to you. . . . We need National Socialist ardor now, not professional ability. I cannot expect this of an officer of the old school such as you." In his dementia Hitler simply could not conceive that providence might let him down; therefore, the directives of the supreme warlord to his forces remained what they had been in the battle for Moscow at the close of 1941—no retreat and no surrender. But where this obstinacy before Moscow had resulted in no more than a costly rebuff, at Stalingrad the outcome was a Nazi fiasco. By the end of November 1942, following Soviet counterattacks, a third of a million Nazi troops found themselves cut off. Denied authority to break out, they were annihilated or captured in the next ten weeks. In all, Hitler lost half a million men at Stalingrad. Beyond question, the Battle of Stalingrad was the most cataclysmic military engagement of the war.

Its significance, however, was enhanced by simultaneous setbacks which befell the Axis in North Africa. On November 1, 1942, the British army broke through Rommel's line at El Alamein in Egypt. The *Afrika Korps*, starved of supplies because of Germany's incomplete armaments program and the demands of the Russian front, was forced into retreat. A week after El Alamein, an Anglo-American armada landed an invading force at the other end of North Africa. At first, the authorities in French Morocco and Algeria, acting on Pétain's orders, resisted. But on November 10, Admiral Darlan, now head of Vichy's armed forces, who was visiting a sick son in Algiers, took it upon himself to sign a cease-fire with the Anglo-Americans. The *Afrika Korps* was trapped between two advancing Allied armies.

After Stalingrad and El Alamein, the Axis was consistently on the defensive. By 1943 the Nazi *Festung* (Fortress) *Europa* began to seem vulnerable to invasion—by the Russians advancing from the east; by the Anglo-Americans who, after the capture of North Africa, would be in a position to cross the Mediterranean and attack what Churchill inelegantly called "Europe's soft underbelly"; and by the western Allies who were being urged by Stalin to breach Hitler's Atlantic Wall in order to take the pressure off the eastern front. Moreover, the longer the war lasted, the greater became the advantage of the grand antifascist coalition as its members—the United States especially—

proceeded to mobilize their vastly superior resources. It promised to be 1918 all over again.

This military outlook put fresh heart, not to mention new recruits, into the resistance movements within nazified Europe. From the moment of occupation, organized resistance had sprung up almost everywhere—the Polish underground, the French *Maquis*, the partisans in Greece and Yugoslavia. Initially, such groups were heavily outnumbered by collaborators who were not restricted to the prewar fascists. With time, however, the anti-Nazis gathered momentum, encouraged by Britain's continued resistance to Hitler in 1940 and shelter to governments in exile, and buoyed by the Soviet Union's entry into the war which brought Europe's communists into the resistance. Above all, the resistance grew in proportion to the rising brutality of Nazi government in the occupied countries. In the Soviet Union, for example, Hitler ruled out any conciliation of the population and thereby any exploitation of latent Russian discontent with the Stalinist autocracy. Instead, the Nazis concentrated on enlisting collaborators among the national minorities of the U.S.S.R. One likely group was the Volga Germans, but Stalin ruthlessly transported them east out of fear they might serve as a fifth column. Another consisted of those western Ukrainians who, in 1929, had founded the Organization of Ukrainian Nationalists along Italian Fascist lines. In actual fact, several thousand Ukrainians, Caucasians, and central Asians did ultimately don German uniform as *Osttruppen*. However, the mass of the Russian people, finding no solace from the Nazis, remained fervently loyal to the Soviet state, with those behind German lines giving aid and comfort to a vigorous partisan action.

The Nazi response to this civilian role in guerrilla warfare was terror—the shooting of hostages, deportations, burnings, and lootings. These tactics were used endlessly and callously in Russia, although the two most notorious episodes took place elsewhere. On May 29, 1942, "Hangman Heydrich," one of the architects of the Jewish final solution and Nazi protector of Bohemia and Moravia, was assassinated in Prague by a bomb thrown by two Czechs sent from London. The assailants first escaped into the Czech underground, engendering a reign of savage Nazi vengeance. Over a thousand Czechs were executed immediately; many members of the Czech resistance, including the two assassins, were killed; and a purge of already decimated Jewry in Prague and Berlin sent another wave of cattle trucks rolling east. Then on June 10, as a calculated warning to all subject peoples, the innocent village of Lidice outside Prague was wiped out. Every male over sixteen was shot and the women and children dispatched to concentration camps. The other unusually cold-blooded Nazi reprisal occurred two years to the day after the Lidice massacre, engulfing the French village of Oradour-sur-Glane. An SS division rounded up the entire population in the square and began searching the empty homes for explosives. Not remarkably, some evidence of *Maquis* presence was unearthed. The men of the village were then herded into barns and the women and children into the church, and the whole place set alight. Those who fled the flames were machine-gunned. Of 652 inhabitants of Oradour, only 10 survived by simulating death.

In the short run, Nazi reprisals often stifled resistance activity; the Czech underground, for instance, never very numerous, was unusually quiescent after mid-1942 lest it provoke another Lidice. Yet, from the long view, Nazi terror was self-defeating in that it guaranteed that the sympathy of the bulk of the oppressed peoples would go to the resistance—an error that was to haunt the Nazis between 1943 and 1945. In the closing stages of the war, the national resistance movements enjoyed enough popular backing to sustain a serious and persistent harassment of the beleaguered Germans, and sometimes even to mount veritable military operations.

In both western and eastern Europe, the leadership of the resistance was left wing and frequently communist. There were various reasons for this: the communist parties, often clandestine before the Nazis arrived, provided a ready-made administrative network for the resistance; the communists had an extra measure of dedication and ruthlessness needed for guerrilla war; and the polarization of European ideologies, stemming largely from the Spanish Civil War, cast the communists as the "natural" foes of fascism. But, above all, the resistance was generically left wing because most of its members felt deeply that out of their struggle and suffering must come a better world than the prewar universe of the Great Depression, which had opened the gates to Hitler and so many other fascists. "From resistance to revolution," declared one French underground paper on its masthead. On the other hand, with the exception of the Soviet partisans, every resistance movement to some extent cut across party lines and included elements of the Right as well as the Left. Inevitably, there was some internecine tension, particularly in Yugoslavia where Marshal Tito's leftist partisans quarreled openly and spectacularly with their monarchist counterparts under Colonel Mihailović. However, for the most part, left- and right-wing antifascists inside occupied Europe cooperated loyally. It was the fulfillment of the Popular Front prospected in 1936, as well as the mirror of the grand diplomatic alliance which since 1941 had embraced the Soviets and the western powers. Furthermore, the range of attitudes within the resistance symbolized all that the fascists were in revolt against. Essentially, fascism was a repudiation of the life style of the nineteenth century; and in the resistance conservatives, liberals, and socialists—the heirs of the main nineteenth-century political traditions—finally banded together against their common enemy.

In a manner of speaking, the resistance was the conscience of Europe, recalling the Continent to its pristine humanist verities. This was nowhere more true than in the two major fascist states, Italy and Germany. And, naturally, the evolution in 1943–44 of substantial opposition to Mussolini and Hitler in their homelands was a further sign of the beginning of the end of European fascism.

Since entering the Second World War in 1940, Fascist Italy had met with one military humiliation after another—in the French Alps, in the Balkans, and in the North African desert. Even the navy, which was reputedly the most efficient arm of Italy's forces, had been crippled by a British aerial attack on Taranto harbor. Unlike the German population who lived well until 1944, the Italians soon experienced serious privation. By the winter of 1942–43, public transport was curtailed, the use of electricity restricted, and on moonlit nights in Rome the street lights switched off. Metal objects ranging from kitchenware to statuary were requisitioned. Besides the rationing of food and clothing, the sale of silk, cotton, and leather goods was banned. The problem of civilian morale was compounded by the existence of a thriving black market in which many prominent Fascists (the Petacci clan, for instance) were known to traffic profitably. Popular discontent surfaced during March 1943 in a series of strikes in Turin and Milan. These were the first independent working-class demonstrations in Italy since 1922 and the first against the Axis war effort anywhere in Europe. A leaflet widely distributed among the strikers called for "bread, peace, and freedom." The regime restored calm temporarily by granting wage increases, but the political overtones of the strikes boded ill for Mussolini's future.

Mussolini displayed his usual querulousness and indecision in a crisis situation. Everyone was to blame except the Duce; the Italian people were "a nation of sheep," and he compared himself to Jesus betrayed. He surrounded himself with sycophantic advisors, younger Fascists whose character had been molded by a Fascist education. They obligingly fed his delusions of infallibility and ultimate Axis victory. But Hitler's was the most baleful influence of all. Whenever Mussolini met the Führer after 1941, he would go full of resolution to advise Hitler to liquidate his costly Russian campaign and to divert a larger share of Axis war matériel to hard-pressed Italy. But invariably, the Nazi leader brushed aside the Duce's advice, and the Germans continued to take more supplies out of Italy than they brought in. Nonetheless, Mussolini always succumbed to the Führer's magic and returned from these conferences in jubilant spirits. In public, Mussolini would then exude confidence, although inwardly he was in a state of nervous tension. His gastric ulcer recurred, and for days on end he was in considerable pain. Mussolini had never shown a liking for the hard grind of administration. Now, when the war required all his attention, he was growing physically as well as temperamentally incompetent.

Against this background of inertia, two opposition groups began to form early in 1943. The first consisted of certain Fascist party hierarchs whose dissatisfaction was crystallized in February by a comprehensive changing of the guard. In an attempt to shift the responsibility for Italy's dismal war record from his own shoulders, Mussolini dismissed all but two of his cabinet. The most prominent scapegoats were Ciano, Grandi, and Bottai, who were dismissed from their respective ministries of foreign affairs, justice, and education. These three would form the hub of the Fascist challenge to the Duce. Their strategy was to use the party apparatus to bring Mussolini to heel, rather in the way the party consuls had dictated to Mussolini in the closing stages of the Matteotti affair. For this reason, they advocated the convocation of the Grand Council of Fascism which Mussolini had not summoned since December 1939.

But while the PNF plot was hatching, another opposition cell was active in the royal palace. King Victor Emmanuel, for some time past, had been resentful of Mussolini's invasions of his prerogative in matters of the royal succession and the conduct of the war. Not until 1943, however, did he perceive a chance to strike back. On behalf of the king, the minister of the royal household, the Duke d'Acquarone, opened contacts with a number of political figures from the pre-Fascist era and also with some of the dissident hierarchs. So the two conspiracies began to dovetail. Neither one was, properly speaking, an anti-Fascist movement; after all, the principal actors were either Fascists or fellow travelers of long standing. Rather, both sets of malcontents were driven to act against Mussolini personally because he appeared incapable of extricating himself and his country from the Axis and a disastrous, unpopular war.

Granted this motivation, it was not surprising that the Allied invasion of Sicily on July 10, 1943, should precipitate a crisis. The Allies met little resistance—often attributed to Mafia complicity although this has been much exaggerated in the telling—and overran Sicily in a week. It could only be a matter of time before an invasion of the Italian mainland; in the meantime, Rome suffered its first air raid. Mussolini was constrained to promise his party lieutenants a session of the Fascist Grand Council, but before this could take place, he went off to meet Hitler at Feltre, north of Venice. On his return to Rome on the twentieth, it was common knowledge that, once more, Mussolini had failed to stand up to the Führer. Thereupon, Grandi circulated a motion he planned to introduce at the upcoming Fascist Grand Council meeting; it called for the reactivation of the legal organs of the Fascist state—the Grand Council itself, the Council of Ministers, the Chamber of Fasces, and the corporations. It also proposed that the king resume sole command of Italy's armed forces. To avoid any charge of treason, Grandi even showed his motion to Mussolini, who apparently failed to grasp its purport. Nevertheless, Grandi was uneasy, and he carried two grenades with him when he entered the Palazzo Venezia for the fateful Grand Council session on the evening of July 24.

The council debate proved to be disjointed in the extreme. Mussolini defended his war policy at length with references to Hitler's loyalty and to an inconsequential Italian victory on the Mediterranean island of Pantelleria, but he made only oblique mention of the recent loss of Sicily. Grandi submitted his motion of no confidence, and Bottai and Ciano spoke briefly in support. In a vain effort to ward off a showdown, Roberto Farinacci, the former PNF secretary, and the current party secretary, Carlo Scorza, both brought forward motions of their own, but they aroused little interest. Tempers began to flare. At one point, a fifteen-minute intermission was called, during which Guido Buffarini, one of the Petacci clan, privately urged Mussolini to arrest Grandi and his supporters. But Mussolini, who had been growing more detached and fatalistic as the meeting wore on, refused to do anything. Eventually at 4 A.M., after nine hours of desultory talk, a vote was taken on Grandi's resolution; it was approved by nineteen to seven.

In a legal sense, the vote in the Fascist Grand Council was of no moment, which was doubtless why Mussolini tolerated it with a relatively good grace. On the other hand, King Victor Emmanuel who, since Mussolini's return from Feltre, was determined to dismiss him, took it as a signal to act. Almost certainly, some of the dissident Fascists anticipated this. On the morrow of the Grand Council session, the oblivious Mussolini played into his enemies' hands by telephoning the royal palace to ask for an interview with the king. Mussolini intended nothing more than a conventional reporting to the monarch such as he had made scores of times since 1922. At 5 P.M. on July 25, he was driven to the Villa Savoia.

Once closeted with the king, Mussolini launched into an account of the military situation. He then turned to the events in the Grand Council, which he described as a purely consultative body. But here, Victor Emmanuel interrupted him and requested his resignation. A new government was planned under Marshal Badoglio, who ironically had won his field marshal's baton for his part in Mussolini's conquest of Ethiopia. The Duce tried to argue, and the king was overheard to say: "I am sorry, I am sorry, but there could have been no other solution." When the stunned Mussolini emerged from the villa, he found that D'Acquarone had made certain arrangements for him. He was approached by a *carabiniere* officer who told him: "His Majesty has charged me with the protection of your person." Whereupon, he was whisked off to prison in an ambulance. As news of Mussolini's downfall spread, there was some celebrating in the streets. Nowhere was there the slightest hint of a Fascist insurrection—damning corroboration of the final bankruptcy of Mussolini's regime.

The new Badoglio government, discreetly termed a "ministry of technicians" to disguise the fact that its members were all former collaborators with Fascism, sought to liquidate Mussolini's catastrophic foreign policy. But it was early September before a deal was struck with the Allies, which provided for simultaneous Italian surrender and Anglo-American landings in southern Italy. The Germans had expected and prepared for Badoglio's desertion of the Axis. In typical blitzkrieg style, they seized Rome and swiftly extended their sway over the entire Italian peninsula north of the battlefront. The king and his ministers fled south and took refuge with the Allies. Several weeks later, the royal government declared war on Nazi Germany.

Meanwhile, the custody of Mussolini's person was proving an embarrassment to the Badoglio regime. The erstwhile Duce, who was ill and tired, would have liked nothing better than to retire to private life in his native Romagna, but he was far too notorious. For one thing, Hitler was anxious to restore Mussolini's political power, which may have been due in part to the Führer's loyalty to the man who had once been his mentor and of late his client. But a more important motive, no doubt, was the need to use Mussolini to keep as many Italians as possible loyal to the Axis. To prevent Mussolini falling into Nazi hands, the Badoglio authorities refused to divulge his whereabouts and moved him rapidly from one *confino* to another. However, a few days after royalist Italy's surrender to the Allies, the Germans finally caught up with Mussolini, who was being held in a resort hotel in the Apennines. A daring rescue by glider was executed by Otto Skorzeny, an Austrian and one of the "intellectual roughnecks" of the SS. Mussolini was first taken to Munich, where he was reunited with his family, and then on to the Führer's headquarters at Rastenburg. Hitler told him he was to return to Nazi-occupied Italy and head a new Fascist administration. Mussolini agreed without enthusiasm. To give him his due, this was in some way a patriotic gesture, for he hoped that his presence in Italy might stand between the full force of Nazi tyranny and the Italian populace.

Mussolini's new regime was officially called the Italian Social Republic, although it has gone down in history as the Salò Republic. It was perforce republican since King Victor Emmanuel had disavowed Mussolini. Its offices were scattered among the villages along the shores of Lake Garda, the major conglomeration being in the small town of Salò. The damp winter chill of the north Italian lakes afflicted Mussolini in spirit and body. When he appeared in Salò or Gargnano, where he had his private home, people noticed that he looked like an old man. Just past his sixtieth birthday, he had lost his one-time fire and vigor and was now a stolid figure who moved with deliberation. His eyesight, too, had grown weak; to read, he required strong glasses and electric light. On the other hand, Mussolini received some competent medical treatment from Dr. Zachariae, a German suggested by Hitler whose choice more often ran to medical quacks. Mussolini was lucky; Zachariae successfully prescribed for anemia and an enlarged liver, and fortified his patient enough for him to grapple with the paper work of Salò.

Those who followed Mussolini on his last political odyssey were a nondescript company. Besides his family, only Clara Petacci of his personal intimates remained loyal. Most of his earlier political cronies had cut themselves off by their stand in the Fascist Grand Council session of July 24–25. In consequence, the principal Salò offices were filled by relatively unknown Fascists, of whom the new party secretary, Alessandro Pavolini, was most influential. The Pavolini clique was characterized by its extreme vindictiveness toward those who had voted against Mussolini in the Grand Council, and it clamored for the punishment of "the criminals of July 25." Their specific *bête noire* was Ciano who, trusting for his safety to his family relationship with Mussolini, had joined the latter in Munich. The Nazis were well aware of Ciano's anti-German barbs which he was accustomed to make in private. In due course, after Mussolini's return to Italy, they were delighted to hand Ciano over to his enemies in the Salò Republic for trial. As for Mussolini, he harbored no discernible rancor against Ciano and the other Fascist hierarchs who had crossed him. But he yielded to Pavolini's importunities, and a special tribunal was set up at Verona.

The Verona trial was a travesty. Of those who had voted for Grandi's motion on July 25, a mere six could be apprehended and charged with treason. Only Ciano and Marshal de Bono, one of the quadrumvirate which had directed the March on Rome in 1922, were well known. During the trial, the prosecution made much of a conspiracy against the Duce, but no proof was adduced to link the accused with a conspiracy; indeed, the alleged plot itself was never substantiated. Nonetheless, all the prisoners were found guilty, with five of them, including Ciano and De Bono, receiving the death sentence. Edda Ciano tried to save her husband's life by offering in exchange his papers and diary with their revelations of Axis diplomacy. Mussolini, although upset by the persecution of his son-in-law, washed his hands of the whole Verona affair. The breach with Edda, who had always been his favorite child, was never healed. The Germans seemed more eager to obtain the compromising diary until Hitler, who disliked Edda Ciano for objecting to his harsh treatment of Italian labor battalions, personally ordered that negotiations be broken off. Leaving behind final appeals to Mussolini and Hitler, she made her way into Switzerland, carrying the diary with her. When published after the war, it proved a mine of information on Fascist Italian foreign policy between 1936 and 1943. No reprieve being granted Ciano and his four condemned colleagues, they were executed in Verona on January 11, 1944, by a Fascist firing squad.

Odious though it was, the Verona bloodbath was almost the sole positive act by the Salò regime. Even so, it was widely believed at the time that the Germans had forced Mussolini to kill his own son-in-law. For, in reality, everything else in the Salò Republic was dictated by Nazi Germany. The appointment of Giovanni Preziosi, one of the few anti-Semitic Italian Fascists from the start, as inspector general of race was an obvious sop to the Nazis. Most often, however, German officials in northern Italy ignored the Salò authorities and governed directly; the German Ministry of Labor arbitrarily conscripted Italians for war work. In October 1943 Berlin declared the whole of northern Italy to be subject to German military government. What rankled most was German conduct in the Alto Adige and the other territories which Italy had inherited from the Hapsburg Empire after World War I. On the heels of the Pact of Steel in 1939, Nazi Germany had formally reaffirmed Italian sovereignty over the Alto Adige, while an agreement was signed to resettle as many Germans as were willing to leave the area. But notwithstanding Himmler's ambitious schemes for resettlement of the *Volksdeutsche*, only 80,000 out of more than 200,000 in the Alto Adige had been relocated by 1943. Then, the collapse of the Mussolinian government in July gave Hitler an excuse to renege on past engagements. In the Alto Adige and the other ex-Austrian lands, Nazi *Gauleiters* were appointed. Many of them were bureaucrats trained in the Austrian empire before 1918; the "Hapsburg revenge" it has been neatly called. They kept the Italian prefects incommunicado with Salò, and disarmed and interned Italian troops in their districts. Mussolini tried to extract from Berlin a clarification of the status of these areas, but none was forthcoming. Yet, it was plain that their de facto annexation to the Third Reich had already taken place.

It was no accident that the Fascist administration was housed far from Rome, nor that Mussolini after July 1943 never set foot again in the Italian capital—although the Allies did not capture Rome until the following summer. It was all symptomatic of the simple truth that the Salò Republic was an Italian government in name only. Hitler's determination to prop up his Fascist partner appeared, in the event, completely self-seeking. If friendship, this was in Hitler's own phrase "a brutal friendship."

Mussolini understood that a humiliating subservience to Nazi Germany was inevitable unless the Salò regime could mount a credible war effort of its own, the achievement of which required the concurrence of all Italians within the jurisdiction of Salò. To cultivate mass allegiance, Mussolini tried to reconvert Italian Fascism to what it had been at the outset in 1919—a radical, populist movement. He was not altogether insincere in this. Having delayed his renunciation of republicanism in 1922 as long as he had dared, it was a real pleasure to resume his attacks on the monarchy in 1943. It was also with reluctance that Mussolini in 1924 had given up hope of reconciliation with the Socialists—and through them with the Italian workers. So it was not out of character when he announced that the Salò Republic would pursue a moderate socialist economic policy. Specifically, workers were to have more say in the management of factories, while the most vital war industries would be nationalized. But, once again, German officials intervened, systematically sabotaging all efforts to change the status quo. Moreover, the Italian proletariat, after more than twenty years of Fascist partnership with the capitalists, responded skeptically to Mussolini's rediscovered socialism.

The Italian people, far from rallying to Mussolini, showed a decided preference for the resistance, a spontaneous popular uprising against the Nazi occupation of most of Italy and against the Salò Republic as the Germans' accomplice. Because of Fascist Italian defeats on the battlefield, the view that Italy was a nation of cowards had increased in currency. Mussolini himself was not above broadcasting the notion to excuse his own shortcomings. The Italian resistance thus became a conscious endeavor to redeem national honor, attracting Italians of every class, walk of life, and shade of opinion—rich and poor, young and old, secular and Catholic, republicans, monarchists, democratic socialists and communists of course, and even a sprinkling of Fascist idealists disenchanted by Mussolini's failure to effect a proper social revolution. The integration of such disparate elements had been Mussolini's unfulfilled objective for two decades; now, ironically, it was accomplished in a matter of months at Mussolini's expense. The place of the resistance in the annals of Italian unity is indicated by the common appellation of the years 1943–45 as the second *risorgimento*.

The resistance was not just a spiritual rebirth for Italians, but a military one also. The partisans, highly disciplined with strategy devised and coordinated through a network of committees of national liberation (*comitati de liberazione nazionale*, or CLN), gave ample proof that Italians could fight and die as bravely as any other people if they thought the cause worthwhile. So successful was guerrilla activity behind the German front that the Allies, inching their way up the Italian peninsula more slowly than expected, came to depend on it absolutely.

By 1944, in fact, the CLN was in a position to bargain with the Allies. In return for their military cooperation, the CLN was able to obtain the replacement of the Badoglio crew with a more genuine anti-Fascist coalition in liberated Italy, and also a promise of a postwar referendum on the Italian monarchy, besmirched by its backing of Mussolini until the eleventh hour.

The resistance movements in Europe at large were inspired by the hope of a reformed postwar world and hatred of the foreign invader. This was so even in France and Italy, where the partisans fought against Vichy and Salò not least because they were Nazi puppet regimes. But in Germany the resistance was of necessity qualitatively different. Resistance in the Third Reich was treason, and nationalism disposed the masses to Hitler—not against him. Some recent investigations of the eponymous "unknown German worker" have unearthed more lingering proletarian opposition to Nazism than was formerly suspected. However, this was largely a matter of preserving a socialist infrastructure and local pamphleteering than of mounting a physical resistance to the regime—if only because the Gestapo within a few years of Hitler's coming to power had removed most left-wing leaders to concentration camps. In the long run, the Nazi police proved so efficient in obliterating all traces of a populist opposition that the historian's appraisal of its scope must remain conjectural.

What was left by way of an activist opposition in Nazi Germany was, in contrast to every other European resistance movement which boasted grass-roots support and leftist ideology, unqualifiedly elitist; its politics were conservative and its moral values based on traditional Christianity. Yet, it was in these upper reaches of German society, from which the German resistance was drawn, that the problem of loyalty to the state assumed its most sensitive form. Not only were obedience, duty, and patriotism inbred in Germany's upper classes, but those who held important administrative offices or who ranked high in the professions had been compelled to swear an oath of personal allegiance to the Führer. Understandably, German resisters were few in number; nevertheless, this anti-Nazi movement has received a large share of attention and admiration. The argument of H. Rothfels's *German Opposition to Hitler* (1948, 1962), for example, is that, given the inhibitions facing the citizen in Hitler's totalitarian state, the presence of any underground at all has to be significant. This view is voiced usually by German conservative historians eager to suggest that the resistance, small though it was, was more representative than Nazism of the "true Germany." If by this phrase one presumes, as many writers do, the pre-1918 hierarchical, paternalistic Germany, then the traditionalists of the resistance did indeed speak for Germany.

Beyond question, the resistance contained superior, possibly the soundest, elements of German life, and sacrifices made in the face of overwhelming odds must not go unrecognized. But, in the final analysis, it may be doubted whether this was a resistance against Nazism per se or whether it was not perhaps a rejection of certain late-blooming fruits of Hitler's rule. For surely it was more than coincidence that no positive action was forthcoming before 1943.

An anti-Nazi resistance did exist earlier. It was centered on the army officer corps, ever ready to despise Hitler as a crude upstart and terrified lest the Führer's foreign and military policy overstep the bounds of prudent realpolitik. We have observed the military's forebodings before the German march into the Rhineland in 1936, and also the weighing by General Beck and a few associates of a coup against Hitler at the time of the Munich Conference in 1938. However, the best chance for these early resistance elements to act came during the "twilight war" of 1939–40. By this point, other German generals beside Beck were contemplating the removal of Hitler, as were important figures in the *Abwehr*, German military intelligence under Admiral Canaris, and in the foreign ministry, notably the state secretary, Baron von Weizsäcker. Outside official circles, some of Germany's old-line conservatives, such as the former mayor of Leipzig, Carl Goerdeler, were now active in the putative resistance movement. The outbreak of a second world war had been greeted by the German people with a noticeable lack of enthusiasm, while Hitler's spectacular victories in the west and on the road to Moscow had not yet swept up the Germans in a tide of false optimism. Before the full fury of the fighting and the emotional bitterness of wartime set in, it was possible to imagine the German resistance and the western Allies working together.

But when the anti-Nazi conspirators contacted London, either directly or through the Vatican, they tended to pitch their expectations high. Arguing that an alternative regime to Nazism required some bribe to offer the German people for deserting Hitler, they hinted that post-Hitlerian Germany be allowed to keep Austria, the Sudetenland, and perhaps even parts of the Polish Corridor. In brief, they wanted much of what the Führer had won but without the Führer himself. The Allies, while not rejecting all such proposals, were disturbed by this apparent chauvinism, and they were also unimpressed by the mere handful of conspirators the resistance could really count on for an anti-Nazi *Putsch*. Although the Allies never broke off contact with the German resistance, after the summer of 1940 the ties became fainter with the passage of time. Finally, in January 1943, Churchill and Roosevelt, meeting at Casablanca, announced that they would accept nothing short of German unconditional surrender. Their main intent was to assure Stalin that the Anglo-Americans would remain in the Second World War until the end. Incidentally, however, they removed the last hope of the German resistance to outflank Hitler by securing preferential treatment from London and Washington.

Left to itself, the German resistance was passive until 1942 when Nazi extremism stirred it into life. Secret police terror and whispers of genocide were responsible for an upsurge of intellectual opposition groups. The coterie of intelligentsia who had been meeting since 1940 at Kreisau, Count Helmut von Moltke's Silesian estate, grew in number. High-mindedly though, the Kreisau Circle forswore violence, even against Hitler. So, too, did the idealist Christian White Rose Society at Munich University, which clandestinely circulated anti-Nazi pamphlets. Such cliques, of course, were quite ineffectual, and were sooner or later rounded up by the Gestapo. For the practical resistance one has to turn back to the army officers, whose motive was less moral and more political. After Stalingrad, Germany's military situation deteriorated dramatically, and because Hitler in his megalomania refused to recognize the limits of German power, there was no rectification in sight. In June 1943, in one of the strangest episodes of the war, Ribbentrop and Molotov met covertly at Kirovograd in the German-held Ukraine; at this abortive conference Nazi Germany was still talking unrealistically about a frontier on the River Dnieper as the price for a separate peace with the Soviets. The Führer's conduct thus bade fair to bring the Red Army into the heart of Europe. It was only when this contingency loomed as a distinct possibility in 1943–44 that numerous conservative anticommunists aligned with the long-term anti-Nazis and, for the first time, contrived a series of plots to kill Hitler.

Hitler, needless to say, was well guarded. The nearest he had come to assassination was a bomb explosion twelve minutes after he left a reunion of *Alte Kämpfer* in Munich's *Bürgerbräukeller* on November 8, 1939, but this was either the work of a brave but lonely individual or else a fake sensation staged by the SS. Once the Führer took up near-permanent residence at *Wolfsschanze*, he was still harder to reach.

Nevertheless, several times in 1943, military members of the resistance got close enough to kill Hitler at the cost of their own lives, which they were willing enough to sacrifice. The problem was not so much the assassination itself but the swift communication throughout the underground that the deed had been done, so that the resistance might have a few hours advantage on the hopefully bewildered Nazis in seizing key offices and establishing a successor government. Moreover, providence really did seem to walk with Hitler. The assassination attempts were plagued with misadventures—detonators that failed to work, sudden shifts in Hitler's timetable which foiled the plotters' well-laid schemes, and so on.

This sort of ill luck continued to dog the German resistance in its supreme bid to remove Hitler on July 20, 1944. On that day a much wounded and decorated officer, Colonel Claus von Stauffenberg, attended a military conference at Hitler's East Prussian headquarters. In his briefcase he carried a charge of explosives. He placed his case beneath the table which the Führer and his generals were gathered around. Excusing himself, he left the meeting and, as he hurried away, the building behind him appeared to disintegrate in a shattering blast. On arriving in Berlin by plane, he telephoned his fellow conspirators the news that Hitler must be dead. What Stauffenberg could not and did not know was that, in his absence from the conference room, his briefcase had been accidently kicked over and put upright again behind a thick table leg which had protected Hitler from the full force of the explosion. This, together with the fact that the walls of the building were blown out, allowing the blast to escape, reduced the toll. Four were killed, but the Führer stumbled out of the wreckage with minor cuts and bruises, damaged ear membranes and, of course, nervous shock. When he recovered his wits, he was in a foul, vengeful mood.

Word of Hitler's escape soon reached Berlin where the *Putschists*, acting on Stauffenberg's message, had revealed themselves and tried to seize the reins of government. They were overwhelmed by the Gestapo and the SS. General Beck, the old anti-Nazi and the conspirators' choice as president of a post-Hitlerian government, was allowed to commit suicide. Stauffenberg and several others were shot in the Defense Ministry courtyard during the evening of July 20. In a way, these were the fortunate ones. Of the 7,000 arrested, probably 5,000 were put to death, with many of the executions anything but swift. There were trials before the People's Court in which Roland Freisler, the Nazi prosecutor, bullied and humiliated the accused. Eight of the ringleaders of July 20 were garroted, and the macabre scene filmed for screening in the Führer's private cinema. The Gestapo net caught up a wide range of resistance personages, including civilians such as Moltke and Goerdeler, who was to have been the new chancellor under Beck. But Hitler's venom was greatest and boundless against the army officers, and he resolved to decimate the entire corps. Many officers, including those who had played no part in Stauffenberg's plot but had known vaguely that something was afoot, came under indictment. One such was the war hero, Rommel, who was persuaded to take his own life. The purge continued until the spring of 1945. When it was over, the self-confident military elite, the perennial state within a German state, had vanished.

In the short run, the incident of July 20, 1944, did not change the course of the Second World War. Afterward, Hitler more than ever assumed personal command of military operations. He put his trust increasingly, not in the Wehrmacht, but in the Waffen SS, the military arm of Himmler's ever-growing empire. By the middle of 1944, the Waffen SS numbered over half a million, recruited almost as much from outside the Reich as inside it. In order to release both regular and SS troops for the front, in October 1944 Hitler ordered the creation of the Volkssturm, a home guard of males above and below the ages of normal military conscription. Meanwhile, Goebbels's propaganda ministry pointed to the Führer's narrow escape as infallible proof of providential blessing. Goebbels also harped on the theme that the German resistance could wring no concessions from the Allies; the Casablanca declaration of unconditional surrender gave the Germans no choice but to fight on. Such propaganda may have assisted the populace to stand up to Allied "area bombing," a calculated strategy to destroy civilian areas and morale, which was widely used in 1944. Its effect, like that of the Luftwaffe blitz on British cities in 1940–41, was to stiffen rather than undermine national resolve.

Yet, the writing was on the wall for the fascist dictators. In two successive Julys, a part of the prefascist power structure in Italy and Germany, respectively, had challenged the supposedly omniscient leader. These rebellions were significant as a symptom, not a cause, of fascist decline. Whether success crowned the antifascist effort as in Italy or failure as in Germany, the original sickness—namely, the military plight of the Axis—continued unabated. Not only the Third Reich but shrinking nazified Europe was running out of men and supplies. Speer's ingenuity might delay but could not avert the day of complete

disintegration which King Victor Emmanuel and Colonel von Stauffenberg had anticipated.

## Götterdämmerung

From the summer of 1944 onward, the advancing Allies, aided by
the now-confident resistance movements, pressed in on Germany from
three sides. The Nazi empire of fascist satellites began to crumble at
the edges. On June 4 the Allies took Rome, thus eroding further the
credibility of Mussolini's Italian Social Republic to the north. Two
days later the Allies at last opened their "second front" in Normandy.
Hitler held back the German tanks until he was sure that the landing
was not a feint; this allowed the Allies to establish their beachhead
from which they broke out in July. The next month Paris fell to a
combination of the *Maquis* and General de Gaulle's Free French who
were part of the Allied forces. At the same time another Allied landing
was made successfully in the south of France. Under these blows the
Vichy regime simply disintegrated. Pétain and Laval made their way
east, eventually taking refuge on German soil. The new French
provisional government under De Gaulle imprisoned as many prominent collaborationists as it could lay its hands on; Maurras was one
so incarcerated. Lesser collaborators were left to the mercy of the irate
French citizenry: girls who had walked out with German soldiers had
their heads shaved; Vichy officials and sympathizers were frequently
executed after a summary trial run by the former resistance, and at
least 10,000 died in the "liberation terror."

But the major dislocations in the Nazi world came from the Red
Army's progress in the east. By the autumn of 1944, Russian troops
were in Belgrade and Warsaw, and those old-guard regimes in eastern
Europe which, out of conviction or compulsion, had joined in the antibolshevik crusade of 1941, now strove desperately to disentangle themselves from the German alliance. The Finns, having advanced into and
been ejected from Eastern Karelia, made overtures for an armistice with
the Russians as early as February 1944. However, not until the old
warhorse, Marshal Mannerheim, was restored as Finnish president did
negotiations pick up. By the terms of the armistice of September 19,
Finland not only left the war but also agreed not to tolerate any
"fascist-type" organization which might disseminate anti-Soviet propaganda. In practice, this meant the final suppression of the IKL.

The pattern was repeated in Rumania, albeit through more direct Soviet intervention. The Rumanian government under Antonescu had been a wholehearted ally of Nazi Germany, giving access to the Ploesti oilfields and supplying troops for the Russian front second in quantity only to the Germans themselves. When the military tide turned clearly against the Axis, King Michael of Rumania found an answer by imitating King Victor Emmanuel's dispensation of Mussolini. On August 23, 1944, King Michael called Antonescu into his study, informed him he was dismissed, and then imprisoned him in a palace vault. There were still a number of Rumanian fascist legionaries in exile in Germany, some in concentration camps, some enrolled in the SS. Out of these elements, the Germans hastily concocted a Rumanian fascist government in exile with Horia Sima at its head. But it never governed a single foot of Rumanian territory for, within a fortnight, the Red Army overran the entire country. Thus, the Iron Guard and the Legion of the Archangel, kept at bay for years by the quasi-fascists, King Carol and Marshal Antonescu, were thwarted to the very end.

Not so Hungary's Arrow Cross. Early in 1944 Hitler suspected correctly that the Hungarian regent, Horthy, was seeking an armistice with the Soviets. On March 19 while Horthy was visiting the Führer, German troops occupied Hungary and the SS moved in to round up the Hungarian Jews. Yet the Horthy regime preserved a semiautonomous existence for another six months until October 15, 1944. On that date the regent, in anticipation of a swift Russian advance on Budapest, called publicly for Hungarian withdrawal from the war. But Hitler would not let Hungary go the way of Rumania; Budapest was one of the hinges in Hitler's planned defense of central Europe. German armored divisions were rushed to Budapest, and indeed the Soviet drive was stalled for several months while the Führer dreamed of a Stalingrad in reverse. Meanwhile, a few hours before Horthy's broadcast in favor of neutrality, SS *Obersturmbannführer* Skorzeny, Mussolini's rescuer, had kidnapped the regent's son and taken him to Germany. Under this pressure Horthy cracked. On October 16 he abdicated and nominated as new head of state the German favorite, Ferenc Szálasi, leader of the fascist Arrow Cross. The Arrow Cross had been held in check for several years by Hungary's historic classes, and its membership during the war had flagged. But now, belatedly, under German patronage, it revived and at last brought under its wing all the diverse splinter groups which made up Hungarian national socialism.

Szálasi honestly tried to establish an independent Hungarian fascist administration. In defiance of Nazi Germany, he insisted on propounding Hungarist-Turanian ideas in foreign policy and promised a corporative social order at home. As for the Jews, he objected to their transportation to death camps, preferring to put them to labor within Hungary. However, these were gestures only for, in truth, Szálasi's regime was just as much a German creature as Mussolini's Salò Republic. Out of deference to Berlin, Szálasi had to accept as colleagues anti-Semites much more crazed than himself. Béla Imrédy's ministerial faction viewed genocide almost as a holy duty and two secretaries of state for Jewish affairs, László Endre and László Baky, cooperated enthusiastically with the German Eichmann. Realizing that they had but little time to destroy their racial enemies, Hungary's national socialists acted with the ruthlessness of desperation. Even by the standards of the final solution, the Nazi-Arrow Cross pogrom of 1944 was remarkable in its ferocity. The rounding-up and dispatch of Jewish victims to Auschwitz and elsewhere was accompanied by wanton butchery and gratuitous torture. In all, 70 percent of Hungary's 800,000 Jews perished in only a few months. Then, in the new year 1945, the Red Army resumed its advance, engulfing swiftly all of Hungary and throttling abruptly the swan song of the Arrow Cross.

The prime Soviet war effort, however, was geared to reaching Berlin across the north German plain, and, ironically, this was facilitated by the final major offensive launched by Hitler as military commander. In December 1944 the Germans counterattacked in the Ardennes, and although the ensuing "battle of the bulge" saw the western Allies pushed back temporarily, it was done at the cost of seriously denuding Germany's eastern front. Once more the hope of a quick knockout blow against the west distracted Hitler from his primal life struggle against the communist danger from the east. And so, in April 1945, the Red Army stood poised to enter the suburbs of Berlin, which was defended mainly by the untrained *Volkssturm* leavened with units of the *Waffen* SS.

Hitler had been forced to leave his East Prussian lair the previous November and, since January, had made his headquarters in a bunker fifty feet beneath the bombed and blackened Reichschancellery. In thirty cramped rooms, eighteen in the *Führerbunker* proper, Hitler lived more than ever divorced from reality. Basically, he could not comprehend that the game was up; his mind dwelled perpetually on miracles and gambits which would salvage victory at the last minute. He set great store by the perfection of the "secret weapon" of which he had boasted throughout the war—the V weapons, flying bombs and rockets, which began to rain on southeastern England in the summer of 1944. But they came too late to arrest the tide of war, and in the following spring, the Allies overran the German launching sites in the Low Countries. The Führer's expectations in the east were even more optimistically bizarre. Late in 1944, he permitted General Vlasov, a Soviet officer captured earlier at Leningrad, to organize a Committee for the Liberation of the Peoples of Russia, and to raise an anti-Soviet liberation army of fifty thousand. Three years earlier, when the ploy might have been practicable, Hitler had ruled it out and his *Einsatzkommandos* had driven the Russian people into Stalin's arms; in 1945, the Vlasov exploit was ludicrous.

Equally fanciful was the reception given the news of President Roosevelt's death on April 12, 1945. In the Reichschancellery bunker, comparison was made with the death in 1762 of the Russian czarina, which had saved Frederick the Great of Prussia from a coalition of his enemies. The horoscopes were eagerly scanned; Himmler by now was a frank believer in astrology, and Goebbels exulted: "My Führer, I congratulate you! Roosevelt is dead. It is written in the stars that the second half of April will be the turning point for us." The hope that the American president's death might upset the Allies' cooperation, vain and foolish though it was, spurred Hitler on to a last flurry of military directives. However, the troops whom he ordered up to the various fronts existed only in his imagination; Nazi reserves had run out. Those who tried to convey this ugly truth to Hitler were dismissed with the ritual taunts of liars, cowards, and traitors.

This cultivation of lunatic fantasies must be attributed in part to the state of Hitler's health. The strain of a quarter of a century of unrelieved politicking topped by four years of personal direction of the Nazi war machine had produced a wreck of a man, grievously sick in body and mind. In October 1944 Hitler had undergone a second operation (the first having been almost a decade before) to remove a polyp from his vocal chords, which left his voice weakened. His entire left side trembled constantly, and when he walked, he was inclined to drag his right leg after him. His hands twitched and could not grasp objects; someone had to place a chair under him whenever he wanted to sit down. His complexion was pallid, although the eyes still burned hypnotically. Hitler may have been suffering from Parkinson's disease, although his symptoms were also those of drug addiction. In the closing stages of his life, Hitler was totally dependent on the pills and injections of Dr. Morell, erstwhile quack specialist in venereal disease. Hitler, in his faddish way, rejected responsible medical opinion, and even condemned his personal surgeon of twelve years standing to death for challenging Morell. In all probability, Morell was slowly poisoning the Führer; for example, he prescribed a mixture of strychnine and belladonna for his patient's stomach cramps. But, in the short run, the medication enabled Hitler to keep going. For that matter, nearly all the denizens of the *Führerbunker* were partaking of Morell's drugs at the end.

In the bunker were gathered the elite of Nazi Germany, "Hitler's Court" as H. Trevor-Roper nicely terms it in his *Last Days of Hitler* (1947, 1962). For most of their adult lives, the members of this entourage had surrendered their will to the Nazi leader and ideology, and the spell of the sick, mad Führer remained strong upon them. Their loyalty was tested—but did not break—when it dawned that Hitler, if he could not have victory, was prepared to bring down Germany and Europe in destruction. He had always promised this. A decade before, he had remarked: "We may be destroyed but if we are, we shall drag a world with us—a world in flames." Early in the Russian campaign, still speaking in his favorite scientific metaphor of fire and ice: "I am as cold as ice in this. If the German people are not willing to take an active part in their self-preservation, good: then they shall cease to exist." In 1945 he tried to apply these words literally in orders to the retreating German armies to destroy factories, railroads, dams, supplies, and everything else of value in their path. For some time, prominent Germans had been discussing means of salvaging the national economy in the event of defeat, and even Himmler and Bormann, behind Hitler's back, had been involved in such talks. But now, of the top Nazis, only the technocrat Speer voiced strong objection to Hitler's nihilistic directives. And although the Führer brooked contradiction from Speer that he would take from nobody else, he refused to rescind his scorched earth policy. For a time, Speer considered ending the insanity by pumping poison gas into the ventilation system of the *Führerbunker*, but he abandoned the scheme as impractical. Instead, in his capacity as minister of armaments, he sent word to his subordinates to disregard Hitler's instructions. By and large, in March and April 1945, Germany's managerial class obeyed Speer rather than the Führer. Moreover, on April 23 Speer flew to Berlin and confessed to Hitler what he had done. Such was the strange but powerful personal bond between the Führer and the ex-architect that Speer was neither shot nor arrested, but allowed to leave the bunker and the German capital unscathed.

While Hitler's court, Speer apart, offered no demur to razing the fatherland, it was clearly nonplussed by the Führer's decision to extend the destruction to his own person. The general expectation in the *Führerbunker* was that Hitler, on April 20, his fifty-sixth birthday, would depart for a planned Nazi redoubt in Bavaria. But the day came and went without a determination. Then, on the twenty-second, it became clear that the German counterattack in relief of Berlin had not materialized, and Hitler announced definitively that his end would be suicide. It was broadcast over the German radio that the Führer would stay in Berlin to the death. For the faithful, it was now a question of whether to join their leader's self-immolation or to carry on his work outside Berlin. Two who chose the latter alternative were the inveterate empire builders within the Nazi movement—Göring and Himmler.

If Hitler were to remove himself, both aspired to the succession. On April 20 Göring had departed with many of his looted art treasures for Berchtesgaden. Then, on hearing of Hitler's suicide resolution, he telegraphed Berlin a request to "assume the full leadership of the Reich, with full freedom of action at home and abroad, as your deputy, in accordance with your decree of June 29, 1941." Himmler acted more secretively. Of late he had eased his persecution of the Jews hoping to persuade the western Allies to negotiate with him as the new Führer; now he traveled north to broach the matter via the Swedish Count Bernadotte. The Anglo-Americans not only dismissed Himmler's overture out of hand but Reuters also publicized it, thus bringing it to Hitler's ears. Hitler was distraught, especially at the dereliction of "der treue Heinrich," while Bormann labored to convince him that Göring's message was an ultimatum. The outcome was that both were expelled from the Nazi party. Himmler's representative in the Reichschancellery, despite being married to Eva Braun's sister, was shot; Göring in distant Bavaria, to his consternation, found himself under SS guard. Göring and Himmler were technically disloyal to Hitler. Yet their scramble for the succession, when there was nothing left to succeed to, was eloquent testimony to the sway the Nazi idea still exercised; Göring and Himmler never ceased to be the automated creatures of a totalitarian society.

On April 26 Russian shells began to fall on the Reichschancellery, and the arrival of the Red Army was expected within days. Nevertheless, Hitler left it until the small hours of the twenty-ninth before preparing his final rites. First, he married Eva Braun, his long-time mistress in a rather passionless love affair, who had insisted on remaining in the bunker. Her existence had as far as possible been hidden from the German people, for Hitler had always ruled out marriage lest it detract from his image as a single-minded instrument of destiny and servant of the Volk. But now that his career was over, the faithful Eva received her reward. Next, he dictated his will and political testament in which he retracted nothing and blamed all, including the Second World War, on the Jews. Accordingly, he charged his successors with "scrupulous observation of the race laws and with merciless opposition to the universal poisoner of all peoples, international Jewry." In a parting jab at the army officer corps, he implied it had lost the war through cowardice: "May it at some future time become part of the German officers' code of honor—as it already is in the case of our navy —that the surrender of a district or town should be impossible and the leaders should march ahead as shining examples loyally fulfilling their duty unto death." As Reich president and supreme commander of the armed forces, Hitler pointedly nominated, not a general, but Admiral Dönitz. Goebbels and Bormann were repaid for their devotion in staying at Hitler's side; Goebbels was named chancellor, and Bormann party minister and executor of Hitler's private estate.

Later on April 29, news arrived of Mussolini's death. Ten days earlier, as Axis strength in northern Italy melted away, the Duce had moved to Milan. There, through the intermediacy of Archbishop Schuster, he tried to come to terms with the CLN, which alone had already liberated most of the Po Valley. But Mussolini, learning that the German high command in Italy was negotiating separately with the Allies, feared a trick and fled with a score of Black Shirts to the mountains north of Milan. He may have had some idea of reaching Switzerland or the rumored Nazi stronghold in Bavaria; more likely, he was simply trying to delay the day of reckoning. A Fascist column assembled by Pavolini was supposed to follow Mussolini, but it never did catch up. So for safety, Mussolini's band joined a German antiaircraft unit en route to the Austrian Tyrol. Traveling along the western shore of Lake Como, the convoy encountered the partisans, who agreed to let the Germans pass after a search for Italian personnel. The partisans may well have suspected Mussolini's presence. At any rate, they found him huddled in a German greatcoat in the back of a truck. With him was Clara Petacci who begged to remain with her paramour, and both of them were incarcerated in a neighboring farmhouse.

When CLN headquarters in Milan heard of Mussolini's capture, the extremists and communists advocated a summary execution. No clear decision on Mussolini's fate was taken, but a communist member of the resistance, who went by the name of Colonel Valerio (his real name was Walter Audisio), was dispatched to bring Mussolini back to Milan. Neither the colonel nor the Milanese communists intended that he be returned alive. In the afternoon of April 28, Valerio reached Mussolini's rural prison where he found the former Duce and la Petacci listless and resigned. They passively accompanied Valerio and two local partisans in a car which sped off ostensibly for Milan. About a mile along the road, Valerio stopped the car and ordered his two prisoners to stand against a stone wall surrounding a villa. They were killed at once by a burst of machine-gun fire. The next day, their bodies, along with those of several other executed Fascists, were hung upside down from the roof of a gasoline station in Milan's Piazzale Loreto, the site of a notorious execution of fifteen hostages ordered by the Nazis in reprisal for partisan activity. To the last, therefore, Mussolini was haunted by the folly of his liaison with Hitler.

Not all the details of Mussolini's abject end reached the *Führerbunker*, but what Hitler did learn strengthened his resolve not to fall into his enemies' hands. The way of his going had to be a *Heldentod*, a hero's death, and an inspiration to later generations of Nazis. Such was the thinking, too, of the archpropagandist Goebbels, who all along had urged Hitler to stay in the bunker and now stage-managed his funeral. It was the afternoon of April 30, with the Red Army only a few blocks from the Reichschancellery, when Hitler committed suicide. There remains some controversy over the exact manner of his death. After he retired with his bride to his private suite, a muffled shot was heard. Hitler was shot in the left temple and, for long, it was presumed by his own hand. However, the official Soviet autopsy, made public a few years ago, states that he also swallowed potassium cyanide. If this were the case, Eva Hitler probably shot her dying husband, either to guard against the poison not being lethal or else to leave the impression that the Führer had died a soldier's death—by the bullet. Finally, Frau Hitler herself took poison. The two bodies were carried into the chancellery garden and placed in shallow graves. Gasoline was poured on them and a conflagration started with a lighted rag. A small group from the bunker, Goebbels and Bormann to the fore, stood briefly at attention with right arms outstretched in the Nazi salute. The ceremony was a conscious reenactment of the *Götterdämmerung* or Twilight of the Gods in Valhalla in Wagner's operatic Ring Cycle. As such, it was a climactic symbol of Nazism's barbaric, pagan *Weltan-*

*schauung*. And the consuming fire was a fitting token of the nihilistic impulse to destroy which had sparked the Nazi movement from the beginning to its close.

On May 2 the Russians overran the Reichschancellery and, a week later, exhumed and carted away the charred remains of Adolf and Eva Hitler. The bodies had been hastily buried and Soviet shelling had so churned up the Reichschancellery garden that identification was difficult. The Russians even seem to have identified the wrong corpse as Hitler's. Yet, for several years, they refused to confirm his death. Possibly Stalin was afraid of giving rise to a Nazi martyr cult—as Hitler himself had intended. But Soviet prevarication notwithstanding, there were too many eyewitnesses around the Reichschancellery on April 30, 1945, to permit doubt about the fact of Hitler's demise.

After Hitler's Nordic burial, Goebbels and Bormann were left in the Reichschancellery. They made a futile effort to negotiate a more palatable agreement than unconditional surrender with the nearby Russians, and then went their separate ways. Goebbels was determined to emulate his master, and he took his entire family in the bunker with him. On May 1 poison was administered to the six young Goebbels children; then the parents took their own lives by shooting. The bodies of Herr and Frau Goebbels, like those of the Hitlers, were burnt in the garden, although due to lack of time and gasoline, it was even more cursorily done than in the Hitlers' case. The same evening, some of the remaining inmates of the bunker tried to break out. Among them was Bormann whose fate was to remain a mystery for many years. As his body was not immediately discovered, speculations of his escape soon proliferated. After the war his presence in Latin America, whither a fair number of middle-rank Nazis fled, was constantly rumored, and one bizarre tale went that all along he was a Soviet agent who had returned to Russia in 1945. But it was always highly improbable that he survived the Berlin inferno, and recently forensic experts have pronounced a skull unearthed in a Berlin railway yard, the scene of fierce fighting in 1945, to be Martin Bormann's; suicide by poison seems to have been his fate, too. With the closing of the Bormann case, the possibility that any top Nazi avoided death or capture at the war's end can sensibly be ruled out.

The two renegades from Hitler's court, Göring and Himmler, both stumbled into western hands. Göring talked his way out of his SS captivity in Bavaria and out of the firing squad which Bormann tried to arrange for him from Berlin. However, he was at large for only a week before he surrendered to the Americans in Austria. As bumptious

Nazi totalitarianism excluded compromise. In World War II the choice lay
between total victory and utter destruction of Germany; the latter came
close to realization. Here is the shattered heart of Nazi Berlin in the summer
of 1945—the shell of Speer's massive Reichschancellery. Beneath lay the
Führerbunker where Hitler spent the last months of his life. To the right
can be seen the Reichschancellery garden where the bodies of Adolf and Eva
Hitler were burned.

as ever, he demanded preferential treatment as an important prisoner.
Meanwhile, Himmler attached himself to Admiral Dönitz's headquarters at Flensburg near the Danish frontier. Dönitz, who had fully
expected to find himself serving Himmler as Hitler's appointed successor, was at a loss what to do with his embarrassing aide. But on

May 6 he plucked up courage and dismissed the *Reichsführer* SS; yet for another fortnight, Himmler hung about Flensburg with a pretentious retinue of 150 SS officers, still under the illusion that he might strike a private deal with British army authorities. Eventually, he fled disguised as a private soldier, with his mustache shaved off and a black patch over one eye. Almost at once, he blundered into a British control post where he was recognized and, while being searched on May 23, he bit into a cyanide capsule hidden in his mouth. In seconds, Himmler, perhaps the most sinister and certainly the most feared of all Hitler's accomplices, was dead.

Even before Göring and Himmler made their respective exits from public life, the Third Reich had given up the struggle. As the new head of the German state, Dönitz first tried to negotiate with the Anglo-Americans alone, but he met with no more success than Himmler, pretender to Hitler's crown, before him. Dönitz was left without choice. On May 7, 1945, German plenipotentiaries appeared at General Eisenhower's headquarters in Reims to sign an instrument of unconditional surrender to all the Allies. The war in Europe thus ended, and with it the epoch of European fascism.

### The Relics of Fascism

The war in which fascism culminated took thirty-five million lives from all causes, twice as many as the First World War. The casualty list included the bulk of the leading fascists themselves. Those in the upper fascist echelons who did survive the fighting then faced retribution at the hands of the victors. In eastern Europe, Szálasi was hanged by the Russians and Antonescu by leftist Rumanians. Horia Sima was probably killed in combat in the closing weeks of the war, but, like Bormann, his precise fate remains somewhat cloudy. In the west, special courts handed out the death penalty in Norway to Quisling, in Holland to Mussert, and in France to Laval, who was forcibly repatriated from a temporary Spanish refuge. Pétain, who voluntarily returned to France, was also condemned to death, but President de Gaulle commuted his sentence to life imprisonment. The ideological guru of Vichy, Charles Maurras, was imprisoned after a hearing before a special tribunal which, mockingly, called up shades of the Dreyfus trial. He was released a sick man in 1952 and died splenetic to the last. The most prominent collaborator to escape scot-free was the Belgian Rexist Degrelle, who to this day relishes the sanctuary of Franco's Spain.

The most sensational disposal of leftover fascists occurred in Germany. There, in accord with the Allies' oft-stated intention, what remained of the Nazi power structure was indicted on four counts: conspiracy to commit crimes against the peace, crimes against the peace, war crimes, and crimes against humanity. The trial of the major German war criminals took place at Nuremberg—the site was chosen because of the memory of the Nazi party rallies held there—between November 20, 1945, and October 1, 1946. There were twenty-one defendants, and a twenty-second, Bormann, was tried *in absentia*. Faced with the grisly evidence of Nazi bestiality—films of mounds of corpses, harrowing eyewitness accounts of mass executions, the records of human guinea pigs used in medical experiments, mementos such as lampshades made out of human skin—most of the accused shrank into cowed, sagging figures; Göring and Ribbentrop, in particular, were greatly reduced from their one-time arrogance. Eleven were sentenced

*Ferenc Szálasi, leader of Hungary's Arrow Cross, was installed by German arms as regent in 1944 and presided over the liquidation of 70 percent of Hungarian Jewry in a matter of months. But, like most of Europe's fascists, he could not survive the collapse of the Third Reich. Seen here imprisoned in 1945, he was later executed.*

WIDE WORLD PHOTOS

to death by hanging; they included Göring (who at the last minute cheated the rope by swallowing the standard cyanide pill), Ribbentrop, Rosenberg, Frank, Sauckel, Streicher, and Seyss-Inquart. Hess received life imprisonment, and Speer and Dönitz, among others, lesser terms. Schacht and Papen were acquitted.

Fair judicial process was always observed before the Nuremberg Tribunal; nevertheless, the Nuremberg judgment was tainted. In the first place, the charges had a distinct ex post facto ring to them. Crimes against the peace, known popularly as "planned aggression," recalled Article 231 of the Versailles treaty, but no person before 1945 had been tried on such a count. Although war crimes were rooted in conventional international law and genocide was covered by the proscription of murder in every civilized legal code, the phrase "crimes against humanity" constituted a sweeping indictment freshly minted for Nuremberg. Moreover, the nations sitting in judgment could hardly be said to have clean hands. On the score of responsibility for the outbreak of World War II, western "positive appeasement" and the Nazi-Soviet nonaggression pact had plainly encouraged and sanctioned Nazi expansion. Then again, not a few Allied actions during the war seemed to fall into the categories of war crimes and crimes against humanity. There was the near-certain Soviet massacre of between four and five thousand Polish officers captured in 1939, whose mass grave was unearthed by the Germans in 1943 in the Katyn Forest near Smolensk. For their part, the Anglo-Americans, increasingly toward the end of the war, had directed their aerial attacks against nonstrategic and civilian targets (the Dresden raids in February 1945 provided the most devastating case), and out of this practice sprang the United States decision to explode the first atomic bombs over Japanese populated areas. The hypocrisies in the Nuremberg Trials were not lost on the German people who dismissed the entire performance as nothing but victors' vengeance.

Unfortunately, German public opinion mattered, for Nuremberg was only the spectacular tip of a larger program of denazification. The shortcomings of the trials cast discredit on the ambitious attempt to reverse twelve years of Nazi brainwashing of the German population. Although all Nazi organizations were outlawed, Nazi laws repealed, and Nazi doctrine expunged from the nation's schoolbooks, the experiment on balance was a failure. As one popular poll reported in November 1947, most Germans still thought Nazism "a good idea, but badly carried out under Hitler." Denazification, anyway, ground to a halt by 1948 amid international tensions. German friendship became a valuable com-

The end of the road for those Nazi leaders who survived the Götterdämmerung of 1945. Photograph shows the accused in the dock (Göring
is leaning forward at end) of the International Tribunal at Nuremberg.

modity in the cold war, and to secure it both the Russians and the
western powers desisted from the unpopular task of reminding the
Germans of their Nazi past.

The fundamental question raised, albeit not answered, by the Nuremberg Trials and denazification procedures was how far down the chain
of command to go in holding individuals responsible for their government's criminal conduct. The charter establishing the Nuremberg Tribunal allowed an accused's plea that he carried out policy framed by
a recognized, de jure government to be used as an extenuating cir-
cumstance in mitigation of sentence. On the other hand, obedience to
a legal superior was not to justify complete exoneration. In consequence, after the trial of the major German war criminals came a
judicial parade before both Allied and German courts of "little Nazis."
The more vicious administrative personnel of the concentration and
extermination camps were condemned to death, while thousands of
lesser Nazi party functionaries were imprisoned. In addition, prison
terms were meted out to businessmen who had employed slave labor,

337

lawyers who had serviced the people's courts, doctors who had endorsed Nazi eugenic theories, and so on. Concurrently, thousands more who had been Nazis or Nazi hangers-on were purged from the German professions and civil service. However, it very quickly became apparent that, in Hitler's totalitarian society, everyone who kept up a career was tinged by Nazism. If all who had paid lip service to Nazism had been proscribed, postwar Germany would have been left quite devoid of professional skills and administrative expertise. Hence, in all zones of occupied Germany, Russian and western, ex-Nazis were employed in the thousands to start the wheels of German society turning again.

Yet, although former fascists and Nazis were inevitably abundant in postwar Europe, fascist organizations and parties have not fared well since 1945. A Nazi cell survived clandestinely in Bavaria under the direction of Artur Axmann, the last Hitler Youth leader, until the Americans flushed it out in December 1945. After this, the unrepentant had to find substitutes for avowedly Nazi-fascist parties. For many in the new one-party regimes of eastern Europe, it proved no great psychological hardship to transfer allegiance from one totalitarian ideology, fascism, to another, communism. Between 1930 and 1933, not a few German communists had switched to the rampant Nazi party; now they made the journey back with equanimity—which goes some way toward explaining the plenitude of ex-Nazis in the East German administration. In contrast, the multiparty systems of western Europe permitted the emergence of parties which pandered to some fascist instincts without calling themselves fascist. The best known have been the *National-demokratische Partei Deutschlands* (NPD) and the *Movimento sociale italiano* (MSI). In prosperous West Germany neofascism has remained a peripheral force, but amid Italy's economic travail it has received enough encouragement to mount terrorist attacks against the democratic regime. Yet so far neither the NPD nor the MSI has reflected the youthful radical idealism which breathed life into interwar fascism. Rather, their strident nationalism and reactionary anticommunism has appealed to an embittered minority of the older generation. Much the same might be said of Sir Oswald Mosley's return to politics after spending most of the Second World War in British jails. In 1948 he founded the Union Movement whose overtones of imperial racism recalled the British Union of Fascists and attracted many former British Black Shirts. The new venture, however, remained an anachronistic cult in an age of anti-imperialism, and Mosley never recaptured his flamboyance of the 1930s.

In the Iberian peninsula, on the other hand, the fascist thread was unbroken by World War II. By avoiding too close a contact with Nazi Germany, fascism in Spain and Portugal escaped the holocaust of 1945. To be a fascist in Madrid or Lisbon remained a guarantee of official acceptance. On the other hand, beginning with the decline in the wartime fortunes of the Axis, Franco and Salazar had been edging toward friendship with the west. The resignation in 1942 of Spain's profascist foreign minister, Serrano Suñer, was the harbinger of a changing Iberian mood. After 1945, for reasons of international politics and trade, the two dictators found it more than ever necessary to curry favor with the United States, Great Britain, and France by de-emphasizing the fascist content of their regimes. In Portugal, fascism had never been more than skin-deep, but the Spanish Falange had been an integral part of Franco's coalition from the start. With the passage of time, however, the Falangists discovered themselves being systematically excluded from the inner councils of the *Caudillo;* some, discomforted, sought greener pastures in Perón's Argentina between 1946 and 1955. In lieu of the Falange, Franco raised to new prominence two old rivals of Spanish fascism, the monarchists and *Opus Dei,* the Catholic lay order.

Yet, one facet of fascism lived on strongly in the Iberian dictatorships—the theory of a corporative state. In 1956 Salazar announced a "second corporative drive" to speed up the industrialization and modernization of his country, although as always in Portugal the corporative inspiration was as much Christian as fascist. In Spain, too, the national syndicates in the 1950s basked in a blaze of governmental publicity. But increasingly, Spanish corporativism has been divorced from its fascist origins and connotations, and the task of national renovation taken from the Falange and entrusted to the middle-class technocrats of *Opus Dei.*

The survival of corporativism in Spain and Portugal, not to mention the belated fascist experiment in Argentina, suggested that fascist notions could linger on even though Europe's fascists had been thrust aside in 1945. In a modest degree, this was true in Italy where fascism had enjoyed its longest innings. The most significant of Mussolini's accomplishments to outlive him has been the Lateran Accords, which were written verbatim into Italy's postwar constitution in 1947. A few other Mussolinian institutions, the *Istituto per la ricostruzione industriale,* for example, have also survived. It has been suggested further that the taste of corporativism in Fascist Italy, and in Vichy France too, prepared these countries for the postwar interventionist state. On the other hand, however, it might equally be argued that a reconciliation of church and state or the growth of a triangular relationship among big business, big labor, and big government was inevitable twentieth-century developments. In this context fascism at best hastened their coming in certain places.

The gist of the matter is that nowhere did fascism leave much of a positive legacy. Its talent, especially after falling under the aegis of Nazi Germany, was more for destruction than construction. The fascists' monuments consisted not in the few public buildings they erected of mock classic design and heroic proportions, but in the shell of Berlin and the ruins of a hundred other cities. In retrospect, fascism's historical function seems to have been the negative one of clearing away old institutions so that others, coming later, might build anew. Thus, in eastern Europe the fascists dragged down with them to destruction their collaborators, the "historic classes." Into the vacuum stepped the communists to implement their blueprint of a collectivist utopia. Analogously, the Italian monarchy, tarnished by twenty-one years' connivance with Mussolini, was swept away in a referendum in 1946, and in its place the Italian republic was ushered in. As for Germany, the Nazis, once in power, deliberately tried to eradicate the old order and went a long way toward succeeding. Above all, the army officer corps, long the bane of German democracy, was annihilated by 1945. The old *Junker* aristocracy was no more, its East Prussian homeland after World War II divided between Poland and Russia. German big business was also caught up in the maelstrom; the Allies, besides indicting many industrialists at Nuremberg, decreed the dissolution of some of Germany's larger cartels. Unlike the officer class and the *Junkers*, the business elite was reestablished within a decade in West Germany. But, in the meantime, the derangement of the traditional power structure caused by Nazism and the war was sufficient to allow a new West German democratic system, under the sponsorship of the western Allies, to make its debut.

Finally, on a larger canvas, the destructive war of nations unleashed by Hitler appeared to put to rest some of Europe's older quarrels. The Führer's monstrous exaggeration of international Social Darwinism called into question the pursuit of national rivalries. This was not reflected on the world stage where the superpowers indulged in their cold war, but European integration, particularly the voluntary integration of west European states, has owed much to the memory of common suffering between 1939 and 1945. The Nazi new order, of course, predicated a united Europe, centralized and controlled from Berlin. But Hitler's exertions to realize this ambition were counter-productive. Inadvertently, he bequeathed the conditions and kindled the will to create a more fraternal Europe in repudiation of the fascist tenets of exclusive group loyalty and endless strife.

# CONCLUSION
# Toward a Definition
# of Fascism

In view of the welter of destruction in which fascism ended, it is often difficult to keep in mind that the fascist movements began as an idealistic cult. The original urge was to escape from the mechanical, money-grubbing life style of the nineteenth century, and to recapture the qualities of passion, heroism, and spirituality. In this sense, there is something to the taunt of the dialectical materialists that Plato was the first fascist.

The fascist critique of the nineteenth century, however, did not stop with the crasser aspects of bourgeois society. Fascism's theoretical attack was directed at the very fundamentals of nineteenth-century civilization, especially the empirical assumptions of liberals and Marxists, who both envisaged progress being achieved through scientific rationalism. Moreover, both regarded contemporary society as fragmented, the liberals emphasizing the atomic citizen and the Marxians class consciousness. Pristine fascism was a reaction against this narrow positivism and the prevailing theories of a pluralistic community. It was surely no accident that the majority of prominent fascists between the world wars were lapsed Catholics, or at least had been brought up in a Catholic at-

342

mosphere. Atavistically, they seemed to hanker after a substitute for the Christian belief which they and the secular modern world had lost—a faith at once idealistic, harmonious, and simplistic. Fascism was to be such a reintegrated world view.

By and large, the fascists came from those social groups which existed on the periphery of the nineteenth-century synthesis, or else became alienated from the existing consensus by the shocks of the Great War and the Great Depression. The youth movement provides a case in point. To many of the generation that came of age between 1910 and 1930, liberalism and even democratic socialism were elderly creeds discredited by the international bungling of 1914–19 and the capitalist collapse of 1929. They turned to leaders with a youthful image: Mussolini, aged thirty-nine when he became Italian premier; Hitler, forty-three on his appointment as German chancellor; Primo de Rivera, merely thirty-three at the time of his execution; junior officers from the First World War such as Dollfuss, Szálasi, and Mosley; and those, like Degrelle and Codreanu, who had been too young to fight in the war.

Another category of outsiders to provide a supply of important fascists consisted of national minorities and populations living on national frontiers—peoples that displayed acute problems of assimilation. The young Hitler in the Hapsburg Empire plainly felt himself part of a German minority cut off from a proper *Grossdeutschland* by Bismarck's policy in 1866. Rosenberg, the self-styled Nazi philosopher of *völkisch* ideas, arrived at his views after an upbringing in a German outpost in the Baltic states, while the number of Nazis to hail from the particularist German state of Bavaria was legion. Among Hungarian fascists, Gömbös was of Swabian German descent and Szálasi of Armenian-Slovak origin. The Rumanian Codreanu also possessed a mixed ancestry —Bavarian, Polish, and Bucovinian. In the case of Italy, Fascism was most successfully pioneered in the borderlands obtained in the dissolution of the Hapsburg Empire. Likewise, Finnish fascism was most intense on the Karelian frontier, while in Rumania fascism got its start at Jassy hard by the frontier province of Bessarabia. Excluded for the most part from the triumphs of nineteenth-century nationalism, the fringe areas and their populations remained with nationalist passions unslaked. Insecure in their attachment to the current nation-state system, local zealots reassured themselves by adopting a tone of strident, sometimes racial, patriotism. These volatile and unfulfilled group loyalties frequently found an outlet in fascism.

Besides an alienated rising generation and frustrated nationalists, not a few intellectuals and artists evinced a thorough disgust with contemporary civilization. Turned off by the deference paid to material success and to popular taste in an industrial age, scholars such as Gentile, Spann, Manoilescu, and writers of the caliber of Brasillach, Drieu la Rochelle, Ezra Pound, Wyndham Lewis, Gottfried Benn were inclined to see in fascism a safeguard of elitist standards and a reassertion of high idealism. Needless to say, the endorsement of such figures lent priceless air of respectability to the fascist movements, especially in the early days. In terms of numbers, however, one suspects that fascism gained most recruits from the squeeze in which the small savers were caught between monopoly capitalism and militant labor. The fate of Germany's *Mittelstand* in the 1920s was merely the most dramatic manifestation of a longer, universal process. The economic losers who found a new psychological security in fascism were more passive followers than, say, the "youth cohort"; nevertheless, their silent support was invaluable to parties operating in the world of mass politics.

Fascism, then, drew on the margins of nineteenth-century society, which became ever wider in the first third of the twentieth century under the impact of irrational philosophies, popular nationalism, and economic instability. Moderation and reasonable compromise, on which the nineteenth-century order claimed to rest, were increasingly difficult to come by, indeed were scorned as craven virtues. The impatient, iconoclastic, and apprehensive mood of the interwar years, so seasonable to fascism's germination, is not easy to capture in print. Perhaps it has been done best in some oft-quoted lines from W. B. Yeats's strangely prophetic poem, "The Second Coming" (1921):

> Turning and turning in the widening gyre
> The falcon cannot hear the falconer;
> Things fall apart; the centre cannot hold;
> Mere anarchy is loosed upon the world,
> The blood-dimmed tide is loosed and everywhere
> The ceremony of innocence is drowned;
> The best lack all conviction, while the worst
> Are full of passionate intensity.

Fascism's comprehensive onslaught on the nineteenth century was mounted from positions on both the right and left of the political spectrum. On the one hand, the fascists' emphasis on hierarchy and obedience at the expense of equality and liberty could not fail to appeal to the Right; and the fascist version of a perfect society, organic and corporate, had intimations of the vanished world of pre-1789 extolled by conservative philosophers. On the other hand, none of the fascist leaders, with the possible exceptions of Primo de Rivera and Mosley, sprang from Europe's aristocracy. Moreover, fascism's collectivist doctrines, offered in lieu of liberal laissez faire, smacked very much of leftist national planning. It might loosely be said that fascist economic theory amounted to socialism to be applied by authoritarian means that the democratic socialists could not stomach. Even the fascist conjunction of nationalism and socialism was a general twentieth-century phenomenon on the left; during the Great Depression especially, many social democrats could be heard speaking in national autarchic accents. In the final resort, however, it is idle to ask whether fascism was a left- or right-wing force; it was far too eclectic for simple categorization.

But whether leftist or rightist, all fascists were putatively radical. They intended to sweep away the debris of all *anciens régimes*. Yet, in practice, most fascist movements found great difficulty in disentangling themselves from the embrace of vested interests. Some never succeeded at all. In general, success or failure in retaining a radical image corresponded to the division of fascism, propounded above, into progressive and regressive ideological schools.

Naturally, traditional power structures wielded most sway in the less advanced European nations, often to the extent of manipulating twentieth-century fascism. This was particularly evident in eastern Europe where the historic classes held a tight grip on the fascist parties in Finland, Rumania and, until 1944, Hungary. In Austria, before 1938, the fascism of Dollfuss and Schuschnigg testified to the abiding influence of the Catholic church. Franco's junta of the Right gobbled up the Falange at the outset of the Spanish Civil War. Even in Fascist Italy, dyarchy, one-party state, and totalitarian boasts notwithstanding, Mussolini never completely amorphized the monarchy or the Vatican or, for that matter, the business community. These ties with an old order, which the fascists were unable to cast off, constituted a bridge whereby fascism in backward areas stayed in touch with certain values from the past. The result of this bridge-building must be seen in intellectual terms. Specifically, the adoption of corporative socioeconomic doctrine kept some fascist movements, at least partially, within the mainstream of European scientific thought and development. For corporativism was, on paper, an enlightened and rational blueprint for modernization; and it represented a large part of fascism's appeal in the Iberian peninsula, and in Italy, Austria, and even eastern Europe before these latter regions succumbed to unscientific, feral racism. There is a paradox in all this: association with conservative elements and traditional modes of thought helped these fascist movements to present a corporative and therefore forward-looking face. But withal, corporative fascism, despite its progressive and syndicalist overtones, was a much less radical version of fascism than that which appeared in the sophisticated German environment.

Of all the countries that went fascist, Germany had undoubtedly experienced the largest dose of modernization—an industrial revolution and urbanization before 1914, and a novel freedom in politics, art, and personal behavior during the Weimar era. The revulsion of many Germans to this sudden access of modernity was extreme, and in Hitler's hands it amounted to an unmitigated rejection of the recent past and present. In the search for a new social harmony, Nazism tied to rekindle the tribal loyalties of a fairy-tale world that had never existed in reality. Nonetheless, the Nazi elite accepted the vision of a brave old world with a visceral intensity which precluded any compromise with conventional forces and opinions. Within five years of Hitler's taking office, *Gleichschaltung* had destroyed the potency of Germany's special interest groups—Junkers, the churches, big business, the legal and teaching professions and, most important, the army officer corps. At the same time, an ambitious campaign was undertaken to brainwash the entire German population. Elaborating on the *völkisch* strain in German culture, the Nazis concocted a veritable counterculture to the *Weltanschauung* of the ages of reason. When, in Michael Hurst's phrase, "the party swallowed the regime," and Nazi ideology began to dictate national policy, Germany had become a totalitarian community. Here, in Nazi Germany, was fascist radicalism with a vengeance. It was no coincidence that the opposition which developed to Hitler's sweeping transformation of Germany was conservative, and Dahrendorf is right in calling Germany's anti-Nazi resistance "counterrevolutionary."

The full totalitarian potential of fascism was only realized within the baleful Hitlerian orbit—inside the Third Reich, in the wartime puppet states of Salò, Szálasi and, in its closing stages, of Vichy. Until the brooding influence of Nazi Germany became overwhelming, the old establishments of Latin and eastern Europe were able to tame fascism, and the liberal politicians of western Europe to keep their fascist movements away from the seats of power altogether. But for the strength of the Danubian *ancien régime*, the Arrow Cross and the Iron Guard may readily be imagined, of their own accord and out of their racist ideologies, emulating Hitler's frenzied, totalitarian society. But it is in the industrial northwest of Europe that a real parallel to the German experience must be sought. If liberalism in France, the Low Countries, and Great Britain had been weaker, and the fascists there able to approach closer to power, would they have embarked on radical, totalitarian experimentation? Did the greater the modernity of a nation really mean the more revolutionary the fascist reaction against the status quo? One suspects that the sole course and justification for fascism in an advanced community was to renounce the contemporary world and its mores without reservation. There were hints of this in the French fascist longing for a legendary *pays réel*, in Mosley's uncharacteristic conversion to anti-Semitism and violence in 1934, and in Degrelle's extravagant election campaign of March 1937. Much must inevitably remain speculative. Whatever slim prospects the western European fascists had of fulfilling their own political philosophy, they were cut short by the outbreak of war in 1939. Henceforth, these fascists were forced willy-nilly into the mold of Nazi German collaborators and sympathizers. Thus, it was in Germany alone that fascism was given the opportunity in a modern setting to reveal its true colors. They were horrifying enough to occasion thanks for the lack of other case studies of radical fascism in action.

In this book fascism has been subdivided into two broad denominations. One species stressed corporativism as a means to modernize backward areas without upsetting the current class structure. The other, less tender toward existing privilege, sought to escape from a detestable modernity by conjuring up fantasies from the past. Neither of these formulas for reintegrating twentieth-century society, however, proved practicable between the world wars. Corporativism, because of a combination of the fascists' own ineptitude and the selfishness of the propertied classes, seldom progressed far beyond a propaganda exercise. Mussolini was the torchbearer of this corporative fascism, and his regime set the pattern for the betrayal of the ideal throughout Europe. Conversely, in Nazi Germany, where the most determined effort was made to flee from the present in a cultural sense, Hitler found it impossible to dispense with the urban-industrial complex which he required to sustain an expansionist foreign policy. Necessarily, the focus of *völkisch* dreaming switched to the underdeveloped "no man's land" between Europe proper and the Soviet Union.

Yet, it was precisely through the failure of these ideological expectations, in the twilight of the fascist epoch, that the inner reality of the major fascist regimes became clear. Thus, in Italy after 1938, Mussolini's government was exposed as opportunistic and corrupt. Its lack of grassroots support was revealed in the abysmal war effort of 1940–43. The socialistic gestures of the Salò Republic were a forlorn and belated effort to return to the populist origins of Italian Fascism. Mussolini's whole career ended in the proverbial, passive whimper, not a bang. In contrast, the closer the Nazi regime came to its end, the more fanatical and nihilistic it grew. Always an ideologue, Hitler from 1941 onward gave himself over utterly to *völkisch* imperatives. Thus it was that the ghastly final solution of the Jewish problem was, for the most part, executed as German troops were retreating on all fronts. And, of course, the Wagnerian soul of Nazism was laid bare in the famous destructive *Götterdämmerung* in the spring of 1945.

In a very real sense, the extremism of Nazi Germany in the Second World War was the apotheosis of fascism. In their totalitarian and impersonal attitude to genocide, the Nazis arrived at the ultimate contradiction of the nineteenth-century value system which exalted the individual. In the Nazi death camps there was neither individual worth nor, more important, individual responsibility. The observation of the homespun philosopher, Eric Hoffer, is apt:

> When we renounce the self and become part of a compact whole, we not only renounce personal advantage but are also rid of personal responsibility. There is no telling to what extremes of cruelty and ruthlessness a man will go when he is freed from the fears, hesitations, doubts and the vague stirrings of decency that go with individual judgment. When we lose our individual independence in the corporateness of a mass movement, we find a new freedom—freedom to hate, bully, lie, torture, murder and betray without shame and remorse (*The True Believer* [1951]).

This is what fascism was all about: the submergence of self in an emotionally perceived and satisfying integral fellowship. Therein, the democracy of belonging was allied to absolute obedience to a creed and its high priests.

Finally, fascism was defined by the manner in which it was overthrown in the international arena. In 1939 Hitler stumbled into war with the liberal-conservative west; two years later, the Führer led the fascist world in a calculated assault on the socialist east. Reluctantly and temporarily, therefore, the three chief political forces to be handed down from the nineteenth century were forced together into an anti-fascist front; the conservative Churchill, the liberal Roosevelt, and the Marxist Stalin engineered the destruction of Hitler's new order. This grand coalition symbolized everything that fascism had tried to refute; its victory was the revenge of the nineteenth century.

# BIBLIOGRAPHICAL ESSAY

It hardly needs to be said that the literature on fascism is by now voluminous. What follows is, of necessity, highly selective and restricted mainly to English-language works; material in other languages is included only if it is of unusual merit or plugs an otherwise unfillable gap. Furthermore, in specifying monographs and articles, I have concentrated on those titles which led me to my conclusion regarding the dual nature of fascism.

## Fascist Words Written and Spoken

Both Duce and Führer have had their pronouncements compiled: Benito Mussolini, *Opera omnia*, eds. E. and D. Susmel, 32 vols. (Florence, 1951–61); *The Speeches of Adolf Hitler, 1922–1939*, ed. N. H. Baynes, 2 vols. (London, 1942), and *Hitler's Words (1922–1943)*, ed. G. W. Prange (Washington, 1944). For the rest of the Hitlerian record, one must turn to Max Domarus, ed., *Hitler: Reden und Proklamationem, 1932–1945*, 2 vols. (Munich, 1965). More illuminating than Hitler's public statements, of course, are his remarks made privately; these may be sampled in E. Calic, ed., *Secret Conversation with Hitler: Two Newly Discovered Interviews, 1931* (New York, 1971), for the period 1932–34 amid the author's analysis in Hermann Rauschning's *Voice of Destruction* (New York, 1940), and for the period of the Second World War in more straightforward fashion in *Hitler Directs His War*, ed. F. Gilbert (New York, 1950), and *Hitler's Table Talk, 1941–1944*, intro. by H. R. Trevor-Roper (London, 1953).

Hitler concocted his memoirs-cum-political credo before he reached power—*Mein Kampf* in 1924–25; the standard English-language version has been edited by J. Chamberlain and S. B. Fay (New York, 1939). (Werner Maser, *Hitler's Mein Kampf*, Eng. trans. [London, 1970], is, incidentally, an account of the vicissitudes of this important book.) Hitler completed another work in 1928 which was not published at the time; appearing subsequently as *Hitler's Secret Book*, Eng. trans. (New York, 1961), it is mostly a reiteration of the foreign policy proposals of *Mein Kampf*. Mussolini's equivalent contributions were made much later in his public career. The famous definition of Fascism which he and Gentile composed for the *Enciclopedia italiana* (1932) appeared in shortened English form as "The Social and Political Doctrine of Fascism," *International Conciliation* no. 306 (January 1935): 5–17. After his dismissal by King Victor Emmanuel, the Duce gave his exculpatory and tendentious account in *The Fall of Mussolini*, ed. M. Ascoli (New York, 1948).

A few of the leaders of other fascist movements have confided their thoughts to paper. The young Sir Oswald Mosley wrote idealistically in *The Greater Britain* (London, 1932), and more gloomily in old age in *My Life* (London, 1969). António Salazar explained his theories of government in a rather heavy-handed book, *Doctrine and Action*, Eng. trans. (London, 1939). Austria's principal fascists understandably have concentrated on the Anschluss problem, the *Heimwehr* chief, Prince Ernst Starhemberg, in *Between Hitler and Mussolini* (London, 1942), and Chancellor Kurt von Schuschnigg in *The Brutal Takeover*, Eng. trans. (New York, 1971).

The fascist lieutenants have supplied a number of books, albeit of mixed value to the historian. Among the Nazis, Joseph Goebbels, as befitted a propaganda minister, was most active in print. There is *My Part in Germany's Fight*, Eng. trans. (London, 1935); more revealing are the extracts from Goebbels's diaries captured by the Allies at the end of the war: *The Early Goebbels Diaries, 1925–1926*, ed. H. Heiber (London, 1962), and *The Goebbels Diaries, 1942–1943*, ed. P. Lochner (Garden City, 1948). *The Ribbentrop Memoirs*, Eng. trans. (London, 1954), written while the author was awaiting execution, explain away Nazi aggression as justifiable antibolshevism. The socialist side of Nazism was presented in a party platform drawn up by Gottfried Feder in 1927; in English, it bears the misleading title of *Hitler's Official Programme* (London, 1934). Similar leftist views inform Otto Strasser's memoir, *Hitler and I*, Eng. trans. (Boston, 1940). Kurt Ludecke, *I Knew Hitler* (New York, 1937), conveys the sense of adventure involved in being a Nazi in the 1920s. Three memoirs which illustrate the willingness of the German establishment to side with Hitler a decade later, as well as the frightening things to be found within the movement, are *Revolution of Nihilism*, Eng. trans. (New York, 1939), by the aristocratic conservative, Hermann Rauschning; *Account Settled*, Eng. trans. (London, 1949), by the businessman, Hjalmar Schacht; and *Inside the Third Reich*, Eng. trans. (New York, 1970), by the architect and technocrat, Albert Speer.

In literary frankness, the Italian counterpart to Speer's book consists of *The Ciano Diaries, 1937–1938*, ed. A. Mayer (London, 1952), and *The Ciano Diaries, 1939–1943*, ed. H. Gibson (New York, 1946). These disclose the cavalier approach to decision-making in Mussolini's Italy and the one-sided nature of the Rome-Berlin Axis. Against Ciano's sardonic perspective, one may set Giovanni Gentile, *Genesis and Structure of Society*, Eng. trans. (Urbana, 1960), an exposition of the "ethical state," which is what one honest intellectual vainly hoped Italian Fascism would become. Other academic blueprints for an ideal fascist society are the Rumanian Mihail Manoilescu's *Theory of Protection and International Trade* (London, 1931), and by the same author, *Le siècle du corporatisme* (Paris, 1934), both prescriptions for the updating of an underdeveloped nation. In contrast, *Back to Reality*, Eng. trans. (London, 1955), written in Vichy France by the French scholar, Gustave Thibon, advocates a reversion to the ancient verities of family and soil.

Lastly, there are a number of paperbacks which contain brief selections from documentary and other primary sources pertaining to fascism. The best anthologies of this type are those edited by G. H. Stein, *Hitler* (Englewood Cliffs, N.J., 1968); J. Remak, *The Nazi Years* (Englewood Cliffs, N.J., 1969); and C. Delzell, *Mediterranean Fascism* (New York, 1970), which includes material from Italy, Spain, and Portugal.

### The General Background of Fascism

Historical surveys of the period covered in this book are innumerable. One-volume works which stand out are J. M. Roberts, *Europe, 1880–1945* (London, 1967); Felix Gilbert, *End of the European Era, 1890 to the Present* (New York, 1970); H. Stuart Hughes, *Contemporary Europe,* 3d ed. (Englewood Cliffs, N.J., 1971). Also highly recommended are the volumes in the "Rise of Modern Europe" series: Carlton J. Hayes, *A Generation of Materialism, 1871–1900* (New York, 1941), was one of the first books to expose the cracks beneath the surface of the nineteenth-century synthesis; and the story is more than adequately carried forward under the self-explanatory titles, *The Great Illusion, 1900–1914* (New York, 1971) by Oron J. Hale, and *A Broken World, 1919–1939* (New York, 1971) by Raymond J. Sontag.

Quite a number of nonhistorians (social scientists, philosophers, etc.) have attempted a broad analysis of twentieth-century civilization and its malaise. In this context, fascism usually appears as one facet of totalitarianism. Several of the following titles in this category have already been discussed in the text: Theodor Adorno et al., *The Authoritarian Personality* (New York, 1950); Hannah Arendt, *Origins of Totalitarianism*, 2d ed. (New York, 1958); Zevedei Barbu, *Democracy and Dictatorship* (New York, 1956); C. Friedrich, ed., *Totalitarianism* (Cambridge, Mass., 1954), a set of essays treating fascism and communism jointly, an approach repeated in *Totalitarianism in Perspective* (New York, 1969) by C. Friedrich, M. Curtis, and B. R. Barber; Erich Fromm, *Escape from Freedom* (New York, 1941); Eric Hoffer, *The True Believer* (New York, 1951), contends that a specific personality type constitutes the followers of fanatical movements such as fascism; Seymour Lipset, *Political Man* (New York, 1960); Barrington Moore, *Social Origins of Dictatorship and Democracy* (Boston, 1966), tries not too successfully to explain fascism as a maneuver of disturbed rural interests; David Riesman, *The Lonely Crowd* (New Haven, 1950); J. L. Talmon, *History of Totalitarian Democracy*, 2 vols. (London, 1952–60).

Then there are those cultural and intellectual overviews which suggest, at least by inference, that fascism sprang out of a collapse of accepted values. Two pessimistic contemporary observers were Oswald Spengler, *Decline of the West*, Eng. trans., 2 vols. (New York, 1926–28), and José Ortega y Gasset, *Revolt of the Masses*, Eng. trans. (New York, 1932). Julien Benda, *The Treason of the Intellectuals*, Eng. trans. (New York, 1928), gave the world the famous phrase to describe the European thinkers' desertion of Enlightenment precepts. An interesting variation on the theme of a drift away from rationalism is offered in Peter Drucker's *The End of Economic Man* (New York, 1939). Two excellent descriptions of the changing artistic and intellectual climate are Gerhard Masur, *Prophets of Yesterday, 1890–1914* (New York, 1961), and H. Stuart Hughes, *Consciousness and Society: The Reconstruction of European Social Thought, 1890–1930* (New York, 1958). Some consequences of the changes detailed in Masur and Hughes are worked out in Alastair Hamilton's *The Appeal of Fascism* (London, 1971), which deals with a cross section of Europe's cultural elite who succumbed to fascist blandishments in the interwar years.

## Modernization

During the 1960s the study of modernization became something of a scholarly cult, inspired to some degree by Walt Rostow's seminal work,

*The Process of Economic Growth* (New York, 1952), and *The Economics of Take-off into Sustained Growth*, ed. W. W. Rostow (New York, 1963). Nevertheless, an acceptable paradigm of modernization has yet to appear. Two brave attempts are C. E. Black, *The Dynamics of Modernization* (New York, 1966), and S. H. Eisenstadt, *Modernization: Protest and Change* (Englewood Cliffs, N.J., 1966). Neither author, however, tries to place the various fascist movements on a scale of modernization, the necessity of which task is cogently presented by Henry A. Turner, "Fascism and Modernization," *World Politics* 24 (1972): 547–64. As I have explained in the preface to this book, A. F. K. Organski, *The Stages of Political Development* (New York, 1965), assays the job in a generic fashion, although his examples of fascism are confined to Germany, Italy, and Argentina. Wolfgang Sauer, "National Socialism: Totalitarianism or Fascism?" *American Historical Review* 73 (1968): 404–24, suggests in passing that the totalitarian quotient of a given fascist movement might depend on the modernity of the environment.

On the relative backwardness of pre-Fascist Italy, which is central to my own thesis, Alexander Gerschenkron, *Economic Backwardness in Historical Perspective* (Cambridge, Mass., 1962), chap. 4: "Notes on the Rate of Industrial Growth in Italy, 1881–1913," is extremely valuable. Charles S. Maier, "Between Taylorism and Technology," *Journal of Contemporary History* 5, no. 1 (1970): 22–61, is an excellent survey of the post-World War I European vogue for American economic rationalization, a frame of mind clearly reflected in the productivist side of early Italian Fascism.

As for the concept of mobilization, often allied to the question of modernity, a good treatment is J. P. Nettl, *Political Mobilization* (London, 1967). Also on the subject of change in modern societies, Talcott Parsons, *Politics and Social Structure* (New York, 1969), has a brief chapter on "Some Sociological Aspects of the Fascist Movements."

## Fascism—Accounts and Interpretations

Broadly speaking, one may distinguish between two approaches to fascism. In the first place, there are those works which examine the different national fascisms in turn, and tend to leave the reader to draw his own conclusions about a general concept of fascism. At the other extreme stand those interpretations which regard fascism as a supranational force and are explicitly concerned with extracting its universal essence. (For what it is worth, this present book has tried to combine these two methods of inquiry.)

In the former genre, pride of place must go to F. L. Carsten, *The Rise of Fascism* (London, 1967). As the title implies, the narratives of the principal fascist episodes stop short of the end of the fascist era—in the Italian case around 1926, and in the German in 1934. But within these limits, it is admirably concise, clear, and informative. Eugen Weber, *Varieties of Fascism* (Princeton, 1964), surveys a number of fascist movements and provides one or two key documents for each. The emphasis is on diversity, and the author comes close to denying a common fascist identity altogether. The same impression is inevitably left by many collections of essays by several authors within one volume. For instance, the first issue of the *Journal of Contemporary History* (1966), was given over to a series of disparate articles on "International Fascism, 1920–1945." S. J. Woolf, ed., *European Fascism* (London, 1968), consists of papers on a dozen variegated national experiences of fascism, and a similar division by nationality provides the framework for the essays in *The European Right*, ed. H. Rogger and E. Weber (Berkeley, 1965), many of which concern fascist parties. Although it is hard to discern any clear-cut definition of fascism in these compilations, many of the individual pieces in the *Journal of Contemporary History*, vol. 1, and in the books edited by Woolf and Rogger/Weber are excellent, and will be cited below under "Fascism by Nation." Other collections of essays worth mentioning include P. Sugar, ed., *Native Fascism in the Successor States* (Santa Barbara, 1971), short analyses of the lesser-known fascist fronts of central and eastern Europe written, interestingly, by scholars from either side of the iron curtain; J. Weiss, ed., *Nazis and Fascists in Europe, 1918–1945* (Chicago, 1969), accounts of Hitlerian and Mussolinian activity composed at the time by writers for the *New York Times*; N. Greene, ed., *Fascism: An Anthology* (New York, 1968), and G. Allardyce, ed., *The Place of Fascism in European History* (Englewood Cliffs, N.J., 1971), are both made up of extracts from scholarly studies of fascism.

Of the more interpretative works on fascism in general, undoubtedly Ernst Nolte, *Three Faces of Fascism: Action Française, Italian Fascism, National Socialism*, Eng. trans. (New York, 1966), represents the most ambitious attempt to construct a fascist typology. Nolte finds the key in fascism's antitranscendence, its rejection of modern progressive thought. The thesis is obviously derived from the Nazi model. Although it offers a credible explanation of Action Française, the argument falls down when applied to Italy, for Nolte is constrained to brush aside the progressive aspects of Mussolini's corporativism. The book is rather heavy going, yet is full of stimulating insights and warrants careful reading. One of the side merits of *Three Faces of Fascism* is that it provoked several useful reviews and historiographical articles. George L. Mosse, for one, in a review article in the *Journal of the History of Ideas* 27 (1966): 621–25, argues that while fascism may have denied "bourgeois transcendence" as Nolte says, it nonetheless created its own inspirational transcendence. George Lichtheim also uses *Three Faces of Fascism* as the starting point for an essay, "The European Civil War," in his *Concept of Ideology* (New York, 1967), pp. 225–37, wherein he stresses the fundamentally antimodernist character of Nazism. Yet another bibliographical survey of Nolte and others is Michael Hurst, "What Is Fascism?" *Historical Journal* 11 (1968): 165–85, which accurately pinpoints fascism as an antiliberal (rather than anti-Marxist) phenomenon, while observing that Nazism in practice became divorced from other fascist movements by its unique totalitarian frenzy.

Whereas Nolte seems to extrapolate too much from Nazi Germany at the cost of misconstruing Italian Fascism, A. James Gregor, *The Ideology of Fascism: The Rationale of Totalitarianism* (New York, 1969), must be criticized for the obverse. He regards Mussolini as a "productionist" and a modernizer able to fulfill his mission only through totalitarian methods. As such, the Duce is seen as the fascist pacemaker, which he certainly was in many respects; but there is little consideration given to the fact that Mussolini's totalitarian revolution never really materialized, and only glancing reference made to the very different antimodernist base of Nazi totalitarianism. In sum, Gregor's version of Italian Fascism seems a forced one tailored to fit a dubious pattern. The failure to differentiate between the Mussolinian and Hitlerian types of fascism also creates a problem in R. H. Kedward's *Fascism in Western Europe, 1900–1945* (London, 1969). Although Kedward includes Nazi Germany within the scope of western European fascism, he accords no recognition to the special character of Hitler's regime; significantly, Austria, where Hitler and Mussolini fought toe to toe for the primacy of their own ideologies, is ignored. On the other hand, Kedward is excellent on the origins of fascism, pointing out that the fascists' attraction rested on their ability to fuse apparently contradictory elements from the nineteenth century—reason and emotion, autocracy and democracy, capitalism and socialism.

John Weiss, *The Fascist Tradition* (New York, 1967), returns to an older interpretation of fascism as a right-wing force, and he emphasizes the fascists' affinity with the traditional opponents of liberalism and socialism. He would appear to give too much weight to the fascist parties' alliances with the power structures and not enough to early fascism's radical ideology—whether or not the latter was realized in practice. Nevertheless, Weiss's view is much more subtle than the standard Marxian assertion that fascism was a tool of vested monopolistic interests—a position which may be sampled in R. Palme Dutt, *Fascism and Social Revolution* (London, 1934). One further effort to provide an overall definition of fascism might be mentioned—*The Nature of Fascism*, edited by S. J. Woolf (London, 1968), and a counterpart to his compilation, *European Fascism*. The essays in *The Nature of Fascism* necessarily vary in approach and quality, and one's verdict on the pieces in a collected work tends to be more than usually subjective. Suffice it to say that this author profited most from the contributions by A. F. K. Organski, "Fascism and Modernization," pp. 19–41, and G. Germani, "Fascism and Class," pp. 65–96.

Inquiries into those fascist movements which postdate World War II have not been wildly successful. The best known is A. Del Boca and M. Giovana, *Fascism Today* (New York, 1969), but the authors cover such a wealth of authoritarian and radical rightist organizations that any concept of fascism is swiftly lost. L. K. Adler and T. G. Patterson, "Red Fascism: The Merger of Nazi Germany and Soviet Russia in the American Image of Totalitarianism, 1930s–1950s," *American Historical Review* 75 (1970): 1046–64, is an interesting article which argues that the cold war after 1945 warped western (and specifically American) understanding of fascism.

## Fascism by Nation

### ITALY

Among the historical surveys of united Italy, two are outstanding: Denis Mack Smith, *Italy: A Modern History*, rev. ed. (Ann Arbor, 1969), mostly a political account, and its economic counterpart, S. B. Clough, *Economic History of Modern Italy* (New York, 1964). Luigi Salvatorelli, *The Risorgimento: Thought and Action*, Eng. trans. (New York, 1970), sums up a century of history with the verdict that Fascism was "the anti-Risorgimento." In his national character sketch, *The Italians* (New York, 1964), Luigi Barzini argues that the mass of the Italian people, being congenitally cynical toward any central authority, were never really taken in by Mussolini.

The shortcomings of the pre-Fascist liberal regime are perhaps best illustrated obliquely in contemporary critiques of parliamentary democracy: Gaetano Mosca, *The Ruling Class*, Eng. trans. (New York, 1939), and Vilfredo Pareto, *The Mind and Society*, Eng. trans., 4 vols. (New York, 1935). And since Mussolini at least claimed to be inspired by the syndicalist teachings of Georges Sorel, the latter's *Reflections on Violence*, Eng. trans. (New York, 1914), is also relevant. Modern scholarship has been kinder to Italian liberals, especially Giolitti: see A. William Salomone, *Italy in the Giolittian Era* (Philadelphia, 1960), and Frank J. Coppa, *Planning, Protectionism, and Politics in Liberal Italy* (Washington, D.C., 1971). On the other hand, Italy's intellectuals on the eve of the First World War come off rather badly in A. J. Thayer's *Italy and the Great*.

*War* (Madison, 1964), many of them as protofascists. A very thorough and rewarding survey of liberal Italy's politics is Christopher Seton-Watson, *Italy from Liberalism to Fascism, 1870–1925* (London, 1967).

Of general books on the Italian Fascist era, Luigi Salvatorelli and Giovanni Mira, *Storia d'Italia nel periodo fascista*, 5th ed. (Turin, 1964), is undoubtedly the best reference work. Federico Chabod, *History of Italian Fascism*, Eng. trans. (London, 1963), really a series of lectures by a distinguished Italian historian, is concerned primarily with how his country's respectable classes came to accept Fascism. Herman Finer, *Mussolini's Italy* (London, 1935), takes a detailed look at Fascist Italy's legal and administrative system. *Under the Axe of Fascism* (New York, 1936) is the best-known title of several by the historian and *fuoruscito*, Gaetano Salvemini, exposing the emptiness and brutality behind the Mussolinian façade. A more recent overall review is Edward R. Tannenbaum, *The Fascist Experience: Italian Society and Culture, 1922–1945* (New York, 1972), which recognizes the early idealism and progressive spirit of many Fascists but leaves no doubt of the PNF's fall from grace in the 1930s. Short surveys of the Italian Fascist era include S. William Halperin, *Mussolini and Italian Fascism* (Princeton, 1964), and Alan Cassels, *Fascist Italy* (New York, 1968).

Biographies of the Duce are plentiful, although no definitive work has yet emerged. Renzo De Felice has aspirations to fill the gap with a multivolume sociopsychological study, three volumes of which have so far appeared—*Mussolini il rivoluzionario; Mussolini il fascista: La conquista del potere; Mussolini il fascista: L'organizzazione dello Stato Fascista* (Turin, 1965–68). They are exhaustive, and the reader tends to lose sight of the forest for the trees. The best biography in English is by Sir Ivone Kirkpatrick, *Mussolini: A Study in Power* (London, 1964). It is strong on Mussolini's rise to power and his foreign policies, weak on the subtleties of corporative doctrine. Laura Fermi, *Mussolini* (Chicago, 1961), is an impressionistic study of certain high points of the Duce's career, and has some interesting speculations on his personal quirks.

Worthwhile specialist studies include Roberto Vivarelli, *Il dopoguerra in Italia e l'avvento del fascismo*, vol. 1 (Naples, 1967–    ). When completed, this will probably be the definitive work on Italy's post-World War I situation. Meanwhile, Angelo Rossi (pseud. for Tasca), *The Rise of Italian Fascism*, Eng. trans. (London, 1938), written from a decidedly leftist position, remains valuable. Adrian Lyttleton, *The Seizure of Power: Fascism in Italy, 1919–1929* (London, 1973), is a densely packed book but invaluable for its careful dissection of each Mussolinian step to dictatorship and its analysis of the regional currents within the PNF. Roberto Farinacci, charged with establishing the one-party regime in 1925–26 although fading from prominence afterward, is the subject of Harry Fornari *Mussolini's Gadfly* (Nashville, 1971). How far the "second wave" of the Fascist revolution carried is a matter of some dispute. S. J. Woolf, editor of *European Fascism*, observes in his own contribution "Italy," pp. 39–60, that after 1932 the prospect of radical domestic change faded rapidly. This is testified to in Michael Ledeen's *Fascist International* (New York, 1972), which charts the growing disillusion of young Fascist idealists, culminating in their unhappy meeting with the racial fascists at Montreux in 1934.

In practice, the question of a Fascist revolution turned on the efficacy of Mussolini's corporative state, a subject which of late has received new and deserved attention. Interest was in part sparked by P. Ungari, *Alfredo Rocco e l'ideologia giuridica del fascismo* (Brescia, 1963). In the English language, two important articles are by Roland Sarti, "Fascist Modernization in Italy," *American Historical Review* 75 (1970): 1029–45, who gives the productivist background, and by Edward R. Tannenbaum who places corporativism in the forefront of "The Goals of Italian Fascism," ibid. 74 (1969): 1183–1204.

From another perspective, the question of the success or failure of the Fascist revolution can be posed in the form: Did Mussolini succeed in establishing a totalitarian society? Dante L. Germino, *The Italian Fascist Party in Power* (Minneapolis, 1959), thinks that he did, although Germino does not take his analysis beyond 1940 when the Duce's totalitarian boast was put to the test. Philip V. Cannistraro, "Mussolini's Cultural Revolution: Fascist or Nationalist?" *Journal of Contemporary History* 7, nos. 3–4: 115–39, questions whether the *stile fascista* was much of an innovation at all. Even more convincingly, Alberto Aquarone, *L' organizzazione dello Stato totalitario* (Turin, 1965), argues that too many interest groups remained too strong in Fascist Italy to allow use of the word "totalitarian." On Italy's businessmen, for example, Roland Sarti's excellent *Fascism and the Industrial Leadership in Italy* (Berkeley, 1971), demonstrates the abiding influence of the *Confindustria*. On the Vatican, see Daniel A. Binchy, *Church and State in Fascist Italy* (New York, 1941), who gives a balanced description of the Lateran Accords and their implementation, while Richard A. Webster, *The Cross and the Fasces* (Stanford, 1960), stresses the preservation of Christian Democracy under cover of the accords. Although not the last word on the subject of the Italian monarchy under Fascism, Robert Katz, *The Fall of the House of Savoy* (New York, 1971), contains useful information.

The role of the intellectuals is analyzed in Emiliana P. Noether, "Italian Intellectuals under Fascism," *Journal of Modern History* 43 (1971): 630–48. The symptomatic position of Benedetto Croce is covered by Chester M. Destler, "Croce and Italian Fascism," ibid. 24 (1952): 382–90. The punishment of *confino* in a backward southern village meted out to recalcitrant intellectuals is graphically pictured in one victim's memoir, Carlo Levi, *Christ Stopped at Eboli*, Eng. trans. (New York, 1947).

In an interesting work which spans domestic and foreign concerns, Dennison I. Rusinow, *Italy's Austrian Heritage* (Oxford, 1969), indicates that the touchstone of Fascist fortunes was to be found in the northeastern provinces gained in 1918. Charles F. Delzell, *Mussolini's Enemies* (Princeton, 1961), chronicles the efforts, made mostly outside Italy, to keep alive an anti-Fascist spirit, which bore fruit in the resistance of 1943–45. On the other hand, John P. Diggins, *Mussolini and Fascism: The View from America* (Princeton, 1972), records the mostly favorable impact made by the Duce on U.S. opinion. Monographs on Fascist Italy's foreign policy before World War II include: Alan Cassels, *Mussolini's Early Diplomacy* (Princeton, 1970); George W. Baer, *Coming of the Italian-Ethiopian War* (Cambridge, Mass., 1967); Elizabeth Wiskemann, *Rome-Berlin Axis*, rev. ed. (London, 1966); Mario Toscano, *Origins of the Pact of Steel* (Baltimore, 1967). The fantasy world in which the ideologues of Berlin and Rome lived is illustrated by D. C. Watt, "The Rome-Berlin Axis, 1936–1940: Myth and Reality," *Review of Politics* 22 (1960): 519–43. This suggests the fatal flaw in Fascist Italy's ambitious diplomacy. As Denis Mack Smith speculates in "Mussolini: Artist in Propaganda," *History Today* 9 (1959): 223–32, the Duce was so successful a salesman that he ended up deluding himself about his country's strength.

GERMANY

One approach to Hitler's National Socialism is to regard it as a product of German history. A. J. P. Taylor, *The Course of German History* (London, 1945), comes close to implying that it was an inevitable outcome of a thousand years of Teutonic development. Despite the narrowness of its announced topic, Fritz Fischer's *Germany's Aims in the First World War*, abridged Eng. trans. (New York, 1967), is another notorious book which seems to imply that some chronic defect in the national character of modern Germany might have produced Nazism. Less contentiously, Friedrich Meinecke, *The German Catastrophe*, Eng. trans. (Cambridge, Mass., 1950), and Ralf Dahrendorf, *Society and Democracy in Germany* (New York, 1967), also relate Nazism to trends in Germany's past, at least as far back as the Second Empire. The most dispassionate and up-to-date account of recent German history is by Hajo Holborn, *History of Modern Germany*, Vol. III: 1840–1945 (New York, 1969).

The specific element in German history to attract major attention is *Volk* culture which, gaining momentum from the romantic movement, flourished throughout the nineteenth century. This was the tradition of Paul de Lagarde, Julius Langbehn, and Möller van den Bruck—which trio provide the subject matter of Fritz Stern's *Politics of Cultural Despair* (Berkeley, 1961). Of the two most blatant racists to make an impact on the German mind, however, neither was a German; Houston Stewart Chamberlain, *Foundations of the Nineteenth Century*, Eng. trans., 2 vols. (London, 1910), was English; Count Joseph de Gobineau, *The Inequality of Human Races*, abridged Eng. trans. (London, 1915), was French. One of the first modern authors to depict Hitler as heir to a *völkisch* tradition was Peter Viereck in *Metapolitics* (New York, 1941). More recently, George L. Mosse, *The Crisis of German Ideology: Intellectual Origins of the Third Reich* (New York, 1964), has become the authoritative work on the topic. Several other books on pre-1914 Germany inevitably touch on the *völkisch* seedtime and look ahead to the Nazi harvest: R. H. Bowen, *German Theories of the Corporate State* (New York, 1947); Klemens von Klemperer, *Germany's New Conservatism* (Princeton, 1957); Hans Kohn, *The Mind of Germany* (New York, 1960); Walter Laqueur, *Young Germany: History of the German Youth Movement* (London, 1961); Peter J. Pulzer, *Rise of Political Anti-Semitism in Germany and Austria* (New York, 1964).

On the crucial period of the Weimar Republic, there are two excellent brief surveys: J. R. P. McKenzie, *Weimar Germany* (London, 1971), and A. J. Nicholls, *Weimar and the Rise of Hitler* (London, 1968). Also very useful is Peter Gay's short review of *Weimar Culture: The Outsider as Insider* (New York, 1968). The background of social and artistic experimentation, against which Nazism reacted so violently, figures prominently in Otto Friedrich's *Before the Deluge: Portrait of Berlin in the 1920s* (New York, 1972). The Bavarian ambience of the Führer's first bid for power is captured in Harold J. Gordon, *Hitler and the Beer Hall Putsch* (Princeton, 1972), G. Pridham, *Hitler's Rise to Power: The Nazi Movement in Bavaria, 1923–1933* (London, 1973) continues the Bavarian Saga, while Jeremy Noakes, *The Nazi Party in Lower Saxony, 1921–1933* (New York, 1972), reminds us of Nazism's increasingly northern orientation after 1923. The continuing militarist strain in German life, Weimar's civilian guise notwithstanding, comes through in Robert G. L. Waite's splendid study of the *Freikorps Vanguard of Nazism* (Cambridge, Mass., 1952).

Hitler's takeover of the Weimar Republic is described definitively, if exhaustingly, in Karl Dietrich Bracher, *Die Auflösung der Weimarer Republik*, 4th ed. (Villingen, 1964), and K. D. Bracher, W. Sauer, and G. Schulz, *Die Nationalsozialistische Machtergreifung* (Cologne, 1962). An English translation of some of the best articles on the Nazi advance originally published in the *Vierteljahrshefte für Zeitgeschichte* is *Republic to Reich: The Making of the Nazi Revolution* (New York, 1972), ed. H. Holborn. The chronology of the Nazi consolidation of power is provided in E. B. Wheaton, *The Nazi Revolution, 1933–1935* (New York, 1968).

Fritz Tobias, *The Reichstag Fire*, Eng. trans. (London, 1963), holds that this crucial event was in all probability set off by a single arsonist without political motivation. Max Gallo explains the motive behind *The Night of the Long Knives*, Eng. trans., (New York, 1972) as Hitler's determination not to be pressured into a hasty "second revolution."

Of the interest groups which aided Hitler's rise, the German businessmen's belated rallying to the Nazi cause is the point of Henry A. Turner's excellent bibliographical article, "Big Business and the Rise of Hitler," *American Historical Review* 75 (1969–70): 56–70. The army officer corps' complicity is explored both in Gordon A. Craig, *Politics of the Prussian Army, 1640–1945*, rev. ed. (New York, 1964), and in F. L. Carsten, *The Reichswehr and Politics, 1918–1933* (Oxford, 1966). Something of an apology for the Reichswehr may be found in Gerhard Ritter, "The Military and Politics in Germany," *Journal of Central European Affairs* 17 (1957–58): 259–71. On the Social Democratic failure to oppose Hitler more energetically, see Gerard Braunthal, "The German Free Trade Unions during the Rise of Nazism," ibid. 15 (1955–56): 339–53. The acquiescence of Germany's academic and intellectual community is explained in part by Fritz K. Ringer, *Decline of the German Mandarins* (Cambridge, Mass., 1970).

Naturally, the major debate has swirled around the nature and extent of the Nazis' mass support. It is often asserted that Nazism was a bourgeois phenomenon and, in this context, H. Lebovics's analysis of the *Mittelstand —Social Conservatism and the Middle Classes in Germany, 1914–1933* (Princeton, 1969)—is instructive. Foremost, however, in arguing that Nazism was a revolt of the middle class is Seymour Lipset; see specifically, "Faschismus," *Kölner Zeitschrift für Soziologie und Sozialpsychologie* 11 (1959): 401–44. On the other hand, K. O'Lessker, "Who Voted for Hitler?" *American Journal of Sociology* 74 (1968–69): 63–69, insists that Nazism appealed to a cross section of the German nation. M. H. Kele, *Nazis and Workers* (Durham, N.C., 1972), stresses Hitler's attractiveness to the proletariat. C. P. Loomis and J. A. Beegle, "The Spread of German Nazism in Rural Areas," *American Sociological Review* 2 (1964): 724–34, also indicate support for Hitler beyond the urban bourgeoisie. Undoubtedly the best analysis, though, is to be found in William S. Allen, *The Nazi Seizure of Power: The Experience of a Single German Town* (Chicago, 1965). As the subtitle says, this is a microcosmic—although probably representative—study. Within its limits, Allen's book presents the evidence of Nazism's broad support with an exactitude lacking in an earlier journalistic sampling of opinion within a small German town, Milton Mayer's *They Thought They Were Free* (Chicago, 1955). The type of individual likely to rise in the National Socialist hierarchy has been examined by Hans Gerth, "The Nazi Party: Its Leadership and Composition," *American Journal of Sociology* 45 (1939–40): 517–41, and by Daniel Lerner, *The*

*Nazi Elite* (Stanford, 1951). Perhaps predictably, he proves to have been an insecure person, often a failure in conventional walks of life.

To survey the entire history of Hitler's Germany and to capture all the complexities of the bizarre experiment is a formidable task—one that yet remains to be done in satisfactory fashion. The most ambitious and famous attempt is William Shirer's *Rise and Fall of the Third Reich* (New York, 1960). Yet, in spite of the author's familiarity with details, the essence of Nazism seems to elude him. Similarly, Richard Grunberger, *The Twelve-Year Reich* (London, 1971), has a quantity of information on every conceivable aspect of life under Nazism, yet lacks an analytical core. T. L. Jarman, *Rise and Fall of Nazi Germany* (London, 1955), is a commendable summary, but its brevity allows only a cursory treatment of many topics. *The Third Reich*, ed. M. Baumont, etc. (London, 1955), and *Nazism and the Third Reich*, ed. H. A. Turner (Chicago, 1972), are collections of first-rate scholarly essays, but are not designed to present a coordinated viewpoint. Karl Dietrich Bracher, *The German Dictatorship*, Eng. trans. (New York, 1970), is thorough on the early years of the Third Reich, thin on the later ones. Franz Neumann, *Behemoth: Structure and Practice of National Socialism* (New York, 1944), is still a useful description of the apparatus of the Nazi state, although marred by an insistence that Hitler was a servant of capitalism.

The absolute dominance of Hitler from beginning to end of the Nazi episode renders a good biography of the Führer virtually synonymous with a history of Nazism. It follows that Alan Bullock's brilliant *Hitler: A Study in Tyranny*, rev. ed. (London, 1962), is arguably the best work on the Nazi movement. The book is an admirable blend of narrative and analysis. R. Payne, *Life and Death of Adolf Hitler* (New York, 1973), and C. Cross, *Adolf Hitler* (London, 1973). The former aspires to be more sensational, the latter is more reliable and balanced; but both lose the Hitlerian personality amid the later narrative of world events. The best book on Hitler's infancy and adolescence is by Bradley F. Smith, *Adolf Hitler: His Family, Childhood and Youth* (Stanford, 1967). The politicization of Hitler up to 1934 is recounted in Konrad Heiden's racy *Der Fuehrer*, Eng. trans. (Boston, 1944), while in contrast P. E. Schramm presents a well-rounded characterization of the Führer at his zenith in *Hitler: The Man and the Military Leader*, Eng. trans. (New York, 1971). Hitler's primacy in the Nazi story is attested to in Dietrich Orlow's definitive *History of the Nazi Party*, 2 vols. (Pittsburgh, 1969–73).

The clue to understanding both Hitler and the Third Reich lies in a recognition of the ideological dynamism at work. E. Jäckel, *Hitler's Weltanschauung*, Eng. trans. (Middletown, 1972), codifies the Führer's prejudices. More briefly and suggestively, H. Holborn, "Origins and Political Character of Nazi Ideology," *Political Science Quarterly* 79 (1964): 542–54, emphasizes the importance of a consistent ideology throughout Hitler's career. Another dimension of the Nazi rationale is supplied in R. Cecil, *Myth of the Master Race: Alfred Rosenberg and Nazi Ideology* (London, 1972). ⸢For what Nazi ideology involved in practice, one should turn to David Schoenbaum's perceptive *Hitler's Social Revolution: Class and Status in Nazi Germany, 1933–1939* (New York, 1966), which may be supplemented by T. W. Mason, "Labour in the Third Reich," *Past and Present*, no. 33 (1966): 112–41. These investigations disclose that Nazi radicalism lay not so much in any class upheaval as in the superimposition of the values of a tribal *Volksgemeinschaft* on the whole German nation. Also in this category may be mentioned Robert Koehl's imaginative parallel between Nazism and antique feudal practices, "The Feudal Aspects of National Socialism," *American Political Science Review* 54 (1960): 921–33.

Nazi fanaticism has understandably aroused the attention of psychoanalysts and social psychologists. Long ago, Erik Erikson, "Hitler's Imagery and German Youth," *Psychiatry* 5 (1942): 475–93, suggested that Hitler and his charisma amounted to a case of protracted infantilism. Also during the Second World War, the American government commissioned Dr. Walter C. Langer to prepare a psychiatric profile of the Führer, which has only recently been released for publication under the title *The Mind of Adolf Hitler* (New York, 1972). Langer's diagnosis laid stress on the subject's deviant sex habits, forecast his suicide two years before it happened, and in the main has been corroborated by at least one other researcher on the frontier of history and psychology: witness R.G. Waite's "Adolf Hitler's Antisemitism," in *The Psychoanalytic Interpretation of History*, ed. B.B. Wolman (New York, 1971), pp. 192–230, and the same author's "Adolf Hitler's Guilt Feelings," *Journal of Interdisciplinary History* 1 (1971): 229–49. Himmler, too, has been the subject of psychoanalytical speculation, notably by Bradley F. Smith, whose *Heinrich Himmler: A Nazi in the Making* (Stanford, 1971), is based in part on a diary the subject kept as a young man. The concentration on these two most passionate anti-Semites, Hitler and Himmler, reflects the psychoanalysts' fascination with the unreasoning Nazi hatred of the Jews. Indeed, Norman Cohn, *Warrant for Genocide* (London, 1967), a history of the forged *Protocols of the Elders of Zion*, interprets Nazi anti-Semitism as western society's mental rejection of its Jewish father figure. There have been several other psychoanalytical forays into the collective Nazi mind, the first in time being Wilhelm Reich's *Mass Psychology of Fascism*, 3d ed., Eng. trans. (New York, 1946), which interprets Nazism in terms of warped sexuality. G. M. Gilbert, *Nuremberg Diary* (New York, 1947), stems from a psychologist's observation of the defendants before the Nuremberg Tribunal, although no very clear Nazi character type emerges. Peter Loewenberg, "The Psychohistorical Origins of the Nazi Youth Cohort," *American Historical Review* 76 (1971): 1457–1502, sees Nazism growing out of a generation deprived of normal parental authority by the Great War and the Great Depression. Finally, Joachim Fest, *The Face of the Third Reich*, Eng. trans. (London, 1970), is a popularized rendering of the more distinctive and deviant traits exhibited by typical Nazis.

As may be imagined, there exist a host of specialized studies on aspects of the Third Reich. Space dictates that only a few can be listed here. Willi Frischauer has adequate if not very penetrative biographies: *The Rise and Fall of Hermann Goering* (New York, 1951), and *Himmler* (New York, 1953). Himmler's empire is portrayed by Gerald Reitlinger, *The SS—Alibi of a Nation* (New York, 1957); Heinz Höhne, *The Order of the Death's Head*, Eng. trans. (London, 1969); and George H. Stein, *The Waffen-SS* (Ithaca, 1965). On Goebbels the best book is Ernest K. Bramsted, *Goebbels and National Socialist Propaganda* (East Lansing, 1965). For other facets of Nazi thought-control, consult Z. A. B. Zeman, *Nazi Propaganda* (London, 1964); Oron J. Hale, *The Captive Press in the Third Reich* (Princeton, 1964); and H. T. Burden, *The Nuremberg Party Rallies, 1923–1939* (New York, 1967). What the Nazis considered sound *völkisch* art may be scrutinized in G. L. Mosse, ed., *Nazi Culture* (New York, 1966). Other Nazi ventures into the arts are treated in D. S. Hull, *Film in the Third Reich* (Berkeley, 1969), and Barbara M. Lane, *Architecture and Politics in Germany, 1918–1945* (Cambridge, Mass., 1968). The subjugation of Germany's businessmen is described, at least up to the outbreak of the Hitler-Schacht argument in 1936, by Arthur Schweitzer, *Big Business in the Third Reich* (Bloomington, 1964); see also T. W. Mason's very good essay, "The Primacy of Politics—Politics and Economics in National Socialist Germany," in *The Nature of Fascism*, pp. 165–95, cited above. William Manchester's lurid *The Arms of Krupp, 1587–1968* (Boston, 1968) contains material on rearmament in the Third Reich. On Nazi relations with the Catholic church, Guenter Lewy, *The Catholic Church and Germany* (New York, 1964), is highly critical of the papacy's acceptance of Nazism at its antibolshevik face value. More restrained in tone, J. S. Conway, *The Nazi Persecution of the Churches* (Toronto, 1968), covers the Protestant denominations, too. As for the army officers, J. W. Wheeler-Bennett, *Nemesis of Power: The German Army in Politics, 1918–1945* (London, 1953), R. J. O'Neill, *The German Army and the Nazi Party, 1933–1939* (London, 1966), H. Deutsch, *Hitler and His Generals: The Hidden Crisis, January–June 1938* (Minneapolis, 1973), all trace their mounting distrust of Hitler and their growing impotence. Edward N. Peterson, *The Limits of Hitler's Power* (Princeton, 1969), tries to suggest that at the grass roots of Bavarian society (the author's regional test case) Nazi influence was less than total, but proves rather that normally the Hitlerian system operated smoothly without too much interference from Berlin.

None of the titles mentioned so far under "Germany" deals directly with three important topics: Hitler's foreign policy, the destruction of the Jews, and the German anti-Nazi resistance. All these issues came to a head in World War II, and therefore relevant works will be found later in this bibliography under "World War II."

THE IBERIAN COUNTRIES

On Spanish fascism one authority leads the field. Stanley Payne's *Falange* (Stanford, 1961) is the definitive book on the subject. The same author's brief survey, *Franco's Spain* (New York, 1967), indicates the Falange's decline since 1945. A touching lament for the tragic Falangist leader, José Antonio Primo de Rivera, is Hugh Thomas's "The Hero in the Empty Room," *Journal of Contemporary History* 1, no. 1 (1966): 174–82. On the right-wing forces which eventually swallowed up Spanish fascism, see R. A. H. Robinson, *Origins of Franco's Spain* (Newton Abbot, 1970). The best works on the Spanish Civil War itself are G. Jackson, *The Spanish Republic and the Civil War* (Princeton, 1965), and H. Thomas, *The Spanish Civil War* (London, 1961). The subject of foreign intervention is covered in Dante A. Puzzo, *Spain and the Great Powers* (New York, 1962). George Orwell, *Homage to Catalonia* (London, 1938), is characteristic of the engagement of some western intellectuals in the Spanish struggle and their subsequent disillusion.

Portuguese fascism receives a balanced treatment in H. Kay, *Salazar and Modern Portugal* (London, 1970). H. Martins, "Portugal," in *European Fascism*, pp. 302–36, admits Salazar's regime to be generically fascist.

AUSTRIA

For the origins of Austrian fascism, one must begin with Andrew G. Whiteside, *Austrian National Socialism before 1918* (The Hague, 1962). This describes not only the environment out of which Hitler sprang, but also the rise of the first Nazi party anywhere. The Catholic corporative background of Austrian fascism is considered in Alfred Diament, *Austrian Catholics and the First Republic* (Princeton, 1960), and also Klemens von Klemperer, *Ignaz Seipel* (Princeton, 1972). Gordon Brook-Shepherd, *Dollfuss* (London, 1961), is not without value despite its hero worship. On the other side of the controversy, the socialist critique of Dollfuss-Schuschnigg authoritarianism is presented in Julius Braunthal's brief *Tragedy of Austria* (London, 1948), and in Charles A. Gulick's massive *Austria from Habsburg to Hitler*, 2 vols. (Berkeley, 1948). The interwar struggle between Austrian corporativists and Nazis is well analyzed in A. G. Whiteside, "Austria," in *The European Right*, pp. 308–63. On the Viennese corporative experiment between 1933 and 1938, see A. Pelinka, *Stand oder Klasse?*

(Vienna, 1972). The most reliable work on the Anschluss, which finally determined that Austrian fascism should be of the Pan-German sort, is Jürgen Gehl, *Austria, Germany, and the Anschluss* (London, 1963).

### EASTERN EUROPE

Probably the most famous work on modern Hungarian history is C. A. Macartney's *October Fifteenth: A History of Modern Hungary, 1929–1945,* 2 vols. (Edinburgh, 1957). In many ways a work of great erudition, it is nevertheless uncritically sympathetic to Admiral Horthy and even to Hungary's fascists. A useful antidote is István Deák, "Hungary," in *The European Right*, pp. 364–407, which establishes clearly the innately racist spirit of Magyar irredentism and fascism. M. Lackó, *Arrow-Cross Men* (Budapest, 1969), has some useful detail on Hungary's main fascist organization, although the narrative ceases with Szálasi's assumption of power in October 1944 and the interpretation follows a narrow Marxist line. The most authoritative if verbose work on Hungarian fascism is N. M. Nagy-Talavera, *Green Shirts and Others* (Stanford, 1970). Although most of the book is devoted to the Hungarian scene, it also takes in the Iron Guard of Rumania. Nagy-Talavera finds a common ground between Hungarian and Rumanian fascists in a ferocious racism and anti-Semitism, and demonstrates that fascism in both countries had considerable mass appeal.

Other studies of Rumanian fascism include Zevedei Barbu's "Rumania," in *European Fascism*, pp. 146–66, which effectively conveys the element of mysticism in Codreanu's Legion of the Archangel Michael and Iron Guard, and Eugen Weber's "Men of the Archangel," *Journal of Contemporary History* 1, no. 1 (1966): 101–26, a skillful reconstruction of the movement's peasant and popular support. On the general background of Rumania between the wars, H. L. Roberts, *Rumania: Political Problems of an Agrarian State* (New Haven, 1951), is most valuable.

For a discussion of Finnish fascism in the English language, the writings of Marvin Rintala are invaluable. Both in his "Finland," in *The European Right*, pp. 408–42, and in *Three Generations* (Bloomington, 1962), fascism is placed in the context of Finnish conservatism and nationalism. On the winter war of 1939–40, when IKL enjoyed a slight revival, see A. F. Upton, *Finland in Crisis* (London, 1964). The best text on twentieth-century Finland is J. Wuorinen, *History of Finland* (New York, 1965).

### FRANCE AND THE LOW COUNTRIES

Inasmuch as Action Française was the progenitor of French fascism, there are two excellent works bearing that title: Eugen Weber, *Action Française* (Stanford, 1962), is the more comprehensive and treats the movement as a serious political exercise; Edward R. Tannenbaum, *Action Française* (New York, 1962), a shorter and more pointed discussion, dismisses Maurras and his colleagues as political dilettantes. The description of French fascism as a vague fever is connoted by R. Girardet's title, "Notes sur l'esprit d'un fascisme français," *Revue Française de Science Politique* 5 (1955): 529–46. The imprecision of French fascist doctrine is also the subject of Robert J. Soucy, "The Nature of Fascism in France," *Journal of Contemporary History* 1, no. 1 (1966): 27–55. The main function of fascism in France was to infect the Right with authoritarian, racist, and backward-longing prejudices. On this process, see René Rémond, *The Right Wing in France*, Eng. trans. (Philadelphia, 1966); E. Weber, "France," in *The European Right*, pp. 71–127; and R. J. Soucy's case history, *Fascism in France: The Case of Maurice Barrès* (Berkeley, 1972). One dimension of the problem was the dilemma of the French conservatives, nationalist but increasingly fascistic, faced by the threat from across the Rhine; this is explored by Charles A. Micaud, *The French Right and Nazi Germany* (Durham, N.C., 1943).

The shortcomings of the Third Republic which made fascist solutions appear credible to many are best examined in Stanley Hoffmann, "Paradoxes of the French Political Community," in *In Search of France* (Cambridge, Mass., 1963), pp. 1–117. William Shirer's *Collapse of the Third Republic* (New York, 1969) is somewhat superficial on France's sociopolitical difficulties. A good résumé of France between the world wars is Nathaniel Greene, *France from Versailles to Vichy* (New York, 1970).

For a survey of the diverse French organizations to which the label "fascist" has been applied, see J. Plumyène and R. Lasierra, *Les fascismes français, 1923–1963* (Paris, 1963). The case of the ex-communist who came closest to creating a mass fascist party in France is treated in Gilbert D. Allardyce, "The Political Transition of Jacques Doriot," *Journal of Contemporary History* 1, no. 1 (1966): 56–74.

Works on Vichy France will be cited below under "World War II."

On fascism in the Low Countries, there is virtually nothing in English save Jean Stengers, "Belgium," in *The European Right*, pp. 128–67. In other tongues, one may consult J. Willequet, "Les fascismes belges," *Revue d'Histoire de la Deuxième Guerre Mondiale*, no. 66 (April, 1967): 85–109, and H. A. Paape, "Le mouvement national-socialiste en Hollande," ibid. pp. 31–60; on Rexism, P. Daye, *Léon Degrelle et le rexisme* (Paris, 1937), and L. Narvaez, *Degrelle m'a dit* (Paris, 1961); and on Flemish fascism, A. De Bruyne, *Joris Van Severen* (Zulte, 1961).

GREAT BRITAIN

Colin Cross, *The Fascists in Britain* (London, 1961), is a sound, straightforward account, which can be supplemented in a few details by Robert

Benewick, *Political Order and Public Violence: A Study of British Fascism* (London, 1969). Mosley's career prior to the foundation of the BUF is well analyzed by Robert Skidelsky, "Great Britain," in *European Fascism*, pp. 231–61. The political maneuverings of the early 1930s are dealt with by W. F. Mandle, "Sir Oswald Mosley's Resignation from the Labour Government," *Historical Studies: Australia and New Zealand* 10 (1961–63): 493–510, and the same author's "The New Party," ibid. 12 (1965–67): 343–55. R. Skidelsky, "The Problem of Mosley: Why a Fascist Failed," *Encounter* (September 1969), pp. 77–88, appraises Mosley's adoption of desperation tactics in 1934.

MISCELLANEOUS

Among minor fascist movements, General O'Duffy's Irish group has received adequate coverage in M. Manning, *The Blueshirts* (Toronto, 1971). Two articles describe two kinds of Russian fascism—one a pre-World War I phenomenon, the other a product of Russian émigrés between the wars: H. Rogger, "Was There a Russian Fascism?" *Journal of Modern History* 36 (1964): 398–415, and E. Oberländer, "The All-Russian Fascist Party," *Journal of Contemporary History* 1, no. 1 (1966): 158–73. W. Wolf, *Faschismus in der Schweiz* (Zurich, 1969), relates all one needs to know of Swiss fascism.

## World War II

The debate over the origins of World War II was launched by A. J. P. Taylor, *Origins of the Second World War* (London, 1961), whose views have been discussed in the text. That Hitler was an opportunist who planned only short, localized wars receives credence from Burton Klein, *Germany's Economic Preparations for War* (Cambridge, Mass., 1959), and E. M. Robertson, *Hitler's Pre-War Policy and Military Plans* (London, 1963). H. W. Koch, "Hitler and the Origins of the Second World War," *Historical Journal* 11 (1968): 125–43, examines some of the well-known documentary evidence for calling Hitler a warmonger and finds it wanting; not unlike Taylor, Koch concludes that the Führer did not anticipate the war that began in 1939. On the other hand, Alan Bullock, "Hitler and the Origins of the Second World War," *Proceedings of the British Academy* 53 (1967): 259–87, is a moderate and sensible attempt to rehabilitate the demonic view of Hitler whom the western powers would have had to fight sooner or later. Indeed, the consensus of scholarly opinion is that World War II must remain Hitler's prime responsibility. Such is the verdict of the most comprehensive review to date of Nazi diplomacy, Hans-Adolf Jacobsen, *Nationalsozialistische Aussenpolitik, 1933–1938* (Frankfurt,

1968), and of Gerhard L. Weinberg, whose *Foreign Policy of Hitler's Germany*, vol. 1 (Chicago, 1970–   ) should become the standard authority in the field once the second volume is published. Shorter treatments which also subscribe to the notion of Hitler's war include Keith Eubank, *Origins of World War II* (New York, 1969), a survey of the entire interwar period, and Christopher Thorne, *Approach of War, 1938–1939* (London, 1967), a crisp account of the four crises leading up to the Second World War.

For an overview of the war in all its complexity, there is nothing better than Gordon Wright's lucid and informed *Ordeal of Total War* (New York, 1968), the concluding volume in the "Rise of Modern Europe" series. It supersedes Louis Snyder's heavily factual *The War* (New York, 1960).

In 1941 the complexion of the Second World War changed with the entry of the U.S.S.R. and the U.S.A. G. L. Weinberg, *Germany and the Soviet Union, 1939–1941* (Leiden, 1954), and A. Hillgruber, *Hitler's Strategie: Politik und Kriegfuehrung, 1940–1941* (Frankfurt, 1965), alike testify to Hitler's obsession with Russia and his determination to turn eastward at the first opportunity. M. van Krefeld, *Hitler's Strategy, 1940–1941: The Balkan Clue* (London, 1973), demolishes the myth that Balkan distractions in the spring of 1941 were responsible for the Wehrmacht's failure to reach Moscow. M. D. Fenyo, *Hitler, Horthy, and Hungary* (New Haven, 1972), describes one diplomatic facet of this *Drang nach Osten*. The Far Eastern dimension of Nazi Germany's global policy is treated by J. Meskill, *Hitler and Japan: The Hollow Alliance* (New York, 1966). The Führer's almost gratuitous declaration of war on the United States after Pearl Harbor was probably motivated by his scorn for a "mongrel" people—see J. C. Compton, *The Swastika and the Eagle* (Boston, 1967)—although H. H. Herwig, "Prelude to *Weltblitzkrieg*," *Journal of Modern History* 43 (1971): 649–68, discerns some rational calculations behind the step. A comprehensive appraisal of Nazi imperialist motivation is Norman Rich's projected two-volume study, *Hitler's War Aims: Ideology, the Nazi State, and the Course of Expansion*, vol. 1 (New York, 1973–   ), which maintains a nice balance between the Führer's *idées fixes* and the exigencies of war.

In Nazi-occupied Europe, collaboration and resistance stood at opposite poles. On the former, D. Littlejohn, *Patriotic Traitors* (London, 1972), has surveyed the whole European scene from 1940 to 1945 with sympathy for many who compromised themselves. The archetypal collaborator, Vidkun Quisling, has recently been the subject of a lively debate; probably the most reliable biography is by P. M. Hayes, *Quisling* (Bloomington, 1972). National case studies of mixed reaction to Nazi occupation are: W. Warmbrunn, *The Dutch under German Occupation* (Stanford, 1963); J. Gérard-Lebois and J. Gotovitch, *L'an 40: La Belgique occupée* (Brussels,

1971); V. Mastny, *The Czechs under Nazi Rule: The Failure of National Resistance, 1939–1942* (New York, 1971); J. A. Armstrong, *Ukrainian Nationalism (1939–1945)*, 2d ed. (New York, 1963).

The special situation of France is described fairly by Robert Aron, *The Vichy Regime*, abridged Eng. trans. (London, 1958). Stanley Hoffmann has written several articles exploring the deeper meaning of Vichy and emphasizing in the process the distinction between Maurrassians and the French nazis; "Quelques Aspects du Régime de Vichy," *Revue Française de Science Politique* 6 (1956): 46–69; "Effects of World War II on French Society and Politics," *French Historical Studies* 2 (1961): 28–63; "Collaborationism in France during World War II," *Journal of Modern History* 40 (1968): 375–95. Richard Griffiths's *Marshal Pétain* (London, 1970) is a sound, not unsympathetic biography; on Laval, the most reputable work is by Geoffrey Warner, *Laval and the Eclipse of France* (London, 1968). Peter Novick, *The Resistance versus Vichy* (New York, 1968), concentrates on the collapse of Vichy and the ensuing purge of collaborators.

For a broad sweep of the anti-Nazi resistance, one should consult Henri Michel's impressive *The Shadow War: Resistance in Europe, 1939–1945*, Eng. trans. (New York, 1972). For the rest, much of resistance literature consists of personal memoirs, anecdotal and difficult to subsume in a bibliography. There are, however, several worthwhile books on the German anti-Nazi opposition—a topic which raises the question, Who were the true Germans? Hans Rothfels, *The German Opposition to Hitler*, rev. ed., Eng. trans. (Chicago, 1962), has no doubt they were the resisters, albeit his admiration is somewhat undiscerning. A more penetrating work is Harold Deutsch, *The Conspiracy against Hitler in the Twilight War* (Minneapolis, 1967), which argues convincingly that the most favorable moment for the resistance to strike was the winter of 1939–40, but that the failings of the resistance caused the opportunity to be missed. *The German Resistance to Hitler* (Berkeley, 1970), ed. H. Graml, a useful set of essays by four German scholars, stresses the conservative and elitist features of most anti-Nazi groups. A workmanlike study with no ax to grind is *Germans against Hitler* (London, 1964) by T. Prittie. The most famous resistance plot, that in the summer of 1944, is covered by R. Manvel and H. Fraenkel, *The July Plot* (London, 1964), and its principal architect portrayed by J. Kramarz, *Stauffenberg*, Eng. trans. (London, 1967).

The Second World War in Europe turned ultimately on the capacity of the Third Reich alone to sustain the war effort. Yet, Alan S. Milward, *The Germany Economy at War* (London, 1965), and Berenice Carroll, *Design for Total War* (The Hague, 1968), both attest that not until 1944 did Nazi Germany go on a total-war footing. The treatment of the conquered countries was dictated more by political ideology than by economic reality. Thus, A. S. Milward, *The New Order and the French Economy* (Oxford, 1970), details the self-defeating efforts to integrate the French economy into a European fascist order. E. Homze, *Foreign Labor in Nazi Germany* (Princeton, 1967), describes the costly and callous transport of millions of foreign workers to Germany.

Meanwhile, during the latter half of the war, Nazi ideology was being taken to its logical conclusion. After launching Operation Barbarossa in 1941, the Nazis set about constructing their ideal *völkisch* community in the underdeveloped east. The savage process is described by Robert Koehl, *RKFVD: German Resettlement and Population Policy, 1939–1945* (Cambridge, Mass., 1957), and Alexander Dallin, *German Rule in Russia, 1941–1945* (London, 1957). Closely related to the application of racial theories in the east was the resolution to embark on the final solution of the Jewish question. K. A. Schleunes, *The Twisted Road to Auschwitz* (Urbana, 1970), examines Nazi anti-Semitism before the outbreak of war and finds no anticipation of genocide—which would seem to ignore some obvious implications in Nazi thought. By contrast, Raul Hilberg, *The Destruction of the European Jews* (Chicago, 1961), and Gerald Reitlinger, *The Final Solution* (New York, 1953), focus on the war years and graphically recount the anti-Semitic holocaust. Anne Frank's *Diary of a Young Girl*, Eng. trans. (New York, 1952), set in wartime Amsterdam, is a moving document of ordinary Jews in hiding. Day-to-day life in a death camp is recalled by a survivor, Eugen Kogon, *Theory and Practice of Hell*, Eng. trans. (New York, 1950). The depersonalized central administration of the system of slaughter is expressed in the subtitle of Hannah Arendt's *Eichmann in Jerusalem: A Report on the Banality of Evil* (New York, 1963).

The decline of the Axis is the setting for F. W. Deakin, *The Brutal Friendship* (London, 1962), a title which aptly summarizes Mussolini's subservience to the Führer between 1943 and 1945. The Duce's inglorious end is told by Roman Dombrowski, *Mussolini—Twilight and Fall*, Eng. trans. (New York, 1956). The fervid atmosphere and lunatic events of the *Führerbunker* in the spring of 1945 are compellingly re-created by H. R. Trevor-Roper, *The Last Days of Hitler*, rev. ed. (London, 1962), although the details of Hitler's suicide are disputed by some questionable evidence since released by the Russians: see L. Bezymenski, *The Death of Adolf Hitler*, Eng. trans. (New York, 1968). The epilogue of the Nazi-Fascist age took place in Nuremberg and received extensive coverage; the most thorough and dispassionate treatment is E. Davidson, *The Trial of the Germans* (New York, 1966).

## Fascism in Fiction and Film

The atmosphere surrounding fascism's rise and the aura which the fascists themselves created are not always easily depicted by the scholar, tied as he is to concrete evidence. Often, it is the literary artist who best captures the intangible. For example, the claustrophobia and anxiety of a totalitarian society are nowhere better conveyed than in Franz Kafka, *The Castle*, Eng. trans. (London, 1930), and *The Trial*, Eng. trans. (London, 1937). Astonishingly, Kafka, a Czech, wrote his novels more than a decade before Hitler made the nightmares a reality. Then, Hitler's rise to power can be examined through fiction. Thomas Mann's *Magic Mountain*, Eng. trans., 2 vols. (London, 1927), reflects metaphorically on Weimar's failure to engage the Germans' enthusiasm. Richard Hughes's, two novels, *Fox in the Attic* and *The Wooden Shepherdess* (London, 1961, 1973), contain an incisive portrayal of the German milieu within which Hitler's steps to power—the beer hall *Putsch*, his trial and imprisonment, his appointment as chancellor, the Night of the Long Knives—are traced. Hans Fallada, *Little Man, What Now?* Eng. trans. (London, 1933), presents a sentimentalized but touching story of the material and psychological impact of the Great Depression on ordinary Germans. A quasi-Marxist view of Hitler's dealings with the German capitalists was put on stage by Bertolt Brecht, *The Resistible Rise of Arturo Ui*, Eng. trans. (New York, 1957); it makes for sprightly entertainment if somewhat dubious history.

Outside Germany, the bored disillusion of western middle-class liberals, some of whom regarded fascism in the abstract as an exciting option, informs Muriel Spark's *The Prime of Miss Jean Brodie* (London, 1961). The Italian people's passive but solid backing of Mussolini's regime in the mid-1930s emerges in Ignazio Silone's tragic novels, *Fontamara*, Eng. trans. (London, 1934), and *Bread and Wine*, Eng. trans. (London, 1936). The panoramic background of the Spanish Civil War is displayed in *The Forging of a Rebel*, Eng. trans. (London, 1973), an autobiographical novel by Arturo Barea. Of innumerable works of fiction about the Second World War, John Hersey's *The Wall* (New York, 1950), a reconstruction of life in Warsaw's Jewish ghetto in 1942–43, comes closest to what Hitler's war was all about.

Some novels with a fascist background have been made into successful films. The Italians seem particularly adept at this. Witness Bernardo Bertolucci's poetic film (1971) of Alberto Moravia's *The Conformist*, Eng. trans. (London, 1957), a psychosexual study of a neurotic intellectual who seeks self-identity by serving dominant Fascism. Equally affecting is Vittorio de Sica's restrained and sensitive cinematic adaptation (1971) of *The Garden of the Finzi-Continis*, Eng. trans. (London, 1965), Giorgio Bassani's tale of the introduction of anti-Semitism into the town of Ferrara. The German scene on the eve of Hitler's appointment as chancellor was vividly caught in Christopher Isherwood's sketches, *Goodbye to Berlin* (London, 1939); these were cast in theatrical form by John Van Druten, *I Am a Camera* (New York, 1952), and were more recently converted again into a film musical, *Cabaret* (1972), which provides a surprisingly effective picture of decadent Weimar. In contrast, De Sica's attempt (1963) to put on the screen Jean Paul Sartre's quasi-existentialist play, *The Condemned of Altona*, Eng. trans. (New York, 1961), scarcely rises above melodrama.

Of original cinematic creations, the Italian social realist school after World War II specialized in representations of the agony of war and resistance following Mussolini's fall; see for instance, Roberto Rossellini's *Open City* (1945) and *General Della Rovere* (1960). Unfortunately, the sensationalism of the Nazi story usually gets the better of filmmakers: a classic case is Luchino Visconti's *The Damned* (1970), an interpretation of Nazism in psychopathic terms, which suffers from too many camera tricks and overstatement of the message. Stanley Kramer's *Judgment at Nuremberg* (1961), in contrast, is a slightly oversimplified but otherwise honest presentation of the issues involved in denazification. *Hitler: The Last Ten Days* (1973) is a faithful if pedestrian rendering by Ennio de Concini of the final lunacy.

In conclusion must be mentioned some documentary films which have come down from the fascist era. In particular, Leni Reifenstahl's classic propaganda vehicles, *Triumph of the Will* (1935) and *Olympiad* (1938), are still available. In a different vein, *Swastika* (1973), directed by Philippe Mora, gives a very human picture of the Führer, partly because it makes use of some interesting home movies taken at Berchtesgaden by Eva Braun; yet withal, it is a searing exposé of the Hitlerian mentality. And another *succès de scandale* on its release, *Le Chagrin et la pitié* (1971), Marcel Ophul's brilliant amalgam of newsreel material from World War II and interviews with participants twenty-five years on, reflects the pervasiveness of French collaboration with the Nazi occupiers and support for Vichy between 1940 and 1944. No doubt, film archives contain a wealth of evidence and the film world a wealth of expertise, as yet barely tapped, to illuminate the diverse fascist experiences.

Since this book was set in proof, several new and relevant titles have come to my notice. P. M. Hayes, *Fascism* (London, 1973), is another effort to capture the abstraction albeit a very disjointed one. Fascist origins are put in intellectual terms, but so many thinkers from two thousand years of Western history are invoked that one is left wondering what, after all, is distinctive about fascism. Autarchy is given as the key to fascism in practice. O-E. Schüdekopf, *Revolutions of Our Time: Fascism* (London, 1973), is a very brief survey pitched at an elementary level. A. Szymanski, "Fascism, Industrialism, and Socialism: The Case of Italy," *Comparative Studies in Society and History* 15, no. 4 (1973): 395–404, provides some statistics to suggest that fascism, while a response to socialism, was not, however, a ploy of big business as many Marxists hold. *Modern Italy,*

edited by E. R. Tannenbaum and E. P. Noether (New York, 1974), takes
as its theme Italy's slow rate of modernization which Fascism was supposed
to hasten. Two more overviews of the Fascist Italian scene are M. Gallo,
*Mussolini's Italy: Twenty Years of the Fascist Era,* Eng. trans. (New York,
1973), and *The Ax Within* (New York, 1974), a collection of essays edited
by R. Sarti. Werner Maser's *Hitler,* Eng. trans. (London, 1973), is less a
conventional biography than a rigorous analysis of certain debatable facets
of the Fuhrer's character and career; it explodes some of the wilder fantasies
about his personal life. S. Milgram, *Obedience to Authority* (New York,
1974), contends on the basis of laboratory tests that the Germans obeyed
Hitler in an "agentic state." In the field of World War II studies, B. A.
Leach, *German Strategy against Russia* (Oxford, 1974), tries to rehabilitate
Hitler's military reputation at the expense of his generals; I. Trunk, *Judenrat*
(London, 1973), describes how the elders of European Jewry were forced
to connive at their own genocide; and R. O. Paxton's *Vichy France: Old
Guard and New Order* (New York, 1972), is an excellent examination of
Pétain's quasi-fascist "national revolution."

Among English-language titles announced but not yet published, the
following sound of most interest: W. Maser, ed., *Hitler's Letters and Notes,*
Eng. trans.; J. Fest, *Hitler,* Eng. trans.; H. P. Blenel, *Strength Through
Joy;* R. Skidelsky, *Oswald Mosley.*

In the film world L. Becker's *Double-Headed Eagle* (1973) is another
dramatic documentary of Hitler's rise; F. Vancini's *Matteotti Affair* (1973)
is a successful fictionalized recreation; and one of the most compelling
portrayals of an imaginary young recruit to fascism to appear on the screen
is *Lacomb, Lucien* (1974), directed by Louis Malle and set in the France
of 1944.

# INDEX